THE HEART OF THE MATTER

Perspectives on Emotion in Marital Therapy

THE HEART OF THE MATTER

Perspectives on Emotion in Marital Therapy

Edited by
Susan M. Johnson, Ed.D.
Leslie S. Greenberg, Ph.D.

BRUNNER/MAZEL *Publishers* • New York

Library of Congress Cataloging-in-Publication Data
The Heart of the matter: perspectives on emotion in marital therapy / edited by
   Susan Johnson and Leslie Greenberg.
            p.   cm.
   Includes bibliographical references and index.
   ISBN 0-87630-741-1
   1. Marital psychotherapy. 2. Emotions. 3. Intimacy (Psychology)
I. Johnson, Susan M. II. Greenberg, Leslie S.
RC488.5.H42 1994
616.89'156—dc20   94-15906
                                                                                CIP

Published by
BRUNNER/MAZEL, INC.
19 Union Square West
New York, New York 10003

Manufactured in the United States of America
10 9 8 7 6 5 4 3 2 1

Contents

Section D: Cognitive and Behaviorally Oriented Approaches

PART III: CONCLUSION

Contributors

Steven R. H. Beach, Ph.D., is Associate Professor at the University of Georgia, Athens. He is the author of numerous articles and co-author of *Depression in Marriage: A Model for Etiology and Treatment* (Guilford, 1990).

Marc J. Blumberg served as a prosecuting attorney for the State of California for nine years and spent three years as Director of Training for the California District Attorney's Association. He is currently completing a doctoral degree in clinical psychology at Temple University.

Mario Cusinato, Ph.D., is a Professor of Psychology at the University of Padova, Italy.

Jay S. Efran, Ph.D., is Professor of Psychology and Director of the Psychological Services Center at Temple University in Philadelphia, where he has also served as Director of Clinical Training. He is the co-author of *Language, Structure, and Change: Frameworks of Meaning in Psychotherapy* (Norton, 1990).

Frank D. Fincham, Ph.D., is Director of Clinical Training at the University of Illinois. He received the Berscheid-Hatfield Award for "sustained, substantial, and distinguished contributions to the field of personal relationships" and is co-author of *Communicating in Relationships: A Guide for Couples and Professionals.*

John M. Gottman, Ph.D., is Professor of Psychology at the University of Washington. He has held a Research Scientist Award from the National Institute of Health since 1979.

Leslie S. Greenberg, Ph.D., is a Professor of Psychology at York University, Canada. He is co-author of *Emotionally Focused Therapy for Couples* (Guilford, 1988) and *Facilitating Emotional Change: The Moment By Moment Process* (Guilford, 1993).

Bernard G. Guerney, Jr., Ph.D., is Director of the National Institute of Relationship Enhancement, Bethesda, Maryland. He conducts live therapy demonstrations, workshops, and training for agencies and group practices, and supervises individuals nationwide.

Cindy Hazan, Ph.D., is a social/developmental psychologist in the Department of Human Development and Family Studies at Cornell University. She studies the developmental transition from parent-child to adult attachment relationships.

Neil S. Jacobson, Ph.D., is a Professor of Psychology and Director of the Center for Clinical Research at the Univerity of Washington. He is co-author of *Marital Interaction: Analysis and Modification* (Guilford, 1984) and *Clinical Handbook of Marital Therapy* (Guilford, 1986).

Susan M. Johnson, Ed.D., is an Associate Professor of Psychology and Psychiatry at the University of Ottawa, Canada, and Director of the Marital and Family Therapy Clinic, Civic Hospital, Ottawa. The co-author of *Emotionally Focused Therapy for Couples* (Guilford, 1988), she is actively engaged in research and clinical training.

Roger Kobak, Ph.D., is a Clinical Psychologist at the University of Delaware. He studies the relation between attachment processes and communication in the parent-teen and marital relationships.

Kelly Koerner is a research assistant at the Center for Clinical Research, University of Washington. She is involved with psychotherapy research on couple therapy, cognitive therapy for depression, and case formulation.

Luciano L'Abate, Ph.D., is Professor Emeritus of Psychology at Georgia State University, Atlanta, and Clinical Director of Multicultural Services for the Cross Keys Counseling Center. He is co-author with Dennis Bagarozzi, Ph.D., of *Sourcebook of Marriage and Family Evaluation* (Brunner/Mazel, 1993).

Sharon Glick Miller, Ph.D., is Director of Family Psychiatry, Department of Psychiatry and Behavioral Medicine, at the University of South Florida.

Robert A. Pierce, Ph.D., is Director of The Therapy Center and Clinical Assistant Professor of Psychiatry (Psychology), University of Rochester Medical School. He is co-author of *Emotional Expression in Psychotherapy* (Gardner, 1993).

Katy Ruckdeschel, M.A., is a doctoral student in clinical psychology at the University of Delaware. Her research focuses on parenting and children's emotional regulation.

Daniel B. Wile, Ph.D., is a psychologist in the private practice of individual and couples therapy in Oakland, California. He has published on psychotherapeutic theory as well as on couples therapy, and has given numerous talks, courses, demonstrations, and workshops on couples therapy.

Preface

Intimate relationships are at the core of our emotional life. There is no other context so infused by and responsive to the ebb and flow of human emotion. A large part of human communication is emotional communication, involving minute signals concerning closeness and distance, and dominance and submission. This information is of central importance in organizing interactions with significant others. In addition, the social interactions most crucial to our senses of well-being, positive adaptation, and physical and emotional health are those that occur with significant others on whom we depend for our sense of security and belonging in the world. This book examines the role of affect in intimate relations and in the redefinition of such relationships in therapy.

It is only relatively recently in human history that family relationships have centered on intimate connectedness rather than on instrumental survival tasks, and even more recently that psychology and psychiatry have begun to concern themselves with understanding the nature of adult love relationships rather than focusing upon the individual and patterns of individual adaptation. The power of the social context in which the individual is embedded has become more and more recognized, both in its ability to foster health and resilience to stress through the mechanisms of confiding and social support, and in its ability to generate and maintain problematic symptoms such as depression, family dysfunction, and other common forms of human unhappiness.

In terms of theories of adult intimacy and the part emotion plays in such relationships, the literature is still sparse and incomplete. Such intimacy can be considered as a replay of family-of-origin conflicts, as a quid pro quo exchange of resources, or as an attachment bond, where innate needs for security and contact are satisfied. These theories, of which the latter seems the most promising, vary in the focus they place on cognition, behavior, motivation, and emotion. Of the three, attachment theory is the most explicit about the role of emotion, viewing it as the primary organizing factor in attachment behaviors. This perspective is congruent with empirical work defining marital distress in which the expression of negative affect and lack of emotional engagement have been found to predict separation and divorce.

Whether health professionals and academics understand love relationships or not, the demand for therapeutic intervention, to help couples conjure up closeness from distance, intimacy from alienation, connection from isolation, empathy from aggression, and respect and equality from power struggles, shows no signs of abating. Here too, in the area of intervention, emotion has only recently been recognized as an essential ingredient in the change process rather than just being part of the problem.

Until recently, the focus in empirically validated approaches to marital therapy has been on cognitive understanding and behavior change. In the practice of marital therapy, the key change strategies have focused on insight into habitual responses learned in past negative relationships, often in the family of origin, or the learning of new skills and behaviors that would have an impact on each partner's emotional experience of the relationship. Even if affective responses were recognized as an important element in marital distress, in therapy they tended to be seen as phenomena to be bypassed or controlled. There was very little written about how to specifically address emotional responses to create change, and no set of clearly specified interventions for working with emotions in marital therapy. Gradually, however, the focus on emotion that developed in the individual therapy field began to have an impact on clinician/researchers in marital therapy. There now exist treatment approaches that focus on affective experience as the main pathway to change in marital therapy, such as our own emotionally focused therapy (EFT), and specified techniques for integrating affect into behavioral and insight approaches (Snyder & Wills, 1989; Baucom, Seyers, & Sher, 1990). The clinician can now find in the literature a variety of techniques that focus on emotion, either teaching expressive skills, labeling affective experience, or using affect to help restructure interactional positions. There are still more questions than answers, however, as to how and when to address and use emotion at specific times in therapy.

This book is an attempt to advance the consideration of emotion in intimate relationships, on both the theoretical and practical levels. It is designed to provide the clinician with insights into how expert therapists of various orientations view and work with affective processes to improve distressed relationships and enhance individual functioning. At a theoretical level, it provides a variety of different perspectives on emotion and suggestions as to how affective processes can influence the disintegration and re-creation of intimate bonds.

In the main body of the book, contributors from different therapeutic traditions have been asked to describe their orientation to emotion in couples therapy, and to explicate, by using case examples, how they address emotion in the process of therapy. The contributions represent then a variety of clinical perspectives, namely, the more cognitive-behavioral approaches, exemplified in the chapters of Beach and Fincham, and Koerner and Jacobson; the empirical perspective on marital distress illustrated by the work of Gottman; the more systemic approaches represented here by Miller, and by Efran and Blumberg; the more humanistic and experiential approaches of Pierce, Guerney, and Cusinato and L'Abate; and the more dynamic ego-analytic and attachment perspectives of Wile, and Kobak, Ruckdeschel, and Hazan. Marital therapists tend by nature to be integrative, perhaps because they have to include interactional perspectives, and so the designations of orientation above are intended to be reflections of the contributors' base perspectives rather than an exclusive and precise categorization. Perspectives not included here, such as traditional object relations perspectives, structural-strategic approaches, and family-of-origin approaches, are omitted because unfortunately it was difficult to find contributors who represented these approaches and were interested in looking at emotion in marital therapy or able to do so. We regret this, especially because one of the goals of this book, following the positive reception of the editors' book *Emotionally Focused Therapy for Couples* (Greenberg & Johnson, 1988) was to invite people from different orientations, even orientations where emotions do not figure, to focus on the role of emotion, which we believe has to be dealt with in some way in every approach to couples therapy. The intent is to present different theoretical assumptions and to pinpoint how these assumptions translate into change strategies and therapeutic interventions. In the last part of the book, we provide a synthesis and critical analysis of the previous chapters and consider various future directions for theory, research, and intervention on emotion in couples therapy.

Our objective is to facilitate and further the dialogue about the place of emotion in intimate relations and in therapies that attempt to redefine such relationships. This will then, we hope, fuel the process of theoretical understanding and the integration of insights derived from different theoretical perspectives. It will also further the explication of intervention techniques and how different perspectives lead to different ways of addressing emotional experience and expression. As a result, research in this area will become more refined and more relevant to the practicing clinician. As the marital therapy field progresses, this kind of dialogue has the potential to allow us to specify how and when to access, control, contain, heighten, and use emotion to achieve specific ends, and to judge when it is more efficient and effective to focus on meaning and cognitive factors or behavioral factors. Since emotion is most powerful and evident in intimate relationships, we can perhaps also use the marital therapy context to understand more about this phenomenon, and thus expand our understanding of and ability to intervene in families and individual therapy. After all, in all therapies emotional relationships are one of the main targets and agents of change.

REFERENCES

Baucom, D. H., Sayers, S. L., & Sher, T. G. (1990). Supplementary behavioral marital therapy with cognitive restructuring and emotional expressiveness training: An outcome investigation. *Journal of Consulting and Clinical Psychology, 58,* 636–645.

Greenberg, L. S., & Johnson, S. M. (1988). *Emotionally focused therapy for couples.* New York: Guilford.

Snyder, D. K., & Wills, R. M. (1989). Behavioral versus insight-oriented marital therapy. Effects on individual and interspousal functioning. *Journal of Consulting and Clinical Psychology, 57,* 39–46.

PART I

INTRODUCTION

1

Emotion in Intimate Relationships: Theory and Implications for Therapy

SUSAN M. JOHNSON and LESLIE S. GREENBERG

The purpose of this book is to expand our understanding of emotion in intimate relationships and begin to delineate different perspectives taken by theorists and clinicians concerning this aspect of experience, which Sartre described as constituting a transformation of the world, particularly as it pertains to our ability to relate to others. The goal of this introduction is then to lay out our perspective on emotion in intimate relationships (the perspective that underlies the theory and practice of emotionally focused therapy [EFT], Greenberg & Johnson, 1988; Johnson & Greenberg, 1994) and to set the scene for the chapters that follow, which present the theoretical perspectives and clinical strategies of leading clinician/scientists in the field of marriage and marital therapy.

Evidence as to the importance of emotion in marriage and marital therapy arises from various sources, empirical, theoretical, and clinical. On an empirical level, recent research into the phenomenon of marital distress has confirmed the key role that emotional experience and expression plays in the definition of relationships. Such research has found that the level of physiological arousal, particularly of husbands, during couple interactions is a powerful predictor of longitudinal marital distress and separation. In addition, facial expressions of emotion, particularly a wife's disgust, a husband's fear, and the unhappiness of both, are an excellent predictor of separation and divorce. The Four Horsemen of the Apocalypse for marriage have been identified as (1) critical anger, (2) contempt, expressed by one spouse, usually the wife, (3) fearful defensiveness, and (4) withdrawal by the other spouse (Gottman, 1991, and this volume). This research, which demonstrates the significance of the facial communication of emotion and physiological emo-

3

tional responses, underlines the power of emotional experience and communication in the regulation of social interaction.

In addition, it has been found that it is not the number of fights, or even the outcome of the fights, that predicts whether couples stay together, but the quality of emotional engagement. Couples can fight, not resolve issues, and sustain a satisfying relationship provided they can stay emotionally engaged rather than becoming distant and defensive (Gottman & Krokoff, 1989). This kind of research presents more and more clearly a picture of marital distress in which the key elements are powerful negative affect and automatic, highly structured negative emotional responses, which elicit reciprocal aversiveness or distance from the partner, creating cycles of anger and alienation. Negative emotional experience and communication appear to become an absorbing state, which overrides other responses and takes over the relationship, making new responses more and more difficult to initiate and maintain. Such cycles may explain why outcome studies of marital therapy find extremely little evidence of spontaneous remission in marital distress. In summary, empirical studies of marital distress underline the power of emotion in couple interaction and signal the necessity for greater understanding and refined intervention techniques in this area.

On a theoretical level, the desirability of a focus on emotion is highlighted by the recent applications of attachment theory to adult love relationships. At present, attachment seems to be the most promising theoretical perspective for understanding adult love (Shaver, Hazan, & Bradshaw, 1988; Johnson, 1986; Johnson & Greenberg, 1994). Attachment theory, as well as focusing on internal representation, sees emotion as the primary signal of the success and failure of attachment and as motivating attachment-seeking behaviors. This may be contrasted, for example, with exchange theory (Thibaut & Kelley, 1959), which views adult intimacy in terms of economic, rational self-interest and quid pro quo contracts. Attachment theory views adult love as an emotional bond addressing innate needs for security, protection, and contact with significant others, conceptualizing such a bond as an emotional tie in which emotional experience and expression organizes attachment behaviors and regulates closeness and distance. The emotional accessibility and responsiveness of the partners form the basis of the bond between them and facilitate emotional engagement and contact. In this framework, attachment and the emotions that organize attachment behaviors are adaptive and serve to form a secure base (Bowlby, 1969, 1988) from which the individual can confront the world. This perspective is congruent with research findings that confiding, intimate relationships buffer individuals against stress and promote mental and physical well-being. Attachment behaviors and associated emotional responses are considered to be innate, and tend to increase in intensity if the bond with the attachment figure is threatened. Typically, in the face of separation, protest and anger, clinging, despair, and detachment follow. The quality of adult attachments is considered to be mediated by strong emotional responses and working models of self and other learned in early attachment contexts. This perspective suggests that marital therapy is obliged to include affect at least as a target of change and, more significantly, to discover and explicate how to use affect in the reorganization of intimate bonds that have gone astray. Otherwise, there is a risk of focusing on more peripheral elements rather than on the central building blocks of intimate relationships; the acquiring of specific relationship skills, for example, may not lead to greater marital happiness or intimacy (Harrell & Guerney, 1976), and insight into the repetitions of past relationships may not produce change in the here and now. Specifically, from an attachment perspective, it is essential in marital therapy to address the emotional responses that organize attachment behaviors and restructure interactions to facilitate accessibility and responsiveness. Rigid negative interactional cycles of hostility and distance, which preclude secure contact and the satisfaction of attachment needs, then give way to cycles of increasing trust, intimate engagement, and the creation of a secure bond. In the early 1980s, we set out to develop and test an approach to couples therapy that focused on reprocessing of partners' emotional responses to facilitate a shift in negative interactional cycles and facilitate secure bonding. Continuing practice and further investigation (Goldman & Greenberg, 1992; James, 1991; Dessaulles, Johnson, Hotz, & Kallos, 1994; Dandeneau & Johnson, 1994; Walker, 1993) have convinced us of the importance of the experience and expression of attachment-related emotions in the creation and repair of intimate bonds.

Clinical developments in the field of psychotherapy in general, and marital therapy in particular, have increasingly recognized the importance of emotion. Generally in psychotherapy, the 1980s saw a growing emphasis on affect and an acknowledgment that a focus on behavior and cognition was necessarily incomplete. Previously when emotion was addressed, it was often acknowledged in clinical theory but glossed over as far as the description of specific affect-oriented interventions was concerned. As Mahoney (1991) has recently pointed out, intense emotionality usually has been seen as something to be discharged, avoided, or controlled, or at most perhaps understood and therefore transcended. Affect has also been described in a general global fashion, rather than differentiated into specific emotions linked to specific interventions in particular contexts. Recently, however, there have been considerable advances in considering the role of affective interventions and processes in therapeutic change in individual therapy (Greenberg & Safran, 1987; Safran & Greenberg, 1991; Stein 1991), and this in turn has encouraged marital therapists to begin addressing the role of affect in this modality.

Marital therapists in the 1970s concerned themselves with delineating marital interventions and were beginning to conduct outcome studies of their effects. However, the lack of specification of interventions, whether focused on behavior, cognition, or affect, continued to be problematic (Gurman &

Kniskern, 1981) and indeed is still an issue in the 1990s (Johnson & Greenberg, 1991). The behavioral marital therapies led the field in describing interventions and validating these interventions empirically. In these approaches, affect was generally considered to be epiphenomenal, a consequence of cognition, and was often seen as an impediment to the process of change, which focused on rational processes such as behavior exchange and the learning of communication and problem-solving skills. A focus on affect was considered to be, at best, inefficient (Jacobson & Margolin, 1979) and often detrimental to therapy. Negative emotion was particularly viewed as dangerous, destructive, and distancing, and therefore the expression of such feelings was to be avoided at all costs (Waring, 1988). The main change strategies, as in individual therapies, involved the expansion of behavioral repertoires, or in the more dynamic therapies, insight into marital dynamics. These approaches tended to focus on what we have termed secondary and instrumental emotions (Greenberg & Safran, 1987; Greenberg & Johnson, 1988) rather than on the role of biologically adaptive, attachment-oriented emotions.

In the 1980s, however, there was a growing acknowledgment among cognitive and behavioral marital therapists that the problems couples brought into marital therapy were emotional in nature, and that the quality of the emotional connection between partners had a great impact on the outcome of therapy (Margolin & Weinstein, 1983; Hahlweg, Schindler, Revenstorf, & Brenglemann, 1984). Marital therapists began to question whether affect could be bypassed or controlled, and assumed to change as a result of modifications in behavior and cognition. Affect began to be seen as a crucial factor in marital adjustment that had to be addressed in therapy (Broderick & O'Leary, 1986). In addition, cognitive-behavioral researchers began to analyze the results of their interventions across studies, concluding that such interventions were less powerful than originally believed, creating improvement in only 50% of couples, and often failing to accomplish the most rigorous goal of marital therapy, that of rendering distressed marriages not only improved but satisfying by the end of treatment (Jacobson et al., 1984). They then began to consider new ways to increase the effectiveness of such interventions by including new elements in treatment.

At the same time, other clinician/researchers were delineating emotionally focused interventions in which emotion was reprocessed and used to change partners' interactional positions in marital relationships (EFT; Greenberg & Johnson, 1986, 1988; Johnson & Greenberg, 1985a, b) and increase intimacy. These investigations suggested that affect was a powerful agent of change in this approach to marital therapy, and also provided some explanation as to why this might be so (Greenberg & Johnson, 1988; Johnson & Greenberg, 1988). In the last part of the 1980s and the present decade, different kinds of interventions focusing upon affect have been included in cognitive-behavioral approaches, including teaching the skills of affective expression (Baucom, Sayers, & Sher, 1990), helping couples label the emotional consequences of their partner's behavior (Jacobson, 1991), including emotion as part of an insight-oriented change strategy (Snyder & Wills, 1989), and more recently (Koerner & Jacobson, this volume) creating an emotional acceptance of differences. In addition, systems theorists have begun to recognize the importance of including emotion in their work. Napier (1988) has included working with emotion as part of family-of-origin work, and Guerin, Fay, Burden, and Kautto (1987) have recognized the destructive role of negative emotions and offer ways of dealing with emptiness and bitterness in marriage.

The process in the field has been one of a growing recognition of the crucial role of affect in intimate relationships, paralleling the recognition of the crucial role of affect in individual functioning and adaption (Greenberg & Safran, 1987; Mahoney, 1991; Frijda, 1988) and an acknowledgment of affect as an essential target of change in marital therapy. In addition, a growing technology of affective interventions has emerged, either as primary interventions or as additional elements in marital therapies that focus primarily on cognition and behavior. The process of specifying and testing different affective interventions has begun, and theoretical formulations of affective change processes have begun to be delineated. Let us now turn to a summary of these theoretical perspectives.

THEORIES OF EMOTION

In the last decade, views on emotion within psychology have changed dramatically. Most broadly, emotions are currently viewed as arising in the course of human action, especially interpersonal interaction, and as providing biologically based solutions to human problems that cannot be managed by cognition alone (Oatley & Jenkins, 1992). Emotion is beginning to be seen as central in understanding both interaction and cognition in that emotion is, first, attentional, influencing the salience of information; second, motivational, influencing goal setting; and third, communicational, regulating interaction with others.

The Nature of Emotion

Emotions are best viewed as involving *action tendencies* that arise as a function of *automatic appraisals* of the relevance of situations to an individual's *basic concerns* (Arnold, 1960; Frijda, 1986; Lazarus, 1982, 1991). Emotions start with the detection of some notable change, often in another person, which acts as a signal to continue processing the input for its personal significance (Scherer, 1984). The continued processing involves first appraising the interpersonal event in relation to one's concerns and then to one's ability to cope with the event.

Emotions, in addition, are seen as being adaptive (Izard, 1979; Frijda, 1986). They govern goal priorities within people, and communicate intentions between people, in ways that promote survival and positive adaptation (Greenberg & Safran, 1987; Greenberg & Johnson, 1988; Oatley & Jenkins, 1992; Safran & Greenberg, 1991). Emotions are best understood as complex syntheses of elements including motivation (in the form of needs and concerns) and cognition (in the form of appraisals), as well as being primary organizers of action and interaction (Greenberg, Rice, & Elliott, 1993; Lazarus, 1991a, b). Discrete primary emotions such as surprise, happiness, anger, sadness, fear, and disgust (Ekman & Friesen, 1975; Izard, 1977) have been shown not just to be internal experience, but also to be action dispositions (Arnold, 1960; Frijda, 1986; Lang, 1984) biologically related to survival and adaptation. These basic primary emotions have, in addition, been shown to be universal, with associated characteristic facial expressions, neuroendocrine patterns, and brain sites.

Emotions have also been shown to influence information processing in higher cognitive areas of the cortex in a variety of ways (Panksepp, 1989). For example, the effects of mood on memory have been investigated (Blaney, 1986), and a mood-congruent memory effect has been reliably found demonstrating that people's moods affect what they recall and what they encode. By comparison, the higher cognitive areas seem to have only modest control over the underlying emotive circuits, although it is clear that thinking can and does have some effect on everyday feelings.

Basic or primary emotions appear to have a distinct nonsymbolic manner of internal signaling that differs from the manner of processing cognitive information. Each emotion signal is discrete, direct, and when clear or intense, does not need to be interpreted to understand its meaning. Rather, it automatically provides meaning and organizes action. The organism is thus provided with innate signals and innate knowledge of the significance of each signal. The interpretation of the signal is not semantic but involves direct appraisal. These emotion-based signals are specifically adaptive because they can rapidly influence behavior without relying on conceptual processing.

Emotions are then a nonsymbolic way of guiding action that do not require a complex inferential process. They are, in fact, an evolutionarily older method of controlling action, with rapid and often effective results. They operate automatically, and human perceptual systems can therefore automatically register information, but signal to consciousness only an emotion toward the object, resulting in a person feeling something toward a person/ situation (e.g., anger) without knowing the reason. Therefore, primary emotions appear to be in-wired, and to be tied to information processing in ways that help persons adapt and survive, enabling them to respond quickly to information that would otherwise take too long to process and delay the evoking of an emotional action tendency. As well as being biologically based action tendencies, emotions are also socially constructed, and constituted by language in that they need to be named and symbolized in awareness. Complex emotional organizations such as feeling "humiliated" or "vulnerable" are biological, psychological, and socially constructed states. As humans learn the proper use of emotional terms such as sad or angry, they learn to make distinctions with respect to situations as well as to physiology and behavior associated with the terms. Emotional language thus involves an understanding of social roles and norms as to how a culture defines different emotional organizations.

The Experience and Expression of Emotion

Emotional experience has been shown to consist of different degrees of cognition and affect, and to involve an integration of many different levels of information (Lazarus, 1982; Leventhal, 1979; Lang, 1983). Consciously experienced feelings are a complex synthesis of a variety of types and sources of information. These feelings seem to be comprised of an integration of at least three measurable systems: a physiologically based expressive-motor system, a semantically based emotional memory system, and a verbally based conceptual system. Thus emotional experience is made up of many components, including the experience of sensory and physiological changes, meaning, and action tendencies, which are all integrated into conscious awareness or the experience of feelings. This complex, information-processing emotion system is seen as providing us with a rich source of complex meaning and with feedback about our reactions to situations in the form of feelings (Greenberg & Safran, 1987). Emotional experience in these models is thus a synthesis constructed from various elements, any one of which primes and resonates with the other elements.

Emotional expression, on the other hand, communicates intentions between people. Such expression has been shown to be both a primary self-regulator, organizing infants' responses to environmental stimuli, and a primary regulator of others' behaviors, by providing affective signals to caretakers to guide their actions (Stern, 1985; Tronick, 1989). Emotional expression is thus fundamentally communicative and serves to regulate social interaction.

To summarize, empirical and conceptual developments in the study of emotion provide support for the existence and the universality of certain discrete primary emotions that are generated by the automatic appraisal of situations in relation to needs. In addition, the schematic emotion system organizes and synthesizes complex high-level incoming information at multiple levels, to provide us both with complex meanings and with feedback about our responses to situations, as well as producing rapid emotional response tendencies that are fundamentally adaptive. It is also clear that affective processes influence attentional allocation and information processing. In addition, affect has been shown to be the infant's primary means of self-regulation and communication.

There has then been an extremely significant shift in attitudes toward emotion, away from a view of emotion as disruptive and disorganizing, toward a view of emotion as part of evolutionary adaption; that is, as an essential and valuable element in human information processing that aids in problem solving and in orienting us to our world, providing us with feedback about the personal significance of events (Izard, 1977; Plutchik & Kellerman, 1980; Tomkins, 1980). This perspective has been echoed by relationship theorists such as Bowlby (1988), who also views emotion as organizing individuals for survival and security.

EMOTION IN INTERACTION

What then are the main perspectives on emotion emerging in the current literature that are particularly relevant to intimate relationships?

1. *Emotional experience and expression is the primary building block of adult intimate relationships.* Other people and our relationships with them provide a primary source of emotional experience for human beings. It appears that evolutionary processes have endowed us with an innate capacity for, and need to, attach to significant others. This results in a sense of felt security when we are close to care givers whom we see as responsive to us and anxiety and anger when we are unwillingly separated from them (Bowlby, 1969). In Western society, we institutionalize this attachment in marriage. We marry primarily to give and receive love, and hope that our long-term intimate relationships will be characterized by this emotion (Broderick, 1981). Responses such as love and caring, as well as other emotions, tend to be a spontaneous reflection of inner experience, rather than mediated by conscious control (Buck, 1984). For this reason, in interaction, partners trust the information conveyed on an emotional level, often nonverbally, rather than more conscious deliberate communication. We also recognize the power of such responses, often experiencing them as happening to us automatically, and refer to them as passions. We use phrases such as "falling in love," rather than viewing love as something we choose or do. Emotional intimacy, characterized by understanding, validation, and caring, is therefore a critical aspect of human coupling.

2. *Emotions, such as love, are adaptive in human functioning.* Love, and caring, although they can be defined in many ways (Sternberg & Barnes, 1988), are essentially part of attachment (Shaver et al., 1988; Johnson, 1986). Attachment, which comprises an emotional tie and a set of proximity-seeking behaviors is organized by emotional responses. Attachment forms a secure base, a source of protection and intimate contact that buffers stress and facilitates positive adaptation and well-being (Hofer, 1984). The emotions that organize attachment are then adaptive and vital in human functioning. A "secure base" is characterized by confidence in the accessibility and respon-

siveness of care givers and a sense of self as lovable and worthy of care. This is learned in a context where the emotional signals of the child are sensitively responded to by care givers, who are emotionally attuned to the infant's responses (Stern, 1985). The processes of empathic attunement to the emotions of another, emotional accessibility, or the willingness to engage emotionally with the other, and responsiveness to the other's emotional cues and needs form the basis of a secure and nurturing adult bond.

Avoidant or anxious attachment, arising from the attachment styles of the partners and the nature of present interactions, inhibits the creation of trust and intimacy and does not provide a secure base from which partners can explore, and effectively interact with, their environment (Johnson & Greenberg, 1994).

3. *Emotion is a primary signaling system.* Emotional communication, especially nonverbal emotional communication, plays a primary role in organizing social interaction. Emotional expression changes the emotional experience and the behavior of the other (Tronick, 1989), and also has the potential to change the subject's experience and behavior, either directly or as a result of the other's response; that is, it is self-regulating and other regulating. Human systems signal their action readiness or dispositions to others by emotional displays. Emotion in humans serves a communicative function from birth. Infants are equipped with a set of adaptive expressive patterns long before their capacities for exclusively human cognitive operations are developed. From birth, infants' ability to communicate their needs, wants, and distress through nonverbal affective channels, such as voice and facial expression, is highly developed. Affective expression organizes the "interpersonal reflex" (Leary, 1959) of the other; that is, it pulls for certain responses. For example, vulnerability tends to disarm, while anger creates distance. The expression of fear and vulnerability, besides evoking compassion, also communicates analogically that there is no danger and therefore no need for defense. Similarly, expressions of sadness and pain communicate a need for support, while newly recognized anger and resentment can help define differences and delineate individual boundaries in a relationship. Levels of closeness-distance and dominance-submission, two critical dimensions of couple interaction, can be modified via affective expression (Greenberg & Johnson, 1988; Johnson & Greenberg, 1994).

4. *Emotion primes and organizes people for action in general, and for interpersonal responses in particular.* The motivational nature of emotion has been recognized by many theorists (Plutchik & Kellerman, 1980; Arnold, 1960; Tomkins, 1980; Frijda, 1988). Emotion may be viewed as a rapid response system, an alarm system, orienting the organism to the features of the outside world as they relate to that organism's safety and well-being. It primes approach and avoidance, attack and flight. The compelling quality of emotional experience focuses the individual, supersedes other concerns and goals, and creates an action tendency that must be either completed or resisted. As

Frijda (1988) suggests, emotion exhibits "control precedence"; it commands a response that other considerations, such as the long-term consequences of expression, are often powerless to inhibit. Distressed marital partners are often aware that they are endangering their relationships by their responses, but find themselves unable to respond in any other way. On the positive side, a partner's tears and congruent expression of vulnerability evoke compassion and a desire to comfort in a compelling and powerful fashion. Tomkins (1980) has also argued that emotions are motivation amplifying: they strengthen and energize motivated action. Thus emotions of fear or joy amplify one's motivation to escape or approach; a feeling of love amplifies the desire to approach and take care of, while anger amplifies the tendency to distance or aggressively protect oneself.

   5. *Emotion plays a powerful role in structuring interactional positions.* Since, as mentioned above, emotion primes and motivates individual responses and, when expressed, organizes social interaction, by pulling for or constraining the response of the other, it plays a very significant role in organizing interactional positions. Emotions are thus critical elements in determining the interactional cycles couples create (Johnson & Greenberg, 1994). In distressed couples, negative strong emotions concerning the spouse tend to become an absorbing state and override responses that do not conform to that affective state (Frijda, 1988), leading to each spouse taking rigid interactional positions. These rigid positions then interact to create self-reinforcing cycles such as pursue/withdraw or attack/defend. The relationship events that constitute such cycles in turn maintain each partner's emotional experience of the relationship. In the above explanation, an intimate relationship is viewed in terms of process; process forms of explanation, in general, seem to be replacing more static structural views of personality and psychological functioning (Mahoney, 1991). Emotion is a powerful part of the process that actively creates and maintains distress or satisfaction in intimate relationships.

   6. *Experienced emotion provides access to needs and desires.* The experience of emotion connects individuals to their intrapsychic longings, needs, and wants. To be unaware of emotions in an intimate relationship is to be cut off from an essential source of information and motivation necessary to construct a satisfying bond. Accessing the despair of loneliness leads naturally to a clear desire for contact and reassurance. Contacting the resentment associated with violations of one's boundaries leads to a clear desire to define these boundaries more clearly. Awareness of one's needs is certainly necessary before a partner can present such needs to a spouse.

   7. *Emotions organize perceptions of self and other.* The self is fundamentally an affective process involving the evaluation of phenomena in terms of their significance for personal well-being. Emotional experience tends to act as a filter, coloring the perceptions of self in relation to other and the other as a partner. Core cognitions and scripts involved in affect-laden self-schemas or working models are accessed and enacted in interactions when partners are

emotionally aroused. These cognitions tend to be more difficult to access, and therefore to reprocess or modify, when the emotion associated with them is absent.

The ongoing construction of personal identity is inextricably intertwined with emotional processes, particularly in the context of interactions with intimate others who are the mirror that allows us to elaborate and refine our model of self (Bowlby, 1988; Guidano, 1987). Couples fight not only about the nature of their relationship and who defines it but, more fundamentally, about how they are defined as people. Emotion is therefore a central organizing element of the self and of the perception of the other.

8. *Emotion links self and system.* Emotion connects us to our needs and longings and to our biological arousal patterns. Emotion as well plays a large part in organizing role relationships between people, and organizing how the self is perceived in relation to significant others. The expression of emotion also evokes responses in others, thereby establishing an interactional system. The unique power of emotion is that it links inner and outer worlds, need, and environmental status in relation to that need; that is, it links self and system. The challenge of therapies that seek to restructure intimate relationships is precisely that they have to deal with the dynamic interaction between external and internal realities. As Sullivan (1953) suggested, an interaction is already an integration of two realities, and these two realities then construct a third interpersonal domain, which is not a mechanical reflection of the first two but is "transformative."

In summary, emotional experience as viewed here is not a primitive, irrational response but a high-level information-processing system, integrating innate biological and emotional needs with past experience, with perceptions of the present environment, and with anticipated interpersonal consequences (Frijda, 1988).

INTERVENTIONS: IMPLICATIONS

The ways to approach emotion in terms of intervention are many and various. It can be a target or an agent of change, or both. It can be a central focus of change strategies in a particular approach (Greenberg & Johnson, 1988; Johnson & Greenberg, 1994), or one part of an approach that focuses more on behavior and/or cognition (Jacobson & Holtzworth-Munroe, 1986). It can be seen as an area of expertise, so the therapist teaches the skills of emotional expression (Baucom et al., 1990), or the skills of negative affect regulation (Lindahl & Markman, 1990). In terms of a release of tension, a couple's therapist might facilitate catharsis in one partner (Pierce, Nichols, & DuBrin, 1983) to create more open communication, or it can be viewed as part of a necessary mourning or grief process. Emotion in a distressed couple can be viewed as basically a maladaptive response to past traumas and conflicts and interpreted on a conceptual level to create insight into the partner's difficulties (Bockus, 1980). It can also be seen as setting goal priorities within and between people, and therefore validated, heightened, resynthesized, and used to reorganize interactions (Greenberg & Johnson, 1988; Johnson & Greenberg, 1994).

What do the theories and principles of emotion in close relationships summarized above suggest in terms of therapeutic interventions?

1. *Emotional experience and expression is a powerful tool for the therapist to use in reorganizing interactional positions.* The essence of marital therapy is that the couple find new ways to be together, to initiate new patterns of interaction, which redefine their relationship. Emotional experience and expression, if clear, congruent, and open, tends to create interactional positions that encourage affective attunement, emotional engagement, accessibility, and responsiveness—that is, a secure bond. If these positions are explicit and flexible, the relationship forms a secure base for both partners and is able to adapt to their changing demands and needs. In a distressed relationship, the expression of primary emotions underlying interactional positions can reorganize the individual's stance toward the other into one that evokes compassion and closeness rather than distance and self-protection. If the other then responds compassionately, a new emotional engagement occurs that modifies partners' perceptions of their partner, and begins a positive cycle of risking, trusting, asking, and responding (Johnson & Greenberg, 1988).

More specifically, the primary emotion (rather than secondary or instrumental emotion [Greenberg & Johnson, 1988]) underlying the positions partners take in most distressed relationships appears to be fear—fears of rejection and abandonment, or fears of loss of autonomy and engulfment. The positions the partners take with each other seem to reflect the level of insecurity in the relationship: the higher the level of fear, the more rigid and self-protective the position, and the more focus there is on regulating this emotion, either intrapsychically (I shut down, numb out, dismiss my feelings) or in the interaction (I cling to you and try to please, or I control you or avoid you). The direct accessing, expression, and owning of such fear allows for a reorganization of self in relation to other (I am not indifferent, I am so afraid of your rejection, I run), and allows for a reorganization of the interaction. In general, sadness, fear, and vulnerability are expressions that can be used to create closeness, while anger and disgust tend to define the boundaries of self more clearly.

2. *Accessing emotion in marital therapy provides partners with specific adaptive information.* Most emotional information generated in couples interaction informs partners of their attachment-related responses to their spouse and their own interpersonal sensitivities and needs. This information is crucial to the maintenance of an intimate relationship. It has been argued elsewhere that generally emotion provides information necessary to optimal functioning in human systems (Safran & Greenberg, 1991). In the area of intimate

relationships, however, this is particularly true, precisely because emotion organizes people for adaptive action in interpersonal environments. The expression of emotion is a primary signaling system and organizes interactions by signaling to partners each person's internal states and intentions. The therapist then needs to raise partners' awareness of their own emotional responses, and of the messages sent and received, in order to clarify what is governing their interactions.

One of the most common scenarios in marital therapy is a partner demanding a particular response in a manner that elicits antithetical behavior from the other partner, such as demanding intimate sharing in a hostile or complaining manner that elicits distance. By facilitating the experiencing of the person's primary emotional response, for example, the desperate desire for contact and fear of abandonment underlying the hostility, the therapist can increase this spouse's awareness of his or her needs, and explicate this partner's helpless rage at the other's distance and inaccessibility. The expression of such emotion, directed and focused by the therapist, then gives the other partner new information about this spouse's responses and reactions.

Awareness of such primary emotional experience provides information to the self about the significance to one's well-being of the spouse's actions, in this case distancing, and information about how one regulates such emotion and responds. Since emotional experience and expression is so rich, in the sense described above, the therapist often legitimizes, validates, and expands such experience. The therapist's empathic attunement to each partner's feelings provides the safety to experience more fully and search for symbols to capture that experience.

Awareness of the emotional messages we send and their potential impact on others is then essential if we are to construct reliable positive relationships and curtail or control negative reactive cycles such as pursue/withdraw or demand/distance, which seem to be endemic in current marital relationships. Indeed, an interpersonal definition of dysfunction is that it essentially involves a communicative style that pulls for negative responses from others, without awareness of, or the taking of responsibility for, this style (Kiesler, 1983).

3. *Intimacy is created by emotional experience and expression.* Marital therapy must then facilitate the experience and expression of emotions that connect partners and foster secure attachment. Love, and generally positive emotional experiences such as security, acceptance, and trust, are crucial to marital happiness. How then does therapy facilitate, create, or evoke these feelings? Three approaches can be identified: maladaptive blocks to love and affection such as negative beliefs about others or the dangers of intimacy can be modified, and love will presumably follow; loving behaviors can be structured by the therapist, as in caring days (Stuart, 1980); or loving feelings such as compassion or tenderness can be evoked by emotional communication in the session (Johnson & Greenberg, 1994), or by specific experiences

such as the sharing of hurts (L'Abate & Sloan, 1984). Whatever the means, the end goal is the generation of intimacy-creating emotional experience. If therapy can create a context of trust and emotional engagement, problems that arise can become a vehicle for intimate connection and sharing (Johnson & Greenberg, 1991). Emotional contact strengthens the bond between partners. The target of change has to be the feelings partners have for each other (Roberts, 1992), particularly if we accept that the real criterion for effectiveness in marital therapy is not only improvement, but the creation of a happy and satisfying relationship by the end of therapy. Behaviors, skills, ideas, can all change, and will all change in successful therapy; however, if caring or love is somehow not rekindled, many of our clients will tell us we have failed. Success in marital therapy is not only less distress, it is also the creation of a positive relationship, that is, one that generates positive affect.

4. *New feelings need to be experienced and expressed to produce change.* It is the expression of *new*, currently synthesized feelings that leads to change, not old, stale, repeatedly expressed feelings. These newly expressed feelings also need to be the primary, most direct experiences felt in the moment and to be free of blame or evaluation. It has been cogently argued that only new emotional experiences can change core emotional themes and the personal meanings inherent in them (Guidiano, 1991). If so, then the primary aim of marital therapy is to provide such experiences. This is done by attending to emerging momentary emotional states that have the potential to alter interactions in marital therapy; such feelings can facilitate contact between partners and access and modify blocks to contact. Thus a momentary look of yearning or fear from a blamer or a withdrawer, if focused on and developed, can alter the person's organization and lead to a new kind of dialogue and emotional contact (Greenberg & Johnson, 1988; Johnson & Greenberg, 1994).

5. *Restructuring emotional bonds is the core concern of marital therapy.* If attachment is the basis of adult love, the goal of therapy is essentially to restructure and strengthen attachment bonds, that is, to reprocess the emotional tie between the couple, and reorganize interactions that concern closeness and security. Emotion activates the attachment system, and attachment behaviors are structured by how this emotion is processed and regulated. No matter what the presenting problem, however pragmatic, the experience of emotion and emotional responses, and how issues of safety, trust, contact, comfort, and intimacy are enacted in the process of interaction, are preeminent. New cycles of interaction, characterized by sensitive responding to attachment needs and emotional attunement (Johnson & Greenberg, 1994), have to be initiated and integrated into the relationship. When this occurs, prototypical bonding events take place, such as when one partner expresses fear or hurt and is comforted, or asks for acceptance and compassion and receives it. Making new agreements, exchanging new resources, and understanding each other better, may be part of this process, but will not, by themselves, achieve the task of therapy.

From this perspective, the therapist's focus will most fruitfully be on bonding issues, particularly contact and safety, and the therapist needs to directly choreograph new bonding events, which are enacted and processed in the session with the therapist's help.

6. *The emotions that organize an intimate relationship are best evoked, aroused, and reprocessed in the session,* that is, they are best experienced rather than discussed or viewed from a distance. The power of emotion tends to compellingly override other priorities and cues, and to take control precedence (Frijda, 1988), particularly in attachment contexts. Unless harnessed and used in therapy, it has the potential to undermine any intervention that requires that attention be shifted from the powerful agenda dictated by emotional responses. Mead (1981) suggests that couples will not use skills such as problem solving if competing behaviors are more salient in the relationship. This may also be true of new insights or affect-regulation strategies. There is surely no more salient competing experience than emotional vulnerability and the protection of that vulnerability, particularly if such emotion is part of an innate survival/security system. In short, if processing emotion is not part of the treatment in marital therapy, it will likely be part of the problem.

7. *Reworking the way the self is defined in relation to the other is an essential part of marital therapy.* Essential self-definitions become available in emotionally charged interactions. Self-definition and relationship definition are two sides of the same coin; they are the dancer and the dance. Emotion, being so closely tied to the nature of self and the salience of external events for the self, is intricately connected to core definitions of self in relation to other, or to working models of self (Bowlby, 1969). In fact, it is difficult to access and formulate such core appraisals of self unless individuals are emotionally aroused. Emotional schemata concerning self tend to be up and running and more available to awareness in emotionally charged interactions with significant others. The therapist tracks and focuses on working models of self as they arise, particularly the self experienced as unlovable and inadequate. These models can then be modified by new interactional experiences such as acceptance and recognition of worth from the other spouse. The therapist can actively choreograph new emotional experiences that allow such models to be reformulated in more positive ways that evoke intimacy and trust (Johnson & Greenberg, 1994).

Since the construction and maintenance of personal identity is intricately connected to attachment processes (Guidiano, 1991), and attachment figures reflect and impact the operating model of self, the integration of less known or accepted aspects of self is particularly fostered by a secure bond with an accepting, acknowledging other. A secure relationship is then the natural arena for reintegrating aspects of self that have been denied or disowned, or simply never formulated. In individual psychotherapy, the emphasis has been on the healing power of the therapist-client relationship; in marital therapy, the emphasis shifts to the healing power of the partners' relationship. The reworking of models of self, as well as the restructuring of emotional schemata representing the self, other, and interpersonal situation, is part of marital therapy and is made possible by accessing and reprocessing emotion with one's partner. It is by interacting with intimate others that the nature of self becomes more clearly defined, articulated, and integrated.

8. *Emotional contact is the touchstone of intimate relationships.* The basis of intimacy is the sharing of emotional vulnerability (L'Abate & Sloan, 1984). Vulnerability shared forges connections between people, as vulnerability experienced and defensively protected creates distance. In marital therapy, the therapist can structure the process of reprocessing and expressing newly synthesized emotions to one's spouse in such a way as to forge a sense of intimate connection between partners (Dandeneau & Johnson, 1994). The therapist's task is then to help partners become emotionally attuned to each other and be able to respond with sensitivity. Intimate self-disclosures lead to affiliative interaction (Greenberg, Ford, Alden, & Johnson, 1993). Heightened emotion activates attachment behaviors, and emotional engagement provides an opportunity for the renewal of the bond between partners, which is experienced as a source of joy and belonging. The therapist then structures new levels of engagement that act as antidotes to alienation and distance.

If this specific kind of engagement is experienced in a secure context, the need for self-protective strategies that limit contact and involvement is also lessened. Behaviors designed to regulate negative affect either intrapsychic or interpersonal, which become automatic, inflexible, and indiscriminate, constrict the individuals' engagement with others and also limit the modification or expansion of perceptions, schemata, and experience (Tronick, 1989). If the therapist structures risk-taking interactions, where vulnerability is shared, this effectively engenders secure connectedness.

9. *Since emotion is a multifaceted phenomenon, it must be differentiated if it is to be used effectively in therapy.* Emotion has been considered as a global uniform phenomenon, for example, as energy to be released, and understandably has therefore been difficult to deal with as a therapeutic agent. It is necessary for the therapist to differentiate levels of emotion, such as primary, secondary, or reactive, and instrumental emotion, since primary emotion, the organism's initial automatic response to the situation, is considered the source of adaptive action and change in therapy.

Interventions also need to be refined. With some couples, it may only be necessary to access underlying emotions to facilitate new interactions; with others, these responses will also need to be reframed (e.g., anger reframed as desperation). In more serious cases, emotional responses may also need to be reprocessed and restructured, as when the fear underlying distance is owned and elaborated. In a few cases, primary emotion, which was adaptive in a past context, will now be maladaptive, and will need to be accessed and modified, for example, the extreme terror and disassociation arising from childhood sexual abuse that preclude the development of trust in intimate relationships.

The therapist also has to track and differentiate the level of emotional experience and expression. Change events in marital therapy have been associated with deeply experienced and elaborated emotion in therapy sessions (Johnson & Greenberg, 1988). Such experience often has to be heightened and elaborated by the therapist, and then integrated into the interaction. Interpersonally, emotional attunement, a moment-to-moment tuning into the other's emotion, and emphatically being with and responding to the other in the experience, is the level of emotional response required for positive bonding experiences. As Stern (1985) describes, in attunement the facial expression of one participant mirrors the affect of the other; this is a different level of experience from the labeling or detached understanding of an affective response. Again, this kind of attunement often needs to be fostered by the therapist, who monitors the way partners respond to each other and process their own experience in the interaction.

10. *Intervention at the level of emotion helps the therapist create the necessary bridge between the intrapsychic and the interpersonal, the social, and the biological.* Marital therapy has to deal with intrapsychic realities and interpersonal realities, and the way these two interact and create each other. Emotion gives the therapist access to the interpersonal and intrapsychic determinants of action, integrating appraisals of relational events with action tendencies and expressive sensory responses. In the emotionally charged interaction between partners, the therapist has operating, in process, in front of him or her, the internal working models of self and other of each partner, the synthesis of motor responses, the emotional schemata and conceptual beliefs about emotion and how to relate, the action tendency inherent in the emotion enacted, and the partner's response to the above, which evokes the positive or negative cycles that define the relationship. There are many entry points and many ways to impact experience and interaction. The emotion is the music that brings the dance alive and engages the dancers; with all the elements present the potential for new choreography is at its height.

REFERENCES

Arnold, M. B. (1960). *Emotion and personality.* New York: Columbia University Press.
Baucom, D. H., Sayers, S. L., & Sher, T. G. (1990) Supplementing behavioral marital therapy with cognitive restructuring and emotional expressiveness training: An outcome investigation. *Journal of Consulting and Clinical Psychology, 58,* 636–645.
Blaney, P. (1986). Affect and memory. *Psychological Bulletin, 99,* 229–246.
Bockus, F. (1980). *Couple therapy.* New York: Aronson.
Bowlby, J. (1969). *Attachment and loss: Vol. 1. Attachment.* New York: Basic Books.
Bowlby, J. (1988). *A secure base.* New York: Basic Books.
Broderick, C. (1981). A method for deviation of areas for assessment in marital relationships. *American Journal of Family Therapy, 9,* 25–34.

Broderick, J. E., & O'Leary, K. D. (1986). Contributions of affect, attitudes and behavior to marital satisfaction. *Journal of Consulting and Clinical Psychology, 54*, 514–517.

Buck, R. (1984). *The communication of emotion.* New York: Guilford.

Butler, S. F., & Strupp, H. H. (1991). The role of affect in time-limited dynamic psychotherapy. In J. D. Safran & L. S. Greenberg (Eds.), *Emotion, psychotherapy and change.* New York: Guilford.

Dandeneau, M., & Johnson, S. M. (1994). Facilitating intimacy: A comparative outcome study of emotionally focused and cognitive interventions. *Journal of Marital and Family Therapy, 20*, 17–33.

Dessaulles, A., Johnson, S. M., Hotz, S., & Kallos, V. (1994). The treatment of clinical depression in the context of marital distress: A preliminary study. *Manuscript in preparation.*

Ekman, P., & Friesen, W. V. (1975). *Unmasking the face.* Englewood Cliffs, NJ: Prentice-Hall.

Frijda, N. H. (1986). *The emotions.* Cambridge, England: Cambridge University Press.

Frijda, N. H. (1988). The laws of emotion. *American Psychologist, 43*, 349–358.

Goldman, A., & Greenberg, L. S. (1992). Comparison of integrated systemic and emotionally focused couples therapy. *Journal of Consulting and Clinical Psychology, 60*, 962–969.

Gottman, J. M. (1991). Predicting the longitudinal course of marriages. *Journal of Marital and Family Therapy, 17*, 3–7.

Gottman, J. M., & Krokoff, L. J. (1989). Marital interaction and satisfaction: A longitudinal view. *Journal of Consulting and Clinical Psychology, 57*, 47–52.

Greenberg, L. S., Ford, C., Alden, L., & Johnson, S. (1993). In-session change in emotionally focused couples therapy. *Journal of Consulting and Clinical Psychology, 61*, 78–84.

Greenberg, L. S., & Johnson, S. M. (1986). Affect in marital therapy. *Journal of Marital and Family Therapy, 12*, 1–10.

Greenberg, L. S., & Johnson, S. M. (1988). *Emotionally focused therapy for couples.* New York: Guilford.

Greenberg, L. S., Rice, L. S., & Elliott, R. (1993). *Facilitating emotional change.* New York: Guilford.

Greenberg, L. S., & Safran, J. D. (1987). *Emotion in psychotherapy.* New York: Guilford.

Guerin, P. J., Fay, L. F., Burden, S. L., & Kautto, J. G. (1987). *The evaluation and treatment of the marital conflict.* New York: Basic Books.

Guidano, V. F. (1987). *Complexity of the self: A developmental approach to psychopathology and therapy.* New York: Guilford.

Guidano, V. F. (1991). Affective change events in a cognitive therapy systems approach. In J. D. Safran & L. S. Greenberg (Eds.) *Emotion, psychotherapy and change* (pp. 50–81). New York: Guilford.

Gurman, A. S., & Kniskern, D. P. (1981). Family therapy outcome research: Knowns and unknowns. In A. S. Gurman & D. P. Kniskern (Eds.), *Handbook of family therapy.* New York: Brunner/Mazel.

Hahlweg, K., Schindler, L., Revenstorf, D., & Brenglemann, J. C. (1984). The Munich marital therapy study. In K. Hahlweg & N. S. Jacobson (Eds.), *Marital Interaction.* New York: Guilford.

Harrell, J., & Guerney, B. (1976). Training marital couples in conflict negotiation skills. In D. H. L. Olson (Ed.), *Treating relationships.* Lake Mills, LA: Graphic.

Hofer, M. A. (1984). Relationships as regulators: A psychobiological perspective on bereavement. *Psychosomatic Medicine, 46*, 183–198.

Izard, C. E. (1977). *Emotion in personality and psychopathology.* New York: Plenum.

Jacobson, N. S. (1991). Towards enhancing the efficacy of marital therapy and marital therapy research. *Journal of Family Psychology, 4*, 373–393.

Jacobson, N. S., Follett, W. C., Revenstorf, D., Baucom, D. H., Hahlweg, K., & Margolin, M. (1984). Variability in outcome and clinical significance of behavioral marital therapy: A reanalysis of outcome data. *Journal of Consulting and Clinical Psychology, 52*, 497–504.

Jacobson, N. S., & Holtzworth-Munroe, A. (1986). Marital therapy: A social learning/cognitive perspective. In N. S. Jacobson & A. S. Gurman (Eds.), *Clinical handbook of marital therapy* (29–70). New York: Guilford.

Jacobson, N. S., & Margolin, G. (1979). *Marital therapy: Strategies based on social learning and behavior exchange principles.* New York: Brunner/Mazel.

James, P. (1991). Effects of communication training component added to an emotionally focused couples therapy. *Journal of Marital and Family Therapy, 17*, 263–276.

Johnson, S. M. (1986). Bonds and bargains: Relationship paradigms and their significance for marital therapy. *Journal of Marital and Family Therapy, 12,* 259–267.

Johnson, S. M., & Greenberg, L. S. (1985a). The differential effects of experiential and problem-solving interventions in resolving marital conflict. *Journal of Consulting and Clinical Psychology, 53,* 175–184.

Johnson, S. M., & Greenberg, L. (1985b). Emotionally focused couples therapy: An outcome study. *Journal of Marital and Family Therapy, 11,* 313–317.

Johnson, S. M., & Greenberg, L. S. (1987). Emotionally focused marital therapy: An overview. *Psychotherapy, 24,* 552–560.

Johnson, S. M., & Greenberg, L. S. (1988). Relating process to outcome in marital therapy. *Journal of Marital and Family Therapy, 14,* 175–183.

Johnson, S. M., & Greenberg, L. S. (1991). There are more things in heaven and earth than are dreamed of in BMT: A reply to Jacobson. *American Journal of Family Psychology, 4,* 407–415.

Johnson, S. M., & Greenberg, L. S. (1994). The emotionally focused approach to problems in adult attachment. In N. S. Jacobson & A. S. Gurman (Eds.), *Clinical handbook of marital therapy* (2nd ed.). New York: Guilford.

Kiesler, D. J. (1983). The 1982 interpersonal circle: A Taxonomy for complementarity in human transactions. *Psychological Review, 90,* 185–214.

L'Abate, L. N., & Sloan, S. (1984). A workshop format to facilitate intimacy in married couples. *Family Relations, 33,* 245–250.

Lang, P. J. (1977). Imagery in therapy. An information processing analysis of fear. *Behavior Therapy, 8,* 862–886.

Lang, P. J. (1983). Cognition in emotion: Concept and action. In C. Izard, J. Kagan, & R. Zajonc (Eds.), *Emotion, cognition and behavior.* Cambridge, England: Cambridge University Press.

Lang, P. J. (1984). The cognitive psychology of emotion: Fear and anxiety. In A. H. Tuma & J. D. Maser (Eds.), *Anxiety and anxiety disorders.* Hillsdale, NJ: Erlbaum.

Lazarus, R. S. (1982). Thoughts on the relations between emotion and cognition. *American Psychologist, 37,* 1010–1019.

Lazarus, R. S. (1991a). Cognition and motivation in emotion. *American Psychologist, 46,* 352–367.

Lazarus, R. S. (1991b). Progress on a cognitive–motivational–relational theory of emotion. *American Psychologist, 46,* 819–834.

Leary, T. (1959). *The interpersonal diagnosis of personality.* New York: Ronald.

Leventhal, H. (1984). A perceptual motor theory of emotion. In L. Berkowitz (Ed.), *Advances in experimental social psychology.* New York: Academic.

Leventhal, H. (1979). A perceptual motor processing model of emotion. In P. Pliner, K.R. Blankstein, & I. M. Spigal (Eds.), *Advances in the study of communication and affect: Vol. 5. Perceptions of emotions in self and others* (pp. 1–46). New York: Plenum.

Lindahl, K. M., & Markman, H. J. (1990). Communication and negative affect regulation in the family. In E. A. Blechman (Ed.), *Emotions and the family: For better or for worse.* Hillsdale, NJ: Erlbaum.

Mahoney, M. J. (1991). *Human change processes: The scientific foundations of psychotherapy.* New York: Basic Books.

Margolin, G., & Weinstein, C. D. (1983). The role of affect in behavioral marital therapy. In L. R. Wolberg, & M. L. Aronson (Eds.), *Group and family therapy.* New York: Brunner/Mazel.

Mead, D. E. (1981). Reciprocity counselling: Practice and research. *Journal of Marital and Family Therapy, 7,* 189–199.

Napier, A. (1988). *The fragile bond.* New York: Harper & Row.

Oatley, K., & Jenkins, J. M. (1992). Human emotions: Function and dysfunction. *Annual Review of Psychology, 43,* 55–85.

Panskepp, J. (1989). The psychobiology of emotions: The animal side of human feelings. *Experimental Brain Research, 18,* 31–55.

Pierce, R. A., Nichols, M. P., & DuBrin, J. R. (1983). *Emotional expression in psychotherapy.* New York: Gardner.

Plutchik, R., & Kellerman, H. (Eds.). (1980). *Emotion: Theory, research and experience, Vol. 1: Theories of emotion.* New York: Academic.

Rapaport, D. (1970). *Emotions and memory.* New York: International Universities Press.

Roberts T. W. (1992). Sexual attraction and romantic love: Forgotten variables in marital therapy. *Journal of Marital and Family Therapy, 18,* 357–364.

Safran, J. D., & Greenberg, L. S. (Eds.). (1991). *Emotion, psychotherapy and change.* New York: Guilford.

Scherer, K. R. (1984). On the nature and function of emotion: A component process approach. In K. F. Scherer & P. Ekman (Eds.), *Approaches to emotion* (pp. 293–317). Hillsdale, NJ: Erlbaum.

Shaver, P., Hazan, C., & Bradshaw, D. (1988). Love as attachment. In R. J. Sternberg & M. L. Barnes (Eds.), *The psychology of love.* New Haven: Yale University Press.

Snyder, D. K., & Wills, R. M. (1989). Behavioral versus insight-oriented marital therapy. Effects on individual and interspousal functioning. *Journal of Consulting and Clinical Psychology, 57,* 39–46.

Stein, R. (1991). *Psychoanalytic theories of affect.* New York: Praeger.

Sternberg, R. L., & Barnes, M. L. (1988). *The psychology of love.* New Haven: Yale University Press.

Stern, D. N. (1985). *The interpersonal world of the infant: A view from psychoanalysis and developmental psychology.* New York: Basic Books.

Stuart, R. B. (1980). *Helping couples change: A social learning approach to marital therapy.* New York: Aronson.

Sullivan, H. S. (1953). *The interpersonal theory of psychiatry.* New York: Norton.

Thibaut, J. W., & Kelley, H. H. (1959). *The social psychology of groups.* New York: Wiley.

Tomkins, S. S. (1980). Affect as amplification: Some modifications in theory. In R. Plutchik & H. Kellerman (Eds.), *Emotion: Theory, research and experience, Vol. 1: Theories of Emotion.* New York: Academic.

Tronick, E. Z. (1989). Emotions and emotional communication in infants. *American Psychologist, 44,* 112–119.

Walker, J. (1993). *Marital interventions with parents of chronically ill children.* Unpublished doctoral dissertation. University of Ottawa, Canada.

Waring, E. M. (1988). *Enhancing marital intimacy through facilitating cognitive self-disclosure.* New York: Brunner/Mazel.

Wile, D. (1981). *Couples therapy: A non-traditional approach.* New York: Wiley.

PART II

AFFECT IN COUPLE RELATIONSHIPS AND THERAPY

SECTION A

Dynamic Approaches: Ego-Analytic and Attachment

2

The Ego-Analytic Approach to Emotion in Couples Therapy

DANIEL B. WILE

Ego analysis developed as an alternative to id analysis. Whereas in id analysis, the crucial issues are "primitive drives" and the defenses against these drives, in ego analysis, the crucial issue is the relationship that people have with themselves about their thoughts, feelings, and wishes—and about their drives and defenses.

From an ego-analytic view, "primitive drives" are consequences of the phobic or rejecting (disapproving, condemning) relationship that people have with themselves about their ordinary feelings. A man is critical of himself for being angry. He thinks he should not be angry, so he suppresses his anger. When his anger eventually reemerges, it does so in an intense and provocative form—he has a tantrum. His rejection of an ordinary feeling (ordinary anger) has resulted in a primitive drive (infantile rage). In viewing primitive drives not as ultimate psychological explanations but as derivatives (distorted products) of something else, ego analysis is similar to Kohut's (1977) self psychology and to the "relational" theories described by Greenberg and Mitchell (1983).

Ego analysis has its roots in Freud (1926); it emerged in the work of Otto Fenichel (1941), and was further developed by Paul Gray (1982) and Bernard Apfelbaum (Apfelbaum, 1977, 1982, 1988; Apfelbaum & Apfelbaum, 1985; Apfelbaum & Gill, 1989). My own work (Wile, 1981, 1984, 1985, 1987, 1988, 1993, in press) follows the line of thinking developed by Apfelbaum.

Ego analysis is not to be confused with Hartmann's and Rapaport's ego psychology. As Apfelbaum (1966, 1983) demonstrated, ego psychology is an extension of id-analytic thinking, whereas ego analysis is an alternative to it.

The purpose of this chapter is to apply ego-analytic thinking to the subject of "emotions." From an ego-analytic viewpoint, the issue is not so much the emotion in itself as the relationship the person has with himself of herself about the emotion.

I shall use the following fictional interchange to talk about the role of emotion in ego-analytic couples therapy. Sally and Rich have come in for their third couples therapy session:

SALLY: [*To Rich*] Why do you always have to get so insanely jealous all the time?

RICH: I don't get jealous.

SALLY: What do you call sulking in the corner for the whole party Saturday night and then the next morning yelling at me for the "horrible crime" of talking to a couple of the men there?

RICH: Anytime I raise my voice just a little, you immediately think I'm yelling.

SALLY: You *were* yelling. You scared the cat.

RICH: I didn't scare the cat; the cat was leaving anyway. I'm tired of your always exaggerating.

SALLY: Well, I'm tired of your always getting jealous.

RICH: I wouldn't get jealous if you didn't have to flirt with every man at every party we go to.

SALLY: You know I don't flirt.

RICH: What do you call laughing like a fool Saturday night at all that man's stupid jokes?

SALLY: I was just being *polite*—the way you're *supposed* to be at parties—you know, friendly.

RICH: You were friendly all right.

SALLY: I wasn't being any friendlier than anyone else—except you, of course. You spent the whole evening sulking in the corner.

RICH: I wasn't sulking. I was just observing.

SALLY: Observing *me*, you mean. You were *spying* on me. How else would you know so much about what I was doing?

RICH: It didn't take spying to see what you were doing. It was obvious. Everyone saw it.

SALLY: Oh? Just what exactly did everyone see?

RICH: They saw you playing up to every man in the room.

SALLY: *Playing up?* Maybe I should have been. It'd be nice to have someone express a little interest in me. You certainly don't.

RICH: Oh, so you admit it. You *were* flirting.

SALLY: I don't admit anything. Can't you listen to what I'm saying?

RICH: Okay, okay, what are you saying?

SALLY: That you haven't shown any interest in me lately.

RICH: You think *that's* an excuse?

SALLY: An excuse for what? I wasn't doing anything *wrong*.

RICH: Every man you talked to, you looked like you were ready to have sex with right then and there.

SALLY: Well, you needn't have worried about it. It's been so long since we've had sex that I've forgotten how it's done.

RICH: What do you mean? We had sex last week.

SALLY: For the first time in 2 months.

RICH: We've had sex *lots* of times in the last 2 months. I keep telling you how I hate it when you exaggerate, but you keep doing it.

SALLY: Well, *I* hate it when you accuse me of flirting.

RICH: Why do you do it then?

SALLY: I *don't* do it.

RICH: You haven't heard a word I've said.

SALLY: You haven't said anything that makes any sense.

RICH: This is stupid. We're getting nowhere.

For the purposes of this chapter, I shall focus on what Sally calls Rich's "insane jealousy"—and what therapists might call morbid jealousy. Different therapists might view this jealousy in the following variety of ways:

- Some therapists would look for damage, deprivation, or abuse in Rich's childhood.
- Other therapists, who see defect or deficiency as providing insufficient explanation, would attribute his problem to a conflict. They might trace his jealousy to an unresolved conflict in childhood.
- Or they might see his jealousy as serving an unconscious purpose, such as protecting against too much intimacy or as energizing the relationship.
- Or they might see Rich as projecting on Sally his own nonmonogamous wishes.
- Or they might see Rich's focus on Sally's behavior (or misbehavior) as a way to explain to himself problems in their relationship—problems that might include his loss of sexual interest in her. Focusing on her flirting might be part of his way of blaming her for their problems.
- Other therapists, looking for Sally's hidden contribution to the problem, might emphasize how she might be functioning as a codependent.
- Or they might see her as covertly reinforcing his jealous behavior because it serves unconscious purposes of her own.
- Other therapists, who see relationships as based on an unconscious marriage contract (an intermeshing of primitive needs of both partners), might see Rich's angry jealousy as part of the contract—or as his reaction to the violation of this contract.
- Still other therapists, who look for an alternative to deficiency or conflict theory, might emphasize the grain of truth in Rich's response (i.e., how he might have reason to be jealous).
- Therapists with a family systems view might see Rich's jealousy as signaling a more general problem in the relationship.
- Or they might construct a genogram to check how jealousy might be a theme in the family through the generations.

- Or they might look for the ways in which Rich's jealousy serves a family or couple purpose, such as maintaining homeostasis (i.e., Rich is the identified patient).
- Still other therapists might view Rich's jealousy in its sociopolitical context (i.e., they might see his jealous demands as simply a clear form of the way men view women as their property).

In this array of possible explanations, it is easy to miss how Rich's morbid jealousy is a result of his inability to experience "simple" or "pure" jealousy. The clue is that Rich's jealousy has been transformed from a feeling ("I feel jealous") to a moral injunction ("She shouldn't be doing what she is doing").

THE LIFE-HISTORY OF A FEELING

At the party the night before, Rich looked across the room and saw Sally engaged in a lively conversation with one of the men there. It was then that Rich had this flash of what I am calling "simple" or "pure" jealousy, which, if he had been able to experience it—that is, put it in words in his own mind—would have come out like this:

RICH: [*To himself*] Wow! I'm really jealous. This is wrenching. I wish it were *me* who Sally was talking to in such a lively way.

We are not used to people feeling jealousy in its simple or pure form—that is, as an ache and a sense of anguish. But if Rich were to talk to himself in this way, he might be able to go to Sally and say:

RICH: You know, it's funny, but standing over there watching you talk to that man, I felt really jealous—*really* jealous. I wish it were me you were talking to with such animation.

Since Rich would be making clear that he was not blaming Sally for arousing his jealousy, Sally would be unlikely to take offense. In fact, she might say something like:

SALLY: That's the best thing I've heard all day. I love it when you're jealous. It really makes me feel loved. So I probably shouldn't tell you that that man is the world's biggest bore and I was glad to find an excuse to get away from him. Of course, if talking to him is going to have such a wonderful effect on you, maybe I should hunt him up and struggle through another conversation.

We typically think of jealousy as potentially damaging to relationships. But here we see it as an occasion for an intimate exchange.

Rich, however, is unable to formulate this feeling of "simple" or "pure" jealousy—he is unable to put it into words in his own mind, much less put it into words for Sally. That is because he feels ashamed of his jealousy. He thinks he is being overly possessive. He thinks Sally should be able to talk however she likes at a party—and to whomever. He sees his jealous feelings as a sign of weakness and immaturity. He feels he should not feel jealous unless there is something clear and concrete to point to, such as an affair or love letter. In a word, he feels *unentitled* to his feelings of "pure" jealousy. He feels there is something wrong with him for having them. There were no models in Rich's family—or in society in general—of people who expressed pure jealousy. He has rarely seen people—not even in the movies or on TV—who felt sufficiently entitled to their pure jealousy that they could go to their partner and say, "You know, it's funny, but standing over there watching you talk to that man, I felt really jealous." Pure jealousy is a feeling that Rich never learned to have.

Rich behaves as people typically do when they feel unentitled to and threatened by a feeling and are thus unable to formulate it. He has what I call "symptoms":

He suddenly feels bored with the party.

He loses his interest in talking to people at the party.

He tells himself, "The Sanchezes always throw such dull parties."

He feels critical of the other guests at the party. He tells himself, "Look at them. They're all so pretentious."

He wishes he were home watching television.

He begins to wonder when it would be okay to leave.

He loses his resolve not to drink.

He loses a little of his good feeling about himself.

He feels a little less attractive—he begins to feels self-conscious about his pot belly.

I know that when we use the word symptoms, we typically think of clearly maladaptive or pathological reactions such as insomnia, loss of appetite, and excessive drinking. But I am using the word in a broader way to include reactions such as feeling bored, wishing you were home, or losing a little of your good feeling about yourself. Rich tells himself:

"Sally shouldn't behave this way."

"She should spend more time with me at parties."

"I know you're supposed to mingle, but this is ridiculous."

"There's something oily about that man."

"I know his type—smooth manner but a lot of hot air."

"Why doesn't Sally see how shallow he is?"

"And why is she standing so close to him?"

"Why does she have to flirt with him?"

"She's trying to *make* me feel jealous."

Rich is doing what people often do when they feel unentitled to or threatened by a feeling. He is externalizing. He turns his attention from what he feels, since it is making him uncomfortable, to what others are doing—or, rather, to what he feels they "should" or "should not" be doing. In other words, he turns his "I" statements into "you" statements (and into "he," "she," and "they" statements). What began as a feeling has turned into a set of complaints and moral recriminations:

- Rich's "I feel jealous" has been transformed into "She shouldn't behave that way—she should stay with me at parties," "I know you're supposed to mingle at parties, but this is ridiculous," and "She's trying to make me feel jealous."
- His "I wish she were talking to *me* that way" has been transformed into "She shouldn't talk to *him* that way."
- His "I wish she weren't talking to him that way" has been transformed into "Why can't she see how shallow he is?" "Why is she standing so close to him?" and "Why does she have to flirt with him?"

Rich's pure jealousy has turned into jealous anger. We often think of anger as intrinsic to jealousy. If a person is jealous, we commonly assume that it means that he or she is angry. But, as we see in this example, jealous anger is a derivative or transformation of pure jealousy. It is a consequence of feeling unentitled to pure jealousy:

Pure jealousy—that is, the jealous feeling in itself—is a longing or ache. It is a wish—here Rich's wish that Sally felt about him the way she seems at the moment to feel about the man she is talking to.

Jealous anger, as I see it, is a transfiguration of pure jealousy. It is the result of Rich's feeling of unentitlement to and discomfort with his jealous feeling and his consequent inability to recognize, accept, and commiserate with himself about it, leading to a shift from a feeling ("I feel jealous") to a moral injunction ("She shouldn't be doing what she is doing").

So now Rich has a new experience: this transformation into a moral injunction, which itself is a new feeling—righteous indignation. He feels moral outrage at what he now sees as Sally's and this man's mistreatment of him. He feels like going up to them and telling them directly:

RICH: [*To the man*] Keep your hands off her; find your own woman.
Rich: [*To Sally*] You're coming home with me right now.

Or even:

RICH: [*To both*] Why don't the two of you go to bed together right now and get
    it over with?

There is no way for him to make such direct statements because he knows
that Sally would think he is being ridiculous—she would laugh at him—and
he would feel like a fool. And he would think that maybe she would be right.
He has a nagging, back-of-the-mind worry that his moral outrage is over-
blown and inappropriate. He is caught up in strong feelings of moral outrage with no way to express them. He does not know what to do—he feels
powerless:

- In an effort to retaliate and get Sally jealous (so he won't feel so powerless), he goes up to the most attractive woman at the party and tries
  to talk with her in an alive and engaged way. But Sally does not seem
  to notice.
- He begins skulking in the corner, shooting poisonous glances in Sally's
  direction, but he cannot tell whether she sees them.
- He tries to think of a way that he can sneak up and eavesdrop on what
  they are saying, but he gives up the idea because he is afraid of being
  noticed.
- He thinks of going outside and letting the air out of that man's tires—
  but he worries about how foolish he would feel if he were caught.
- He has the passing thought of leaving suddenly, and taking the car,
  without telling Sally. But he fears that she would just get a ride home
  with that man.
- He gets another drink.
- He goes from skulking to sulking.

When Rich is finally alone with Sally in the car on the drive home, he still
cannot tell her anything. What would he say? The last time he accused her
of flirting, they had an awful fight, after which they did not speak for days.
Just as his pure jealousy turned to moral outrage, his moral outrage now
turns to smoldering rage. And what further upsets him is that Sally seems
totally unaware of all he is going through. She does not even seem to notice
his silence.

Later that night, he gets into bed as if Sally were not in it. He lies in bed
with his back to her. He tosses and turns, not minding how much his shaking
the bed might disturb Sally's sleep. In fact, he hopes that the shaking will
disturb her sleep. He is upset that his shaking of the bed *doesn't* disturb her

sleep. He feels enraged that she can sleep when he cannot. And when she awakens the next morning—seemingly oblivious to all he is going through—it is more than he can stand. He no longer cares whether she will see him as ridiculous and laugh at him. He blows up.

Rich's feeling of unentitlement to his *pure jealousy* resulted in its turning into *moral outrage*, which, since he was unable find an adequate way to express it, turned into *smoldering rage*, which, when he finally reached the point where he no longer cared, turned into *explosive rage*.

THEORETICAL ORIENTATION TO EMOTION

An "emotion"—that is, what we experience, think of, and call an emotion—is not just the emotion in itself. It is also the relationship we have with ourselves *about* the emotion: our comfort or discomfort with it, our sense of entitlement or unentitlement to it, and our ability or inability to give it adequate expression.

> When we feel *entitled* to and unthreatened by an emotion, we experience it in an unmodified (i.e., pure) form. If Rich had felt entitled to his ordinary jealous feeling, he would have experienced it as the wish, ache, and longing that pure jealousy is. He would have been able to say to himself, "Wow! I'm really jealous. I wish Sally were talking to me in the engaged way in which she's talking to that man."

> When we feel *unentitled* to or threatened by an emotion, we experience not the emotion itself but the consequence of our feeling of threat and unentitlement to it—and that is the emotion. Rich never experienced pure jealousy. What he experienced instead was his anxiety and conflict about it and the states of mind he went through in reaction to it. These states of mind included sudden loss of interest in the party, moral outrage, feelings of helplessness, smothered rage, and explosive rage.

In an emotion such as jealousy, we rarely see the emotion we think we see. What we call jealousy is largely our feelings about, struggles with, and reactions to our jealousy. Similarly, what we call "depression" is, in part, our reaction to the sadness, despair, and sense of loss, failure, or inadequacy that generates the depression and, in part, our reaction to the depression. We feel depressed about being depressed. We feel self-hate for being depressed. We see our depression as a sign of failure and moral weakness. We chastise ourselves for "giving in to the depression," "wallowing in self-pity," and "feeling sorry for ourselves." We think we should look at the glass as half full rather than as half empty. We feel we should not be depressed—that we have no reason to be or, if we do have reason, that we should be able to surmount it—or, at least, that we should be over it by now. We feel that we are "doing it to ourselves."

In their concept of self-talk, which, in the case of depression, means negative self-talk, cognitive therapists speak essentially about the relationship (i.e., the ongoing conversation) that people have with themselves about themselves and about their feelings. Depression is, in part, the negative self-talk (the harsh, punitive, aversive, or abusive relationship that people have with themselves) about whatever it is that produces the depression and, in part, the negative self-talk about the depression itself.

Similarly, part of panic is typically panic about panic; that is, the fear of having another panic attack—it is fear of fear.

There are moments, of course, when we do experience the pure emotion. Let us take the example of joy. There are moments when we feel pure joy. Interspersed among such moments, however, are feelings about the feeling, and about ourselves for having the feeling. We feel pleased and fortunate that we feel joy. We feel guilty or superior that we feel joy when others do not. We feel sadness (longing, melancholy, ache) about not feeling joy earlier or more often, for not being able to get more out of it, or for not being able to make it last. An Olympic gold medal winner said that there is nothing like the joy in the first 10 minutes following the victory. The fact that such an achievement produced only 10 minutes of pure joy suggests the evanescence of the experience.

Crucial to the experience of joy is its contrast with ordinary life—a contrast that is partly responsible for people crying when they feel joy. Their joy increases their awareness of the frustrations, disappointments, and struggles of their ordinary life. And then there is the negative aftereffect, anticlimax, letdown, or hangover that Solomon (1980) says typically follows pleasurable (joyful) events.

So, with joy, as with other emotions, a major part of the experience is the states of mind that we pass through in relation to the joy. In this relationship that we have with ourselves about our emotions, emotions turn into other emotions. Since Rich felt unentitled to his pure jealousy and, as a result, was unable to formulate it and confide in Sally about it, he shifted to a new emotion: moral outrage.

It is a common belief that feelings or emotions exist in different layers; that is, feelings are buried under other feelings. For example, anger might be buried under hurt or hurt under anger. In ego-analytic thinking we emphasize, instead, how feelings turn into other feelings. A person feels hurt. If this person cannot "occupy" or "inhabit" the feeling—that is, if he or she feels uncomfortable with or unentitled to it—this hurt might turn into anger, which, if the person feels uncomfortable with it, might turn into detachment. In a similar way:

Guilt can turn into blame of others, which can turn into a renewed and intensified sense of guilt.

Powerlessness can turn into fantasies of omnipotence, which can turn into a renewed and intensified sense of powerlessness.

Grief can turn into emotional withdrawal.

Ego analysis is based on this idea of emotions turning into other emotions. At any moment, a person has a leading-edge, uppermost, major and immediate feeling that

if the person feels *unentitled* to it and is *unable to formulate* it, results in a new leading-edge feeling of one type (e.g., Rich's pure jealousy turned into moral outrage);

and, if the person feels *entitled* to it and is *able to formulate* it, results in a new leading-edge feeling of another type (e.g., Rich's pure jealousy could have led to a sense of intimacy).

The ego-analytic approach provides greater precision than do traditional approaches since it includes the relationship we have with ourselves about our feelings. It includes, in particular, the moment-to-moment variations in our sense of entitlement or unentitlement to our feelings. A person who behaves in passive-aggressive ways is traditionally seen as deep down really very angry. From an ego-analytic perspective, however, this person is seen, not as deep down very angry, but as deep down very afraid of this anger; that is, as uncomfortable with or self-critical about this anger, as feeling unentitled to the anger, or as too worried about displeasing, hurting, or provoking others to be able to show anger directly. This is the crucial (and, in that sense, the deepest) issue at the moment: the *inhibition* against the anger, not the anger itself. The ego-analytic idea of a leading-edge feeling helps the therapist focus on what is crucial at the moment.

Therapists often distinguish between surface or superficial feelings and more important deep feelings. From an ego-analytic view, the surface feeling *is* the important feeling—it is the leading-edge feeling. The ego-analytic concept of a leading-edge feeling, by predisposing the therapist to search at any given moment for what is crucial, enables the therapist to notice, for example, that what is crucial in passive-aggressive behavior is not the "aggressive" part (i.e., the anger), but the "passive" part (i.e., the inhibition against expressing anger).

The therapist's task is to track the sequence of leading-edge feelings. In the case of Rich, at a given moment, the leading-edge feeling was jealous ache ("pure" jealousy). The next moment it was moral outrage in reaction to this jealous ache. The next moment it was self-blame for feeling moral outrage in reaction to this jealous ache. The next moment it was anger at Sally for behaving in a way that led to this self-blame for this moral outrage in reaction to the jealous ache. The next moment it was self-blame for feeling angry at Sally. Each of these feelings was in turn the crucial feeling.

EMOTION IN THE CONTEXT OF COUPLE RELATIONSHIPS AND COUPLE PROBLEMS

Subjective life is an ongoing series of leading-edge feelings in which each feeling is an occasion either to connect with yourself or to become alienated from yourself. Each feeling is also an occasion to connect with or become alienated from your partner. Each feeling in the ongoing series of leading-edge feelings that Rich had—his pure jealousy, boredom, moral outrage, smothered rage, and explosive rage—was an opportunity to connect with or disconnect from himself. And it was an opportunity to connect with Sally (to confide in her about what he was feeling) or an occasion for further alienation.

The problem, of course, is that Rich did not have the perspective to be able to confide in Sally about his jealousy, moral outrage, smothered rage, and so on—and so he was unable to use these feelings as an opportunity to connect with her. Here is how it might sound, however, if he had been able to confide in or connect with her about some of them:

RICH: [*To Sally*] I don't know what's come over me, but I suddenly feel insanely jealous. I'm convinced that you don't care about me at all and that you wish you were married to that man you were just talking to. I've been imagining all kinds of things I can do to get even. I know this might sound ridiculous to you—in fact, I'm afraid to tell you about it because I'm scared you will laugh at me. Even worse, I'm afraid you'll agree with me. But right now I really believe that you've lost all your feeling for me....This is not a good time to be me.

It is difficult to imagine Rich and Sally working out a relationship in which he could talk with her in this way. So, when I say that people can use their leading-edge feelings as an opportunity to connect with their partners, I am talking about an ideal.

We can now arrive at a new definition of a couple relationship: a couple relationship is the relationship the partners have with one another about the continuous series of leading-edge feelings simultaneously being generated within each. Ideally, partners would be able to use one another as resources in dealing with the leading-edge feelings to which they feel unentitled.

1.   Rich would be using Sally as a resource if, for example, he were to confide in her that he is afraid that she will see his jealousy as ridiculous and laugh at him. If Sally were not to laugh but, instead, to sympathize with him, Rich would feel a connection with her.
2.   Rich might be able to internalize Sally's sympathetic attitude. Seeing the tolerance and forgiveness that she feels toward him about his jealousy might enable him to feel more tolerant and forgiving toward himself about it. If so, Sally's attitude would enable Rich to feel a greater connection with himself.

3.   If Sally were to tell Rich that his willingness to tell her about his feelings made her feel loved—that is, if she were to respond to Rich's confiding in her about his feeling of jealousy by confiding in him about a feeling of her own—the result might be a moment of intimacy. The deepest kind of intimacy results from letting your partner in on the main thing that you are feeling and feeling your partner understands, and your partner doing likewise.

To summarize these points, in an ideal relationship, people can use their feelings to connect to their partners, and they can use their partners to connect to their feelings. In a nonideal relationship, partners can do neither of these things. They are unable to talk about their feelings or, if they are able, their partners do not listen, become withdrawn, get upset, offer unwanted advice, or criticize (e.g., "You shouldn't be so immature," "You shouldn't let things bother you so much," or "You shouldn't worry about things you can do nothing about").

A partner is thus a way to connect to or disconnect from yourself—and to connect to or disconnect from your emotions. An emotion is a way to connect to or disconnect from yourself—and to connect to or disconnect from your partner. This property of an emotion for such connecting or disconnecting is so crucial that I include it as part of the definition of an emotion. I define an emotion as not only the emotion in itself, but also how we relate to ourselves and to our partners about the emotion; that is, how the emotion enables us to connect with, or leads us to disconnect from, ourselves and our partners.

In the relationship that Rich had with Sally about his jealousy, Rich feared that Sally would laugh at him for feeling jealous. So he kept his feeling to himself and became grim, alienated, sulky, provocative, and, finally, explosive. In the relationship that Rich ideally could have with Sally about his jealousy, Rich would not fear that Sally would laugh at him for feeling jealous. When he saw Sally talking to that man and felt a jealous ache, Rich would feel that Sally would understand and sympathize. And feeling that Sally would understand and sympathize, Rich would not become grim, alienated, sulky, provocative, and explosive. His jealous ache would be replaced by a feeling of being connected to Sally because he felt she would understand and sympathize.

THEORETICAL VIEW ON THE PART EMOTION PLAYS IN THE CHANGE PROCESS IN COUPLES THERAPY

In ego-analytic thinking, the distinction between thoughts and feelings or between feelings and emotions is unimportant compared to what is important, which is to discover what has immediate hold on the person's attention; that is, what is on the leading edge. (Ego analysis is similar to Gestalt therapy in its focus on the leading edge; that is, on what has immediate hold on the person's attention.) I use the word "feelings" (the best word I could think of) to refer to what is on the leading edge. And these "feelings" that I say are on the leading edge can take the form of thoughts, beliefs, emotions, wishes, sensations, urges, feelings (in the narrow sense), and so on. From an ego-analytic viewpoint, emotions constitute a somewhat arbitrary subdivision in the more crucial general category of feelings.

A major task at any given moment in a couples therapy session is to formulate the leading-edge feelings of each partner. The ultimate goal is to improve the relationship the partners have with themselves and with one another about their ongoing series of leading-edge feelings—that is, to enable the partners to use their feelings as opportunities to connect with themselves and with one another rather than as occasions for disconnection and alienation.

HOW THESE THEORETICAL ASSUMPTIONS TRANSLATE INTO A BASIC SET OF CHANGE PRINCIPLES AND STRATEGIES

To demonstrate how I try to connect people to their own and their partner's leading-edge feelings, let us return to the fictional couples therapy session with Sally and Rich. I could start anywhere in this session (in actual practice I am likely to have intervened earlier). For convenience, however, I shall start at the point we left off. What follows is what Sally and Rich had just said.

RICH: I told you how I hate it when you exaggerate, but you keep doing it.
SALLY: Well, *I* hate it when you accuse me of flirting.
RICH: Why do you do it then?
SALLY: I don't do it.
RICH: You haven't heard a word I've said.
SALLY: You haven't said anything that makes any sense.
RICH: This is stupid. We're getting nowhere.

I try to formulate Sally and Rich's leading-edge feeling as follows:

THERAPIST: I take it that this is one of the moments in which, as you were telling me last time, you feel hopeless about getting the other to listen and so you snap at one another in frustration.

My purpose here is to get Sally and Rich to talk about their shared frustration. I am trying to engage them in a metaconversation.

SALLY: I'm tired of this fight.
RICH: Me too. I'm ready to stop.
SALLY: That's fine with me.

Sally and Rich are correcting (updating) my formulation of their leading-edge feelings. They are saying that they are beyond the snapping-at-one-another phase, that they are tired of the fight and want to stop.

THERAPIST: And when you're "tired of the fight" and are "ready to stop," what usually happens then?
SALLY: We stop talking entirely.
RICH: It gets pretty quiet....
SALLY: Like last night on the way home from the party.
RICH: It was awful.

Sally and Rich are connecting about how they felt disconnected (alienated) last night.

SALLY: Of course, it was pretty quiet even before the party.
RICH: [*To therapist*] We hardly said anything in the car on the way to the party. [*He suddenly sits up straighter.*] In fact, that's why I got so jealous. (*To Sally*) You didn't say two words to me in the car and then, as soon as we got to the party, you couldn't stop talking to that man.
SALLY: [*Defending herself*] It was a party—you're supposed to be chatty.
RICH: Well, you didn't have to play up to him the way you did.
SALLY: Do we have to go into that again? I thought you said you wanted to stop fighting.
RICH: [*Wearily*] I do.

Sally and Rich have just passed through several leading-edge feelings:

Lament: "It gets pretty quiet." "We hardly said anything in the car on the way over to the party." "Of course, it was pretty quiet even before the party."

Relief (in figuring out why he felt jealous): "In fact, that's why I got so jealous."

Anger: "You didn't say two words to me in the car and then, as soon as we got to the party, you couldn't stop talking to that man." "It was a party—you're supposed to be chatty." "Well, you didn't have to play up to him the way you did." "Do we have to go into that again? I thought you said you wanted to *stop* fighting."

Weariness: "I do."

From this sequence of leading-edge feelings, any of which might be useful to pursue, I pick the one that I think most directly hints at crucial unspoken feelings:

THERAPIST: What was that you said, Rich, about feeling jealous because Sally seemed to have so little to say to you in the car and so much to say to that man at the party?

I am trying to focus on the leading-edge feeling that precipitated Rich's jealousy last night.

RICH: Well, you should have seen the two of them laughing it up.

Rich is defending himself (he is justifying his jealous reaction), which means that he is fighting off an accusation—whether he feels it is coming from me or from himself—that he should not have gotten jealous.

THERAPIST: [*To Rich*] Yes, I didn't mean that you shouldn't have gotten jealous.
SALLY: Well, *I* think he shouldn't have gotten jealous. I was only being chatty with that man, for goodness sake.

Sally is apparently smarting from Rich's "You should have seen the two of them laughing it up."

THERAPIST: [*To Sally*] Yes, you don't like being blamed for Rich's jealousy when you feel you were just doing what a person should do at a party—be chatty.
SALLY: [*To Rich*] Listen to that man.
THERAPIST: And Rich, something really struck you about the contrast between Sally's chattiness with the man at the party and the nonchattiness between the two of you in the car.
RICH: Yes, listen to that man.
THERAPIST: So let's look at that. When you saw Sally talking to that man, you felt...what? Left out? Abandoned? Neglected? Angry?
RICH: A little of all those things, and also sad.
THERAPIST: Sad?
RICH: The way Sally was talking to that man—that's the way we used to talk.
SALLY: [*Quietly*] Yes, I know. We had endless things to say to one another—we used to talk for hours.
RICH: I miss it.
SALLY: Me too.

Sally and Rich are momentarily connecting about Rich's feeling: his sadness. But just momentarily:

SALLY: [*To Rich*] If you were feeling sad, why didn't you tell me?

Sally has shifted from one leading-edge feeling (commiserating) to another (criticizing Rich for failing to tell her he was feeling sad).

RICH: I couldn't tell you. I didn't know it myself—I just figured it out now. But even if I had been able to tell you, it wouldn't have done any good. You would have criticized me for not telling you sooner. And we'd have gotten into a fight.

SALLY: You're probably right.

THERAPIST: Well, let's see how it would have gone. [*To Rich*] Let's say that you knew that you felt sad and, last night at the party, you tried to talk to Sally about it. What would you say to her? What words would you use?

RICH: I don't know.

THERAPIST: Well, you could say what you and Sally just said here. You could say, "I felt jealous seeing you talking to that man. But I just realized that all along I've been feeling something else, without even knowing it. I've been feeling sad. And your talking to that man made me realize it—because it reminded me of the way we used to talk. We had endless things to say to one another. It was wonderful—we'd go on for hours. And I really miss it. That's what makes me sad."

SALLY: [*To therapist*] If Rich were to say all that, I'd fall over in a faint. I'd never expect to hear that from him. [*To Rich*] And then I'd get up and throw my arms around you, and I'd tell you that I've been missing it too.

RICH: Well, I wish I had been able to say it then.

There is, of course, a risk in my making this statement for Rich: he might feel like a failure for not being able to make it himself in the first place. I try to reduce this risk by telling Rich and Sally that such a statement is an ideal—hardly anyone would be able to make it.

My purpose is to give Sally and Rich a taste of what it would be like if they could appeal to one another as resources in dealing with their leading-edge feelings. I want to give them a goal to work toward, even if it is difficult, or even impossible, to achieve.

This brief therapeutic interchange demonstrates three main ways I try to improve partners' abilities to use one another as resources in dealing with the series of leading-edge feelings being continuously generated within each. These three main ways are the following:

1. *Focusing on the leading-edge feelings that the partners have from moment to moment right there in the session.* For example, early in the exchange, I said to Sally and Rich:

THERAPIST: I take it that this is one of the moments in which, as you were telling me last time, you feel hopeless about getting the other to listen and so you snap at one another in frustration.

2. *Focusing on crucial leading-edge feelings that occurred earlier in the session, earlier in the week, or earlier in their relationship.* For example, in the middle of this interchange, I said to Rich:

THERAPIST: What was that you said, Rich, about feeling jealous because Sally seemed to have so little to say to you in the car and so much to say to that man at the party?

3. *Demonstrating the conversation they might have were they able to appeal to one another as resources in dealing with their leading-edge feelings.* For example, near the end of the interchange, I said to Rich:

THERAPIST: Well, you could say what you and Sally just said here. You could say, "I felt jealous seeing you talking to that man. But I just realized that all along I've been feeling something else, without even knowing it. I've been feeling sad. And your talking to that man made me realize it because it reminded me of the way we used to talk. We had endless things to say to one another. It was wonderful—we'd go on for hours. And I really miss it. That's what makes me sad."

THE DIFFERENT ROLES THAT EMOTIONAL EXPERIENCE PLAYS IN THERAPY AT DIFFERENT TIMES

Certain emotional experiences such as certain types of anger, defensiveness, and moral outrage can be impediments to couples therapy, which became feasible only when

> therapists discovered ways to interrupt the accusation and defensiveness in which partners frequently engage when seen in therapy together. Before then, many therapists who experimented with seeing the partners in conjoint therapy shrugged their shoulders when the partners started to fight, concluded that couples therapy was unworkable, and recommended that one or both partners go into long-term individual psychotherapy.
>
> Accusation and defensiveness remain the biggest practical problems of couples therapy today. Couples therapy is in essence an experiment to see whether, in the couples therapy setting, the partners will be able to talk in a less accusing and a less defensive way than they do at home— or, if they don't talk much at all at home, whether in the couples therapy setting they will be able to talk. In some cases, the experiment fails. The partners get into the kind of slashing, unmanageable fights in the office that they do at home. (Wile, 1993, p. 120)

So, certain types of emotional reactions (i.e., certain types of anger and defensiveness) play a negative role in therapy. However, the partners' emotional reactions are what couples therapy—and the relationship—are all about. In a manner of speaking, the partners' emotional reactions are the relationship.

According to ego-analytic thinking, the basic issue is the lack of a sense of entitlement to feelings. But what about slashing, unmanageable fights—the kind of fights that lead therapists to diagnose one or both of the partners as "borderline" or "narcissistic." Some might say that the problem in such cases is that the partners feel *too entitled* to their feelings—that is, to their anger.

However, it is only to an outsider that these partners seem too entitled to their anger. The partners' experience is not of anger but of helpless rage—which is why the fight is slashing and unmanageable. Neither partner feels he or she is having sufficient impact. Each feels more provoked by the verbal blows he or she is receiving than satisfied by the ones he or she is landing. Each feels more done in than doing in, more victim than aggressor.

SPECIFIC INTERVENTIONS THAT HEIGHTEN OR DAMPEN EMOTIONAL RESPONSES

Since the *presence* of certain emotional responses—for example, particular forms of intense anger—leads to problems for our clients, we try to find ways to dampen these responses. Since the *absence* of certain emotional responses leads to problems—for example, mutual withdrawal and devitalization—we try to heighten emotional responses.

My way of dampening or heightening emotional responses is to formulate leading-edge feelings, since, as I see it, both the eruptive anger (that we seek to dampen) and the mutual withdrawal (that we deal with by attempting to heighten emotional responses) are *symptoms*; that is, they result from an inability to formulate leading-edge feelings.

SUMMARY

A couple relationship is the relationship the partners have with one another about the continuous series of leading-edge feelings or emotions simultaneously being generated within each. Emotions, especially certain forms of anger and anxiety, can make couples therapy unworkable. But emotions are also what couples therapy and the relationship are all about. Ideally, partners can use their feelings to connect to their partners, and they can use their partners to connect to their feelings. When people are unable to connect to their feelings, they express symptomatic feelings, which are then often taken as their basic feelings. When, as is typically the case, we are unable to connect to our jealous aches, we express moral outrage, which is then taken as jealousy. In other words, what we have come to think of as jealousy is really a symptomatic form of jealousy: moral outrage.

The goal of therapy is to improve the relationship that partners have with themselves and with one another about their ongoing series of leading-edge feelings—that is, to use their feelings as an opportunity to connect with themselves and with one another rather than as an occasion for disconnection and alienation. The way I try to achieve this goal is by (1) tracing the leading-edge *Sum* feelings that the partners have from moment to moment right there in the session; (2) pinpointing crucial leading-edge feelings from earlier in the session, the week, or their life together; and (3) giving partners a taste of the conversations they might have were they able to appeal to one another as resources in dealing with their leading-edge feelings.

REFERENCES

Apfelbaum, B. (1966). On ego psychology: A critique of the structural approach to psychoanalysis. *International Journal of Psychoanalysis, 47*, 451–475.

Apfelbaum, B. (1977). A contribution to the development of the behavioral-analytic sex therapy model. *Journal of Sex and Marital Therapy, 3*, 128–138.

Apfelbaum, B. (1982). The clinical necessity for Kohut's self theory. *Voices, 18*, 43–49.

Apfelbaum, B. (1983). Introduction to the symposium Ego Analysis and Ego Psychology. Presented at the American Psychological Association Convention, Anaheim, CA.

Apfelbaum, B. (1988). An ego-analytic perspective on desire disorders. In S. Leiblum & L. Rosen (Eds.), *Sexual desire disorders* (pp. 75–104). New York: Guilford.

Apfelbaum, B., & Apfelbaum, C. (1985). The ego-analytic approach to sexual apathy. In D. C. Goldberg (Ed.), *Contemporary marriage handbook* (pp. 439–481). Homewood, IL: Dorsey.

Apfelbaum, B., & Gill, M. M. (1989). Ego analysis and the relativity of defense: Technical implications of the structural theory. *Journal of the American Psychoanalytic Association, 37*, 1071–1096.

Fenichel, O. (1941). *Problems of psychoanalytic technique*. New York: Psychoanalytic Quarterly.

Freud, S. (1959). Inhibitions, symptoms and anxiety. *Standard edition* (Vol. 20; pp. 77–174). London: Hogarth (Original work published 1926)

Gray, P. (1982). "Developmental lag" in the evolution of technique for psychoanalysis of neurotic conflict. *Journal of the American Psychoanalytic Association, 30*, 621–655.

Greenberg, J. R., & Mitchell, S. A. (1983). *Object relations in psychoanalytic theory*. Cambridge, MA: Harvard University Press.

Kohut, H. (1977). *The restoration of the self*. New York: International Universities Press.

Solomon, R. L. (1980). The opponent-process theory of acquired motivation: The costs of pleasure and the benefits of pain. *American Psychologist, 35*(8), 691–712.

Wile, D. B. (1981). *Couples therapy: A nontraditional approach*. New York: Wiley.

Wile, D. B. (1984). Kohut, Kernberg, and accusatory interpretations. *Psychotherapy: Theory, Research, Practice, and Training, 21*(3), 353–364.

Wile, D. B. (1985). Psychotherapy by precedent: Unexamined legacies from pre-1920 psychoanalysis. *Psychotherapy: Theory, Research, Practice, and Training), 22*(4), 793–802.

Wile, D. B. (1987). An even more offensive theory. In W. Dryden (Ed.), *Key cases in psychotherapy* (pp. 78–182). London: Croom-Helm.

Wile, D. B. (1988). *After the honeymoon: How conflict can improve your relationship*. New York: Wiley.

Wile, D. B. (1993). *After the fight: A night in the life of a couple*. New York: Guilford.

Wile, D. B. (in press). The ego-analytic approach to couples therapy. In N. S. Jacobson & A. S. Gurman (Eds.), *Clinical handbook of marital therapy* (2nd ed.). New York: Guilford.

3

From Symptom to Signal: An Attachment View of Emotion in Marital Therapy

ROGER KOBAK, KATY RUCKDESCHEL, and
CINDY HAZAN

Christine and Rick presented for treatment at a point of considerable distress. Rick was unemployed, Christine had contemplated divorce, and both were uncertain about their future. Although they demonstrated a willingness to change, they continued to enact the pattern that had led them to several trial separations. That is, Rick's concerns about his unemployment often led him to withdraw. Christine dealt with much of her concern about Rick's availability by focusing on specifics about where he might find a job, and whether she could manage the dislocation involved in moving to a new community. Rick responded to these concerns defensively, with resentment and a sense that his loss of employment had made Christine unhappy. Her unhappiness about moving suggested to him that the house was more important to her than her relationship with him. Thus, Rick and Christine were locked into a pursue/withdraw cycle. She tended to pursue him with ineffective strategies such as criticism and complaints, and he interpreted her depressed, accusatory manner as indicating her unhappiness with their marriage. Feeling ineffective in his attempts to reassure Christine, Rick withdrew further, which only added to Christine's fears about his availability. Christine and Rick's problems are typical of many distressed marriages that are marked by escalating negative exchanges, demand/withdraw interactions, and mutual fears about partners' availability.

Studies of marital communication have yielded a well-replicated set of findings consistent with Christine and Rick's pattern. Distressed couples are prone to engage in reciprocated negative emotion during laboratory problem-solving discussions. Whereas codes that assessed the content of marital interaction such as agreement-disagreement ratios usually failed to discriminate between distressed and nondistressed couples, the amount of negative and neutral affect that couples maintained during problem solving did discriminate (Gottman, 1979). In well-functioning relationships, couples often express negative affect but in relatively brief sequences that are not reciprocated by partners (Schaap, 1984). In contrast, distressed couples are prone to escalating negative affective exchanges, and their communications are more frequently accompanied by negative affect (Gottman & Krokoff, 1989) .

Pursue/withdraw patterns are also prevalent in distressed marriages (Christensen, 1988; Gottman & Levenson, 1986). These patterns are often initiated when one spouse pursues the other in critical or accusatory ways that paradoxically increase the likelihood of the other partner's withdrawing. Once again, these interaction cycles are often emotionally charged with anger, eliciting a defensive response. The well-documented evidence for reciprocated negative affect exchanges and pursue/withdraw patterns in marital distress leave important questions unanswered. For instance, what are the origins and functions of these symptoms? Are negative emotions the by-products of communication difficulties that need to be contained or managed so that successful communication can be sustained (Fruzzetti & Jacobson, 1991)? Or do negative emotions play a useful or adaptive role in marital communication? Questions such as these point to the need for theories that can provide an explicit account of emotional processes in marital relationships.

In this chapter, we argue that these symptoms of marital distress can be viewed as distorted attachment signals. Conceptualized in this way, symptoms can be viewed as sensible reactions to attachment-related fears and expectations. That is, when spouses begin to view their partners as unavailable and/or unresponsive, normal attachment feelings of anger, fear, and sadness become prone to defensive distortions that reduce couples' capacity for effective problem solving. Thus, attachment theory orients the marital therapist toward viewing symptoms of marital distress as distorted expressions of normal attachment emotions. As a result, treatment focuses on linking symptomatic expressions to attachment-related fears, so that partners can openly acknowledge their concerns about each other's availability and commitment. As partners increase their understanding and communication of attachment concerns, emotions become signals that facilitate rather than hinder intimacy and problem solving.

ATTACHMENT IN PARENT-CHILD AND MARITAL RELATIONSHIPS

Bowlby (1969, 1973) initially developed attachment theory as a framework for understanding why infants form emotional bonds with their care givers and why they experience profound emotional reactions when those bonds are disrupted. Adopting an ethological control theory perspective, Bowlby conceived of attachment as a behavioral control system that monitors access to and responsiveness of an adult care giver. The overriding goal of the attachment system is to maintain access to an attachment figure within comfortable limits. Although the individual continuously monitors the whereabouts of the attachment figure (Bretherton, 1980), concerns for increasing access to the attachment figure vary from one situation to another. During normal times, attachment concerns may be evident only through brief checks or communications with the care giver that allow the individual to carry on other activities. At other times, when the individual is frightened or tired, attachment concerns become central, and maintaining access to the care giver takes precedence over other activities.

When the individual perceives a threat to the care giver's availability, restoring access to the care giver is likely to completely override other concerns. Bowlby's initial studies of children's responses to separations provided dramatic evidence for how the attachment system becomes active when the care giver is perceived as unavailable. In observing young children who were experiencing prolonged separations from their parents, Robertson and Bowlby (1952) documented a series of phases in children's responses to separation, beginning with an emergency protest, that gradually gave way to despair, and then over several days led to detachment. Perceived threats to a care giver's *psychological* availability may also elicit attachment reactions. In studying infants and their mothers, Ainsworth, Blehar, Waters, and Wall (1978) discovered that although a mother may be physically available, her psychological availability and responsiveness to her infant's signals may vary dramatically.

Even more extreme threats to parental availability have been documented in clinical populations. Bowlby (1979) has called attention to how parental statements that threaten to send a child away, to commit suicide, or to withdraw emotional support may elicit the child's attachment concerns and problematic behaviors that often lead to clinical referrals. Even more severe disturbances may arise from situations in which the parent becomes a source of danger to the child through abusive behavior (Main & Hesse, 1990; Main & Solomon, 1986). Another extreme reaction could result from prolonged dysfunctional conflict, in which unresolved anger and rejecting responses jeopardize perceptions of the attachment figure's availability. In this sense, attachment concerns are likely to be activated in any distressed relationship in which partners have become chronically unavailable to one another.

During late adolescence and adulthood, individuals often form enduring attachment bonds with peers (Weiss, 1982). Once formed, adult attachment bonds serve similar functions to childhood attachments by providing the individual with a safe haven during times of distress and a secure base for facing the adult challenges. However, compared with parent-child relationships, adult attachment relationships involve a relatively complex meshing of attachment with other behavioral systems. First, whereas in parent-child relationships, the parent normally serves as the care giver to the child, adult attachments are marked by reciprocal care-giving roles. Thus, in addition to monitoring access and turning to the partner during times of distress, adults must also be available and responsive to their partners' needs for comfort and support. As a result, adult attachment partners must move between attachment and care-giving roles. Second, the reciprocity of adult relationships places greater emphasis on partners' abilities in managing and accommodating goal conflicts. Successful accommodation draws on partners' abilities to problem-solve and talk about areas of disagreement in a manner that maintains a sense of cooperation, or what Bowlby (1969) termed a "goal-corrected partnership." Finally, adult attachment relationships often involve integrating the attachment and sexual behavioral systems (Ainsworth, 1989) .

Attachment thus represents an important component of marital relationships that must be integrated and coordinated with problem-solving and sexual concerns. In day-to-day interactions, attachment concerns usually operate in the background of partners' awareness, while problem-solving concerns tend to occupy the foreground. Only during periods of transition or disruption do attachment processes usually come to the fore. In describing attachment in adult relationships, researchers have naturally gravitated toward these periods of transition. For instance, Hazan and Shaver (1987) have sketched the parallels between the formation of infant and adult attachment bonds by examining links between infant research and adults' experiences of falling in love. Robert Weiss (1975) used attachment theory to understand adults' responses to marital separations and divorce, and Bowlby (1981) drew extensively on literature about the death of a spouse in his study of response to loss and grieving. By focusing on periods of transition, these studies offer glimpses into the processes through which adults' perceptions of partners' availability are shaped and changed.

The central goal of the attachment system in both childhood and adulthood centers on keeping access to the attachment figure within comfortable limits. By focusing on individuals' primary concern with maintaining access to their attachment figures, Bowlby's theory provides an integrative account of how cognitive, behavioral, and emotional processes are coordinated in the service of monitoring and maintaining the marital bond (Johnson, 1986). From this perspective, emotions offer valuable clues to partners' underlying assumptions of each others' availability and responsiveness. In this sense, the new interest in the role of emotions in marital relationships points to attachment processes that have previously received relatively little attention from marital researchers. Kobak and Hazan (1991) have begun to examine the interplay between attachment processes and problem-solving communication.

The guiding hypothesis of this research is that a partner's confidence in a spouse's availability will both facilitate and be enhanced by successful problem-solving communication. That is, when partners feel assured of each other's availability, they are free to disagree with each other without disagreements escalating into reciprocal negative exchanges. In contrast, when partners are unsure of each other's availability and responsiveness, they are more prone to expressing blaming or rejecting anger during the course of problem-solving discussions (Kobak & Hazan, 1991). These findings suggest that attachment concerns may accompany the well-documented links between problem-solving communication and marital satisfaction.

Evidence for the role of attachment processes in marital distress also comes from clinical theory and intervention. Greenberg and Johnson (1988) have pioneered in using experiential and systemic theories for understanding emotion processes in distressed marriages. Their emotionally focused approach to marital therapy (EFT) makes a critical distinction between primary and secondary emotions. Primary emotions such as anger, fear, or sadness are seen as adaptive when they signal needs for contact or support in the marital relationship. Secondary emotions are viewed as reactive and motivated by self-protective concerns. For instance, anger that normally motivates constructive assertion is transformed into hostile accusations, or fear that normally elicits support is transformed into desperate and demanding behavior. In distressed marriages, secondary emotions tend to dominate interaction and awareness, and the goal of the therapist is to access hidden primary emotions. In accessing primary emotions, the therapist directs couples' attention to disowned aspects of experience that involve vulnerability and need for contact. Gaining access to these unacknowledged aspects of self allows partners to respond with support and to renew their confidence in each other's availability. Increased confidence in turn promotes more flexible and adaptive problem solving. The EFT approach is remarkably consistent with an attachment approach and offers a specification of the emotional processes that maintain attachment relationships.

Attachment theory offers a useful framework that can incorporate and build upon an EFT approach to marital therapy. In the next section, we will begin to sketch the role that emotions play in attachment functioning. This sketch will specify the adaptive signal function of emotions and illustrate how emotions serve to monitor and maintain access to attachment figures. We will also introduce the critical construct of working models. These models are generalized expectations for a care giver's availability that are derived from numerous relationship episodes. Working models serve a critical control function in regulating attachment feelings and behavior. Once established, they orient the individual to future interactions and guide the development of strategies for maintaining the attachment relationship. We will suggest that working models have important implications for how individuals process attachment information. Different levels of information processing account for how individuals express emotion, update working models, and bring emotional action tendencies under more effective cognitive control.

AN INFORMATION-PROCESSING VIEW OF EMOTIONS IN ATTACHMENT RELATIONSHIPS

Bowlby (1969) viewed emotions as serving critical appraisal, motivational, and communication functions in maintaining attachment relationships. We think that these interrelated functions of emotion may be best understood as operating at different levels for processing information within the attachment system (see Johnson & Greenberg, 1994). Leventhal's (1979) perceptual-motor theory of emotion provides a useful way of conceptualizing these different levels of information processing. He suggests that emotional experience is the product of expressive-motor, schematic memory, and conceptual levels of processing. These multiple levels function in an interdependent fashion such that, for example, activation of expressive-motor information may spread to the schematic and conceptual levels. For the most part, only the conceptual level is under conscious cognitive control, while expressive-motor and schematic processing operate in an automated or preconscious manner. As a result, it is possible for one to be clenching one's jaw at an expressive-motor level and yet be unaware of this information at a conceptual level. This kind of dissociation between levels of information processing accounts for the possibility of unconscious feeling.

By viewing the attachment system as incorporating multiple levels of information processing, it becomes possible to describe the variation and complexity of attachment thoughts, feelings, and behavior. Expressive-motor reactions tend to be the most automated aspects of attachment functioning and are the level at which emotions can be most readily seen as serving an adaptive signal function. These expressions of emotion can be viewed as adaptive insofar as they serve a "primary" strategy of monitoring and maintaining access to the attachment figure (Main, 1990). These expressive-motor processes provide valuable information about an individual's perception and predisposition in a particular situation. For instance, a primary attachment emotion such as fear indicates that a situation is perceived as dangerous and/or threatening. Fear is expressed through a variety of expressive-motor processes, ranging from facial expression to body posture, and the presence of fear leads to strong dispositions to shrink from the source of danger and to approach a protective care giver. Fear also motivates approach tendencies that are expressed through behaviors such as approaching, reaching, grasping, and clinging to the attachment figure (Bowlby, 1969).

Anger can also serve as a primary emotion that serves to restore access to the attachment figure. It accompanies perceptions that something or someone is an obstacle to care givers' availability. Infants frequently perceive separations as threats to a care giver's availability and express anger in the form of "separation protest." This "protest" motivates quick actions intended to overcome obstacles to the care giver's availability or, in the case of separation, to prevent the parent from leaving. If protest fails to deter the parent from leaving, anger may be redirected toward the door or physical objects that separate the child from the parent. Anger thus serves an adaptive function in helping the child to focus attention on obstacles to the care giver's availability, and in motivating actions intended to overcome these difficulties. Sadness or despair accompanies perceptions that attempts to regain access to the attachment figure are futile or hopeless. As protest fails to bring the attachment figure, the individual reevaluates the separation as beyond his or her control and moves into despair. Despair motivates action toward withdrawal and conservation of effort. Joy accompanies perceptions that access to a care giver can be reestablished and moves the individual to sustain interaction once contact is achieved.

Primary attachment emotions not only motivate attachment behavior but also communicate valuable information to the care-giving partner. These expressive-motor signals tend to elicit appropriate care-giving responses naturally. Most people respond to fear and distress with protective and comforting responses. Anger, if it is understood as a communication about the importance of the relationship, often leads the care giver to reconsider goals and plans in an effort to accommodate attachment concerns. Sadness tends to elicit soft and soothing responses, while joy serves to elicit shared positive affect that allows for mutual enjoyment and satisfaction. When emotions are expressed directly and the action tendencies associated with these feelings are understood as expressions of the individual's attachment concerns, signals can lead to responses that are considered, sensitive, and contingent. Emotional communication at an expressive-motor level thus serves to foster open and harmonious exchanges in attachment relationships.

The expression of primary emotions and action tendencies is shaped by the individual's history of interactions with attachment figures that are stored in schematic memory. Through repeated exchanges with care givers at times when the attachment system is activated, the individual develops expectations or *working models* for care-giver responses. Thus, specific interactions are stored at the level of schematic memory in working models. This level of processing provides an automatic and efficient way of anticipating care-giver response at times when the individual may be frightened, challenged, or facing conflict. These forecasts have tremendous psychological and emotional import. Expectations for availability and responsiveness promote confident feelings, whereas expectations for lack of availability foster anxiety. Working models of attachment figures thus combine cognitive appraisals of an attachment figure's availability with emotional processes that signal safety or danger into what Safran and Greenberg (1986) describe as "hot cognitions."

Working models influence how the individual enters new situations and interprets a care giver's behavior. If the individual develops a working model that forecasts care-giver responsiveness and understanding, he or she will approach new situations with confidence (Bowlby, 1988; Sroufe & Fleeson,

1986). Thus, situations that some might find challenging or intimidating will be met with a sense of optimism that increases the likelihood of positive outcomes. In a similar manner, positive expectancies about a partner lead to selective processing of information in situations of conflict or disagreement. For instance, an individual with a secure working model will tend to attribute positive intentions to a partner and discount negativity (Markman & Notarius, 1987). This positive bias will influence subsequent behavior in a way that minimizes the likelihood of negative responses and increases opportunities for cooperation. Thus, positive expectancies tend to produce reactions that increase the likelihood that those expectations about a partner will be confirmed.

Leventhal's (1979) third level of conceptual processing refers to an individual's ideas and propositional knowledge about emotion . This level of processing allows the individual to develop and to evaluate beliefs about attachment feelings and concerns. For instance, beliefs may center on the importance of attachment relationships. When attachment concerns are valued and acknowledged at a conceptual processing level, expressive-motor signals can be smoothly integrated into conversations. Thus, a spouse can express anger about a departure openly by saying "I don't want you to leave," or "I miss you." Such statements indicate that anger functions in the context of valuing the relationship and anger is cognitively connected with concerns about the partner's availability. By valuing and articulating attachment concerns, the individual increases the likelihood that anger will be met with a supportive and understanding response. Emotions thus serve as signals for maintaining the attachment relationship.

Conceptual processing also creates opportunities to bring both expressive motor tendencies and working models under increased cognitive control. By reflecting on and talking about feelings, the individual can examine action tendencies that had previously been confined to the expressive-motor level of processing. Thus, fears can be identified and actions toward seeking proximity or fleeing sources of danger may be delayed. Anger associated with frustrated attachment need may be verbally expressed rather than acted out toward the care giver. The advantage of verbalizing anger is that it makes it understandable in the context of valuing the attachment relationship. If anger serves as a signal of frustration over lack of access to the care giver, the individual can monitor this signal, modulate the expression of anger, and consider alternative plans for overcoming the sources of frustration. Thus, anger may motivate constructive or planned action rather than impulsive outbursts. The individual's access to attachment concerns and ability to verbalize the importance of the relationship with the attachment figure thus create a context that gives negative emotions such as anger positive meaning and purpose. As long as the individual's attachment concerns are valued and acknowledged at a conceptual level, anger is a functional emotion that can serve a positive role in restoring access to the attachment figure.

Conceptual processing also makes it possible for individuals to examine working models that are stored in schematic memory. For instance, individuals may identify tacit assumptions that they make about a partner's availability. Once such assumptions are identified, the individual can review their validity and consistency. In this review process, the individual's attachment-related memories and cognitions can be reconsidered, and assumptions that are no longer consistent with current experience can be modified or replaced. As a result, the individual gains increased cognitive control over working models. By reviewing insecure working models and examining how these models guide current perceptions and expectations, spouses may be able to control negative consequences of their own behavior and consider information that disconfirms their negative expectations. Through a process of revision, negative expectations can be gradually replaced with more positive expectations for a partner's availability.

SECURE WORKING MODELS AND EMOTIONS AS SIGNALS

Working models influence how emotions are processed and expressed in attachment relationships. When working models are secure and forecast caregiver availability, the individual can develop a primary strategy for regulating the attachment system that uses direct and open expressive-motor signals to restore and maintain confidence in the care giver's availability. Secure strategies guide and organize expressive-motor information with positive expectancies for care-giver responses. In addition, a secure strategy facilitates access to information stored in schematic memory in order to review and update working models. Thus, a secure strategy allows different levels of information processing to be coordinated in the service of maintaining access to the attachment figure. The notion that secure working models facilitate open exchange of information between the expressive-motor, schematic, and conceptual levels of processing helps to account for a diverse set of findings that mark well-functioning marriages.

Working models that forecast understanding responses from the attachment figure provide the individual with confidence that open expression of emotional signals will play a useful function in maintaining the relationship. Thus, when the individual becomes concerned with care-giver availability, fear, sadness, and anger lead to actions that are clearly linked to attachment concerns and that are likely to produce a reassuring or comforting response. The fluid movement between tendency and action assures that these expressions will serve as attachment signals to a responsive partner. When negative emotions are clearly linked to concerns with availability, a partner can more easily respond in a way that alleviates distress. For instance, when anger is clearly tied to an uninvited disruption in the relationship, anger becomes an expression of concern about the relationship rather than an attack on the partner. As a result, a partner can respond in a manner that increases closeness and intimacy. Similarly, sadness that is tied to concerns about missing the partner can be easily addressed through increased availability and support. Thus, expressive-motor tendencies signal concerns about the partner's availability. These signals usually lead to responses that confirm the individual's confidence in a partner's availability.

Fluid access to expressive-motor information allows negative emotions to be directly expressed and clearly linked to attachment concerns. Direct expression makes effective response possible, and, as a result, negative affective states are relatively short-lived. Thus, in situations that elicit fear, the individual can effectively signal the attachment figure and gain support. In situations that are difficult or challenging, the individual can actively seek help from a spouse, which leads to a renewed confidence. In situations involving conflicts, anger may motivate engagement and contribute to increased understanding between spouses. Gottman and Krokoff (1989) found that couples who engaged in conflict and openly expressed anger showed *increases* in marital satisfaction during a 3-year follow-up. These partners could thus express anger in a manner that contributed to increased relationship satisfaction. In these couples, anger facilitated engagement and focusing on an issue.

Direct access to expressive-motor signals and schematic memory makes important information available for conceptual processing. First, when expressive-motor signals are available for consideration, the individual gains increased cognitive control over these action tendencies. Knowing that one is angry makes it possible to take responsibility for previously unacknowledged consequences of sarcastic or critical comments. Second, access to information stored in schematic memory allows the individual to review and consider the evidence from which working models are derived. For instance, a spouse might be able to think, "Maybe, I'm overly sensitive and am expecting the worst." By reviewing expectations and assumptions, one partner can correct misguided or self-defeating assumptions about the other. This capacity to acknowledge mistaken attributions and to reevaluate emotional responses may restore understanding and acceptance in relationships following problematic reactions. When working models are available for conceptual processing, an individual's perspectives on self and other are "open" to new information. Thus, secure strategies allow spouses to update their image of their partner as new information becomes available.

Secure working models free the individual to engage in more cognitive exploration (Main, 1991). As a result, secure individuals can explore alternative perspectives on issues that are offered by their partners. This capacity for perspective taking may be a critical conceptual skill for cooperative problem solving that allows partners to take each other's concerns into account and to creatively negotiate joint plans and solutions to goal conflicts. The ability to adopt the frame of reference of the other person and to see the world through the other person's eyes provides the individual with new information that can help him or her develop a more accurate and realistic working model. Thus, perspective taking and open-mindedness produce interactions that tend to confirm partners' sense of availability and confidence in their ability to resolve conflicts. Mistaken assumptions and interpretations can be reconsidered and revised, and through the process of communication new levels of understanding can be achieved.

Secure working models may also increase individuals' capacities for engaging in nonattachment activities. When individuals are confident in each other's availability, they spend less time monitoring and attempting to increase access to their care giver. Thus, they are free to attend to other matters. Ainsworth and colleagues (1987) described this phenomenon in infants who could use their attachment figures as a secure base to facilitate exploration. When infants were confident in their care givers' availability, they showed more spontaneous and engaged play and exploratory activity. In adult relationships, secure working models may increase a couple's ability to successfully engage in nonattachment activities. When couples are confident in each other's availability, they can fully engage in exploratory, problem-solving, parenting, or sexual activities. Successful engagement in these activities can increase a couple's sense of cooperative partnership and ability to use their relationship to develop new aspects of self. In this sense, a secure relationship serves as a secure base for adult exploration and development.

In summary, secure working models facilitate open access to emotional information that is critical for engagement, communication, and problem solving in marital relationships. This exchange of information promotes open communication and motivates activities that confirm the individual's confidence in his or her partner. When emotions serve as signals, attachment concerns are dealt with competently and effectively and the individual is free to attend to other matters such as parenting or problem solving. In contrast, when access to emotions is restricted, attachment concerns remain unacknowledged and these concerns may become hidden agendas that interfere with other aspects of marital communication. As a result, attachment-related emotions may be expressed in distorted or symptomatic ways that reduce the likelihood of receiving an understanding response.

EMOTIONS AS SYMPTOMS OF INSECURE WORKING MODELS

When working models are secure, threats to the care giver's availability activate primary emotions of fear and anger that serve to restore the attachment bond. However, when working models forecast negative responses, direct expression of fear and anger may be associated with expectations for rejecting or unpredictable responses. As a result, the individual must somehow alter or manipulate primary attachment emotions to reduce anticipated negative consequences of engaging the partner. To cope with this situation, the individual must develop alternative or *secondary strategies* for modulating, suppressing, or distorting attachment-related signals. These defensive and self-protective efforts are a desperate attempt to make the best of a bad situation. Because the individual must cope both with anxiety related to negative expectations about the attachment figure and with inhibiting emotional signals, he or she may be prone to experiencing considerable dysfunctional emotion and high levels of physiological arousal.

Studies of infant attachment illustrate the development of secondary strategies (Main, 1990). For instance, when a child anticipates rejection from a care giver, the child may develop a strategy of *deactivating* the attachment system. Such a strategy involves minimizing approach tendencies and the expression of primary feelings. Behaviorally, approach tendencies may be transformed into turning away or ignoring the care giver at times when the attachment system is activated. Ainsworth and colleagues (1978) identified this strategy among infants who avoided contact with their mothers following a stressful separation. At the level of emotions, this defensive strategy requires overriding primary attachment emotions that no longer serve a useful function. This strategy can also be maintained through attention deployment. By systematically shifting attention away from the attachment figure, the child selectively excludes information that would elicit attachment concerns and minimizes the expression of primary attachment emotions (Cassidy & Kobak, 1988). Interactions with the parent acquire a matter-of-fact quality, and the child maintains the relationship in a polite but neutral manner. Primary attachment tendencies toward contact seeking and protest are hidden.

Another secondary strategy may develop when working models forecast inconsistent care-giver response (Main, Kaplan, & Cassidy, 1985). Because primary attachment actions and signals fail to produce consistent response, the individual may maintain the attachment in a hyperactivated state. These individuals may exaggerate primary signals in an attempt to increase the likelihood of care-giver response. This strategy toward *hyperactivating* the attachment system may also result in increased monitoring or hypervigilance toward the care giver. When these exaggerated appeals still fail to produce consistent care-giver response, resentment and anxiety may accompany contact-seeking attempts. Hyperactivating strategies often leave the child preoccupied with the attachment relationship in ways that undermine the development of exploratory competence.

In distressed marriages, deactivating and hyperactivating strategies may develop as spouses begin to anticipate rejection or lack of response from each other. The demand/withdraw cycles that are frequently evident in distressed relationships often develop as desperate attempts to improve a relationship that might be threatened by dissolution. As one partner becomes anxious about the other partner's commitment, he or she may become hypervigilant toward the other and exaggerate concerns about the other's availability. Such pursuit often elicits a complementary deactivating strategy from the other partner characterized by withdrawal or stonewalling. Thus, secondary strategies develop as attempts to stabilize a relationship in which partners have become insecure about each other's availability, and at times these pursue/ withdraw cycles may be partially successful in creating predictable patterns of interactions that alleviate some anxiety.

Although they may yield predictable patterns of marital interaction, secondary attachment strategies may be especially vulnerable to breaking down during periods of conflict and transition. Times of change challenge all couples in their ability to accommodate to each other and actively draw on problem-solving skills. When working models are secure, couples can engage in open communication that focuses on the issue at hand and yields to accommodation between spouses. However, when models are insecure, day-to-day issues and conflicts may take on meanings that are more related to attachment concerns than to the matter under discussion. Attachment concerns thus become evident when normal conflicts become invested with high levels of dysfunctional emotion.

When fears about a partner's availability are strategically transformed into pursuing or withdrawing behavior, primary attachment emotions of fear and anger often become disconnected from the attachment concerns that elicited them. For instance, when approach tendencies are replaced by systematic attempts to ignore or avoid the attachment figure, it may not be apparent that avoidance is motivated out of fear of potential conflict. Similarly, when angry protest toward an attachment figure is redirected toward objects or less powerful individuals, the relation between aggressive behavior and attachment concerns may be hidden from view. As primary emotions are inhibited or manipulated, they become disconnected or split off from the attachment concerns that activate them, and they are expressed in ways that reduce their signal value. As a result, dysfunctional anger, sadness, or fear tends to be readily apparent, while attachment concerns are hidden or ambiguous. Failure to connect expressive-motor symptoms to underlying attachment fears may further confirm partners' negative expectations.

As primary attachment emotions are transformed into blaming and coercive expressions, these dysfunctional emotions dominate partners' awareness and lead to reciprocated negative-affect cycles. Anger that would normally be directed toward protesting lack of access to a partner may be redirected toward the partner. When partners are blamed for relationship difficulties, problem solving tends to take the form of what Wile (1981) describes as accusatory thinking. Accusatory thinking can take a variety of forms that have been well documented in research on distressed couples. Coercive behavior results from angry attempts to change a partner's behavior. Behavior therapists have often called attention to distressed couples' tendencies to use negative reinforcement such as criticism and threats as ways of trying to influence partners (Jacobson & Margolin, 1979). These aversive control efforts almost invariably result in declines in marital satisfaction and may re-

sult in reciprocated coercive responses. Cognitive therapists have emphasized how accusatory thinking may lead to distortions in how one partner
perceives the other (Beck, 1988).

Distorted expressions of attachment emotions may also reduce the clarity
of problem-solving communication. When primary attachment feelings of
fear, sadness, and anger are disconnected from concerns about a partner's
availability, these emotions are communicated in ways that reduce the likelihood of a sensitive or understanding response. Insecure spouses may express their opinions vaguely, talk too much, or divert attention from difficult
topics. When partners become fearful about each other's availability, they
may become even less direct and more self-protective. Fear motivates indirect communication, and indirect communications open the door to increased
misunderstandings. For example, a wife who is afraid that her husband cares
about his work more than her may start complaining about his job. Since her
fears are not directly acknowledged, her husband's responses almost inevitably leave her feeling that she has failed to get her point across. Thus, attachment concerns become a "hidden agenda" that undermines her ability
to communicate effectively. This leads to increased frustration, and further complaining.

Lack of clarity about attachment agendas leaves listeners more attuned to
the demanding or attacking quality of a partner's statements. The husband
may respond to his wife's anger, rather than to her unacknowledged fears
about his availability. In defending himself and his concerns about work, he
unknowingly confirms his wife's fears that he does not love her. In turn, the
wife's own concerns about the husband's job may lead to deaf spots in her
ability to listen to his concerns about work. Fears that the job is more important than she is may lead her to become less available to her husband. Thus,
insecurity in one spouse can lead to communication that fosters insecurity in
the other spouse. Studies of marital communication have documented that
in distressed relationships speakers consistently rate their intended messages
as more positive than their partners rate the impact of the messages (Gottman,
Markman, & Notarius, 1977; Kahn, 1970; Noller, 1981). Thus, speakers may
be unaware of their own communication difficulties while expecting their
partners to grasp their messages. This bias may foster disappointment in the
partner and contribute to more accusatory thinking.

As a couple's problem-solving communications deteriorate, anxiety about
partners' availability increases while thoughts about openly discussing attachment concerns leave partners with a painful sense of vulnerability and
danger. As a result, primary attachment feelings and concerns may systematically be ignored, omitted, or falsified (Bowlby, 1973). For instance, couples
may selectively ignore their own attachment feelings and redirect conversations to practical problems. By systematically excluding attachment-related
fear, anger, and sadness from discussion, these spouses may choose to emphasize their own independence or objectivity. As a result, disagreements

become occasions for finding the right solution to the problem, and a partner's failure to agree may be attributed to failure to be reasonable or rational. To the extent that feelings are discussed, they are seen as getting in the way of achieving a solution to the couples' problems.

When communication becomes defensive and accusatory, spouses' abilities to troubleshoot for mistaken assumptions and misunderstandings are often restricted. As a result, negative expectations continue to influence communication, but these expectations are not available for inspection. This inability to evaluate and correct mistaken assumptions drastically increases the likelihood of attribution errors. A spouse's anxiety about the other's response is likely to put him or her on the alert for danger signals that require vigilance and quick response. As a result, when processing ambiguous signals, an individual with an insecure model is more likely to jump to conclusions that may negatively distort the meaning of the partner's behavior. For instance, insecure models may lead an individual to incorrectly perceive rejection when a partner is preoccupied with other matters, or to mistakenly assume anger or lack of concern when a spouse is tense and anxious. Studies indicate that distressed couples attribute negative relationship events to global features of the relationship, to internal aspects of the partner, and to self-serving or egocentric biases that minimize their own responsibility for relationship difficulties (Bradbury & Fincham, 1987).

Compared with cognitive-behavioral approaches, an attachment perspective provides a more complete understanding of how cognitions about an attachment figure's availability guide emotional communications. While cognitive-behaviorists have focused on the mistakes that individuals make in their thinking about partners and relationship issues (Beck, 1988), they focus less on what is not being communicated when couples are in an accusatory mode. When the focus is on primary emotions and their role in secure attachment relationships, it becomes clearer how accusatory thinking represents a defensive distortion of underlying primary emotions. By viewing emotions as symptoms, the clinician can use distorted thinking as clues to underlying primary feelings. By accessing these feelings, the therapist can direct attention to information that can allow couples to revise insecure working models and to open communication in marital relationships.

MARITAL THERAPY—ACCESSING AND REVISING INSECURE WORKING MODELS

Given the multiple self-defeating and self-confirming ways that insecure models may influence marital interaction, the central challenge of therapy from an attachment perspective is to make rigid negative models of self and partner available for review and revision. This requires that the therapist access information that couples have selectively excluded from processing, sustain attention to this new information, and facilitate couples' abilities to incorporate and use this information in moving toward more accurate, integrated working models of self and partner. Insofar as symptoms represent distorted expressions of primary attachment feelings, they provide a natural focus for therapeutic intervention. By linking symptomatic emotions to the insecure working models that elicited them, the therapist helps the couple gain a new understanding of their relationship difficulties as motivated by fear and efforts at defensive self-protection. As a result, symptoms become intelligible and the insecure working models and fears that guided symptomatic expressions become available for revision.

Marital therapists are initially confronted with the challenge of managing the rigid and destructive patterns of interaction that characterize most forms of marital distress. Our attachment perspective views these rigid and destructive patterns as the product of secondary strategies that result from fears about partner's availability and responsiveness. Since self-protective biases prevent partners from acknowledging their own role in maintaining secondary strategies, the therapist must help couples to identify and bring these self-defeating patterns under greater cognitive control. Different forms of marital intervention have developed specific techniques to accomplish this task. Most generally, therapists establish control over couples' exchanges and point out how partners' behaviors are linked in self-defeating ways. Communication therapists attribute spouses' problems to dysfunctional patterns of communication, while the EFT approach uses relationship themes such as pursue/withdraw to call attention to how each individual's behavior perpetuates relationship distress. The value of these interventions lies in moving spouses from narrow, egocentric views of the marital problems to a broader perspective that assigns mutual responsibility for relationship difficulties. By establishing a greater sense of perspective and control, these initial interventions also provide couples with relief from aversive and escalating negative affect.

In addition to increasing cognitive control over dysfunctional behavior, the therapist must provide spouses with a sense of support and safety. To this end, the therapist needs to listen and to validate each spouse's experience in a way that makes the symptomatic behavior of each understandable as a distorted expression of normal attachment feelings and concerns. By listening and responding to partners' complaints in a nonaccusatory manner, the therapist provides a model of how to break the cycle of escalating blame and allows partners to move toward a nondefensive posture in the therapy session. In listening to clients, the therapist makes extensive use of spouses' expressive-motor cues to "decode" primary attachment emotions of fear, anger, and sadness. By selectively attending to these signals, the therapist can make distorted expressions of primary action tendencies available for discussion and examination. The challenge of this phase of therapy is to accept and validate each partner's experience without taking sides in marital disputes. If the therapist succeeds in this phase, spouses will experience increased acceptance that will allow them to gradually move away from rigid and defensive views of the relationship.

As the therapist establishes a sense of safety in the sessions, more difficult and anxiety-provoking issues can be addressed. In this phase, the therapist actively encourages exploration of difficult topics and begins to explore hidden attachment fears. Accessing insecure models becomes a central goal of treatment in this phase. To access insecure models the therapist must redirect attention from externally focused blame toward awareness of how insecure working models are guiding experience and perception. Since insecure models are premised on fears about a partner's availability, the therapist directs spouses toward acknowledging these fears so that their role in maintaining dysfunctional interactions can be examined. In this phase, the therapist serves as a secure base from which each partner can move toward increased self-exploration and increased tolerance for difficult feelings and vulnerabilities. This type of focus has been well developed in the EFT approach (Johnson & Greenberg, 1994; Greenberg & Johnson, 1988). Their use of experiential techniques and evocative responding provides valuable therapeutic tools for helping spouses to access insecure working models.

Fear and anxiety that accompany concerns about partners' availability may motivate self-protective efforts to exclude these concerns from awareness. To access insecure models, the therapist searches for critical moments when these models are actively guiding spouses' perceptions and behavior. High levels of affective intensity and increasing symptomatic expressions of emotion often provide clues that insecure models are operative. Disagreements that rapidly escalate in an accusatory direction or moments of sadness and withdrawal may signal concerns about a partner's availability. By monitoring these affective moments, the therapist can time interventions designed to help clients explore inner experience and the perceptions of the situation that are leading to symptomatic negative affect. For instance, as a wife starts to complain about her husband's new job, angry withdrawal by the husband can provide a focus for exploring underlying perceptions of the wife's behavior and the husband's fears about her availability. Similarly, the wife's complaining can be explored to articulate perceptions of the husband's lack of availability.

Working models also are operative at moments in attachment relationships when partners need support and comfort. A husband's feelings of weakness at moments of stress, or a wife's sense of isolation in her relationships with friends, provides obvious opportunities for relying on the spouse for care. When couples have difficulty acknowledging their needs at these moments, or turning to a partner for support, insecure models are operative and perceptions of a partner's availability can be fruitfully explored. Once again, symptomatic avoidant or stoic behavior provides a clue that insecure models are guiding perception and behavior.

Couples' reports of relationship events provide another valuable opportunity to access insecure working models. In therapy sessions, spouses often recount these episodes to justify accusatory thinking or lack of trust in the partner. One spouse's account usually brings forward an alternative version from the partner. Both accounts are usually motivated by defensive self-justification. These alternative versions of negative relationship episodes offer the therapist an opportunity to explore the partners' underlying perceptions and feelings in a way that makes their working models available for review. By directing attention to the affective reactions and concerns about the partner's availability, the therapist can increase spouses' awareness of how insecure models guide behavior. Once insecure models are accessed, spouses may reinterpret their own and their partners' behavior. Step-by-step reliving of these events thus offers opportunities to identify the role that negative expectations and fears about the partner's availability played in how the event was perceived and responded to.

Direct expression of fear or hurt provides a critical test of whether an insecure model has been successfully accessed in a session. These feelings almost invariably accompany spouses' appraisals that a partner is unavailable or unresponsive. As the therapist moves toward exploration of these fears, spouses may indicate a sense of discomfort and want to shift the topic. When these hesitations are explored, spouses often express beliefs that their fears are inappropriate or that their partner will trivialize or discount the validity of their fears. The therapist must remain sensitive to these concerns, while supportively exploring and maintaining a focus on accessing attachment fears. Subtle indications that a stoic or angry posture is giving way to more basic fears should receive attention from the therapist and can be amplified through evocative responding (Greenberg & Johnson, 1988). When access to fears is achieved, the client's mode of processing changes toward a softening that allows more openness, greater depth of processing, and a sense of relief. These moments in treatment are critical for testing the degree to which the self is lovable and the partner is available.

Once insecure models and accompanying fears are accessed, clients must integrate this new information into a revised understanding of the relationship. In this process, spouses gain new awareness of the role that insecure models play in marital difficulties. At this point, symptoms that had become cognitively disconnected from the attachment concerns can be linked to the working models and relationship events that elicited them. Thus, complaining or accusatory thinking can be understood as desperate responses to fears about a partner's commitment to the relationship. By expressing attachment fears directly, individuals make new information available to their partners that allow them to reevaluate the meaning of symptomatic behaviors. Symptoms of marital distress now become clues to attachment fears that were previously hidden or excluded from conversation. As the role of insecure models in guiding dysfunctional patterns of marital interaction becomes a part of spouses' awareness, symptoms become less rigid, communication becomes more direct, and attachment fears are disconfirmed. This process of revising insecure models is a gradual one. Partners may initially discount new information that is inconsistent with previous expectations. However, to the extent that insecure models and fears are experienced and validated, attention is keenly focused on this new information, and consequently it is more likely to be integrated into the revised models.

By focusing attention on insecure models, the therapist creates a context in which couples can test and possibly disconfirm negative expectations. When an individual accesses and actively experiences hidden fears, this vulnerable moment naturally signals the need for a sensitive and understanding response. Initially, the therapist may provide much of the understanding and sensitive responding to each partner's fears. This is often necessary because partners tend to carry grudges and resentment that make it difficult for them to respond to distress in each other. However, as therapy progresses, moments of acknowledging fear provide partners with opportunities to respond in a way that accepts and validates the other's concerns. Thus, emotion can be turned into a powerful communicative signal that elicits a care-giving response. To the extent that partners respond with care giving, insecure expectations about a partner's insensitivity and lack of availability are disconfirmed and fears are turned from symptoms to signals that enhance communication.

Finally, as partners begin to gain confidence in each other's availability, they can use primary attachment emotions to openly communicate their concerns and further consolidate their commitment to the relationship. Thus, fear, anger, and sadness can be directly expressed, concerns about attachment can be openly acknowledged, and disagreements can be understood as a normal part of marital problem solving. As communication becomes more direct, partners may become more effective at reading each other's signals and responding in a manner that further restores confidence in each other's responsiveness and availability. Thus, at a certain point in treatment, normal attachment emotions serve to restore trust and become a part of a positive self-confirming cycle. As a result, disagreements become less charged and partners can tolerate and accept differing points of view without adopting defensive or accusatory postures. Attachment behavior may become more apparent in these relationships as ordinary concerns and vulnerabilities motivate partners to reach out and seek support from each other. Thus, primary emotions may motivate new and alternative forms of behavior that can be validated within the changing marital relationship.

Open communication provides a critical marker of the revision process. Ideally, the therapeutic process of disconfirming insecure models should increase awareness that signals may often be ambiguous and perspectives are only partial. This recognition should lead spouses to check out their perceptions with their partner more frequently. The importance of maintaining this open perspective has been recognized in different approaches to marital therapy. Communication approaches stress the importance of "troubleshoot-ing" and "checking out" processes as ways of maintaining an open posture in marital relationships. Beck's cognitive approach places an emphasis on helping partners to adopt a more humble, tentative attitude about the accu-racy of their own appraisals about their partners. From our attachment per-spective, this attitude about working models develops at the conceptual level of information processing. When partners are secure, they increase their ca-pacities to "metamonitor" their working models in a way that leaves the models open for testing and reevaluation (Kobak & Cole, in press; Main, 1991).

The therapist in this approach uses attachment theory as a guide for ac-cessing, focusing, and processing new information in marital sessions. By gaining access to attachment information that had previously been excluded or distorted, couples can revise working models and reestablish confidence in the relationship. As a result, clients should become more successful in us-ing attachment emotions as signals and in openly discussing attachment-related concerns and fears. Increased confidence also increases spouses' openness to examining their own perceptions and responsibilities and al-lows them to attend more completely to their partners' point of view. When confidence in the partner's availability increases, normal conflicts and points of disagreement can be considered without activating attachment fears. Thus, by accessing hidden fears, fostering interactions that end in understanding, and highlighting the importance of attachment-related concerns, the thera-pist provides distressed couples with a more positive and hopeful view of their relationship.

CASE EXAMPLE

At the point that Christine and Rick began treatment, their pursue/with-draw dynamic and mutual distrust had brought them to the verge of separa-tion. Christine had stayed with friends for 3 weeks, then returned home with a renewed commitment to seek help. Initially, the therapist explored each spouse's experience of the brief separation and encouraged them to focus on what had led them to a decision to stay together. As Christine and Rick dis-cussed the experience of being separated, they each reported how the pros-pect of ending the relationship had led them to realize that they needed each other. Rick and Christine were encouraged to express their attachment con-cerns and their renewed commitment to the marriage. This helped to pro-vide the couple with a sense of hope. From this vantage point, the therapist suggested that the couple consider the difficulties that had jeopardized their relationship and motivated their decision to separate. Therapy began by re-viewing the history of interactions that led to the couple's decision to sepa-rate. As the couple discussed their difficulties, they reenacted their dysfunctional patterns and defensive efforts to manage attachment fears. Fears about each other's availability were not directly or openly discussed. Christine's fears that Rick's job was more important to him than she was were hidden behind expressed concerns about moving and changing jobs. Rick's fears that Christine's unhappiness was a sign that he had failed as a husband were hidden behind expressed concerns about how they would sell their house and manage a move to a new location. These insecure working models and unexpressed fears undermined their ability to maintain constructive problem solving. As they talked about selling the house, getting a job, or moving, they became trapped in an unproductive pursue/withdraw cycle. As Christine complained, Rick became depressed and angry. Both partners felt misunderstood, and resentments about past failures prevented each from turning to the other for support.

In the early sessions, the therapist focused on accessing insecure working models and their accompanying fears. When Christine complained about the possibility of Rick's getting a new job that required them to move, the therapist explored for hidden fears that motivated her complaints. Christine had some difficulty with accessing and articulating her fears, but as she explored her anxieties, she brought up past moves when she had felt isolated and when Rick's preoccupation with his job had made him unavailable to her. As she identified her fear of isolation, the therapist pointed out that when she complained, part of what she was asking was whether she was more important to Rick than his job; with every complaint, there was a question of "do you love me?" With assistance, Christine gradually came to acknowledge her fear of being lonely. She was reluctant to experience these feelings, and tended to try to avoid them, but as her tolerance for these feelings increased, she softened, and was able to acknowledge her fear.

Initially, Rick had difficulty responding to Christine's attachment-related fears. He tended to interpret her concerns as further expressions of her unhappiness, for which he blamed himself. For instance, as Christine related an incident in which she had feared being alone, Rick responded by becoming annoyed. In exploring their reactions, Rick was able to state his perception that Christine was criticizing him with her story and Christine acknowledged fears of being alone. The therapist linked Rick's feeling rejected to his withdrawal and Christine's feeling alone to her blaming. In this process, the couple increased their awareness of how unacknowledged fears perpetuated their symptomatic pattern of blame and withdrawal that left Rick angry and Christine feeling even more alone and unsupported. As Rick became better able to interpret Christine's depression and complaints as a sign that she needed reassurance, he was able to change his own behavior to support Christine, rather than withdraw. He was pleased to discover that suspending his tendency to take a logical, withdrawing approach in response to Christine's complaining, and instead acting empathically, sitting with Christine and holding her hand, seemed to work! Christine agreed that Rick was very comforting. When she reached out to him instead of complaining, he was consoling and reassuring; feeling less criticized, Rick was less likely to withdraw.

As Christine began to express her attachment fears more directly, therapy moved toward exploring Rick's insecure models and attachment fears. When Christine entered the session appearing depressed, Rick tried desperately and without success to cheer her up. In response to Christine's expression of need, and fearing the implications of her unhappiness, Rick tended to stifle his own feelings of anxiety and fear and take a stoic stance that prevented him from asking for reassurance or support. However, as each of these sessions progressed, it became apparent that Rick was, in fact, feeling quite depressed himself. The therapist used Rick's nonverbal symptoms of depression and withdrawal as clues for prompting Rick to explore his feelings. With help, Rick began to articulate underlying fears about losing Christine and about being inadequate as a husband. He showed some improvement in being able to express his fears, at one point saying to Christine, " I don't want to go by the wayside like your [estranged] sister did."

As Christine became stronger and more certain of herself and of Rick's support, she started to express her fears in nonaccusatory ways. She reported that she tried to point out to Rick that "it's not your doing that I'm depressed." As Christine responded with increased understanding of Rick's fears, Rick, reassured by her support, moved toward increased confidence in Christine's availability and commitment. Thus, Rick and Christine showed increased access to insecure models, were able to express attachment fears openly, and, as a result, were less prone to rigidly reenacting their initial accusatory pursue/withdraw cycle. In place of these secondary strategies, Rick and Christine were gaining increased abilities to acknowledge fears and to support each other. Rick was less reactive to and defensive about Christine's unhappiness and was better able to listen to and support her. Thus, awareness of their insecure working models permitted Christine and Rick to begin to modify these models, so that both could trust in the other's commitment and availability and expand their giving and receiving care.

Despite movement toward more open expression of attachment fears, insecure working models must be repeatedly accessed in order to be disconfirmed. As treatment progressed, both Christine and Rick demonstrated increased awareness of how fears influenced their daily interactions. In one session, Christine reported a problematic reaction she experienced when Rick returned from a business trip. Christine perceived Rick's excitement as a sign that he was entering a preoccupied phase, and she panicked. In exploring her reaction, she noted that Rick was hyper at the end of the week and this reminded her of how he had acted before many of their fights that had led to threats of divorce. She connected her high level of anxiety to these expectations derived from past experience, and the therapist validated these concerns as an indication of her concern for Rick's availability. Christine often hesitated to bring up these fears out of expectations that Rick would not understand and think of them as silly and neurotic. These expectations led her to devalue her own attachment-related signals, and both increased and confirmed her sense of isolation. During the course of therapy, these insecure working models based on real past experiences may lead to reoccurring fears that need to be repeatedly and explicitly discussed and disconfirmed.

Through voicing fears about each other's availability, Christine and Rick were able to access and validate new aspects of themselves in the marital relationship. As treatment neared termination, both Christine and Rick continued to be concerned about each other's availability. Christine continued to fear being left alone by Rick, and Rick continued to fear failing in the marriage and losing Christine. However, by repeatedly accessing these fears, both Christine and Rick had increased their awareness of these issues and their control over the symptomatic expressions. Thus, Christine's complaining and Rick's compulsive care giving were now linked to underlying attachment fears, and these fears were now available for discussion and disconfirmation. As a result, symptoms of complaining, withdrawal, and depression were now under increased cognitive control. Christine and Rick reflected this new perspective with a sense of humor about their tendencies that made them more accepting of each other and less prone to reacting with accusatory thinking. As a result, symptoms became signals to both self and partner of unexpressed attachment concerns. Rick's need for support that had been completely masked by his compulsive care giving and Christine's need for reassurance and contact could now be more directly expressed and responded to within the marital relationship. Defensive postures were now replaced with understanding of and increased tolerance for each partner's symptomatic or idiosyncratic tendencies.

CONCLUSION

During the past two decades, therapists and researchers have provided extensive descriptions of dysfunctional marriages. Features of marital distress including poor communication, reciprocated negative affect, and demand/withdraw cycles have been documented and targeted for research and intervention. Yet the focus on dysfunction fails to address basic questions about the constructive role that emotions play in maintaining and repairing marital relationships. We think attachment theory holds considerable promise as a guide to understanding the role of emotions in marital functioning and how these emotions become problematic in distressed relationships. That is, when spouses begin to view their partners as unavailable and/or unresponsive, normal attachment feelings of anger, fear, and sadness become prone to defensive distortions that reduce couples' capacity for effective problem solving. Thus, attachment theory orients the marital therapist toward understanding symptoms of marital distress as distorted expressions of normal attachment concerns. The goal of treatment then becomes one of understanding dysfunctional symptomatic expressions, so that partners can acknowledge their more fundamental concerns about each other's availability and commitment. As partners increase their understanding of attachment concerns and communicate more successfully with each other, emotions become valuable signals that facilitate rather than hinder problem-solving communication.

REFERENCES

Ainsworth, M. D. S. (1989). Attachments beyond infancy. *American Psychologist, 44,* 709–716.

Ainsworth, M. D. S., Bell, S. M., & Stayton, D. J. (1971). Individual differences in the strange situation behavior of one-year-olds. In H. R. Schaffer (Ed.), *The origins of human social relations* (pp. 17–57). New York: Academic.

Ainsworth, M. D. S., Blehar, M. C., Waters, E., & Wall, S. (1978). *Patterns of attachment: A psychological study of the strange situation.* Hillsdale, NJ: Erlbaum.

Bartholomew, K., & Horowitz, L. M. (1991). Attachment styles among young adults: A four-category model. *Journal of Social and Personality Psychology, 61,* 226–244.

Beck, A. T. (1988). *Love is never enough.* New York: Harper & Row.

Bowlby, J. (1969). *Attachment and loss: Vol. 1. Attachment.* New York: Basic Books.

Bowlby, J. (1973). *Attachment and loss: Vol. 2. Separation.* New York: Basic Books.

Bowlby, J. (1979). On knowing what you are not supposed to know and feeling what you are not supposed to feel. *Canadian Journal of Psychiatry, 24,* 403–408.

Bowlby, J. (1981). *Attachment and loss: Vol. 3. Loss, sadness and depression.* New York: Basic Books.

Bowlby, J. (1988). *A secure base: Parent-child attachment and healthy human development.* New York: Basic Books.

Bradbury, T., & Fincham, F. (1987). Affect and cognition in close relationships: Toward an integrative model. *Cognition and Emotion, 1,* 59–87.

Bretherton, I. (1980). Young children in stressful situations: The supporting role of attachment figures and unfamiliar care givers. In G. V. Coelho & P. J. Ahmen (Eds.), *Uprooting and development* (pp. 179–210). New York: Plenum.

Bretherton, I. (1985). Attachment theory: Retrospect and prospect. In I. Bretherton & E. Waters (Eds.), Growing points in attachment theory and research (pp. 3–38). *Monographs for the Society for Research in Child Development, 50* (1–2, Serial No. 209).

Bretherton, I. (1990). Open communication and internal working models: Their role in the development of attachment relationships. In R. A. Thompson (Ed.), *Nebraska Symposium on Motivation: Socioemotional Development* (pp. 57–113). Lincoln: University of Nebraska Press.

Cassidy, J., & Kobak, R. (1988). Avoidance and its relation to other defensive processes. In J. Belsky & T. Neworski (Eds.), *Clinical implications of attachment.* Hillsdale, NJ: Erlbaum.

Christensen, A. (1988). Dysfunctional interaction patterns in couples. In P. Noller & M. A. Fitzpatrick (Eds.), *Perspectives on marital interaction* (pp. 31–52). Clevedon, England: Multilingual Matters.

Fruzzetti, A. E., & Jacobson, N. S. (1990). Toward a behavioral conceptualization of adult intimacy: Implications for marital therapy. In E. A. Blechman (Ed.), *Emotions and the family: For better or for worse* (pp. 117–135). Hillsdale, NJ: Erlbaum.

Gottman, J. (1979). *Marital interaction: An experimental investigation.* New York: Academic.

Gottman, J., Markman, H., & Notarius, C. (1977). The topography of marital conflict: A sequential analysis of verbal and nonverbal behavior. *Journal of Personality and Social Psychology, 34,* 14–23.

Gottman, J. M. (1991). Predicting the longitudinal course of marriages. *Journal of Marriage and the Family, 17,* 3–7.

Gottman, J. M., & Krokoff, L. J. (1989). Marital interaction and satisfaction: A longitudinal view. *Journal of Consulting and Clinical Psychology, 57,* 47–52.

Gottman, J. M., & Levenson, R. W. (1986). Assessing the role of emotion in marriage. *Behavioral Assessment, 8,* 31–48.

Greenberg, L. S., & Johnson, S. M. (1988). *Emotionally focused therapy for couples.* New York: Guilford.

Greenberg, M. T., & Speltz, M. L. (1988). Attachment and the ontogeny of conduct problems. In J. Belsky & T. Nezworski (Eds.), *Clinical implications of attachment* (pp. 177–218). Hillsdale, NJ: Erlbaum.

Hazan, C., & Shaver, P. (1987). Romantic love conceptualized as an attachment process. *Journal of Personality and Social Psychology, 52,* 511–524.

Jacobson, N. S., & Margolin, G. (1979). *Marital therapy: Strategies based on social learning and behavior exchange principles.* New York: Brunner/Mazel.

Johnson, S. (1986). Bonds or bargains: Relationship paradigms and their significance for marital therapy. *Journal of Marital and Family Therapy, 12,* 259–267.

Johnson, S., & Greenberg, L. (1994). The emotionally focused approach to problems in adult attachment. In N. S. Jacobson & A. S. Gurman (Eds.), *Clinical handbook of marital therapy* (2nd ed.) New York: Guilford.

Kahn, M. (1970). Nonverbal communication and marital satisfaction. *Family Process, 9,* 449–456.

Kobak, R., & Hazan, C. (1991). Attachment in marriage: Effects of security and accuracy of working models. *Journal of Personality and Social Psychology, 60,* 861–869.

Kobak, R., & Cole, H. (in press). Attachment and meta-monitoring: Implications for adolescent autonomy and psychopathology. In D. Cicchetti & S. Toth (Eds.), *Rochester Symposium on Development and Psychopathology: Disorders of the Self.* Rochester, NY: University of Rochester Press.

Leventhal, H. (1979). A perceptual-motor processing model of emotion. In P. Pliner, K. Blankstein, & I. M. Spigel (Eds.), *Perception of emotion in self and others* (Vol. 5). New York: Plenum.

Main, M. (1981). Avoidance in the service of proximity: A working paper. In K. Immelmann, G. Barlow, L. Petrinovitch, & M. Main (Eds.), *Behavioral development: The Bielefeld interdisciplinary project* (pp. 651–693). New York: Cambridge University Press.

Main, M. (1990). Cross-cultural studies of attachment organization: Recent studies, changing methodologies, and the concept of conditional strategies. *Human Development, 33,* 48–61.

Main, M. (1991). Metacognitive knowledge, metacognitive monitoring and singular (coherent) vs. multiple (incoherent) models of attachment. In J. S. Stevenson-Hinde, C. M. Parkes, & P. Marris (Eds.), *Attachment across the lifecycle* (pp. 127–159). London: Routledge.

Main, M., & Hesse, E. (1990). Parents' unresolved traumatic experiences are related to infant disorganized attachment status: Is frightened and/or frightening parental behavior the linking mechanism? In M. Greenberg, D. Cicchetti, & E. M. Cummings (Eds.), *Attachment in the preschool years: Theory, research and intervention* (pp. 161–184). Chicago: University of Chicago Press.

Main, M., Kaplan, N., & Cassidy, J. (1985). Security in infancy, childhood and adulthood: A move to the level of representation. In I. Bretherton & E. Waters (Eds.), *Growing points of attachment theory and research* (pp. 66–106). *Monographs of the Society for Research in Child Development, 50* (1–2, Serial No. 209).

Main, M., & Solomon, J. (1986). Discovery of an insecure-disorganized/disoriented attachment pattern. In M. Yogman & T. B. Brazelton (Eds.), *Affective development in infancy* (pp. 95–124). Norwood, NJ: Ablex.

Markman, H., & Notarius, C. (1987). Coding marital and family interaction: Current status. In T. Jacob (Ed.), *Family interaction and psychopathology: Theories, methods and findings.* New York: Plenum.

Marvin, R. S. (1977). An ethological-cognitive model for the attenuation of mother-child attachment behavior. In T. M. Alloway, L. Krames, & P. Pliner (Eds.), *Advances in the study of communication and affect: Vol. 3. The development of social attachments* (pp. 25–60). New York: Plenum.

Noller, P. (1981). Gender and marital adjustment level differences in decoding messages from spouses and strangers. *Journal of Personality and Social Psychology, 41,* 272–278.

Robertson, J., & Bowlby, J. (1952). Responses of young children to separation from their mothers. *Courrier du Centre International de L'Enfance, 2,* 131–142.

Safran, J. D., & Greenberg, L. S. (1986). Hot cognition and psychotherapy process: An information processing/ecological approach. In P. Kendall (Ed.), *Advances in cognitive behavioral research and therapy* (Vol. 5). New York: Academic.

Schaap, C. (1984). A comparison of the interaction of distressed and nondistressed married couples in a laboratory situation: Literature survey, methodological issues, and an empirical investigation. In K. Hahlweg & N. S. Jacobson (Eds.), *Marital interaction: Analysis and modification* (pp. 133–158). New York: Guilford.

Sroufe, L. A. (1989). Relationships, self, and individual adaptation. In A. J. Sameroff & R. N. Emde (Eds.), *Relationship disturbances in early childhood* (pp. 97–124). New York: Basic Books.

Sroufe, L. A., & Fleeson, J. (1986). Attachment and the construction of relationships. In W. W. Hartup & Z. Rubin (Eds.), *The nature and development of relationships*. Hillsdale, NJ: Erlbaum.

Weiss, R. S. (1975). *Marital separation*. New York: Basic Books.

Weiss, R. S. (1982). Attachment in adult life. In C. M. Parkes & J. Stevenson-Hinde (Eds.), *The place of attachment in human behavior* (pp. 171–184). New York: Basic Books.

Wile, D. B. (1981). *Couples therapy: A nontraditional approach*. New York: Wiley.

SECTION B

Humanistic and Experiential Approaches

4

Helping Couples Make Authentic Emotional Contact

ROBERT A. PIERCE

> *It must be considered that there is nothing more*
> *difficult to carry out, nor more doubtful of success,*
> *nor more dangerous to handle, than to institute a new*
> *order of things.*
>
> —*Niccolo Machiavelli*

> *The quality of thinking that got us into this is not*
> *sufficient to get us out of it.*
>
> —*Albert Einstein*

People do not fall in love and get married so they can hurt, frighten, and disappoint each other. They get together because they sense something mysteriously familiar, sexy, exhilarating, or comforting when they are with each other. Couples often report that in their falling-in-love phase, they felt better about themselves and more complete than ever before. When these same couples come to see us for help, they are still powerful generators of feelings for each other, and they still exert a strong influence on each other's self-esteem. The feelings are more painful, however, and the partner is more likely a source of negative than positive self-regard.

Between that first bright promise and the present disappointment, hurt, and distance, some very complex emotional adaptations have occurred that we need to understand and alter. These adaptations often limit and narrow emotional contact and authenticity in order to control some very painful feelings. These adaptations help the partners feel less rageful, anxious, or hurt by making them less emotionally connected and providing them with less access to pleasure and delight.

If this is the problem, then the therapist's job is to facilitate authentic and useful emotional contact between the partners. By the time they see us, many couples have minimal contact with each other. Others have highly repetitive and ritualized contact. They may be polite or they may fight, or one may pick and criticize while the other distances. Some who have wild fights may look as though they are emotionally engaged, yet over time a listener can hear the fight as a set piece played over and over again, without any real connection. None of these couples is having authentic and useful emotional contact. It's our job as therapists to help them do that, and it's my job in this chapter to present some ideas about how we can help them.

While most therapeutic approaches include some attention to emotional factors, some approaches view affective experience and expression as a major lever for change (Perls, Hefferline, & Goodman, 1951; Pierce, Nichols, & DuBrin, 1983; Greenberg & Safran, 1984; Hendrix, 1988; Denton, 1991; Roberts, 1992). The thesis of this chapter is that fear of feelings underlies a great deal of marital discord, and that easing that fear can move couples toward more satisfying contact.

To do this, we need to help clients work their way back to their more basic feelings from the defensive manifestations these feelings have taken. Rigid patterns of withdrawal or pursuit, criticism, overwork, or excessive child-focus are examples of these defensive manifestations, as well as one-note feelings where, for example, one person is always angry and the other always hurt. Our job is to create a safe enough environment and provide the right tools so couples can discover the deeper, more basic feelings that once connected them.

In order to go further with this distinction between our basic and most genuine feelings and others that are more derived or defensive, we first have to understand what we mean by emotions. Emotions are the felt components of action tendencies, based on a person's appraisal of self in relation to environment. Psychophysiologial concomitants are part of the emotional state, and each emotion implies an action in relation to the environment. For example, a man who is bereaved wants to find and be reunited with the person he is missing. When we are embarrassed we want to "drop through the floor"—hide, so people will not see the shameful flaw that has just been exposed. These action tendencies are a central part of any emotion and are part of what makes emotions seem risky and potentially out of control.

Emotions imply behavior, sometimes unacceptable beahvior. We have a way we want to present ourselves to others and even to ourselves. Someone hurts us and we feel like crying, but we don't want that person to know how important he or she is to us or how vulnerable we feel, so we try to hide our trembling lips and brimming eyes. If we cannot hide embarrassing feelings, we may say "my feelings betrayed me." That is, they kept me from presenting to others the picture of myself I wanted to present. It is this tension between what we feel and what we want to feel that fuels many marital struggles.

We are afraid of what it means to have certain feelings—what it means to us or to our partners. And so we do sleight-of-mind tricks with our emotions, some conscious, some not so conscious, to try to make things better. It is helpful to remember, incidentially, that no matter how troublesome the results, our intention is almost always to make things better. Let us look at some of these sleight-of-mind tricks we pull on ourselves and on those we love.

BASIC, BLOCKED, AND TRANSFORMED FEELINGS

People may be more or less aware of the emotion they are experiencing. When people are largely unaware of the feeling they are implicitly experiencing, we say the feeling is *blocked*. Sometimes one feeling is swiftly turned into another, presumably less threatening, feeling. The original feeling is called the *basic* feeling, and the derivative feeling is called the *transformed* feeling. Most of us know "transformer" as a box that transforms electricity from one form to another; it is not very visual. But the toys called transformers can be transformed from a superhero, say, to a car. They literally change forms as you watch. This is more what a feeling transformation is, except usually it happens much faster.

Consider Bill and Sue, in bed one night, trying to make love. Sex is suddenly not working out. Bill's erection is shrinking. He doesn't know why. He's embarrassed. "What's wrong? What will she think? I'm supposed to be hard. What's wrong with me?" These are his thoughts. What he says is: "Guess I must be tired. Maybe I drank too much. Sorry."

Sue says, "It's okay. It's nice just to be close. We made love last night. Maybe it's too soon."

Bill's shame makes him vigilant. He wonders, "Is there some condescension in what she said? Does she think I'm over the hill?" He cannot accept Sue's assurance. He cannot let it go. He covers his shame with anger. "Don't be so condescending, for Christ's sake! Maybe if you didn't bitch at me so much and weren't on the phone with your girlfriends all the time, I'd feel sexier toward you." Strange as this may seem, we all have an empathic grasp of the wacky logic of feelings that makes such a transformation understandable, if regrettable. The basic feeling here, largely blocked, is shame. In an effort to preserve his self-esteem, Bill transformed his shame into anger.

But getting mad instead of feeling ashamed or frightened is only one of the many defensive transformations we see in our clients, our friends, and ourselves. We frequently see people who are angry at their mates and do a little dance that ends up as fear. The swift, unconscious transformation goes something like "I'm mad at Jim, but if I show it, he'll get mad at me and that scares me." It is hard to know whether the fear is more of her own anger or of her mate's, but either way it gets transformed into fear. This particular transformation, anger into fear, is a common one. People do an amazing number of things just to avoid the catastrophic possibility that someone might get mad at them! Another example of a defensive transformation is the transformation of sadness into fear. A spouse who has been abandoned by a parent or previous lover may carry a great deal of sadness about the earlier loss, but experience it mostly as fear that the current partner will leave. He may behave like a fearful "Klingon," seeking repeated reassurance and thus drive his wife away. If he could have shared his loss and sadness with her, she could have comforted him and better understood his need for reassurance.

There are many such transformations that occur in couples. Some do not do much harm, but others are corrosive of the relationship. One therapeutic implication of this is that helping couples recognize and accept their basic feelings avoids the trouble caused by transformations like the ones above, which make matters worse. Greenberg and Johnson (1986b) make a similar point when they say, "It's not people's feelings and wants that cause problems in marrige...but the disowning or disallowing of these feelings and wants that leads to ineffective communication and escalating interactions cycles" (p. 258).

Shame

The only emotion people never seem to transform other feelings *into* is shame. We may experience our loneliness as lust, our sadness as anger, or our anger as fear. But we never seem to choose shame. Shame is always unwelcome. For a long time, our field was preoccupied with guilt and paid little attention to shame. Lewis (1971) and Tomkins (1963) were lonely voices. In the past few years, however, a number of good books have appeared describing the corrosive effects of shame (Kaufman, 1989; Nichols, 1991; Nathanson, 1992). It is clear now what a large role shame plays as the root of a great deal of pain and miscommunication in couples. Shame separates people. We look down, cover our faces, look away, and go away when we feel shame. We also try to ward it off by arguing, getting mad, and blaming. But that only shames the other and leads to endless fights about who is to blame. Wiping dirt off yourself and onto your partner is a very costly way to get clean.

Let's start with an argument based on shame. A couple in their late twenties, struggling with a new baby, his beginning career in accounting, and her half-time work as a programmer, basically like each other and do fairly well, given the demands of their lives. They were visiting friends for the evening to see their friends' big new house. They said they would bring a pizza along. She could seldom find the kind she used to have back home, with a very thin crust, and asked her husband to get one of those. He said, "I'll get it at Luigi's. He's a client of mine." When she opened the box and said, "Jeez, look at this crust! It's real thick!" he blew up at her, got very angry, said she was never satisfied. As he was winding down, she said, "Why are you being so mean to me?" He said, "Why am *I* being so mean to *you*? Why are *you* being so mean to *me*?" She said, "Whaddya mean, mean to you? All I said was the crust is thick." Later, he apologized for blowing up, and she accepted his apology, and they made up. But a lot of what seemed to be going on was bypassed—primarily a sense of shame. Shame for getting a pizza with a thick crust? No. Shame for not being a good provider. Her mild criticism about the pizza crystallized his existing concerns about whether his newly formed practice would be adequate to his family's needs, whether they could buy as big a house as their friends', and whether he could feel okay about himself as a provider (that is, a potent, competent man) if his wife had to work part-time as well as take care of the new baby. The comment about the crust triggered these feelings and caused his shame, and he warded off that very painful feeling the way people often do. He got mad.

Shame, by its nature, hides and divides. Tears can bring people together and anger can be a foundation for assertiveness and respect. But shame causes problems because it is so painful to recognize, accept, and admit to, and there is such a temptation to shift the blame. When working affectively with couples where shame is a major dynamic, the therapist must always be on the look-out for self-esteem sinkholes—pockets of self-disgust and feelings of inadequacy and worthlessness. At times, these coexist with an otherwise fairly adequate sense of self-respect.

The main tools a therapist needs to bring to this work is a sense of humor and the ability to appreciate both the client's strengths and the client's mesmerizing belief that everyone who does not yet know what a fool she is will know very soon. And they all will laugh. The therapist needs to be able to experience the world from as close to the client's perspective as possible, and to put that experience into a larger context, a context that shapes and gives broader meaning to the client's subjective view.

An important predictor of good outcomes is how willing the partners are, or can become, to engage each other, talk, deal openly, rather than withdraw (Gottman & Krokoff, 1989; Gottman, 1993; Johnson & Greenberg, 1991; Smith, Vivian, & O'Leary, 1990). Fox (1991) has pointed out that even anger, as much trouble as it causes us, is basically an "approach" emotion. Shame, however, moves us away from our partners and makes us cautious; it is an avoidance emotion. Let's take a look now at shame's companion—fear.

Fear

Fear is a feeling that most couples experience more as a deadened *defense against fear* than as directly felt sweating palms and pounding heart. Fear keeps many couples stuck in unrewarding relationship cycles. To break out, they would need to do things that frighten them—confront their partners, for example, or share feelings of vulnerability. Overcoming fear and being able to share feelings of vulnerability can move a couple ahead. It *is* a risk, though, and the partner may not take the hoped-for next step toward empathy, but may instead use the partner's acknowledgment of vulnerability or apology as a weapon in the next fight. There are certain basic fears that are almost invariably involved in couples' troubles.

Fear of Being Left

Being left feels bad to almost everyone. Yet lots of couples threaten to leave each other, especially during fights. One couple, early in their marriage, left each other so regularly after fights, that they had to negotiate who "got" to leave on a particular evening. They had a driveway only wide enough for one car, so it was a major act of trust on the husband's part when he got home first and put his car in the driveway, knowing she would pull in behind him when she got home, and he would be unable to leave during that evening's fight. Conversely, if he parked on the street, that was evidence that he was planning to leave her that night, and could, itself, become the basis for a fight.

Fear of Humiliation

We are all afraid of being known and found to be laughable, disgusting, bad, or incompetent. These are all essentially fears of being shamed. We have already talked about how awful shame feels, and most of us have early warning devices that let us know if shame is in the vicinity. This usually registers as fear—fear of being seen by important others as foolish, dirty, bad, or stupid—in some very basic way as "not okay," as with the young accountant in the example above.

Fear of Being Controlled; Loss of Autonomy

A woman told a story about her successful physician-husband who, at times, liked giving up control and playing a passive role with her, especially in bed. She would sometimes initiate this type of sex play and called it "taking the bull by the horn." Most other times, he was busily engaged with what Adler called "masculine protest," emphasizing his power and importance and how much he had to take care of others weaker than himself. Whether sexually or in vulnerable conversations, or when he was sick and she'd bring him comfort, there were times when he relished feeling small, protected, and cared for. But that was a role he could permit himself only sometimes, when things were just right. One day, shortly after he had enthusiastically taken up golf, his wife came to him and asked if he would like her to "take the bull by the horn." He looked torn for a moment, as though he wanted to, but wasn't quite ready to let go. He said, "Okay, but first I gotta wash my clubs." They both laughed, and she said, "Okay, when you get your club good and clean, I'll meet you in the bedroom."

Fear of Criticism

Most of us dread criticism, especially when it comes from people close to us, to whom we've shown ourselves most openly, and who are, therefore, in a position to hurt us most by what they say. Gottman (1993) now has video-taped evidence of a process we've all seen in our clients in which one part-ner, often the wife, wants more attention than she's getting from her husband. She criticizes him for that or other flaws, and he responds by withdrawing, intensifying the conflict, making her feel more isolated and hence more criti-cal. This criticism/withdrawal cycle is at the root of a great deal of marital unhappiness. It's worth noting that *fear* of criticism is key to this cycle. Criti-cism alone does not cause withdrawal. At times, when the partner hearing the criticism is able to stay present, listen, and respond, the critcisim/with-drawal cycle does not occur. One of the strengths of Hendrix's (1988) ap-proach is that it gives the couple a sturdy framework that allows one to listen while the other talks. It prescribes behaviors that contain criticism and an-ger, making withdrawal less likely. Counterattack is, of course, another com-mon response to criticism, which, like withdrawal, does not work very well. It, too, is triggered by fear. So fear of criticisim is the basis for lots of marital trouble, and learning how to manage it is an important part of marital therapy.

The principle thesis of this chapter is that the effort to avoid feelings is often more costly to a relationship than the feelings themselves. Each of the fears we have described operates to limit openness and sharing between part-ners and to circumscribe the full range of choice these people would other-wise have. These fears narrow life, and with a goal of making it less dangerous, they also make it less enjoyable. Let's look at how each of us comes to view certain feelings as dangerous and requiring defenses.

THE MEANING FILTER

All our feelings are based on the present, more or less objective reality we face as viewed through the filter of our earlier life experience. Early experi-ence is a lens through which we see the world and with which we make sense of it. We could think of it as a meaning filter. This meaning filter is a prism of life's scars and lessons through which we view everything, includ-ing our partner's behavior. This filter is affected by such transitory factors as mood, level of energy, and stress, and by such long-term influences as social norms, family upbringing, sex-role training, intelligence, and temperament. When two people fall in love and become a couple, each brings his or her own meaning filter into the relationship and views self and partner through this lens. It is as if when our mate speaks to us, we do not actually see or hear that real person, but rather a video image of him or her that has been muted, blurred, distorted, or colorized. From time to time, the signal is interrupted by the imposition of scenes from *The Donna Reed Show* or *Who's Afraid of Virginia Woolf?* It's a wonder we do as well with each other as we do.

A lot of the work we do with couples involves this meaning filter. Part of our effort is aimed at eliminating the distortions, and part at recognizing them and understanding them so they can be corrected. Ideally, the clarification of feelings is so deep and complete that partners truly and deeply shift their perception of the other. For example, one of them may say, "I no longer think of the time you spend with your children as a threat to me. I can now see it as a part of the same deep love you feel for me. It's not against me or instead of me. It's a part of you that I have come to love and respect." Other times, however, the change is not as deep but still useful: "I know you love your children and want to spend time with them. I'm still afraid sometimes that they will take up all of your time, but mostly I trust you to remember and care about me. I don't need to control the time you spend with them."

Either of these outcomes is useful, and both represent significant work on the meaning filter, although one clearly is more thorough. While all our feelings involve us as active "meaning makers," responding to our environment in individual ways, still it's often useful to make a rough distinction between those feelings that can be fairly well understood on the basis of present reality, and those that seem to tap powerful veins of childhood experience. When an apparently mild slight elicits a powerful rage response, we can assume that the present circumstances matched and reactivated much more damaging assaults from early family experience. This transference-like process typically begins when a couple falls in love, finding in each other ecstatic union and blissful feelings of finally being at home and understood. The lovers see each other through a very positive but very distorted meaning filter in which all the best features of early care givers seem present in the beloved. It is not surprising, then, when they become disillusioned with each other, that the disappointment, hurt, and anger would be very great.

At such times, it's hard to communicate well because each person is looking at the same process—let's say a fight—through very different filters. Is he always critical of her no matter how hard she tries? Or does she undermine everything he asks of her? Both, probably, but it's often useful to try to attend to one person's experience at a time. "We're both a mess right now, but I'll try to put my mess behind me for a few minutes and listen to you tell me about your mess. I'll try to see our mess from your point of view." This is a more adaptive response than arguing, as people sometimes do, with near-Talmudic distinctions and scholarship, about who is more of a mess and why. The discovery that we are all hurting children can be a powerful vehicle for building compassion and understanding between two people who love and disappoint each other. Used aggressively, however, it causes shame and inhibits risk taking.

From one perspective, feelings make obvious sense. Their adaptive value is clear. Our ancestors were propelled by their fear to run away when faced with saber-tooth tigers. Their cousins, who felt no fear, had few descendants.

Fear of real and present danger is rational—it leads to adaptive behavior. In our more complex, largely interpersonal environment today, however, we see lots of ways our feelings lead us astray. We cannot hit or usually even yell at the people who make us mad. And when we feel fear, we try hard not to shake, or wet our pants. Since few of us escape childhood without learning painful lessons about the cost of showing our feelings, most of us have a patchwork of rules and beliefs about what feelings can be expressed under what circumstances. This network of habits and beliefs is an understandable response to our histories. If a child gets hit for getting angry, or is laughed at for crying, we would see the inhibitions of those emotions as an understandable adaptation to that environment. The child has learned to block certain feelings and transform others into feelings or behavior more likely to be acceptable to others. Unfortunately, these lessons often stay as part of the operating software when the environment has materially changed. So this patchwork of ideas about feelings, formed under difficult circumstances by two people with different learning histories, is a part of what we work with when we work with couples.

Most people leave home with unfinished business; their agendas begin to unfold when they establish their own families, even if that family is only a couple and their golden retriever. They form their new families with dreams, often unstated, of carrying on a family tradition, or doing right, this time around,what was done wrong in the families they came from. Partners also bring to current relationships painful memories of how earlier relationships failed, as well as presumptions about how to be in this new relationship so things will turn out better. All of these agendas are powerful sources of feelings, and since each member of the couple has unfinished business and related agendas, there is lots of room for conflict.

We have all wondered, at times, at the remarkable frequency with which people choose as mates partners who are incredibly "wrong" for them— much "worse" than if they had been assigned by chance. He was pained by his mother's frequent absences, yet marries a flight attendant. She was the caretaker in her family, yet chooses a man with alcoholism and a poor work history. Is it masochism, "chemistry," or an effort to resolve unfinished childhood business? Whatever the explanation, we not only have different sensitivities and emotional blindspots than our spouses, but often the very ones that are the most challenging, requiring the greatest flexibility and resourcefulness.

The central idea here is that the basic feelings we have always make sense— if they are understood fully—and that there are good reasons, as well, for those feelings. These distorting processes and the fear of feelings that usually goes with them cause couples trouble, and an important solution to this trouble is to find, express, share, and understand each other's feelings in an atmosphere as free of blame as possible.

Autonomy, Shame, and Blame

To try out some of these ideas on a real-life couple, let's eavesdrop on Anne and Alan. Anne is telling her husband, Alan, about a discovery she made while talking with her sister. Anne and Alan's conversation went something like this:

ANNE: I realized today, after talking with Sheila, that I'm mad at you about something I haven't told you about.

ALAN: What's that?

ANNE: Well, remember the other night when you were over at Bill's house and you called to ask me about staying longer to watch the game with him? I felt there was no way I could win. You were asking my permission, and I could be a bitchy mom and say no or be manipulated into saying yes to something I wasn't happy with.

ALAN: Jesus Christ! I wasn't asking your *permission*, I was trying to talk with you about how that would work out for you! Could you go to sleep if I wasn't there? Would it feel bad to you? I wasn't asking your goddamned *permission*!

ANNE: I knew I shouldn't have brought this up. You're not listening to me. You're just getting all pissed off!

ALAN: Of course I'm getting pissed off! You're seeing me as this baby who has to ask his mommy for permission to play at his little friend's house. It's a very demeaning picture of me. I'm *not gonna* like it!

ANNE: Well, look what you're doing to me! You ask me in front of Bill. It's not a real choice because if I *did* want you to come home earlier, *which*, by the way, I *didn't*, I couldn't say that without you and Bill saying what a controlling bitch I was. So, it feels to me like it's this fancy manipulation to do what you want and put me in a place where I can't get mad at you, and you look like this really thoughtful good guy who is being so considerate.

One notable feature of this dialogue is what might be called its "steepness of slope." That is, this previously casual conversation turned angry very quickly, particularly for Alan. He hadn't been angry earlier, hadn't had a "bad day." Something in that short paragraph of Anne's explanation of what had made her mad sent Alan into orbit. And he tells us which of Anne's words—"asking my permission." When he hears that Anne perceives his call as asking her permission, he is presented with a view of his call, and implicitly of himself, that he finds extremely unpalatable. He gets as mad as he does because three forces come together at this point. First, it is a humiliating picture of himself, which, with some hyperbole and noticeable lack of developmental precision, he characterizes as "this baby who has to ask his mommy for permission to play at his little friend's house." No one older than 10 would relish this as part of his or her self-concept. So Alan *transforms* his basic feeling, shame, into anger. Second, Alan's anger is fueled by a recognition of the truth, near-truth, or possible truth of this view. If Anne had said she was angry because he had used poor grammar during the phone call, Alan might be perplexed, but he would not likely be angry. She struck a sore spot. And third, the sore spot had to do with earlier relationships in Alan's life—his relationship with the aunt who raised him and with his first wife. In both of these relationships, he had been dealing with someone who was quite controlling, and his adaptations to them involved being compliant and appeasing them. He had often been afraid to state clearly what he wanted, and he later came to feel ashamed that he either manipulated to get what he wanted or simply sacrificed his other needs for his need for attachment and peace. He resolved never to let that happen again and began his relationship with Anne determined not to deny his own needs in exchange for peace or to be less than honest with her about what he wanted. So, when Alan heard Anne say "permission," he was not only shamed but also frightened at this confrontation, with its implication that an important agenda he had brought into this relationship was at risk.

What about Anne? Where did her anger come from? She tells us that she felt cornered, without a real choice. Later in the conversation, she reminded Alan that in her earlier marriage, her first husband manipulated her with various illnesses, deficiencies, and inabilities that made it hard for her to state clearly what she wanted and to pursue it. Her ex-husband was very competent at being incompetent, which fit neatly into the role she had practiced in her family of origin as the overfunctioning helper. When she met Alan, Anne thought, "Here, at last, is someone strong and assertive. I won't have to baby him or hold back about what I want." So, when she hears him on the phone asking about whether to stay longer at his friend's house, two demons are set loose. First, she is angry at Alan because she senses in his call a view of herself that is quite uncomplimentary. "He wouldn't call and ask me if he didn't think I was critical and controlling." In addition, she is angered by a sense that Alan's request provides the appearance of choice, but not the reality. She believes that if she were to exercise the option Alan offers her, for her to suggest that Alan come home early, she would pay some price—he would view her as controlling or perhaps harbor a quiet, lingering resentment. Second, and perhaps more speculatively, she may have been uncomfortable with her needs to be protected, to be chosen, and to be cared for. Having functioned in earlier relationships as the caretaker may suggest some discomfort with her own dependent needs. So when Alan called asking would it be okay if he was late, she may have been confronted with his awareness of her need to be cared for. She may have felt ashamed, seeing in herself a need to be taken care of—a need she had so long ago dissociated from her sense of self and seen mainly in others.

So Anne feels angry when Alan calls, for reasons not too different from what makes Alan angry. Both hope that in this relationship they can overcome some painful experiences encountered in earlier family and relationship scenarios. Each feels this hope threatened, and each faces painful negative self-perceptions: Alan's root feeling is mostly shame about being "a baby asking his mommy's permission," and also some fear that he's replaying an old, painful role. He transforms these feelings into anger. Anne, too, starts with shame and fear, both about the possibility of again being seen as controlling and about the fear that her dependency needs will be seen by Alan as too much or not okay. Like Alan, she swiftly transforms these basic feelings into anger.

A related topic that this argument brings up is whether it is a good idea to share feelings with one's partner. As long as the idea has been around that it is good to share your feelings, people have been using their most recent examples as evidence for one side or the other in this epic debate. Here Anne joins this issue, saying, "I knew I shouldn't have brought this up." Is she right? Well, she would have had a more peaceful day if she hadn't brought it up, and so, presumably, would Alan. It is not a situation where she was giving herself headaches or ulcers by holding it in. Yet some important areas of conflict were aired, and that could be good, depending on what happens next. If they end up exploring and better understanding each other's sensitivities about being a "baby" or "controlling," that could help. Especially so because it's very useful to be able to communicate successfully about the boundary where individual and couple meet. Things will be much better if Anne and Alan can negotiate individual needs and couple needs without being distracted by ancient quarrels with other people and the threat of being seen in painfully uncomplimentary ways by each other.

I believe there are four interrelated tasks that couples are continually working on, and that when they are being successful with these tasks, they are likely to enjoy being with each other. Since Anne and Alan's story illustrates these tasks, this is a good place to talk about them.

1. *Self-Esteem*. Each person needs to feel fairly good about himself or herself and see a reasonable measure of respect coming from the other. This is a lot of what Alan and Anne were fighting about. They were each saying, "I can't stand it when you see me in such an uncomplimentary way."

2. *Autonomy*. Each member of the couple needs to experience a workable amount of room in the relationship for individual interests and pursuits. Alan's call was an effort to negotiate with Anne about his interests vis-à-vis hers. Implicitly or explicitly, this negotiation occurs regularly. We only notice it when it does not go well.

3. *Intimacy*. Each person needs to find in the relationship closeness, sharing, and support. Anne and Alan were groping for a balance of autonomy and intimacy in this story. These two needs can actually be thought of as one: creating a boundary/connection between the members of the couple that has a kind and degree of permeability that satisfies both people. It is like having a river running between two cities with bridges over it. In a satisfying relationship, the width of the river provides enough autonomy, and the number and accessibility of the bridges provide enough connection, access, and intimacy.

4. *Boundary Around the Couple.* A couple must also find a good place to set boundaries between themselves and others. A common example is the need to negotiate how much contact they have with friends, children, and work associates. In each of these areas, there are very large differences among successful couples in how these boundaries are drawn. What is just barely enough intimacy for one couple may be way too much for another. Some couples see their parents once a year, some every Sunday. Although the Anne and Alan story does not bear directly on this task, conflict began when Alan called Anne to negotiate about a specific instance related to this boundary—extending an agreement about visiting a friend. At least part of Anne's anger had to do with the semipublic aspect of this conversation. "What will Bill think of me if I ask Alan to come home?" Something that, from her point of view, should have been done within the couple boundary, was being done outside it.

In summary, a couple needs to maintain the self-respect of each member while successfully balancing intimacy and autonomy. They must also find boundaries that work both between themselves and also between themselves and the rest of the world.

AN IDEAL FEELING-KNOWING SEQUENCE

Most couples we actually work with are gnarly and complex. We talk about alcohol use or job loss, or how best to use those last three HMO visits. Other couples are so chaotic, we spend our time getting one just to stay in the room while the other one talks. But other times, we have a chance to see, in pure culture, the steps of a productive emotional dialogue. This is what happened with Doug and Jodi.

The Problem

Doug and Jodi have been angry a lot recently, especially since Jodi's mother became sick. They try to talk, but each feels blamed and misunderstood. They distance, then try again.

The Solution (4 Steps)

Step 1

In their couple session, Doug and Jodi finally have the argument they had been avoiding. They say what they feel strongly, with a minimum of disparagement toward the other. Doug says, "You are never around for me anymore. You're always thinking of your mother. Then when I try to talk with you about her, you shut me out. I'm hurt and pissed off." Jodi replies, "I take care of you in so many other ways. *Once*, I get preoccupied and you can't stand it. It makes me mad that when I want to lean on you a little, *you* get mad."

Step 2

As their argument ends, Doug hears that his hurt and feeling of abandonment is much stronger than his rage. He explores his sense of abandonment in other, earlier situations, feels his sadness, and cries. He also feels shame ("What is wrong with me that people keep leaving me?"), and emerges with an awareness that most of his current pain was caused, not by his wife's actual behavior, but by the excess meaning it had for him because of how it restimulated early painful losses and brought that unfinished business into the present. This allows him to view Jodi's behavior much more compassionately. She is no longer someone who mostly is leaving him. She is now a friend who is very frightened that her mom may die, and when he can see her this way, he wants to give her the support she needs. Actually, two good things happen synergistically here. His ability to see her hurt and need (1) diminishes the chances that he will later reinterpret her behavior as primarily an abandonment of him; and (2) enhances his ability to listen well to her concerns about her mother. This, in turn, makes it easier for her to attend to him lovingly—another good example of how the better things go, the better things go.

Step 3

Jodi goes through a similar process. She yells about how angry she is at Doug for letting her down just when she needs help most. She, too, goes back to earlier times, talks about how often and how early she became the "mother's helper" and supporter of others, how she was always hoping that someone would take the cue and do the same for her. It was hard for her to ask. Now, with her mother sick, she hoped that Doug would see her fear and take care of her. When he did not, she got mad. As she expressed the layers of anger, hurt, and shame, she comes to see Doug more accurately. He is not mostly a taker who cannot give to her, but her friend and partner who is scared of being left and who can respond fairly well when she is able to say more clearly what she wants.

Step 4

The therapist helps build bridges between Doug and Jodi that could be thought of as "cognitive empathy." The therapist gives them a way of viewing themselves, anchored in the strong feelings they shared, which can help them behave more rationally when those old practiced defenses creep back in. The therapist wants to help them build a cognitive structure. The therapist says, "So, you can see now that Jodi's distancing, which feels so bad to you, is mostly coming from worry about her mother?" Doug says he can. "And that some may also come from her hurt or anger that you don't approach her in a certain way that would feel good to her, but that she has a hard time asking for?" "Yeah, I can." "So, the next time that happens and you see yourself start to get mad and feel hurt, you could try doing something different. Maybe you could say to yourself something like, 'It's understandable, given my history, that this would be hard for me, but let's see what we can do differently this time.' Then you could approach her, ask if she'd like to talk about it, or give her a hug. You don't know yet what's going to work. The idea would be to approach her and somehow offer help because that's what she made clear today she needs." The therapist then talks with Jodi about her need to state more clearly what she wants from Doug, and to try not to take it as a personal affront if he does not know what she wants without being asked. She may also remind Jodi to try to keep in mind that Doug has a sensitive spot around being left, and that if she can attend to that, he will probably be a better friend. The idea here is to create a sturdy set of simple thoughts that can be used as a guide for behavior when the feelings of empathy, generated in the session, have diminished.

The ideal sequence could be summarized as: problem→feeling→deeper feeling→historical connections→new awareness about self and partner→improved cognitive structure for guiding future behavior.

As mentioned earlier, this example of the feeling-knowing sequence is complete and less cluttered with other issues than is often the case. Doug and Jodi are not character disordered, their distress is more acute than chronic, and they are able to do two important tasks: follow their feelings from a present to a past stimulus and take responsibility for their part in an interaction. Many couples are more stuck: stuck in a blaming stance or stuck in their roles, or too afraid of their feelings to go into them enough to get through them. That is why in practice, at least in my practice, this ideal movement from problem to solution is seldom approached in any particular session. In a good session, some connections are made at an emotional level between present and past, and one or both clients become aware of how those feelings affect their relationship. But often we work at very basic tasks—learning to listen to each other, learning to accurately name feelings, and finding mutually agreeable ways to express feelings. I spend a lot of time getting couples to speak frankly with each other about their anger. Other couples who may *look* more engaged, fight constantly but never listen and are not truly any more engaged with each other than the quiet, shut-down ones who are afraid to confront each other.

So, if this is the general road map of where we want to go with emotional expression in couples work, what are the specifics? What techniques, what ways of thinking, can help us do the job?

TECHNIQUES FOR ENHANCING FEELING EXPRESSION

Enhancing a couple's expression of feeling can mean a few different things. For the inhibited, cautious couple, it can mean getting them to experience their feelings more fully and also to express more directly to each other what they do feel. It also means helping a husband hear his wife's new, riskier feelings without becoming so upset that she gets frightened and retreats to the safe old way. For the perpetually angry, critical couple, it can mean muting the usual war chants and finding their hurt or shame or fear instead. We want to help couples express real feelings, especially feelings that are new, or that have previously been ignored or rejected by the spouse. We could imagine the sharing of feelings between partners as conversation. There is a natural movement from feeling to feeling as each responds to the other. A repetitious, one-note feeling exchange is as stuck as a one-thought conversation.

Before looking at specific techniques, let's begin with three general principles we can use to guide our feeling work with couples.

1. *A wife and husband feel much more about each other than they do about their therapist.* This self-evident proposition has some important implications. One is that if partners speak directly to each other and look at each other, they are likely to feel more than if they are looking at, and speaking to, the therapist. That means we have a way to titrate their feelings, generally focusing them on each other to increase emotional resonance, but occasionally asking them to speak to us to tone things down if they are, for example, chaotically angry with each other. An extension of this principle involves suggesting brief sentences for the partners to say to each other that state more boldly what they have been saying indirectly. So, if a man is telling the therapist stories about his wife that cast her in a negative light, the therapist can often help deepen their emotional experience by (1) asking him to speak directly to his wife; and (2) suggesting that he say something short and punchy, like "I feel like criticizing you today" or "I'm mad at you" rather than going on with his criticism. Even though his wife has just heard the therapist suggest the phrase, it can still have lots of evocative meaning for her when she hears her husband saying it. She may answer, "What's making you so mad?" or "How do you think *I* feel?", and start a lively conversation that will help them be engaged as well as married. A related phenomenon is how thick the transference is between spouses, how much of the energy is between them, and how puny their connections are with us compared to each other.

2. *Clients often know what they feel even when they say they don't.* Frequently we see a situation and believe we know what each member of the couple is feeling. This belief often helps us move clients toward a better awareness of their feelings. But sometimes we are wrong, and sometimes there is another layer of feeling to deal with first. We need to be careful to stay close to our clients' experience and not be blinded by our preconceptions. Even when people say they don't know what they feel, or come up with something like

"confused" as an answer to "What do you feel?", it's important to remember that when people feel safe enough and are listened to carefully, they usually find their way to important feelings. It may take a while to help them slowly work through their defenses, but eventually they will find their feelings, and often we'll be surprised. The feelings they find are not always the ones we expected.

3. *Some feelings are more useful than others.* Of course we are supposed to value whatever feelings our clients share with us, but some are more likely to lead to change than others. When a man tells his partner for the thirty-seventh time that he's afraid she'll leave him, something new is probably needed. But, if he finds that behind all that abandonment fear, he's really angry at her, that has promise of moving the dialogue along. There are times, particularly with grief, when people seem to need a lot of time to express feelings vigorously and repeatedly. Even here, though, a careful listener can hear movement. "I can't stand it" is different from "I should have visited him more," which is different from "We had such wonderful times together." And even if the next thought goes back to "I can't stand it," we are likely to view this as evolving, useful work unless there are several repeating cycles just alike. Only then do we say the mourner is stuck in his or her grief and try to intervene. With couples, even more because there are two participants, we expect a dialogue that moves and evolves. So, when it sounds like 5-year-olds in the back seat of a car on a long road trip ("Yes, you are!" "No, I'm not!" "Yes, you are!" "No, I'm not!"), we look eagerly for the next feeling and think hard what we can do to jog the record needle into a new groove.

With these three general strategies in mind, let's look at some more specific techniques. The techniques discussed here are a few of the hundreds that can be used to help couples get unstuck from their emotional ruts. They are illustrative only and by no means exhaustive.

Focus on Feelings

This technique has many forms. Its essence is simply to draw the couple's attention to their feelings. Clients often stay distant from their feelings by planning, describing, justifying, complaining, wondering, and even arguing. Often, all we have to do is ask, "How does it feel?" or "What would you like to tell her?" Other times, statements like "You look pretty sad," or "Tell him how hard it's been," help a couple find their feelings. Then we need to stay alert, so that when we get a response that deflects ("I feel confused" or "I don't know"), we pursue until we get a new feeling in which there is a workable match between words and other facial and postural cues. Recently, a man whose wife was leaving him described the past weekend when his wife had moved her things out of the house as "entertaining" and "a circus." He was smiling what Gottman (1991) calls a "miserable smile," in which his mouth smiled but his eyes did not. It did not take a very taxing confrontation to get him to see the denial of his pain in the words he had been using, and to admit to the painfulness of his wife's leaving. Sometimes it's a much harder job than it was with this man to get past whatever defenses a person or a couple characteristically uses to stay away from unpleasant feelings. At other times, however, it is simply a matter of bringing the couple's attention to the *feeling* level when they may have been *problem solving* or *story telling*. Basically this technique consists of simply focusing awareness on feelings. It is basic, but very useful.

Let's look at this technique using as our example, "The Eggshell Couple." A couple, married 3 years, each from a chaotic, critical, and sometimes violent family, came to see me shortly after the birth of their baby. They loved each other and were determined to have the family they were creating be harmonious. They tried so hard not to criticize each other or have angry words! When, inevitably, an insignificant "Have you had a chance to finish the laundry?" slipped out, the other would feel hurt/shamed/devastated/angry. This was especially true of the husband. One night he cooked dinner. She decided her chicken wasn't quite done, so she put it in the microwave. In response, he hung his head for an hour or two and was completely silent. In talking about it with them, he first minimized his response ("I felt a little disappointed"). But at my request, she described his behavior in enough detail so he had to recognize that he had been very upset. When I pursued *how* he felt, he told me *why* he felt it. ("I think if she had pointed it out in the kitchen, I wouldn't have felt so bad, but since it was after the 'presentation' in the dining room, it felt worse.") This is the point where "gentle pursuit" is needed—persistence without impatience.

THERAPIST: So, those are the *circumstances* that led to your feeling disappointed or whatever. What I'm interested in is how it *felt* to be inside your skin right then as Georgia took her chicken to the zapper.
HUSBAND: It felt bad. I don't know how else to describe it.
THERAPIST: It looks like hanging your head was an important part of how you were feeling.
HUSBAND: Yeah, I think it was.
THERAPIST: Would you be willing to sit there now and hang your head like you did then? [*He hangs his head in a caricatured way, exaggerating and smiling.*] Okay, but that's actually probably more extreme than you actually did?
HUSBAND: [*Looking out from under his lowered eyebrows*] Yeah, a bit!
THERAPIST: See if you can modify it so it's as realistic as possible. [*He does. No one speaks for almost a minute.*] What are you feeling now?
HUSBAND: It's strange. I feel embarrassed. [*More silence*]
THERAPIST: Is that how you felt that night?
HUSBAND: Yeah, it is. That's so weird. I actually feel embarrassed now, a lot like I did then.

We then pursued his embarrassment, what critical thoughts he imagined his wife was having, and what names he was calling himself. None of this rang a bell. At one point, I made a guess about what the really nutty, childish, irrational thoughts might be that the critical voice in his head was saying. "Is it like, 'You're no good! You can't even cook! If you really cared about Georgia, you wouldn't serve her such junk,' like that?" Then he brightened up. "No, it's like, 'she at least can take care of herself. If you serve her some bad food that will make her sick, she can do something about it, but little Jane can't. You could have hurt her with food like that. You're a bad father!' like that." Now here someone could say, "Sounds like he's mad at his kid and maybe his wife. He wants to poison them. That's what all the shame is about." Maybe so, maybe not. But this man would run out of the room if I even suggested that. What matters here is that in response to my inaccurate guess about what self-condemning thoughts he had, he was able to recognize/remember what his actual thoughts had been that brought on his shame attack. He was able to take a big step involving knowing and sharing an important feeling. Later I asked him to imagine that someone had been standing in the corner of the dining room, saying the thoughts he had in his head. Who would it be? He immediately said his older sister, Karen, and that led us to a useful and pretty lively conversation about the constant barrage of critical comments from her over the years as he was growing up. I suggested that the next time he "goes down the rabbit hole," his wife might try asking him if he had heard from Karen recently. That made them both laugh, and laughter frequently signals a useful change in set. If his wife uses this or some similar comments the next time he gets caught up in a shame-based retreat, it may help him recover if he is not too far into it. This is an example of what we earlier called "cognitive empathy"—a specific strategy for use at home, which is based on an understanding achieved in the session.

This story, incidentally, also illustrates a couple of useful lessons. One is the value of persistence. We spent the whole session on this incident, beginning with their report of the event, then pursuit of what he felt, an experiment with posture to recreate the feeling, naming the feeling, finding the thoughts that support the feeling, and finding some of the historical roots of his shame response. Finally we developed a strategy to use at home to cope with similar attacks in the future. At various points, we felt stuck. What sounds direct and smooth when summarized was actually choppy, with stops, starts, and dead ends. It frequently takes a number of tries to help a couple move on to a new feeling level. And it is usually hard to know ahead of time what will work. We need to be flexible and persistent in trying to find an intervention that works.

Another lesson from this story is the usefulness of posture and movement as entries to feelings. Many of us spend much of our therapy time as "talking heads," missing valuable opportunities to tap the "wisdom of the body," to help couples find and deepen their feeling expression and also nurture each other in new ways. Finally, it is worth noting that at times, making a guess about what some internal voice is saying can be useful even when the guess is wrong. Although the content of my guess was wrong, it was specific, strongly stated, and stated as someone else's voice—it was an imaginary but verbatim quote. His response had all those same qualities, although the content was quite different. I modeled the form. He supplied the content.

Eliciting Feelings Through Suggested Behavior

There are habits and rigidities in how we do things that keep us in a safe rut. If I put my pants on starting with my left leg instead of my right leg, it feels quite different. I'm out of my habit and experiencing things differently. These habits allow us to go through the day without pondering each move. But they can also narrow our range of experiencing and feeling. Couples, too, develop these structured behaviors—"This is how we greet, sleep, cook together." When, in therapy, we discover how some of these habits are functioning to contain feelings, we can ask our clients to purposely alter these habits and then work with the feelings that emerge.

One day I was working with a couple in which the wife, Linda, had a very hard time enjoying, or even tolerating, physical proximity to or touch with her husband, Roger. She had mentioned a couple of things she especially disliked involving his "coming up behind me." I asked her to stand up and have Roger stand away from her and slowly approach. She was asked to say when she began to feel uncomfortable. Roger approached from different directions, and we found that she could tolerate having him a lot closer when he was in front of her than behind her. When I asked them to see what she would feel if he crossed that comfort line and got closer to her, she found that she became much more uncomfortable when he was behind her than in front of her. She shivered, held herself, looked behind her as much as she could, and had a hard time physically standing still and not moving away. She could have ended the tension by moving to a comfortable distance but she stayed with the experience and felt her fear. Three things resulted from this: (1) Linda used this information in her work with her individual therapist to further explore traumatic events in her troubled family history; (2) at home, Roger made a point of approaching Linda from the front and found that did make a difference—she was somewhat more available; and (3) I began to wonder what Linda and Roger would feel if I asked *her* to reach out to *him*. So the next "experience inducer" I asked them to try was for him to sit still while she reached out and touched his face and head. Since they mostly functioned with him as pursuer and her as distancer, I sought to break the habit and see what they would feel if *she* were the pursuer. As she began to touch his face, she looked squeamish, as though she were touching a slimy, wormy creature. She pulled her hand back quickly after touching Roger's face and looked at me as if to say, "Is that enough?" I said how pleased I was that we had found a road into her fear and that, while of course it was up to her, I hoped she would continue. As she proceeded ("Jeez, that feels funny!"), I urged her to shape her hand to fit his face, to stroke his cheek gently, and to touch the back of his neck tenderly. Despite her fear, tentativeness, and occasional withdrawal, I could see that she was feeling some of the loving feelings that go with these touches. It was not empty compliance. She was struggling with loving him. That is what made it useful. Roger, by the way, was skeptical at first but gradually gave himself to it and began to smile and enjoy Linda's touch. As she settled in a bit to touching him, I asked if they remembered when they first got together, what they each had seen in the other that they liked and wanted. As they told their stories of meeting and first dates, they were warmer and more generous toward each other than they had been previously, and they brought some of that warmth into their lives together during the following week.

In this example, two prescribed experiences were used, each with two phases. The first exercise in which Roger stood at various distances from Linda, in front of, beside, and behind her, resulted in a sort of map of Linda's comfort zone. In the second phase, I asked Roger to encroach on her comfort zone to see what feelings that elicited. In the second exercise, Linda touched Roger's face and head, and in the second phase of that, I asked them to add the sharing of memories of their early times together.

The ideas underlying this kind of intervention are fairly simple: people faced with feelings they deem dangerous or uncomfortable (Linda's fear as Roger approached) avoid the uncomfortable feeling by constricting their behavior in some way (not letting him near her, not touching him tenderly). This solution to one problem is the basis for another problem (Roger and Linda were not having much loving contact). The prescription temporarily undoes the behavioral constriction and allows the previously feared feeling to surface. Often partial extinction of the fear response occurs because the fear actually felt is not as strong or noxious as the client expected. Other times it is a very strong response, but the client can tolerate it because it is viewed as an experiment and therefore temporary—"Yes, I'm scared and shaky, but that's all right. I can tolerate it for awhile."

The second set of exercises in which Linda touched Roger's face lovingly, and I asked them to talk about how they met and fell in love, brought up some interesting questions. Therapists of a dynamic or affective orientation usually assume that when work has been done on eliminating difficulties, positive responses will spontaneously emerge: when we help them with their anger and hate, our clients will find their own way to the warmth and love. Recently, however, some good arguments have been made for the need for "re-romanticizing" relationships (Hendrix, 1988) and for romantic love as "a primary emotion which can function as an independent variable or a change agent" (Roberts, 1992, p. 360). Asking people to touch each other as they did when they fell in love can elicit some of those romantic feelings. So can talking about the early days of their relationship. It's important that when we ask people to experience these tender moments, we do what we can to create an environment where an angry or bitter response is unlikely.

These prescriptions can be for exercises the couple conducts in the session or between sessions at home. In either case, there are two good possible outcomes. One is that the prescribed behavior feels fairly easy to do and simply expands the couple's ways of being with each other. More likely, it stirs up feelings we can work with, and that path should also lead to a fuller range of feelings—more of their selves being available to each other. As for negative outcomes, there are basically two. The most common by far is that they do not do the exercise or subvert it. An opportunity is lost. Less frequently, the feelings generated seem too big or out of control, and the couple goes back to their safe rut more certain than before that feelings are dangerous and that they should be kept hidden. Anne expressed this view, although in a different context, when she said, "I knew I shouldn't have brought it up."

One way to think up the sorts of prescriptions I'm talking about here is to look for rigidities in how couples relate. Maybe they talk in long paragraphs with little spontaneous back-and-forth exchange. Maybe they do not make eye contact, or they always have some household emergency to discuss before they can talk about themselves. Perhaps one is always the angry one or the injured one or the competent rescuer. Whenever these roles or styles seem fixed, there is a possibility to concoct an exercise that requires them to behave contrary to them; and if they are willing to try, and the therapist persists in keeping them on task, something useful is likely to result. The part about keeping them on track is very important. I find it much easier to think up these prescriptions than to resist the blandishments and distractions that often follow. I frequently find, a few minutes after I suggest one of these prescriptions, that I have followed the couple down some other fascinating hall of mirrors and we have all evaded the exercise.

Directed Dialogue

Couple therapists often ask clients to talk with each other rather than with the therapist. This tends to keep the energy between the partners and lessens the likelihood of the therapist becoming a third person triangled into their relationship to provide stability at the cost of intimacy. When the therapist directs a couple to talk to each other, clients often say, "We already know this," or "It wouldn't do any good. I've already told her and she doesn't care." Other times the speaker starts out talking to the spouse, then shifts eye contact to the therapist and pronouns change from "you" to "him" or "her." It is not easy for therapists trained to be empathic to firmly look away from the spouse who tries to talk with us. Nevertheless, that is an effective way to turn them back toward each other.

But having them talk to each other is only half the battle. The other half is getting them to feel. When I ask a couple to tell each other their feelings, they often explain and justify instead. Then another rule of politeness and empathy needs to be broken. I need to interrupt them and say, "Tell Ellen what you *felt* when she said that." The answer is often, "I felt it was unfair." Putting "I feel" at the beginning of a sentence is no guarantee that a feeling will follow. So more persistence is needed—warm, patient, and insistent. "So when she said that, it seemed very unfair to you. You couldn't see how she could say that. And how did that *feel* to you? What went on inside?" "I felt stupid, I guess. I didn't like it that she thought that about me. I didn't like it." "Stupid" and "didn't like it" are closer to being feelings than "unfair." "Stupid" suggests shame, and "didn't like it" may cover either shame or anger. Now, in order to move this man deeper into his feelings, the therapist has invited him to talk with him (the therapist) and thus break off the dialogue he had been asked to have with his wife. It is important to get back to direct dialogue between them. "Okay, tell Ellen that you didn't like it when she said that to you and you felt stupid." When the husband says this to Ellen, the therapist listens to Ellen's response and makes sure that it has at least as much feeling in it as did her husband's statement to her. At this point, it does not matter much what the feeling is. It is the therapist's job to keep focusing on the feeling component, get the partners to address it to each other, and, as much as possible, shift blaming statements into ownership-of-feelings statements. For example, "The kids are having trouble in school because you shout and yell all the time" would be better as "I feel mad (or scared) when you yell. I don't like it."

When we can keep clients talking to each other and keep them focused on telling their feelings, the conversation will naturally deepen and progress. They each have unspoken feelings they are afraid of sharing. As the conversation progresses, there is a fairly natural movement to deeper feelings if a reasonable level of listening and safety is present. As a way to illustrate some of these ideas about technique and to see how some of the theoretical concepts discussed are used in practice, let's use a particular session for illustration.

EXAMPLE: INCREASING EMOTIONAL EXPRESSIVENESS

This session begins with, and is based on, directed dialogue and predominantly deals with focusing feelings. There are issues of self-esteem, intimacy, and boundaries around the couple. It illustrates a part of the feeling-expressive sequence we discussed earlier, although there are no historical connections made in this session. Because both members of the couple are feeling-avoiders, all the focus is on increasing the level of feelings. We do not have to worry about them overdoing it and losing control!

The clients, Sam and Diane, are a couple in their forties who have worked with me for over 2 years. They came to me suffering from DMS (Dead Marriage Syndrome) and its accompanying illness, LRTTK (Let's Relate Through the Kids). Their children are doing better now because Sam and Diane have made some progress in being with and enjoying each other, thus taking some pressure off the children. At this point, they have a relationship that might best be described as companionable without being very intimate. Sex is okay and nothing is terrible. They still, however, manage their negative affects mostly by distancing, and so they lack passion and verve in their life together and watch a lot of television. For them, DMS is not cured, but rather held tenuously at bay.

This recent session is unusual in a couple of ways. One is that, uncharacteristically, I set its initial direction, and the other is that it was better than most. We got to a deeper feeling level than usual, and there was an unfolding affective development that can easily be followed. Most of our sessions were somewhat choppier than this one.

I (Bob) had just sat down with Diane and Sam. There is often some banter as we find our way to the day's agenda. This time Diane began.

DIANE: [*Jokingly to Bob*] Well, what do you want to talk about today?
BOB: Well, I actually do have some thoughts about that. I was listening to some tapes of our sessions the other day.
DIANE: Uh, oh, did we do something wrong?
SAM: I bet he's cooking up something new.
DIANE: [*Mock horror*] Oh, no! Not something new!
BOB: Yeah. Something new! I'm gonna keep my mouth shut for a change! When I was listening to that tape, I couldn't believe how much I talked! I hardly let you guys get a word in edgewise.
DIANE: Jeez, I hope he doesn't make us talk to each other!
SAM: What...?
BOB: That's exactly what I have in mind! I want to get a lot further back, out of it more, and have you talk to each other.
SAM: We can do that at home!
BOB: Yeah, but do you?
DIANE: Well, no, not actually! [*All three of us laugh hard. This is something they have been struggling with for a long time.*]
BOB: Well, I'd like you to...Well, first, would you move your chairs so you're looking at each other? [*They tentatively turn their chairs a little more toward each other.*] Come on, keep turning! [*Bob makes a turning motion with his hand.*] More, more, more! [*They finally, giggling, get their chairs turned toward each other, turn their heads toward Bob, and wait uneasily.*]
BOB: Okay, good. Now we each have a big job to do but I have the hardest job. My job is to keep my mouth shut. Your jobs are to talk to each other about something important. [*Pause*]
DIANE: That's all?

BOB: Yep. [*Pause*]

SAM: Just anything?

BOB: Well, I hope it's not whether to get a new washing machine...[*This is a response to an old shaggy-dog story that is a symbol of the kind of dull, go-nowhere conversations Diane and Sam sometimes have.*]...and ideally I hope it generates feelings and makes you a little uncomfortable. [*Pause*]

There ensues about 5 minutes of settling in. Questions about what to talk about, how long they need to do it, and so on. It reminded me of bedtime when my children were young, and their requests for "one more story," a drink of water, and one last trip to the bathroom. The only difference was that there was anxiety behind Diane and Sam's delaying tactics. They feared the kind of intimacy I was suggesting and had organized their lives so there was little room for it.

With this couple, my general goal almost always was to surface feelings, to increase their intimacy, and to help them relate as personally as possible to each other. I had realized that my talking in earlier sessions was not doing that. I had entered into their let's-keep-it-safe system. So I wanted to get out and get them talking to each other. The delay is evidence of how hard it is to break these patterns.

DIANE: Okay, I've got something.

SAM: Good.

DIANE: When I go out some nights to meetings...No, that's not what I mean...Some nights I go out to meetings and some nights I don't.

SAM: Right...

DIANE: When you're home with Sally and Burt [*their children, ages 10 and 12*]...[*pauses, turning to Bob*]...what am I trying to say? I don't know...this is stupid. [*Bob points to Sam, indicating that she should look at her husband and address him.*] Um...[*giggle*]...I mean does it? Sometimes I wonder if it makes any difference to you whether I'm there or not. [*These last words come out in a rush.*]

SAM: Sure it does. We like having you there. [*Diane looks at Bob as if to say, "See what I mean?" Bob points to Sam. Pause.*]

SAM: I don't really know why you'd ask that. [*Sam looks over at Bob, maybe to ask for help or for a quick "Look what I have to put up with."*] You know...just...what was it? Tuesday night, Burt said how much he liked it nights Mom was home. We all want you home.

DIANE: I guess I don't see why. You're watching TV with the kids and I'm on the computer in the study. What difference does it make to you if I'm home or not?

At this point, I'm pleased I started the session as I did. These are unusually open statements for Diane. She typically couches these thoughts in a more critical form, or at least a more veiled form, and is less vulnerable and less clear about wanting something from Sam.

In terms of the four tasks mentioned earlier, three are clearly involved here: *self-esteem*, *intimacy*, and *boundaries around the couple*. Diane is working on self-esteem in what she views as a situation at home where her presence seems not to matter much to Sam. She is apparently seeking a statement she can believe about her importance to him, and implicitly his wish for intimacy with *her* specifically, apart from the rest of the family.

In this, she is trying to draw a boundary between herself and Sam on the one hand, and the children on the other. Back to the session.

SAM: It's just nice having everybody home.

DIANE: [*Rising tone, angrier*] That's the point! It doesn't matter that *I'm* there, just that "everybody" is there...Can't you see the difference? I don't know, if you can't see *that*, I don't know what would...what would do it?...how could I get you to see it? It just...sometimes you just seem like this *big block* sitting there! Refusing to see, refusing to budge.

SAM: [*Placating, good guy, eyebrows raised*] Jeez, honey! That's pretty strong! [*Eyes to me, like "Look at this wild woman I have to deal with"*] I dunno. I *said* I was glad you were there. Maybe I didn't phrase it just right. Jeez! [*Pause. He looks down at his knees, then over to Bob.*] Is this what...? Is this what you wanted to have happen?

BOB: Something like this. Stay with it. [*Bob points to Diane.*] Tell her what's happening for you now.

SAM: I don't...like this very much. All I did was say it was nice to have...it's nice when we're all together. What's so bad about that?

DIANE: I don't know. Maybe I overreacted...sometimes it just feels like there's you and the kids and the house and the TV, and then there's...*accessories*, those little nice extras like popcorn, cider, and me. It's nicer if I'm around, but it doesn't really matter that much.

SAM: Now listen! [*Sam's trying a sterner tone here.*] I said to you last week we ought to go out, remember? Just the two of us, and what did you say? [*Pause. Diane doesn't like it when Sam gets prosecutorial and asks her to testify against herself.*] Remember? We were in the kitchen? And I said...I asked you about getting ...that we'd get together over the weekend ...?

DIANE: I certainly didn't get the sense you meant *me*..."just the two of us..."

SAM: Well, I did.

DIANE: Actually, I do remember now! You said maybe *we* [*sarcastically*] could go see *Aladdin* or *Free Willy*. I mean, really, Sam [*laughing now*] is that *date* material? That's the Disney Channel...That's...you know, that's family stuff [*turning to Bob*]. I rest my case! This man does not value me separately from the "family unit."

Diane has been sounding uncharacteristically strong and self-confident as her anger and sense of being right have built during the last few exchanges.

In the last sentence, she has gotten witty and dropped away a bit from her anger. While I do not see Diane's anger as the most basic layer of her feelings, it is pretty new to hear it from her in such a clear and straight form, so my goal is to help her stick with it, and hopefully get through to the next layer, probably hurt or shame about not being valued. So I decide here to intervene.

BOB: Diane, try telling Sam, "You don't value me."
DIANE: He doesn't.
BOB: Tell him...say it directly to Sam.
DIANE: You don't value me. [*Pause*] You don't. [*Pause*]
SAM: Jesus! Nothing is enough for you. I said I wanted to go out and you've...Oh shit! You've gotta take your microscope out and examine it for flaws. And if it...if everything isn't exactly perfect, then it's no good!
DIANE: [*Interrupting*] It's not a question of *perfect*. It's whether you wanted to go out with *me* or the whole family...it's about...it's about whether I matter to you and to tell you the truth, I doubt it...*I really do!* [*Pause*]

So far I've succeeded in getting a couple who felt okay a few minutes ago to be angry and to blame, criticize and make each other feel bad. She's more aware of not being valued by him, and he's feeling angry and hurt, as though all his efforts have no value to her. They both feel worse. This is the sort of stuff that gives emotional expression a bad name. We've plowed up the field. Now it's time to plant.

BOB: What I'd like to do is see if we can break this into two parts. Diane has some anger and hurt about not feeling valued, and Sam has some...something, hurt or anger, I guess, about not having your efforts...your moves toward Diane recognized or appreciated? Is that roughly right?
DIANE: It is for me.
SAM: Close enough.
BOB: Okay. I'd like to ask Diane to talk with you, Sam, and tell you how she feels and have you sit and listen to her. Don't argue. You'll have a chance later to tell your feelings. Try not to even argue in your head. Just listen, okay?
SAM: Okay, [*uncertainly*] I'll try.
BOB: And Diane, talk mostly about how *you feel*. Just let it roll. Let it go.
DIANE: Okay. [*Pause*] I don't know. It feels like I've mostly said it...I just don't get the feeling that you ...that I matter much to you. I think if I went away and somebody brought in groceries and did the household things I usually do [*aside to Bob*], which, by the way, I do a lot less of than I used to. [*Bob points to Sam, indicating she should continue to address him.*] Oh...this is hard...I don't know. Maybe this is all in my head. Maybe Sam should start.

SAM: [*To Bob*] You know, I hate to see you make a big something out of nothing. Maybe we're overthinking this. I'd hate to see...hate to see you make Diane say something she doesn't even feel.

BOB: You mean like how mad she is at you? [*They all laugh. Bob goes on.*] It's perfectly understandable to me that you guys would be nervous about what I'm asking you to do. There are good reasons you two have cooperated so long in avoiding conflict and expressions of anger with each other. And I think what I just saw was a great example of that. I heard some conflict, hurt feelings, and pushed you to show them. Diane starts, gets scared, says "You first," and you, Sam, are a very helpful, cooperative partner, rescuing the fair maiden from a tough spot. And also, of course, preventing your own self from getting mugged! You know what I'm saying? [*Diane nods with recognition. Sam, less certainly.*] I think you'd miss an opportunity you've worked hard to get to if you stop now. I think you'll be able to deal with what comes up. Just try for a few minutes to block the exits. [*Pause*] Okay?

A lot of work with feelings is like this: doing something to facilitate feelings, then trying to block exits as clients come up with various schemes to avoid the feelings.

SAM: [*Lightly*] So, you don't think I should be her "knight in shining armor"?

BOB: I think right now the "knight" and the "fair maiden" have an ordeal to go through that will make their love stronger...ready?

DIANE: Ready.

SAM: Ready.

BOB: Okay. Let's go back to where you [*Diane*] were telling Sam that if you weren't there, it wouldn't really matter much to him.

DIANE: Well, it does make me mad. It's hard to feel important when you pay so little attention to *me* specifically...

SAM: Like what? [*A bit defensively*]

BOB: [*To Sam*] Just listen.

DIANE: Well, that walk the other night, for example. [*Diane describes a scene in which Sam asks her to go for a walk after dinner. She says okay. He then asks their children to accompany them. It ends up with their son running, Diane walking, and Sam on a bike, riding next to his son for awhile, and then circling back to ride next to Diane. Sam interrupts a couple of times to correct details, but they are in essential agreement about what happened on the walk.*]

BOB: Okay. It sounds like the outline of what happened is clear. You each have different views of how...how it got to be that way. Now we are at the really good part...where Diane can concentrate on what she felt then and what she feels now. So just listen, Sam, to how your friend feels. Later she will listen to you.

SAM: Okay. Go. I'm listening.

DIANE: I felt like you were humoring me. You looked like a rubber band about to break, going back and forth between Burt and me. It was almost funny...

BOB: Tell Sam your hurt feelings.

DIANE: I *did* hurt. I could see you didn't want to be with me. At one point...by the pond...when you went up ahead to Burt? [*Sam nods.*] I remember right then thinking, "This is what life is. My son is running and getting strong. My husband is going away from me...wanting to be somewhere else...and I'm plodding along with this old brown jacket wrapped around me...feeling...[*Long pause, a tear rolls down her cheek*]. I just felt so old and alone [*Cries harder*]. [*Sam puts his hand on Diane's hand. She ignores it for a minute, then moves her hand away and looks at Sam. Her words have an angrier sound now.*] I don't want comfort right now. I feel bad. I felt bad then. Patting my hand isn't gonna help. I just... I just basically...I see that you don't want me to be mad, but I don't see that you *actually want* anything from me. On that walk, I could see it so clearly. I really believe you wanted to be with Burt but you came back to me so I wouldn't *get mad*. [*Clear angry tone now.*] You didn't *want* me. You wanted to keep me from getting mad! Sam, I want to be with someone who wants to be with me. I feel *so* unattractive. [*Diane cries some more silently. It looks like she would sob if she felt a little safer. Instead, she wraps her arms around herself as if she's cold. Then she looks up at Sam.*] You know...in some...I just feel helpless in a way. I'm mad and I'm sad about you not loving me or paying atten—I don't know...*seeing* me. And the helpless part is I don't know how to make that different. I don't see any opening. I can't run as fast as Burt, and I don't like science as much as Sally...so I distance and get critical, and I know that doesn't really do any good. [*Long pause*] So, I just get...I just end up feeling helpless. [*Long pause. Diane looks at Bob and Sam as though she is through, then she gets curious about a look on Sam's face. She looks a couple of times.*] What's up?

SAM: I feel sad. [*Long pause. Sam starts to cry.*] That picture of you walking down the road with that ratty old coat on, thinking this is what your life is...I just...it makes me so *sad*. [*Sam pauses, then goes on.*] And that picture of me riding away from you...I can almost see what I looked like, pedaling after Burt and away from you...[*Diane takes Sam's hand now and looks at him warmly.*] It makes me feel sort of foolish...[*Long pause, crying*] and sad for you...and I suppose in a way, for me, too [*Long pause, crying silently*]...I'm sorry, Toots, that doesn't sound like a very fun walk. It's...I...It's not...that's not what I want for us...either of us.

[*At this point, Diane reaches over and tries to hug Sam in his chair. That doesn't work, so they stand up and hug. He holds her very tightly, cries some more, and says he loves her. She squeezes him and kisses him, but does not say she loves him. These are words that make her feel very vulnerable, and she's said them to him only a few times in 16 years of marriage. After a few minutes, they sit back down, both looking softer, both have been crying. They move their chairs closer and hold hands, looking at Bob tentatively.]*

BOB: What you guys are doing is very heartwarming...[*Pause*]...very nice to see...Why don't you tell each other what happened for each of you?

SAM: What happened for me is that...it's like...it's like I got transported into Diane's brain and I'm looking at the world from her eyes and everything just looked so different. I saw myself in an unpleasant light, really almost pathetic in a way...chasing Burt and ignoring you. And that picture of you walking with that brown coat wrapped around you, feeling sad and alone...I still feel sad when I think of that. I feel sad that you feel so alone and un...unsought I guess...That must be what you meant when you hated it that I said "we" wanted you home...I felt like you were being really picky about "*I* want you home," rather than *we* want you home. And then, suddenly, I could see what you meant with that story about the walk. [*Bob and Sam both look at Diane and wait.*]

DIANE: Well, first of all, I really appreciate how much that picture meant to you. I was surprised and happy that it did. I guess I still feel a degree of cautiousness that I wish I could get by. You're being very...I don't know...I have hardly ever seen you this way. And I like it. I don't want to discourage you from it. I just...I guess I just don't...can't let myself have quite as much enthusiasm. I wish I could.

SAM: Well, you've been bundled up in that jacket against a cold wind for a long time. One sunny moment isn't necessarily going to change everything. [*Diane nods appreciatively. Hugs Sam again.*]

BOB: Diane, I'd like to get back to you for a minute or two...I guess I'm curious about what it's been like having Sam describe this experience where he sees things so much from what he believes is your point of view. Did that feel good?

DIANE: Mostly it felt *great*! Very different and wonderful...It...it was the complete opposite of what I'd been describing—he was hearing me and I *did* matter to him. [*Smiling at Sam. Pause.*] I suppose there's a cautious part that says "watch out"...maybe nothing will really change." Sort of like "time will tell."

I asked Diane if she still felt angry at Sam. She said she did not presently, but assumed that she would again if she felt discounted by Sam. I urged her to notice any such moments, talk with Sam about them, and bring them into our sessions. I asked Sam to pay attention to his pronouns; does he find it easier to talk with Diane about "us" and "we" than "me" and "I"? I reminded them of work we had done previously, linking these present-day issues each has to some sensitivities from their family histories that make Sam tentative about direct intimate contact and that make Diane vulnerable to feelings of unimportance and a sense of dismissal.

So, what can we learn from the session about using emotional expression in couples work? First, while this session is not particularly notable for the amount of emotional expression it contains, it is quite unusual to have someone so powerfully take the role of the other. People are usually pretty attached to their own viewpoints, so the degree to which Sam came to see and appreciate Diane's pain is unusual.

The main technique I used was Directed Dialogue, focusing them on each other most of the time, on their feelings, and at one point, specifying what Diane was to say ("You don't value me"). At another point, I asked Sam to listen to Diane without arguing back. That is when he was able to connect with her empathically. Other than that, most of my comments were structuring, eliciting of humor, interpreting, and reframing. Near the end I made some suggestions, things to notice and try at home. Probably the specific technique I used most frequently is pointing to indicate that the person speaking should address his or her partner rather than me.

One notable absence from this session is any reference to early family history. It would be easy to imagine ways this session could productively have dealt with Diane's sensitivity to not being valued, by connecting this feeling to her early and fairly troubled family history. Similarly, Sam's difficulty in letting things get intimate and personal could be understood as an adaptation he made to his intrusive parents. These sorts of connections are important but did not happen to be part of this session.

Perhaps the best thing about this session is how well it illustrates a major change process initiated by the right kind of emotional expression. By that I mean emotional expression that is new, risky, and reveals a deeper layer of feelings. Diane had to choose first whether to say anything to Sam about her feelings. Then she had to risk being mad at him and take the risk that he would get mad back at her. Then she had to keep going until she found her hurt and sadness. Her reward for all this hard work was to have her husband see her in a new light that makes him appreciative of her needs and aware of how his behavior had hurt and distanced her. Denton (1991) describes an earlier study by Greenberg, James, and Conry (1988) summarizing the change process this way: "the strongest change factor they identified was that when spouse A expressed underlying feelings, B's perception of A changed." That, quite clearly, is what happened here with Sam and Diane.

SUMMARY

When two people fall in love and become a couple, they unleash extremely powerful forces. These forces create more love and altruism and more hate and disappointment than exist in any other human relationship. If we are to help distressed couples, we need to deal with these powerful feelings that tap both biological needs and early family imperatives.

To do this, we must help our clients distinguish between their most basic feelings and the defensive elaborations of these feelings. Our basic feelings bring us together and add to our empathic understanding of each other. It is our defensive feelings and the behavior that springs from them that keep us apart. When Sam could hear Diane's hurt beneath her anger, he felt drawn to her. When, earlier, he heard only her criticism or felt her distance, he fled to the children and dismissed her.

For a relationship to work, partners must be able to maintain self-esteem as they work out a balance of their needs for autonomy and intimacy. They must cooperate in drawing a boundary between themselves and others that provides both enough privacy for the couple and enough contact with others.

Couples view each other through filters that can be quite distorting, either positively or negatively. Our work with them needs to recognize these distortions and gradually lessen them by making affective connections between important early family events and current issues in the couple. There are various techniques we can use to help our clients find and express their feelings. Many of these are based on the idea that there is a great deal of energy bonding partners together and that focused dialogue with each other is a powerful door to feelings.

Our most basic job as therapists is to find ways to help our clients risk talking with each other, see and move past their prickly or slippery defenses, and find the strong bonding feelings that brought them together.

REFERENCES

Denton, W. H. (1991). The role of affect in marital therapy. *Journal of Marital and Family Therapy*, *17*, 257–261.

Fox, N. (1991). If it's not left, it's right. *American Psychologist, 46*, 863–872.

Gottman, J. M. (1991). Predicting the longitudinal course of marriage. *Journal of Marital and Family Therapy, 17*, 3–7.

Gottman, J. M. (1993). A theory of marital dissolution and stability. *Journal of Family Psychology, 7*, 57–75.

Gottman, J. M., & Krokoff, L. J. (1989). Marital interaction and satisfaction: A longitudinal view. *Journal of Consulting and Clinical Psychology, 57*, 47–52.

Gottman, J. M., & Levenson, R. W. (1985). Assessing the role of emotion in marriage. *Behavioral Assessment, 8*, 31–48.

Greenberg, L. S., James, P. & Conry, R. (1988) Perceived change processess in emotionally focused couple therapy. *Family Psychology, 2*, 4–23.

Greenberg, L. S., & Johnson, S. M. (1986a). Affect in marital therapy. *Journal of Marital and Family Therapy, 12*, 1–9.

Greenberg, L. S., & Johnson, S. M. (1986b). Emotionally focused couples therapy. In N. S. Jacobson & A. S. Gurman (Eds.), *Clinical handbook of marital therapy*. New York: Guilford.

Greenberg, L. S., & Safran, J. D. (1984). Integrating affect and cognition: A perspective on the process of therapeutic change. *Cognitive Therapy and Research, 8*, 557–578.

Hendrix, H. (1988). *Getting the love you want: A guide for couples*. New York: Harper & Row.

Johnson, S. M., & Greenberg, L. S. (1987). Emotionally focused marital therapy: An overview. *Psychotherapy, 24*, 552–560.

Johnson, S. M., & Greenberg, L. S. (1991). There are more things in heaven and earth than are dreamed of in B.M.T.: A response to Jacobson. *Journal of Family Psychology, 4,* 407–415.

Kaufman, G. (1989). *The psychology of shame: Theory and treatment of shame-based syndromes.* New York: Springer.

Lazarus, R. S. (1991). Progress on a cognitive-motivational-rational theory of emotion. *American Psychologist, 46,* 819–823.

Lewis, H. B. (1971). *Shame and guilt in neurosis.* New York: International Universities Press.

Nathanson, D. L. (1992). *Shame and pride: Affect, sex and the birth of the self.* New York: Norton.

Nichols, M. P. (1991). *No place to hide: Facing shame so we can find self-respect.* New York: Simon & Schuster.

Perls, R., Hefferline, R., & Goodman, P. (1951). *Gestalt therapy.* New York: Julian.

Pierce, R. A., Nichols, M. P., & DuBrin, J. R. (1983). *Emotional expression in psychotherapy.* New York: Gardner.

Roberts, T.W. (1992). Sexual attraction and romantic love: Forgotten variables in marital therapy. *Journal of Marital and Family Therapy, 18,* 357–364.

Smith, D. A., Vivian, D., & O'Leary, K. D. (1990). Longitudinal prediction of marital discord from premarital expressions of affect. *Journal of Consulting and Clinical Psychology, 58,* 790–798.

Tomkins, S. S. (1963). *Affect, imagery, consciousness: II. The negative affects.* New York: Springer.

5

A Spiral Model of Intimacy

MARIO CUSINATO and LUCIANO L'ABATE

The purpose of this chapter is to present an upward spiral model of intimacy that represents the revision of a previously published model that defined intimacy as the sharing of hurts (L'Abate, 1986). The downward side of this model is either fear of intimacy in borderline cases or couples (Descutner & Thelen, 1991) or complete inability to be intimate, as in abusive-apathetic (i.e., neglectful) relationships.

From the results of previous research using a Sharing of Hurts Scale (Stevens & L'Abate, 1989), five factors emerged to provide a nomological network for sharing of hurts itself: (a) private values; (b) vulnerability; (c) social desirability; (d) imperfection; and (e) sharing hurts proper. This scale was found to have satisfactory concurrent validity with other established scales of intimacy, like the Personal Assessment of Intimacy in a Relationship (PAIR) by Schaefer and Olson (1981), the Interpersonal Relationship Scale (IRS) by Guerney (1977), and the Intimacy Questionnaire by Waring (1983). It should be noted also that our definition of intimacy is much more specific and concrete than other definitions, which are either multifactorial, as in Schaefer and Olson's case, or are generally vague, covering one general measure of relationship satisfaction, as in Waring's case, or equating (and in some ways trivializing) intimacy with "social support" (Reis, 1990).

In looking over our previous, monofactorial conceptualization of intimacy as the sharing of hurts, it seemed to us that intimacy represents a more complex area of study than what is encompassed by the five factors we originally found (Whitbourne & Ebmeyer, 1990). Consequently, we started a program of research that would not only create a new instrument for evaluation, but would also coordinate the creation of this instrument with the creation of a preventive, paratherapeutic workbook program for couples based on regular weekly, written homework assignments (L'Abate, 1990, 1992). The revision of the original model assumes that intimacy is most likely to be viewed within a context of : (a) commitment to the relationship; (b) equality of importance between partners; and (c) reciprocity and mutuality of resources exchanged between partners.

PREREQUISITES FOR INTIMACY: STRUCTURAL (RELATIONSHIP) FACTORS

Personal and dyadic functionality is one of the major if not *the* major prerequisite for intimacy (Galvin & Brommel, 1991; Heath, 1991; L'Abate, 1994; Reis, 1990). Intimacy is found normatively in functional couples, encompassing at the outside no more than 25% of most interdependent relationships, with certainly no more than half of these being at the highest level of intimacy as we define it. It may be found, perhaps sporadically and inconsistently, in conflictful (reactively repetitive) relationships, which comprise at least 50% of most interdependent relationships, and is not present at all in most abusive-apathetic ones, which represent the remaining 25% of the total (L'Abate, 1986, 1994).

This functionality, however, derives from at least two sets of fundamental abilities that need to be present to set in motion the ever growing spiral of intimacy. Unless these two sets of abilities are present and active, it is doubtful whether intimacy, in the way we define it, will be found. These sets relate to the ability to love (and to like one's partner) and the ability to negotiate (Table 5-1). The ability to love is composed of the attribution of importance to self and to an intimate other (i.e., partner), and by emotional availability, being close to oneself and to one's partner when the going gets rough. This ability covers a dimension of *distance* defined by extremes in approach-avoidance. The ability to negotiate covers a dimension of *control* defined by extremes in discharge-delay. In this chapter, we shall concentrate solely on the ability to love and to be intimate.

Table 5-1. *Summary of a Developmental Theory of Interpersonal Competence Underlying a Spiral Model of Intimacy*

	Modality	Prerequisites	Enhancement Factors
Ability to Love	Being	Commitment Equality Reciprocity	Communicating Values Respect for Feelings Accepting Limitations Affirming Potentialities Sharing Hurts Forgiving Errors
Ability to Negotiate	Doing Having		Authority vs Responsibility Orchestrated vs Instrumental Decisions Content—Doing & Having

Adapted from L'Abate, 1986.

To be able to negotiate, one needs to be in control of oneself and be able to approach conflictful issues rationally rather than emotionally. Issues of love, such as how we feel toward those we love and who love us, are not negotiable. We do not negotiate how we feel, even though we may negotiate how these feelings may be expressed. To problem-solve, to make decisions, and essentially to negotiate is a process requiring rational skills. These skills are developed from one's ability to delay action and from thinking through various sides of a conflictful issue. Issues of love require our relying on our feelings and emotions, although it would be helpful if we were able, ideally, to do both, love and negotiate. Functionality in couples, among many other factors, implies being able to separate sharply issues of love from issues of negotiation. Dysfunctionality in couples means, among other factors, confusing, diffusing, and fusing nonnegotiable issues of love from negotiable issues (services, information, goods, and money), as in: "If you loved me you would do ..." or "If you loved me you would buy me ..."

Within the ability to love, three prerequisite or antecedent factors are deemed necessary (but probably not sufficient in themselves) for the development of intimacy, and they are: (a) commitment to the relationship; (b) equality of importance between partners but differentness (i.e., complementarity) in functions; and (c) reciprocity in the exchange of resources.

Recently, Stafford and Canary (1991) presented significant data, at both theoretical and statistical levels, to support a model of close relationships that differentiated between what they called relationship versus maintenance factors. By relationship they meant those structural factors that are basic to the initial exchange characteristics of a relationship, consisting of commitment, liking, and control mutuality. By maintenance they meant those process factors that allow a relationship to develop and to evolve toward greater closeness, consisting of positivity, openness, assurances, network, and task sharing.

In line with that formulation, what we consider as prerequisites to a close relationship would be relationship factors in their model. While our model includes commitment in the same way that Stafford and Canary define it, there may be some overlap between their definition of control mutuality, which we define as reciprocity. We would consider liking as a different variable that would be part of antecedent factors, like the ability to love. By the same token, while they take equality for granted or do not measure it, we consider it as an important, structural prerequisite for our model. Positivity is implied by the fact that it is predicated to be present in functional couples and absent or inadequate in dysfunctional ones, just like intimacy (L'Abate, 1994). Negativity would be more characteristic of dysfunctional couples. Eventually, of course, we may need to distinguish between personal and dyadic prerequisites or antecedents before dealing with the factors that enhance intimacy.

The present model is part of a theory of personality development in interpersonal competence. As Table 5-1 shows, the abilities to love and to negotiate are considered fundamental to the establishment of intimate relationships. However, it is important to distinguish between receptively subjective experience (what and how we feel about someone at the input side) and expressively visible output (how we show and share our love toward that person). Many abusively symbiotic individuals, for instance, report that they experience a great deal of love toward the very person they have abused. Does that mean that their acts discount their experience? Are they lying? Of course not. It just means that we humans are not always consistent in how we express outwardly what we feel inwardly. Especially in dysfunctional relationships, there is no one-to-one correspondence between experience on one side, the receptive side, and expression at the output side, because there is a host of intervening factors that need to be considered, such as time, thinking, and incubation effects, between these two extremes.

Hence, between the experiencing of love on the receptive, input side and the expressing of love on the output side, we need to consider certain intervening prerequisites. These prerequisites are mostly cognitive, and they need to be interpolated between the two sides, the subjectively receptive, emotionally experiencing one and the objectively expressive, behavioral one, in order to make sense of how we become, or fail to become, intimate. Thus, this chapter is also an elaboration of one segment of the original theory of personality development, as applied to the function of intimacy in close relationships.

Commitment

No relationship can last unless partners are in some way or another committed to its perpetuity. What does this commitment consist of? It may be stubbornness or a determination not to give up. It may be sheer rigidity, a need to see the relationship completed because a broken relationship may be equated with personal inadequacy. It may consist of sheer naivete and dependency that frames divorce as an unpleasant and unwarranted alternative. It may be based on seeing the many positives in the relationship that have been obscured by the negativity of stress or of the partner, who may be more invested in ending the relationship. Naturally, commitment needs to be a two-way street for both partners.

When one peruses the literature, one finds a great many references to the importance of commitment, but very little else in terms of agreement about what it means. Kelley (1983), for instance, in commenting about the lack of consistency about definitions of commitment, noted: "Beyond endorsing the relevance of commitment for behavioral consistency and stability ... the writings about the concept show little uniformity" (p. 288).

Most definitions of commitment, within the context of monadic psychology, imply "the pledging or binding of oneself, as in committing oneself to a course of action" (Kiesler, 1970, p. 26) or "to behavioral acts" (p. 31). Kelley (1983) essentially defines it by stressing that commitment means persistence. "A person committed to an activity is expected to persist in it until the underlying goal is achieved" (p. 287). Hence, for Kelley, the major property of commitment is *duration*. This property is obtained by *adherence* to the positives of the relationship with a parallel discounting or belittlement of the negatives.

Within the context of relational psychology, Schwartz and Merten (1980) define commitment as "loving... in a complete and irrevocable manner— there can be no hidden escape clauses and no deception about the depth and reality of that feeling.... There are no ifs, ands, or buts" (p. 214). Rusbult (1983) found that commitment is indeed related positively to the degree of satisfaction and investment put in the relationship, while Sabatelli (1984) found that commitment was strongly related to equity and fulfilled expectations in the marriage. Sabatelli and Cecil-Pigo (1985) maintain that commitment is critical to the stability of a relationship, increasing the amount of dyadic cohesion, and reducing the number of alternatives sought by both partners. Other research (Lund, 1985) supports Sabatelli and Cecil-Pigo's contention that commitment predicted relational stability better than "love."

Brickman (1987) suggests that in a committed relationship there is an underlying sense of duty and obligation to the relationship as well as excitement about seeing it through. Sternberg (1987), in fact, includes commitment among the three factors defining love, intimacy and passion being the other two, but not necessarily in this order. More recently, Fiske and Chiriboga (1990) equate intimacy with commitment (pp. 242–257) as "an increased willingness ... to yield [our] subjective selves to others above and beyond any expectation of reciprocity" (p. 255). This willingness to yield one's self is tantamount, in our view, to unconditional love, that is, giving up expectations of "perfect" performance, production, and problem-solving in the self and in loved ones and valuing as a primary priority being available emotionally to oneself and to one's partner instead (L'Abate, 1986, 1994).

Scanzoni, Polonko, Teachman, and Thompson (1989), in true social learning fashion, related commitment to sexual gratification and to the accumulation of "intrinsic" gratifications. Consequently, a relationship ceases when these gratifications and "perhaps ... extrinsic ones decreased as well" (pp. 98–104). We take strong exception with this view. We have seen many "miserable" couples, among them the "terrible twosomes," who continue their self-defeating, demeaning relationships in spite of the absence of visible or invisible gratifications. We do not think that a social learning approach, limited to rewards and the absence thereof, is sufficient to account for why couples stay together or split.

Commitment to a relationship, of course, wanting that relationship to continue and endure, is not enough. Where does commitment end and overdependency begin? Commitment should be qualified as "commitment to a positive, mutually rewarding relationship" (Kelley, 1983, p. 267). As Kelley argued, there can be love without commitment and commitment without love. We cannot equate the two processes. When both factors, love and commitment, are present, however, one can predict that it is more likely that the relationship will be characterized by "strong, frequent, and diverse interdependence that lasts over a considerable period of time."

Equality

Once we assert the importance of equality as one of the requirements for intimacy, we need to answer the question: "Equality of what?" We would maintain, on the basis of many considerations, that this equality refers to equality of importance. The attribution of importance is one way of expressing love, in addition to intimacy proper (L'Abate, 1994). This attribution may take place directly or indirectly, consistently or inconsistently, verbally or nonverbally.

Functional couples show this attribution in many consistently clear ways, while dysfunctional couples either show it inconsistently or else fail to show it at all. This attribution is expressed by paying attention to the partner's feelings, thinking, and behaviors as being all important. If one pays attention to these component parts, a message is given to the whole individual as to his or her importance. Functional couples pay attention to both parts and the whole, while dysfunctional couples tend to discount, put down, and disparage parts as well as the whole through abuse and apathy, discounting, deriding, and denigrating what and how the partner feels, thinks, and acts. In other words, functional couples deal with each other as persons, while dysfunctional couples deal with each other as objects or as part-objects.

Once equality of importance for both partners is established, then it follows that each partner's differentness is valued and stressed, allowing each partner to be herself/himself, within accepted and agreed-upon limits of mutually acceptable behavior. Thus, instrumental complementarity in intimate relationships works best when it is based on such equality. It works least when instrumentality in functions and roles is equated with extent of importance and when one partner's priorities (i.e., work, career) are used to denigrate or diminish the other's roles and functions (i.e., housework, taking care of children).

Reciprocity

Reciprocity is to functional couples what reactivity is to dysfunctional ones (L'Abate, 1986). Polarized couples, where commitment is present in one partner and absent in the other, show how important a factor reciprocity is. There cannot be reciprocity without commitment to the relationship and affirmation of equality in the importance of both partners. Reciprocity means following the Golden Rule in treating one's partner the way one wants to be treated. This treatment implies kindness, courtesy, helpfulness, and respect for the partner's rights, including personal foibles and fears. It also stresses our inherent fallibility in hurting those we love and who love us, our vulnerability to our being hurt by them, and neediness in wanting closeness from the very ones we have either hurt or who have hurt us (L'Abate, 1986, 1994). We are not hurt by people we do not care about. Reciprocity refers not only to actions but also to attitudes, such as valuing the partner's strengths as well as weaknesses as being the expression of humanness in its multifarious manifestations.

Houle and Kiely (1984), however, made the important distinction between reciprocity as "tit-for-tat" (where one's behavior is contingent on the other's) versus mutuality (where the positive behavior of one partner's is not contingent on the other's). We would agree that, indeed, mutuality represents a higher order of reciprocity, if we were to define reciprocity as contingent behavior. Our definition, however, would also encompass mutuality in the sense that, if partners were to follow the Golden Rule as originally defined, they would behave well on most occasions and usually in a noncontingent fashion. Each partner would tend to behave at his/her best regardless of the partner's behavior and, indeed, especially when the partner is at his or her worst ("Just because my partner robs banks does not give me the right to rob banks as well!").

FACTORS ENHANCING INTIMACY

Once the three prerequisites for intimacy are satisfied, an upward spiral enhancing intimacy takes place according to a sequence of at least six steps: (a) communicating personal values; (b) respecting each other's feelings; (c) accepting personal limitations; (d) affirming of respective potentialities; (e) sharing of hurts and fears of being hurt; and (f) forgiving errors.

Communicating Personal Values

Each of us needs to express to our partner our values, our difficulties, our experiences, no matter how painful, without, however, feeling coerced to do so. Otherwise, the level of intimacy in the couple would be damaged. It is within the context of love and freedom that one partner confides and shares with the other. This expression and sharing are always partial and never total. If in some way total sharing is claimed, both partners aim at a "fusion" that may damage personal individuality. For instance, to communicate personal factors fully, one needs to assert the necessity of accepting equality in the sense of the importance of the self and of the partner. This sense of importance needs to acknowledge not only the value of differences in functions but also the importance of whatever each partner does in her or his way to enhance the relationship. Thus, taking care of a household and children is just as important as getting a paycheck and enhancing one's career. Without this basic, individual, and dyadic sense of importance, it would be difficult, if not impossible, to proceed to the next step in the relationship (L'Abate, 1994).

Respecting Each Other's Feelings

To avoid fusion, diffusion, and confusion between partners, it is important to stress the importance of personal individuality ("I take care of and I am responsible for my feelings. As much as I love you, I cannot take care of and be responsible for yours"). Aside from valuing limitations, errors, and positive qualities, each individual partner has the right to be whatever she/ he wants to be, without, however, interfering with or depreciating the partner as a fully functioning individual. If feelings or other aspects of the partner's personality, like thinking or behavior, are put down, it does not take much to generalize negatively from one particular aspect to the whole person, as in many dysfunctional couples.

The central nucleus of this individuality is represented by one's feelings, tastes, preferences, memories, aesthetic and spiritual sensitivities, sense of ethnic, religious, and family history, and especially pride. The couple's intimacy is directly related to the presence of respect in this personal realm. Without such reciprocal respect there cannot be intimacy. There can be a legal or economic arrangement, an adaptation with practical advantages for living together, or reciprocal using, but no intimacy in the sense of sharing hurts and fears of being hurt, a process that allows sharing of joys.

Respect for each other's individuality and personality takes place within the context of self-acceptance and respect. How can we respect others if we do not respect ourselves? Often times, we may subordinate personal respect for many exigencies of conjugal life, like eating well, being physically comfortable, achieving professional success, giving and receiving costly gifts, stressing performance or production at the expense of presence, that is, being emotionally available to self and to partner. Respect for each other's feelings, thoughts, and actions implies appreciation of feelings for both partners. When I respect my partner's feelings I am asserting their importance because I want my partner to respect and appreciate the importance of my feelings. By stressing the importance of feelings, we are also affirming the importance of the person whose feelings are expressed, accepted, and eventually shared (L'Abate, 1994).

The importance of feelings in relationships was not always appreciated by many researchers. As Clark (1988) commented on this topic:

> researchers primarily interested in emotion have typically studied it in nonsocial contexts, examining processes that seem more intra than in-

terpersonal.... Moreover, until recently, relationship researchers have tended to neglect emotion, in large part owing to the tendency, noted earlier, to study initial encounters between strangers—interactions characterized by little emotion.... With the recent upswing in studies of close relationships, interest in emotion has grown. (p. 619)

The issue here is: What kind of emotions? The second author has maintained for some time that the emotion basic to intimacy and close interpersonal relationships, as found in the family, is *hurt*. Hurt is, indeed, the basic emotion that is common to all human existence. Hurt consists of the collection of all the painful experiences, traumatic losses, occasional or chronic failures, inevitable rejections, and direct and indirect putdowns we all experience in our lifetimes. The second author has argued that hurt is especially linked to the appropriate or inappropriate expression of feelings (L'Abate, 1977, 1986, 1994). We all experience hurts. However, we all differ in how we express them. Some of us can do it positively, some of us do it negatively and destructively. Ultimately, their positive expression should lead to the increased closeness between partners. Negative expression of hurt feelings, of course, would lead to greater distance, conflict, and possible breakup in many relationships.

Unfortunately, this sharing has been distorted by cultural norms that seep even into the psychological literature. For instance, many introductory psychology textbooks still divide emotions into negative and positive ones, without differentiating the experience of emotions at the input side from the expression of emotions at the output side. Experiencing emotions is a process that takes place without value judgment as to its positivity/negativity. What we feel belongs to us and is part of us. No one can or should detract from, discount, or degrade these feelings. There is nothing negative about our experiencing any kind of emotion. The expression of hurtful feelings, however, can vary along dimensions of appropriateness, destructiveness, and enhancement. There is a limited range of feelings we experience, but there is an almost infinite range of options in expressing these feelings. Again, as Clark (1988) concluded in her review:

> The notion that emotional self-expression might lie at the heart of the disclosure component of intimacy helps to integrate this literature with its traditional counterpart, nonverbal involvement ... it seems reasonable to expect that emotional self-revelation includes nonverbal components. (p. 629)

Again, here, language gets in the way. Just as most researchers have failed to specify that disclosure in intimacy consists of sharing hurts, so-called nonverbal components refer to the bottom line of intimacy—*crying together*. If I feel bad about my partner's painful experiences, I want to be available to him or her when he or she is down. I would do it for two reasons: I cannot share the highs without sharing the lows, and I want my partner to be available to me when I am down. When we cry together, and our tears express directly and openly what we are experiencing, we are congruent in expressing what we feel, both verbally and nonverbally.

This process does not need to be followed literally. We can hurt and cry without tears. However, it is important that we and our partners know that we are sharing their hurtful experiences with them. How else can we reassure them otherwise? Partners do not need to cry together at the same time. However, they need to be convinced that their partner is available to them in times of need. This process takes place most of the time in conductive-creative intimate relationships. It takes place, sometimes, in reactive-repetitive relationships. It does not usually take place in relationships characterized by abuse or apathy or neglect (L'Abate, 1986, 1994).

Accepting Personal Limitations

This factor could also be called "vulnerability." In this dimension we are referring to unconditional love as originally stated by Carl Rogers ("regard") and paraphrased by L'Abate (1986) as "seeing the good." The most essential aspect of unconditional love implies a reciprocal acceptance of each other's limitations ("Warts and all"; "In sickness and in health"), with an implied capacity for forgiveness. Self/other acceptance seems to be the core of reciprocity according to the Golden Rule, which acknowledges the ever present limitations of human nature along a variety of dimensions—physical, intellectual, personal, emotional, and professional.

Such an acceptance is founded on the solidarity of seeing ourselves as fallible, vulnerable, and needy pilgrims along the same hard journey. As human beings, we all are limited and we are all imperfect. Accepting and helping each other allows us to go beyond those limitations and to accept them in a more mature fashion. The marital partnership is a paradigmatic expression of such a solidarity. Indeed, between two people tied by a conjugal relationship, such a reciprocal acceptance takes place in a very special and particular way. Solidarity between the two is sustained and motivated by reciprocal love, that is, by the reciprocal valuing of each positive quality and by the *explicit and concrete* acceptance of each other's limitations—fallibility, vulnerability, and neediness.

These limitations are restricted not solely to those found initially during the courtship or honeymoon phases, but also to the new limitations that crop up and are uncovered and discovered, sometimes dramatically or traumatically, in the process and progress of close and prolonged living together. "For better or for worse" does imply growing old, getting sick, and meeting unexpected but inevitable traumas and losses. It takes a strong person to admit to personal limitations and to what are perceived as shortcomings or frailties. Admitting to errors may make one feel vulnerable to retaliation, revenge, and, ultimately, rejection from the partner. Many individuals are fearful of presenting the jugular vein, so to speak, for fear of having it pierced by the partner. Consequently, they never achieve intimacy with any partner. If they have never experienced intimacy in their families of origin ("Did you ever see your parents cry together?"), how can they express it in their families of procreation? This is one of the most frequently used explanations by many clinical couples to excuse their inability to express and share their limitations.

Affirming Respective Potentialities

In intimate (committed, close, and prolonged) relationships, each partner favors the personal and potential growth of the other and, indeed, stimulates the positives, the hidden or downplayed strengths of the partner. In this process of encouragement, one partner makes it easy for the other to actualize these hidden or downplayed potentials into concrete and specific behaviors. This seeing of the good (L'Abate, 1986) implies the use of all the personal and interpersonal resources available to the couple as individuals in their own right. Thus, this is one of the many processes where the individuality of the partner is not only valued, but also maximized to the utmost.

For instance, after their children reached the third grade, it became apparent to a wife that down the road, while her husband would be enjoying his work and career, she would be facing an empty nest and empty time. Unwilling to join other women in playing cards as a future pursuit, she decided to go back to graduate school. She would have never graduated if it were not for the continuous and unrelenting encouragement of her husband, who valued her intellectual skills, her emotional sensitivity, and her caring for other people. While she was initially fearful to compete emotionally and intellectually in a graduate environment, he repeatedly reassured her about her inherently strong analytical skills that would serve her well in such an environment. Without this support, she would not have even attempted to enter graduate school, let alone finish it. This story, of course, is repeated every day in practically any college and university of this nation. The downside is that a spouse from a blue collar or incomplete educational background may become very fearful of the possible educational achievement of his or her spouse and directly and indirectly sabotage any attempts at education that may make the other spouse more independent!

Sharing of Hurts and Fears of Being Hurt

This, of course, is the key factor in reaching and maintaining intimacy in the real sense of the word. This aspect of intimacy is at the very core of the definition of intimacy as "the sharing of hurts and of fears of being hurt" (L'Abate, 1986). It implies *being* emotionally available to oneself and to one's partner, without demands for *doing* or *having* anything ("Be with me now when I am hurting"). Without emotional availability, intimacy would be superficial and, therefore, occasional, sporadic, and short-lived. Who likes to be hurt? We all are fearful not only in the physical but also, and especially, in the emotional sense. A physical wound can be patched up, but what about an emotional hurt? How long does that last? Millions of abused children suffer from that abuse—physical, sexual, or verbal—for the rest of their lives and end up repeating that abuse in some other form or another.

The sharing of hurts is also the most difficult achievement in conjugal living. In fact, many dysfunctional couples find it difficult, if not impossible, to say congruently: "I hurt." Hurting means experiencing and congruently expressing one's hurts and expecting the other to respond empathetically to them. This sharing lessens the experience of hurt and provides comfort. Sharing hurts is the bottom line of loving someone, because loving means giving someone the power to hurt us and to be hurt by us. How else do we "know" we love someone? We do not give that power to people we do not love. Consequently, intimacy is usually reached in fully functioning couples where equality of importance and reciprocity of respect are practiced, but it becomes questionable in semifunctional couples, and practically nonexistent in dysfunctional couples (L'Abate, 1986, 1994; L'Abate & L'Abate, 1979).

Forgiving Errors

One important aspect of intimacy is represented by the capacity to forgive and tolerate one's own as well as one's partner's imperfections (L'Abate, 1986). This aspect of intimacy was one that the original model did not highlight sufficiently and that needed stressing in this revision. The etymological roots of forgiveness are found in its combination of two parts—for-give—that is, to give a gift many times over, and to respond to an error, in either self or in the partner, with a nonerror ("Just because I behaved like a fool yesterday does not give me the freedom to behave like a fool today"). Forgiveness implies letting go of demands for performance, perfection, production, or problem-solving in the self and in loved ones. In therapy, this forgiveness, in addition to "seeing the good," seems to be one of the prerequisites for "unconditional regard," that is, accepting and valuing clients as they are, hurt human beings whose best try was not sufficient to get them what they wanted. Essentially, forgiveness, aside from its seemingly theological connotations, implies a process of acceptance, accepting oneself as well as accepting others as they are.

One reason for forgiveness can be found in the human solidarity mentioned earlier. The experience of forgiveness becomes concrete when two persons tied by a close and prolonged relationship can find attitudes and behaviors that tend to avoid judging the trivial and the banal, becoming aware of judging only what is important for the primacy of the relationship, within a context of flexibility rather than rigidity ("I am so stupid, that when I forgive myself for my immense stupidity, I can forgive anybody, except perhaps Adolf Hitler").

Within these parameters, there is a vast gamut of unlimited forgiveness, involving dedramatizing, letting go, mutual verification and checking out, acknowledgment, not throwing up to each other past errors, being patient, avoiding nasty "You" statements, threats, excuses, mind reading, blackmail or bribery, ultimatums, and trying out new behaviors to correct previous errors (L'Abate, 1994).

THERAPEUTIC CONSIDERATIONS

The ordering of the above factors suggests the sequence that we think is necessary to follow when intervening in intimacy (L'Abate, 1986; L'Abate & McHenry, 1983). Once a couple is over the initial crisis or reason for referral, they are ready to learn negotiation skills. Only after they learn to negotiate are they able to become intimate, in the sense of becoming and being emotionally available to each other. Being emotionally available means being able to get in touch with one's hurts when one's partner is hurting. However, only strong people can allow themselves to be "weak," in the sense that only relatively mature (i.e., "strong"), individuals can allow themselves to be vulnerable and show and share their relative "weaknesses." People who do not have enough strength to be weak cannot allow themselves to admit or show their vulnerability, because, from past experiences, they are afraid that their feelings will be discounted and trampled on.

A sequence of interventions has been elaborated further to include four stages (L'Abate, 1990): (a) reduction of crisis or reason for referral (for most couples, this reason is usually fighting or arguing); (b) dealing with underlying antecedents for the arguing or fighting, like depression, anxiety, or acting out; (c) teaching negotiation skills; and (d) helping couples become more intimate. This sequence is supported by the work of Doherty, Colangelo, and Hovander (1991), who, on the basis of a tripartite model of inclusion (bonding and organization), control (influence and power during conflict), and intimacy (open self-disclosure and close personal exchanges), suggested a similar sequence to set "priorities in treatment: issues of inclusion take precedence over issues of control, which in turn take precedence over issues of intimacy" (p. 227). If, indeed, it takes a fairly if not fully functioning couple to achieve intimacy, then it would stand to reason that intimacy is best dealt with toward the ending phases of therapy, when emotional issues of abandonment, termination, dependence, and loss come to the fore in one way or another.

More recently, based on the work of Pennebaker (1990), and in a way that is more consistent with the centrality of hurt (L'Abate, 1994) the second author has begun to ask all clients, whether individuals, couples, or parents of children, to write about their past and present hurts, from the very beginning of therapy. After an individual list is made, each client is asked to discuss it with the partner, or with a friend for single individuals, or with the therapist for individuals with no friends, and then elaborate in writing about the most traumatic hurts on the list. This process requires selecting and prioritizing which hurts were the most traumatic to the self and to the relationship.

From this assignment, it is easier to progress to an exercise for couples that consists of their facing each other, closing their eyes, and holding hands. They are then told to concentrate on their hurts and as soon as the weight and volume of these hurts becomes overwhelming for them, to say: "I hurt." They are to repeat this statement until an emotional catharsis follows, in which affect breaks through and they start crying. The important issue here is to see how the partner reacts to the other's disclosure. Three possibilities can take place: (a) neither partner can say and express the feeling; (b) one partner can but the other partner cannot; or (c) both partners can express the feeling and come together to share it (L'Abate, 1986). The value of this exercise is not only therapeutic but also diagnostic, because it allows the couple (and the therapist) to see where they are in regard to intimacy and sharing feelings. Most often, at the beginning of therapy, neither partner can complete this exercise successfully. If the therapy has progressed well, then both partners can complete it successfully.

A different approach, already taken by the first author, consists of developing programmed homework assignments, based on the model presented here. These lessons, to be answered in writing by both partners, allow one to remediate paratherapeutically (i.e., in addition to therapy) any deficiencies in any of these areas of intimacy in couples. They can be added also as parapreventive (i.e., in addition to prevention) lessons to any social skills enrichment or psychoeducational training program for couples (L'Abate, 1986, 1990, 1992; L'Abate & Platzman, 1991).

CONCLUSION

This model of intimacy suggests that intimacy may or may not be an instantaneous process. In some couples, it may be instantaneous; in others, it may take years to develop. In some, intimacy may wax and wane and may never be reached fully. In others, it may stand as an unshakable foundation regardless of life's struggles. There is no single or easy path to intimacy. Only a few couples, perhaps no more than 5% to 15% of the total committed or married population, may experience it without a struggle. another percentage, maybe 25% to 30% of the total population, may experience it at specific events, like funerals, marriages, or accidents and sickness. The rest of the population may not be able to experience it at all and may do whatever they can to avoid it altogether.

REFERENCES

Brickman, P. (1987). *Commitment, conflict, and caring.* Englewood Cliffs, N. J.: Prentice-Hall.

Clark, M. S. (1988). Interpersonal processes in close relationships. *Annual Review of Psychology, 39,* 609–672.

Descutner, C. J., & Thelen, M. H. (1991). Development and validation of a fear-of-intimacy scale. *Psychological Assessment, 3,* 218–225.

Doherty, W. J., Colangelo, N., & Hovander, D. (1991). Priority setting in family change and clinical practice: The family FIRO model. *Family Process, 30,* 227–240.

Fiske, M., & Chiriboga, D. A. (1990). *Change and continuity in adult life.* San Francisco: Jossey-Bass.

Foa, U., & Foa, E. (1974). *Societal structures of the mind.* Springfield, IL: Thomas.

Galvin, K. M., & Brommel, B. J. (1991). *Family communication: Cohesion and change.* New York: HarperCollins.

Guerney, B., Jr. (1977). *Relationship enhancement: Skill training programs for therapy problem prevention and enrichment.* San Francisco: Jossey-Bass.

Heath, D. H. (1991). *Fulfilling lives: Paths to maturity and success.* San Francisco: Jossey-Bass.

Houle, J., & Kiely, M. C. (1984). Intimacy: A little-understood stage of development. *Canada's Mental Health, 32,* 7–11.

Kelley, H. H. (1983). Love and commitment. In H. H. Kelley, E. Berscheid, A. Christensen, J. H. Harvey, T. L. Huston, G. Levinger, E. McClintock, L. A. Peplau, & D. R. Peterson (Eds.), *Close Relationships* (pp. 265–314). New York: Freeman.

Kiesler, C. A. (1971). *The Psychology of commitment: Experiments linking behavior to belief.* New York: Academic.

L'Abate, L. (1976). *Understanding and helping the individual in the family.* New York: Grune & Stratton.

L'Abate, L. (1977). Intimacy is sharing hurt feelings: A reply to David Mace. *Journal of Marriage and Family Counseling, 3,* 13–16.

L'Abate, L. (1986). *Systemic family therapy.* New York: Brunner/Mazel.

L'Abate, L. (1990). *Building family competence: Primary and secondary prevention strategies.* Newbury Park, CA: Sage.

L'Abate, L. (1992). *Programmed writing: A self-administered approach for interventions with individuals, couples, and families.* Pacific Grove, CA: Brooks/Cole.

L'Abate, L. (1994). *A theory of personality development.* New York: Wiley.

L'Abate, L., & L'Abate, B. L. (1979). The paradoxes of intimacy. *Family Therapy, 6,* 175–184.

L'Abate, L., & McHenry, S. (1983). *Handbook of marital interventions.* New York: Grune & Stratton.

L'Abate, L., & Platzman, K. (1991). The practice of programmed writing (PW) in therapy and prevention with families. *American Journal of Family Therapy, 19,* 3–13.

Lund, M. (1985). The development of investment and commitment scales for predicting continuity of personal relationships. *Journal of Social and Personal Relationships, 2,* 3–23.

Pennebaker, J. W. (1990). *Opening up: The healing power of confiding in others.* New York: Morrow.

Reis, H. T. (1990). The role of intimacy in interpersonal relations. *Journal of Social and Clinical Psychology, 9,* 15–30.

Rusbult, C. E. (1983). A longitudinal test of the investment model: The development (and deterioration) of satisfaction and commitment in heterosexual involvements. *Journal of Personality and Social Psychology, 45,* 101–117.

Sabatelli, R. M. (1984). The marital comparison index: A measure for assessing outcomes relative to expectations. *Journal of Marriage and the Family, 47,* 931–937.

Sabatelli, R. M., & Cecil-Pigo, E. F. (1985). Relational interdependence and commitment in marriage. *Journal of Marriage and the Family, 47,* 931–937.

Scanzoni, J., Polonko, K., Teachman, J., & Thompson, L. (1989). *The sexual bond: Rethinking families and close relationships.* Newbury Park, CA: Sage.

Schaefer, M. T., & Olson, D. H. (1981). *PAIR inventory scoring manual.* Department of Social Science, University of Minnesota, Minneapolis.

Schwartz, G., & Merten, D. (1980). *Love and Commitment.* Newbury Park, CA: Sage.

Sloan, S. Z., & L'Abate, L. (1985). Intimacy. In L. L'Abate (Ed.), *Handbook of Family Psychology and Therapy* (pp. 405–427). Pacific Grove, CA: Sage.

Smedes, L. B. (1988). *Caring and commitment: Learning to live the love we promise.* San Francisco: Harper & Row.

Stafford, L., & Canary, D. J. (1991). Maintenance strategies and romantic relationship type, gender and relational characteristics. *Journal of Social and Personal Relationships, 8,* 217–242.

Sternberg, R. J. (1987). *The triangle of love: Intimacy, passion, commitment.* New York: Basic Books.

Stevens, F. E., & L'Abate, L. (1989). Validity and reliability of a theory-derived measure of intimacy. *American Journal of Family Therapy, 17,* 359–368.

Waring, E. M. (1983). *Scoring manual for the WIQ.* Department of Psychiatry, School of Medicine, University of Western Ontario, London, Ontario, Canada.

Whitbourne, S.K., & Ebmeyer, J. B. (1990). *Identity and intimacy in marriage: A study of couples.* New York: Springer-Verlag.

6

The Role of Emotion in Relationship Enhancement Marital/Family Therapy

BERNARD G. GUERNEY, JR.

Emotion, the life force, is also the death force. I believe that at the level of humankind emotion is the force that, by mediating between the environment and the actions of our forebears, determined who lived and who died, shaping our genes and making the human race what it is. At the interpersonal level, emotion is the force that, by mediating between ourselves and our social world, shapes our relationships and hence our personalities. At the personal level, the unemotional life is not worth living.

Emotion plays a key role in every type of therapy. The only question is whether that role is acknowledged and consciously used or simply acts outside the therapist's design and control, in which case it will almost certainly work against the effectiveness of the therapy. Relationship enhancement (RE) theory integrates psychodynamic, behavioral, humanistic, and interpersonal principles and methods within a skill-training, multilevel systems framework (Guerney, 1977, 1983; Guerney & Ford, 1993). This integration accords emotion a major role in every aspect of the therapeutic strategy and process.

Following Staats and Eifert (1990), RE theory defines emotions as responses in the limbic system of the central nervous system. These internal responses reflect both innate and learned patterns. They in turn serve as internal stimuli for action. These stimuli are the components of the emotion complex of which we sometimes become aware (Staats & Eifert, 1990, p. 544). I suggest reserving the term "feelings" for this stimulus aspect of emotion. Memory traces (often not conscious) of positive emotions provide the incentive, when we later encounter a similar person-context system, for repeating those thoughts and actions that occurred prior to their arousal. Negative emotions operate similarly, but as incentives for avoiding rather than approaching the associated external stimuli and for inhibiting rather than repeating preceding behaviors.

Through learning, the meanings of words become stimuli eliciting emotion. Other events associated with positive or negative meanings may take on positive or negative incentive values accordingly. Moreover, one set of meanings may lend positive or negative value to another set (Staats & Eifert, 1990, p. 550b). (I would hypothesize that the majority of phobias are based not on external stimuli, as simple behaviorism would suggest, but rather on a complex chain of self-stimulated thinking-imagining that elicits fear.) Finally, it is my view that *through internal associative processes, symbols, and perhaps even metaphors, may take on emotional and incentive values and that they may influence and be influenced by emotion.*

If this associative linkage involving associations, symbols, and metaphors is acknowledged as valid, then, in my view, *many major barriers between psychodynamic and behavioral theory disappear.* The behaviorists are no longer limiting themselves so much to overt behavior. They have begun to get serious about the territory of our insides—the "black box." Cognitions were the first to be recognized. Now—may the saints preserve us—emotions are starting to sneak in. Some "behaviorists" like Staats and Eifert are busily speculating about how the black box may be wired. So-called behaviorists are starting to acknowledge that there are complex mutually causative linkages between cognitions, emotion, and behavior. They may yet come to acknowledge that emotionally influenced associations among words, symbols, and metaphors also may influence behavior, at times—especially at times one is dealing with people's problems—with only indirect and perhaps minimal connections to stimuli and reinforcements.

When the black box is seen to include that sort of wiring, then many of Freud's observations and conclusions would no longer be inconsistent with "behavioral" thinking. Much of Freud's thinking might still be considered imprecise and wrongly "languaged," but no longer basically inconsistent. Personally, I think that decades from now many of Freud's insights will be "discovered" by behaviorists, who will of course have new names for them, and quite possibly no knowledge that Freud was there first. As with the breakthroughs of Dollard and Miller (1950), but perhaps in a more detailed, sophisticated way, "behavioral" theory will then become behavioral-cognitive-affective theory. Meeting scientific standards the psychodynamicists themselves probably never will achieve, these neobehaviorists, with or without acknowledgment, will then explain rather than reject many psychodynamic insights. Such a development may result in dramatic improvement in therapeutic theory and practice.

It follows from the theoretical positions mentioned earlier, that thoughts, or "self-talk" if that is your preference, may elicit emotions. But often outside our awareness, the reverse is true, and is equally important for our personal and interpersonal development: emotions elicit and shape the nature of our thoughts and our self-concept, our anticipations of future interpersonal events, and our actions.

Much of the emotional-related forces that govern this shaping are elicited by the meanings we perceive in the behavior of significant others in our life. So, to a large extent, it is the meanings we perceive in the actions of others that shape our emotional lives, our self-concepts, and our personalities. *It is when, and only when, therapists can change the nature of a client's interpersonal interactions with significant others that they can produce fundamental, enduring changes in personality.*

Relationship enhancement theory includes the psychodynamic concept of defense mechanisms as they relate to emotion. That is, people defend themselves against perceptions and thoughts that arouse intolerable emotions. In the main, RE theory accepts the explanations of each of the classic Freudian defense mechanisms in terms of learning theory as initiated by Dollard and Miller (1950). Repression is learned through a negative reinforcement process in which forgetting reduces the feeling of anxiety and, I would add, other unwanted feelings. I define defense mechanisms as "anti-mnemonic devices to assist intensely motivated forgetting."

Equally important are the psychodynamic concepts that hold that people may pay heavy prices for such repression. Though outside of awareness, suppressed and repressed emotions continue to influence us in many ways. Unfortunately, however, this influence is mainly in one direction, since that which remains outside of awareness is largely uninfluenced by current experience and circumstances; that is why it is necessary to bring repressed/suppressed feelings into awareness and expression. The distortions of internal and external realities make it more difficult for us to fully understand and accurately predict our own or others' behaviors and, more important, to fully value ourselves and/or others. Thus, repression may lead to a wide variety of physical, emotional, and interpersonal problems, including some of the most-difficult-to-overcome types of marital difficulties.

The main instigators of the need to repress have been and are one's intimates and the values and emotion-thought-behavioral connections they have instilled in us. In RE theory, intimates also are viewed as being the most important *allies* the therapist has in undoing suppression/repression and the reality distortions they produce, and in preventing future repressions from developing (Guerney, 1969). It is the power of intimates to generate stronger feelings—positive and negative—than anyone else, including the therapist, that gives them this exceptional leverage for harming or helping.

ROLE OF EMOTION IN MARRIAGE AND MARITAL DISTRESS

Emotion conceives, develops, and nurtures marriage, and emotion is the only thing that can kill it. Sometimes it does so by striking a single blow, literally. Sometimes, as in an affair, emotion kills fairly quickly, but only after a period of torture. More often, the torture is prolonged, and the death of the marriage follows after countless pinpricks have over months or years escalated into razor slashes and, finally, the fatal dagger thrusts. Often it kills very slowly, accompanied more by gnawing chronic pain than acute distress, through malnutrition created by withdrawal and neglect.

The conception, birth, and nurturance of marriage is based on three of six social emotions (of 14 basic emotions) identified by Ford (1987). These three emotions, each shown in three levels of feeling, build and strengthen a marriage through the desire to avoid and the negative reinforcement properties of (1) *loneliness-sorrow-grief*, and the incentive power and reinforcement properties of both (2) *sexual arousal-pleasure-excitement* and (3) *acceptance-affection-love*.

The remaining three of the six social emotions, the three marriage-killer emotions, are *embarrassment-shame (guilt)-humiliation, resentment-jealousy-hostility*, and *scorn-contempt-disdain*. These operate to bring about loneliness-sorrow-grief, and to reduce or eliminate sexual arousal-pleasure-excitement and acceptance-affection-love, often in the very sequence shown here. However, these killer emotions would not go after the victim on their own initiative, so to speak. They are just the hit men. The emotion that "sets up" the marriage, the one that puts out the contract, does not appear on the above list; nor does it appear among the emotions that make up Plutchik's eight basic emotional patterns (Ford, 1987, p. 523). Frankly, I do not know why—perhaps because it would not be considered a primary or basic emotion, although, to my way of thinking, it is perhaps the most basic of all the emotions. To me, it is so basic that it underlies not only much aggression but, by its defeat, all of our most pleasant and productive emotions, including the emotion that causes us to laugh. And when it comes to destroying marriages, to me it is the *capo de tuttu capi*, the Professor Moriarty, the archenemy, of marriage. It is *frustration*.

Frustration is aroused when any of the emotional needs you hope your partner will help you meet go unmet. It is what steadily builds, while you hope your partner will come to see what needs to be done to meet your needs; see it, you hope, by the light of love alone, without your having to say anything about it. It is what continues to expand, like a red star, a sun whose sustaining sources of energy are almost depleted, as you then start to let your partner know—indirectly, of course, by hints and digs—what needs to be done. And your partner still fails to come through. So the dying sun finally explodes into a supernova of demands, and then threats. You strike out, wanting to hurt your partner as much as you feel hurt. Or, if you are terrified either of your own anger or of your partner's retaliation, the red star implodes into an incredibly shrunken, heavy, hard, impenetrable white dwarf of bitter withdrawal.

A feeling is a call to action. Frustration is one of the loudest. When the action taken is inaction—*when the call is suppressed*—frustration only feeds upon itself and grows. The feelings that eventually result are discouragement-depression. When the actions taken are ones that fail to provide the emotional gratification that would dispel the frustration, the eventual feelings are annoyance-anger-rage, resentment-hostility, and—when even hope vanishes—scorn-contempt-disdain.

It is a tragedy that so few people know how to harness frustration and other related negative feelings, such as annoyance, resentment, anger, boredom, downheartedness, dislike, wariness, and loneliness, to make them do positive work. They have never learned that *negative feelings serve the same purpose in protecting and enhancing their psychosocial welfare as pain provides for their physical welfare.* They do not see these feelings as heaven-sent warnings that something must be changed or more serious damage will result. It is the role of the RE therapist to teach them the skills to draw productive relationship-changing power from these emotions instead of doing things that escalate them and may end in the destruction of the relationship and in serious psychic damage to the individuals involved.

THE ROLE OF EMOTION IN THERAPY

The role of emotion in therapy begins even before clients contact therapists. Emotion creates the uncomfortable feelings that motivate clients to seek relief and satisfaction through therapy. Then, after the intake interview and the first therapy session or two, it is their emotions more than their intellect that make clients decide whether or not they will remain with that therapist, seek another, or discontinue therapy entirely. Therefore, how the professional handles the intake and the first few sessions (i.e., what emotions and feelings the professional stimulates in the client during that time) largely determines whether there will or will not be even the opportunity to continue the therapeutic effort.

In articles, one often reads the statistic that the *average* marital or family therapy case is terminated after about three or four therapy sessions, which means that a great many couples do not even make it into the second therapy session! I think the early dropout statistic reflects the fact that a great many marital/family therapists follow theories and strategies that (a) do not sufficiently attend to client emotions, and (b) do not include a systematic way either to avoid those negative and discouraging emotions that lead to quitting or to encourage those emotions that would lead to a comfortable, trusting relationship with the therapist, confidence in the type of therapy being experienced, and strengthened hope about the viability of the marital relationship.

Relationship enhancement therapy does attempt in a systematic way to foster the emotions that lead to trust, confidence, and hope. Obviously, you cannot facilitate change if your client stops coming. So, the first principle of therapeutic strategy should be "Do nothing to stimulate emotions that will drive your client from therapy." I have identified a "dozen deadly sins" that even experienced marital therapists commit fairly frequently that stimulate emotions that directly or indirectly are likely to lead to premature termination (Guerney, 1991).

Once therapy is under way, the major assumptions underlying RE therapy that have a bearing on the role of emotions are as follows:

1. The central client of the marital therapist is neither the individual nor the marriage, but the relationship itself. This remains true even when the marital therapist is doing Unilateral RE Marital Therapy (i.e., seeing only one member of the pair for marital therapy). However, out of ethical principle, the marital relationship should not be protected at the cost of the growth of either individual within it.

Improving the intimate relationship will promote individual development. Fostering the growth of the individual *in and through the relationship* will also improve the relationship. Note that the statement does not necessarily include the growth that may take place in separate individual therapy. Thus, *when relationship improvement is the major objective, the growth of the individual and that of the relationship are best handled in an integrated way.* This is consistent with the multilevel systems theoretical framework of RE therapy (Guerney & Ford, 1993).

2. It is desirable for the individual, and for relationships, for individuals to express their feelings to one another as fully, openly, and forcefully as is consistent with implementing *all* of their own most important personal and interpersonal values, goals, and priorities, providing that these do not include harming others.

3. Some of the most important characteristics of a good, loving couple relationship are honesty, compassion, trust, security, loyalty, fairness, and a desire to accommodate to each other's wishes. All of these characteristics are enhanced when there is an exchange of feelings tempered with as much compassion and consideration for the feelings of one's partner as is consistent with honestly communicating one's wishes concerning the other's behaviors.

4. Given that the skill exists to accomplish compassionate and considerate expression of one's feelings, then mutual accommodation, fairness, and the other characteristics of a good intimate relationship are most readily facilitated when the exchange of feelings occurs at the *most intense* level. That is, if the behavior of one's spouse gives rise to anger, it is better to express anger than annoyance; if the behavior of one's spouse gives rise to rage, the more quickly one can express rage, and not merely anger, the better. If one feels hopeless and depressed about the relationship, the sooner that feeling is expressed, instead of merely discouragement, the better.

5. Given that the skill exists to accomplish compassionate expression of one's feelings, then the above-mentioned characteristics of a good relationship are best facilitated by expressing the *deepest* levels of one's feelings. For

example, in the instance of any intimate couple who, whether they realize it or not, are still in love, no matter how intense the hostility, at progressively deeper levels one is likely to find that (a) the hostility is present because of anger; (b) the anger has arisen because of frustration; (c) the frustration is due to, let us say, feeling rejected or neglected; (d) the rejection or neglect provoked the anger and frustration because of a (frustrated) longing for closeness with and affection from the other partner; and (e) the longing for closeness with and affection from the partner exists because of a feeling of strong love for the partner. Thus, given appropriate skills, the earlier and more intensely the clients express their negative emotions, the sooner they will be able to come back in contact with their love, and the more quickly and more certain it is that the troublesome issues, whatever they are, will be resolved and the relationship improved.

Should the case be that the desire to preserve the relationship exists out of self-deception or for any one of a number of other reasons (e.g., financial necessity or religious conviction), one may not find love at the deepest level. Indeed, for one or both parties, one may find only stone-cold ashes where fire once existed, and no true desire to relight the fire. What then? In my view, it should not be the goal of a couple's therapist to preserve relationships in a particular legal status or at a particular level of physical proximity, but rather the goal should be to *improve* the relationship in terms of the sorts of characteristics mentioned above, central to which is honesty tempered by compassion. Hence, for improving the relationship, the expression of the deepest level of feelings, again with great skill in compassionate expression, remains the most desirable course even when the deepest level includes disclosing the absence of love and may result in divorce. The key thing about which everyone, including the therapist, should be sure, is that the decision to break apart an intimate relationship has been made on the basis of an honest exploration of *all* pertinent feelings, not alone on the basis of raw anger and hostility or frustration and despair.

6. The neural patterns created by our perceptions, past emotions, feelings, and behavior color our current perceptions, emotions, feelings, and behavior. Some of these neurological traces distort our perceptual abilities rather than facilitate them. Such distortions play a role in creating the problems that bring couples to therapy. Such distortions are corrected when clients discover their true feelings and express them, at their most intense and deepest levels, to an empathic, accepting partner. The most frequently used RE techniques are designed to accomplish exactly that. However, on occasion with certain couples, one reaches a point in the therapeutic process when less frequently used RE procedures, which will be discussed later, are called for.

Among the instances calling for the use of less routine RE techniques are ones in which the neurological traces of past emotions remain powerful enough to go beyond coloration into very serious distortions of current realities. We refer here not to distortions of psychotic proportions but to thoughts and feelings nevertheless obviously different from those that most people would have in response to the verbalizations and behaviors of the partner. Henceforth, let us call our hypothetical clients in this chapter Dan and Sue, and our hypothetical RE therapist, Dr. Joan Smith. The feelings, and/or the lack of to-be-expected feelings, that Dan is experiencing "make sense" neither to Sue, to Dr. Smith, nor, when he is brought down to the deepest *then- accessible* level of his feelings, to Dan either. At that point, it seems appropriate to assume that although the distortions are taking place in the present, the reasons for them lie buried in the past. (It is not advisable to make such an assumption until this situation arises, because regardless of history or the therapist's hypotheses, past problems, even severe ones, may not be a problematic factor in the current relationship. And even if the therapist were infallible, it would probably not be advisable to search for the possible relevance of past problems to the relationship until the individual who must find the hidden feelings, and their relationship to the present, is directly motivated—by experiencing a specific mystery—to seek to discover and reexperience them.)

In a long-standing relationship, the traumatic event(s) may have taken place with the partner. Examples would be a wife who felt she had been severely betrayed, or taken great advantage of on one occasion, or psychologically and emotionally abused or abandoned for many years. In such instances, it would be unexpressed rage that is creating the current distortions. For example, such a wife may be incapable of recognizing that her husband has true remorse over what he has done (because now he has been made emotionally aware of his wife's deepest feelings) or of accepting the fact that her husband does truly love her deeply and is willing to do whatever is necessary to rekindle her love. As long as the rage and hostility remain repressed, such a wife will be numb to her underlying positive feelings, and she will be unable to acknowledge the importance of significant positive steps her husband has taken to win back her love by changing his life-style. Such acknowledgment is simply too incompatible with her unconscious, inhibited rage. And that rage, lying as it does outside of awareness, would not be significantly reduced by the new events.

Or, the emotion creating the current mysterious reactions may come from the still-more-distant past; in that case, it would very frequently have occurred in childhood, probably in the family of origin. Physical and sexual abuse are the most frequent culprits in creating unexpressed, repressed, or suppressed feelings and impulses powerful enough to create significant difficult-to-correct distortions more than a decade later.

7. Given certain conditions, the best person to assist the therapist in helping a client reexperience suppressed or repressed feelings is the person toward whom the feeling is directed. The reason is that, under the right conditions, that person's presence can serve as a stimulus helping to bring the feelings to awareness. One of the necessary conditions is that the person aiming to do the reexperiencing is not too frightened or inhibited by the other's presence to be willing to try to recapture the feelings with that person there.

Another condition is that the person who had originally elicited the suppressed or repressed feelings has acquired a sufficiently high level of the appropriate therapeutic attitudes and empathic skills to be able to maintain them under such trying conditions. (I would very much like to put this assumption to the test with victims of parental sexual and physical abuse in interaction with the abusing parent, but have not yet had that opportunity.) Hence, given that *both* people have the appropriate skills, and it can be done under the direct supervision of the therapist, it is best for the individual and for the relationship if intensely negative feelings are expressed directly to the partner or member of the family of origin who stimulated them. With appropriate skills in use, this affords the best possible opportunity for the person expressing the feelings to fully experience catharsis, and for the person who stimulated the feelings to become aware of and to acknowledge the negative feelings and, later on, to explain, to express remorse, and to seek forgiveness or, if these fail to materialize, inadvertently to help the victim realize that the idea of a positive, emotionally intimate relationship with the perpetrator is unrealistic. This maximizes chances for constructive (although on occasion not immediately pleasant or previously wished-for) developments on the part of both parties and the relationship between them. (There is an array of RE techniques to use in promoting such catharsis and self-exploration. The methods are selected according to the traumatized client's needs and the potential helping partner's skill level and emotional capabilities for providing empathic acceptance at the moment. The procedures range from having the helping partner provide all the empathic acceptance, with the therapist being entirely silent or just providing the helping partner with some coaching; through having the therapist provide the empathic acceptance, with the potential helping partner present but silent; to having the therapist see the traumatized client without the potential helping partner even being present.)

The principles and practices that flow from the assumptions just described are summarized in the following section.

THERAPEUTIC PRINCIPLES AND STRATEGIES

In light of the importance attributed to the early emotional reactions of clients, beginning with the intake, if not earlier, RE therapists respond empathically to almost every emotionally significant statement the client addresses to them. This begins to *build the confidence, trust, and psychological security that foster bonding and confidence.* In the arena of psychotherapy and marital/family therapy, although some client resistance stems from the need to keep what is suppressed and repressed from entering awareness, I maintain that the major portion of client resistance stems, unnecessarily, from the misguided behaviors of therapists.

Of the therapeutic strategies that create client defensiveness, make it more difficult to retain clients in therapy, and make it more difficult for clients to bring to awareness and to express the feelings that they need to express, the most ubiquitous is adherence to the medical model of delivering psychosocial services (e.g., Guerney, Stollak, & Guerney, 1970; 1982). It is followed by adherents of all the leading family therapy approaches, and although behaviorally oriented marital/family therapists eschew the "disease" component of the medical model, they generally follow the medical model in other respects.

By assiduously avoiding as many aspects of the medical model as possible, especially that part of it that calls for determining specifically wherein "the problems lie," RE avoids many of the types of resistance that make it difficult to retain clients in therapy, and to obtain open, honest expressions of feeling. In my view, it is the problem-finding analytic, probing, questioning, interpretive therapist activity that creates most of the distortions and resistance marital therapists face. The difference between RE and other approaches are very large in this regard. For example, therapists from two other orientations and I recently were given the task of describing how we would react *therapeutically* to the same hypothetical case involving marital and family problems. The reactions of the representatives of the other two approaches, by actual paragraph count, were 50% and 80% concerned with diagnostic issues; as the RE representative, my count was about 5%, with 95% devoted to the therapeutic process (Fraillon, Guerney, Kirschner, & Kirschner, 1990).

In RE therapy, except to determine whether referral, medication, or the like is required, which is almost always limited to the intake session, there is virtually no attempt by the therapist to probe or question in order to find out what is *wrong* with a client or a relationship; no attempt to decide whether responsibility for a difficulty resides with Dan or Sue, or both; and no attempt to determine the ways in which Dan or Sue or both should change their behaviors to make things better. (Generally, the only significant changes we advocate are that clients learn the skills, and the skills are presented as something special—that is, virtually no one today acquires them naturally—rather than as something required to remedy special deficiencies on their part. With these skills, applied under the therapist's supervision, they know that it is they themselves who will search for and resolve their problem, although we stand ready to help in other ways as well should they or the therapist feel it is required.)

As a result of not feeling analyzed, judged, or pressured by the therapist to improve faults, clients are less defensive and have little concern with putting their best foot forward for the therapist at the expense of being fully honest with themselves or with their partner about their reactions and feelings. They know that the therapist's general orientation is to be a skill coach, and to assist them to deal with content from their insides out, rather than from the therapist's viewpoint in.

In addition to avoiding the negative feelings of anxiety and defensiveness created by the appearance to clients of judgmentalness that unavoidably arises from diagnostic, prescriptive, and other aspects of the medical model, the RE approach seeks systematically to develop positive feelings in clients. In the earliest phase of therapy, RE therapists seek to develop in clients a *positive feeling triad*: feelings of hope, confidence, and trust toward themselves and the therapeutic process. RE therapists do that, first of all, by consistently responding empathically to the deepest, often unstated, levels of feeling phenomenologically recognizable by the clients. Here is an example of how this is done at intake, when it is the therapist rather than the partner who is spoken to, and who responds empathically.

HUSBAND: In the early years of our marriage, she was real nice, it was great. But, since kids came on the scene, and then even worse after she got to working, she's gotten bitchier and bitchier. Seems I can't do a thing that's right.

THERAPIST: Right now, it seems like everything you do gets you in trouble. And, that makes you sore in turn. [*Husband nods vigorously.*] *Really* mad. And you miss the days when she was loving. [*Husband nods.*] There is a real longing for that love. And you also miss your own feelings of love for her. [*Husband nods, tears up.*] A whole lot. It may get buried under a lot of anger, but underneath the love is still there.

HUSBAND: [*Somewhat choked up*] Yes it is.

THERAPIST: It's still *very* strong.

HUSBAND: Yes, it is.

The positive feeling triad is also developed in this early stage of intake/ therapy because RE therapists elicit the clients' goals. The goals solicited include not only what they want to eliminate, but their objectives, what they want to accomplish, their relationship ideals, so to speak. RE therapists make it clear, largely on the basis of the role they take and what they do and do not do, that they are assisting the couple toward *their* goals, rather than ones that they themselves determine based on their analysis of the couple's individual or interactive problems.

Another part of creating feelings of hope, trust, and confidence early on is that RE therapists also are entirely open and forthcoming about how they plan to act with the clients and what they expect of them and of the therapeutic process. This includes having therapists tell the clients exactly how long it probably will take to accomplish all the goals agreed upon (see Guerney, 1977, p. 71ff, for an explanation of what I have labeled a "time-designated" format).

The positive feeling triad is further strengthened by the fact that RE therapists relate and speak to clients in exactly the same way that they are teaching the clients to deal with each other. Such isomorphism is more obvious and complete in RE therapy than in other types of couple therapy. For example, few therapists would advocate that clients use with each other such techniques as paradoxical instruction or reframing. In fact, in using such methods therapists are adopting a stance toward their clients of "Don't do as I do." We believe the "Do as I do" aspect of RE contributes very significantly to the clients' feelings of trust and confidence in the therapist and the therapy, and, hence, to their staying and improving in therapy.

Another way in which RE therapy seeks to stimulate the kinds of feelings that encourage perseverance and constructive change in therapy is to structure the therapy so that clients gain a sense of hope, trust, and confidence in their *partner* as early as possible. This is accomplished in two major ways. The first is by seeing to it, through RE topic selection procedures and the coaching clients get when they practice the basic skills they are taught, that the clients quickly learn of the positive feelings they have toward one another. The second way is to make sure that early in therapy some specific plan for enhancing the relationship is worked out and implemented, or that some critical and pressing conflict/problem is resolved in a way that all parties feel is as fair to themselves and as beneficial to the relationship as possible. (The enhancement issue would be used in a time-designated format, the pressing problem in time-limited or crisis-intervention RE formats.)

In the time-designated RE format, clients who argue bitterly are initially given brief training in exercising restraint at home on negative interactions. It is made clear that such restraint is sought only until they have learned enough of the skills to allow them to work more effectively on their problems. For example, the therapist might say to clients who fight bitterly, "Neither of you has succeeded up to now in improving the situation, or changing what you don't like in your partner's behavior, and it is not likely that you will do any better until we have taught you the skills you need to resolve your problems. Instead, I wonder if it would be possible for you during the next week or two, to just treat each other more or less as you would a guest in your home. Or if that would not work, just sort of stay away from each other?" It is further suggested that if this fails to prevent anger, they express themselves along these lines: "Look, I'm really mad, but because of Dr. S.'s advice, I'm going to go for a walk and we'll wait until we have the skills to discuss this constructively." They are also advised that they should then and there write down on a Relationship Questionnaire what the problem/conflict was about so that it could be considered as a topic for possible discussion in the weeks ahead. The clients are then asked to provide a couple of examples of the deeds or statements of their partner that typically trigger an argument. These triggers are role-played briefly, with clients giving the new recommended response to their partner instead of their habitual responses. The therapist reinforces them enthusiastically for their agreement and willingness to attempt this new behavior and for their success in rehearsing it.

The positive feeling triad with respect to the interpersonal triad of self, partner, and therapist is protected and strengthened by having clients select topics at those levels of difficulty that the couple's skills will allow them to handle with minimum assistance from the therapist. The positive emotion

triad is further strengthened by having the clients resolve some of these problems without the therapist being present. They do this by using the skills at
home, with only indirect supervision from the therapist based on self-report and
on audiotape segments played briefly in the session. With each conflict/prob-
lem resolved, the couple's mutual hope, trust, and confidence grow stronger.

Another way of building and maintaining positive feelings is for the therapist to see to it that each conflict/problem is clearly resolved before proceeding to the next one. (When a more fundamental problem arises during a
discussion, and skill levels are adequate, clients are encouraged to pursue to
its resolution the more fundamental problem in place of the one that is less
important.) The assumption underlying the idea of completing the resolution of an issue before proceeding to the next, carrying it over from session to
session if necessary, is that the positive feeling we are discussing will decline
if a long period of time is spent wandering from one issue to the next without
an obvious progression toward deeper levels and without any definitive reso-
lutions being reached.

Moreover, the emotional benefits derived from the fact that a specific time
frame was set at intake to resolve the couple's problems and reach their goals
will begin to be replaced by frustration and discouragement if such mean-
dering is permitted. It might seem to therapists operating in theoretical frameworks other than RE that if clients meander, they are responsible—not the
therapist. RE theory leads to the view that it is the therapist and the therapist's
methods that will, at the emotional level, take the blame and pay the price
for a client's frustration. Moreover, from the RE perspective, that is as it
should be.

It is very important that the clients also perceive that their progress toward resolving their *deepest* problems is orderly and rapid. In traditional
marital/family therapies, by default or otherwise, the topic very frequently
is determined session by session by the spontaneous choice of the clients. RE
theory holds that if a therapist allows such selection by saliency, clients often
will unconsciously make sure that they always have ready what I call the
"fight of the week"—a seemingly pressing and important conflict—about
which to talk. Though doubtless unaware of it, the reason they come pre-
pared in that manner is precisely to keep from having to deal with their most
important—and therefore most anxiety-producing—issues. While they deal
with such "hot" but relatively superficial issues, their unsolved fundamental
problems will keep them well supplied with genuine and attention-grabbing
issues indefinitely. Little else gets solved permanently unless the most fundamental problems are solved; so eventually clients get discouraged, and the
therapy, to say nothing of the marriage, falls apart.

What makes a problem more rather than less fundamental? From the RE
perspective, the greater the number of incidents, events, and circumstances
that stem from it, and the more it threatens the continuation of the relationship and the growth of honesty and compassion between the partners, the

more fundamental the problem may be considered to be. An example follows of levels of a problem from an RE, and we think most anybody's, perspective. The levels move from the relatively superficial to the more fundamental. The example is presented as a wife might phrase the problem to the marital therapist. *Dan spent much too much money on a stereo setup this week; he doesn't know how to shop for value; he's not careful about money; he's impulsive; he's selfish; he doesn't believe in saving money for the future; he doesn't worry enough about the children's educational future; he doesn't care about my future either should anything happen to him; I'm not sure how much he thinks of me as a person outside of my meeting his needs; I'm not sure if he still loves me; I think he may be having an affair; I think he may want a divorce; I'm not sure if I still love him; I'm not sure anyone loves me; I'm not sure anyone could ever love me; I don't like myself; I don't think I could ever like myself; I hate myself, and always will; maybe I don't deserve to live; death right now would seem to provide me with peace and everything else I want; before I kill myself, I might want to kill him; while you two went to look at your new office computer, I put cyanide in the coffee he just finished; and the coffee you just finished.*

So, unless the therapist is concerned that clients will drop out if a very salient topic is not handled immediately, or the clients are being encouraged to avoid emotionally loaded topics because they are first learning the skills, a criteria other than saliency is used to select a topic. That criteria is whether the problem is a fundamental one, one of emotional depth that affects many other areas of the relationship. If this criteria has not been put into play earlier, it is called into play shortly after clients have well-learned Empathic, Expressive, Discussion/Negotiation, Problem/Conflict Resolution, and Facilitation skills, and while they are still in the process of learning Changing-Self, Changing-Others, Transfer/Generalization, and Maintenance skills (see Guerney, 1989, for a description of these skills). Once the criteria of fundamental importance is brought into play, the RE therapist, unless the clients can make a very persuasive case for doing otherwise, insists that the clients discuss the topics that they, with the therapist's consultation, have previously and thoughtfully decided were their deepest and most fundamental problems. It also should be noted here that the RE skills themselves are designed to pull clients toward deeper and deeper levels, of which they may initially have been unaware. Therefore, topics that are considered to be most fundamental may shift over time.

Let us move now to another area of consideration: should the therapist ever seek to dampen clients' emotions? In RE therapy, deep emotions may sometimes not arise for a while as the result of the general decision made by the therapist early in the time-designated format of RE therapy to recommend delaying the discussion of deep topics so that clients may concentrate better on learning RE skills. Also, the therapist would discourage launching a discussion of deep negative feelings as a session is close to ending. But generally speaking, once an emotion *has* arisen, there is no thought of dampening it. There is only one direction in which the RE therapist wishes to proceed—that of helping the clients to become aware of and to express most intensely the deepest level of feelings associated with the initial feeling. (If the emotion is one that is not in line with an appropriate progression of the problem discussion—e.g., it is directed toward the therapist or the therapy— the therapist uses a technique called Troubleshooting (Guerney, 1977), which concludes with redirecting the client back to an appropriate type of discussion with the client's partner.)

The RE techniques of accomplishing this have, at their core, the therapist's empathy with the client. RE theory holds that in therapy, regardless of theoretical orientation, expression of feelings by clients at their most intense and deepest levels is accomplished in the surest and quickest way, with the most beneficial long-term results and the fewest possible harmful side effects, by avoiding certain therapeutic techniques. These include asking open- or closed-ended questions, indirect leads, and interpreting. Instead, it is preferred that the therapist use direct, educationally based instruction and reflect deeper levels of unstated feelings. We view the latter as the hallmark of genuine, unconditional, compassionate empathic responding.

Experience has made me realize that few therapists consider empathy in the same way that it is used in RE therapies. Clients and therapists trained in empathy as it is used in RE view it as flowing out of a complete, though time-limited, absence of self, a complete identification with the heart, guts, and soul of the other person. The way to achieve empathy is, at a particular moment, to enter into another person's world so completely as to think and feel, albeit perhaps not to the same degree, what at that moment the other person is thinking and feeling, and hence to experience identification, oneness, with that person. It is that oneness that sometimes allows the empathizer to speak for the other person in ways the other immediately recognizes as more than what he or she, up to that moment, could have expressed. What many therapists seem to regard as synonymous with empathy—paraphrasing or mirroring what the other person has said—we train our clients to try their best not to do. Paraphrasing or mirroring prevents empathy because it sets the wrong goal for the empathizer, encourages the wrong emotional tone, and does little if anything to further the other person's self-acceptance or self-understanding. In fact, hearing paraphrasing repeatedly, and, of course, not experiencing the compassion that is engendered by the identification with the other that makes true empathy possible, very frequently makes the recipient feel that he or she is at the receiving end of word games or mind games, and that the paraphraser is insincere or lacks genuine interest. If that happens, the other person is hurt rather than helped.

Using the educational approach to start the process of eliciting suppressed or repressed emotion will be illustrated in the "Case Example" section of this chapter. When any statements at all are made by other parties during that type of self-exploration, they would be empathic responses. Empathic responses also continuously help to clarify and bring out underlying and deeper feelings in the ordinary course of RE couple therapy. That process was illustrated earlier, in the example where the therapist helped the husband to call to mind and to feel at that particular moment the positive feelings underlying his anger toward his wife. Here we will illustrate its use by a wife rather than a therapist, through a dialogue showing her husband's beginning recognition of anger and, most important, the fear/anxiety that prevents the full recognition and expression of his anger; anxiety that promotes withdrawal in the service of escaping anger. (More actual emoting of anger would occur later, with the help of Modeling from the therapist in accord with the wife's preference for having her husband express anger instead of withdrawing and her consequent reinforcement of the direct expression of anger rather than indirect expressions.)

HUSBAND: No. I don't withdraw because I'm angry. I withdraw because I don't see any point in continuing to discuss an issue, let alone argue about it, when we aren't getting anywhere. When it's clear we are just never going to see eye to eye on something, I like to let it alone right there.

WIFE: So your withdrawal is a rational act and not a result of anger. You just don't want to remain in conflict with me when you know it's not going to lead anywhere. You don't like it when the heat starts to build up without any light being generated.

HUSBAND: That's right, exactly.

WIFE: It's important to you to keep things as peaceful as possible, especially when you know we're not going to agree anyway.

HUSBAND: Exactly.

WIFE: When things aren't moving toward any rational solution and I start to get mad, you want to end it right there.

HUSBAND: Yes. What would be the point of us getting all steamed up for nothing?

WIFE: So when I keep going on like that—being mad—to you it's like, "Why won't she stop?" It's irritating.

HUSBAND: Yes, it is.

WIFE: Annoying.

HUSBAND: Yes.

WIFE: You can feel some annoyance building up, some anger about to begin, and you want to nip it in the bud.

HUSBAND: Yes. I don't like the feeling. Never have.

WIFE: There's a certain amount of anxiety about really getting angry.

HUSBAND: That's true.

WIFE: A fear of your anger and of mine, too, because my anger starts to trigger yours.

HUSBAND: Yes.

As the above dialogue illustrates, routine RE procedure used to assist clients to express their deepest levels of feeling is to *have the intimate, rather than the therapist, provide the empathy whenever possible.* For example, Sue would provide that helping function, whenever her skill level was such as to be able to handle the emotions being generated within herself and within Dan, with routine supervisory help from the therapist. Such routine help includes, predominantly, Modeling or Prompting for the Expresser, or Modeling or Prompting for the Empathic Responder. When it is judged in advance that Dan or Sue will have too much difficulty, or when that proves unexpectedly to be the case, the therapist brings into play less frequently used RE techniques, such as Becoming for the Expresser or Laundering (Snyder & Guerney, in press), to assist clients to reach and express their deepest level of feeling.

The effect of empathic responding is, first, to clarify and deepen the feeling and enhance the client's ability to express emotions openly and fully. In the process of clarification and emotional expression, the emotion changes and other emotions replace them that, in turn, are deepened, clarified, and change. Thus, for example, if annoyance is responded to empathically, anger might surface; if anger is responded to empathically, rage may surface; if rage is responded to empathically, fury or hostility may emerge; and when that is responded to empathically—especially if the person who is the target of the hostility is the one who is being empathic—then, if such feelings also exist, expressions of concern, compassion, and love toward that same person follow naturally.

Many would see the movement from fury and hostility toward one's empathic partner to expression of concern, compassion, and love as a great and surprising leap. But our experience is that deep, prolonged empathy frequently produces abrupt turnarounds in feelings and in perceptions of oneself and others: for example, blaming others changes to self-blame, denial to intense guilt, intense guilt to self-acceptance, and even hatred to love. Deep, compassionate empathy from a person you love, especially in the face of your own rage, acts like a powerful drug, a renew-love potion if you will. Psychopaths and sadists excepted, it seems almost impossible for a person to remain hostile for more than 30 to 60 minutes in the face of sustained, deeply compassionate empathy from a loved one. And what emerges after some such time are compassion, concern, forgiveness, and love. (The process may have to be repeated many times where the anger has run long and deep.) It is well for therapists, especially marital therapists, to frequently remind themselves that, as Somerset Maugham observed, there is only a razor's edge between love and hate. The distance can be as short when moving back to love as when moving away from it.

So, deepening awareness and expressing emotions under conditions of unconditional, compassionate acknowledgment bring into play other feelings. These, in the case of intimates who do in fact love each other, turn out in the end to be concern, compassion, affection, and love. If very strong negative emotions exist and cannot emerge into the light of day, or are not compassionately acknowledged by their target, the positive feelings are much less likely ever to fully emerge either.

If, and when, it becomes evident that, say, Sue has feelings no one would expect her to have, or conversely fails to have feelings that almost anyone would expect her to have under a particular set of interpersonal circumstances, that will represent a mystery to all concerned. Dr. Smith will then suggest that an effort be made to recapture feelings from the past that could conceivably be related to that mystery. If Dr. Smith has some idea as to the general area in which such repressed or strongly suppressed feelings may lie—perhaps, for example, long-past physical or sexual abuse—and neither Sue nor Dan has any other ideas, Dr. Smith might educate Sue about suppression/repression and suggest that Sue attempt to recapture feelings about that aspect of her life.

Frequently, because of the natural resistance to exposing oneself to the very pain that caused the suppression/repression in the first place, it is necessary to explain the rationale for doing this, to repeat the instructions, and to encourage the client several times before the client actually begins to recapture the feelings. Once it does happen, it is amazing how often the much-scorned "hydraulic" Freudian metaphor does seem apropos: the rush of feelings is like water through a burst dam. Insight, changes in perceptions of self, and changes in perceptions of one's partner often follow. Needless to say, one has to allow sufficient time for the person to submerge and resurface from such an experience, and the effort should not even be attempted if one does not have ample time in which to work. Once the dam breaks, usually the best empathic response one can give is an "awe-full" silence, as the person may commence an emotion-filled reexperience and soliloquy lasting a half hour or more. The nonverbal empathy and support the partner, or, if necessary, the therapist, can give is considerable, and verbal empathy usually precedes and follows the emotional reexperience.

Relationship enhancement theory holds that the best person to provide empathic support in such situations, as well as in less dramatic ones, is the person who created the emotion to begin with, and the next best one is another intimate, such as a spouse. In addition to the reasons earlier indicated, being a midwife to such a rebirth of emotion, and the birth of new feelings and perceptions that often follows it, has a very strong bonding effect. It seems highly desirable that an intimate, in this case the spouse, receive the benefit of such bonding rather than the therapist, since it is highly therapeutic for a relationship. Also, having an intimate such as the spouse be completely accepting and understanding, despite the revelation of events and/or feelings the individual considers shameful, is much more therapeutic than if the acceptance comes from a therapist, who after all is being *paid* to be accepting and who, in any case, could not match the emotional power of acceptance by a mother, father, husband, or wife.

Moreover, no mere retelling of what happened, and certainly no mere sharing of the intellectual fruits of the event, can convey to intimates what they see for themselves in the power of the emotions. As a result of being the midwife at an emotional rebirth, intimates can develop a depth of understanding and a level of compassion not possible in any other way. For similar reasons, if an intimate cannot play this therapeutic role because of a lack of skill or insufficient emotional strength, the next best thing is to have the intimate silently present while the therapist does so. Finally, if the person who needs to reexperience past emotions requires privacy with the therapist to do so, it is desirable for that client and the therapist to inform the intimate about the experience and its fruits as soon as possible, while the emotional component remains fresh.

CASE EXAMPLE

As a case example, I've chosen one that demonstrates the expression of deep emotion out of the past to unblock progress in a marital therapy case. The pseudonyms we shall use are Ann and Bob, a blue-collar couple in their thirties, each divorced, and with two children from her prior marriage. They had been married about 5 years, and a couple of years back had marital counseling, which they considered unsuccessful. They were now on the verge of divorce, with Ann indicating that unless her husband made many drastic changes, she would divorce him. They had many problems, but all involved the need for Bob to make drastic changes in the way he behaved in a wide variety of areas. Bob regarded his wife highly and was eager to preserve the marriage. The only good thing that Ann could bring herself to say about her husband was that he was a steady, if not a good, provider. The transcript chosen was made from a videotape of the fifteenth therapy session. By this point, both were highly skilled and had resolved many issues, both through discussion within the therapist's office and at home, and most of these involved agreements on Bob's part to change various aspects of his behavior— the way he dressed, his willingness to help around the house, his interaction with the children and friends, the way he spoke to Ann, and so on. However, it had become evident to all concerned that these changes did not succeed in warming Ann's feelings toward Bob or decreasing her icy criticalness. Every change made seemed only to lead to new requests for changes. On many occasions, Bob revealed his very deep feelings of love and high regard. Ann showed no satisfaction and no reciprocity at those times. They seemed to serve simply to renew her determination to make more changes in Bob. This puzzled us all. So I explained to Ann how past emotional experiences may block or distort current feelings and encouraged her to explore and attempt to reexperience past feelings that might relate in some unknown way to these (lack of) feelings. She chose to try to recapture her feelings of sexual abuse at the hands of her father, which began when she was a preteenager. This effort had begun the preceding week, and when she came in this week for the couple's fifteenth session, she indicated that she had to force herself to come because of the unpleasant feelings explored the week before. She talked about needing to heal a wound and feeling "hollow" as a result of that session. I asked her to speak to Bob about those feelings and asked Bob to remain solely in the Empathic mode.

The following transcript involves only a few omissions to shorten the text (indicated by dots or explained in brackets). The descriptions of mood (in capital letters) come not from the author, but from the transcriptionist (a layperson), who was given a comprehensive list of feeling-related adjectives to use to describe what she heard on the audiotape.

ANN: OPEN: I guess some of the things that I said or found out about myself is [*sic*] like digging really deep with a shovel in the dirt and uprooting. But you didn't fill the hole back in, so it's just open and there. I couldn't remember the question he [*the therapist*] kept asking me and got me frustrated then. [*There had been no specific questions, only the suggestion that she try to be specific about her feelings.*] I thought of some feelings; they were feelings that I had to get to, and, umm, I guess that's the kind of hollow feeling. INSECURE: I remember thinking when I left, well I had found out some more feelings or whatever about not respecting myself [*trailed off here*], but, umm, I guess if you find out bad things about yourself, you want to replace that with the good things, or something to kind of make it kind of fill it in, umm, or be able to change it or fix it or something. And, I don't feel that I have done that.

THERAPIST: SENSITIVE: Ann, could you again be more specific about these bad things, what the things were that made you feel bad about yourself. [*Ann well understands that specificity is the second guideline of Expressive skill, and in other contexts, she had not had any difficulty in complying with that guideline.*]

ANN: FEARFUL: Umm, I umm, just when you said that I feel like I'm gonna cry again. I don't know what triggers that or why. ENRAGED: I hate that! What does that? You did it last week, too! There was just something that was said and then all of a sudden I need to cry and I don't understand why. I don't know why! [*crying now*]. WOUNDED: What the bad things about myself are—I think that's it—the things that I found out that I didn't like about myself. Why is that so hard? I guess I always think that I'm a good person and I'm not bad, but somehow I must feel that I'm bad, umm, and that I've done bad things. And that must be really hard to accept. I don't know! FRAGILE: Umm, not respecting myself, that was something that I remember was very hard to say and to think about. And just say it, you know. Because when you say it out loud, it kind of makes it, umm, *there*! And I, I don't want to do that, I don't want to think about it and have to look at, and categorize, and say, well, certain things were bad and certain things were good. PAINED: But it's like [here in the therapy sessions] I can't just talk about the things that happened; it's like I have to *label* them. So, I must *feel* that they're bad or they're good, so I have to *say* whether they're bad or they're good and [*trailing off*]. TENSE: I know I *hated* myself for putting up with what I put up with, with my father, and I [*trailing off again—deep sigh*], and I wanted to get away from it and I couldn't. And I thought of running away, but I didn't have any place to go and [*trailing off*]. INSECURE: But I think that's worse, to have to stay and hate yourself and not stop it and, umm, *just not like yourself*! That's really bad. And to have to live with yourself and then, on top of it, to have to *prove* yourself to your parents, you know, [to prove] that you are a good person, or that you are smart, or that you can do something when they'd call me dumb and stuff. HURT: And then I know I started to believe it. REGRETFUL: I guess I always felt I had to prove myself to them somehow, but I never quite was able to. And when I didn't do well in school, and I was grounded for a 9-week period because I didn't do well in school and stayed in my room all the time and, ummm [*trailing off, sighing*]. I know—for business school—I knew that they—I did it for them, but then I didn't go through with it. And, of course, disappointed them again. And felt awful about myself again, and then when I married John [*her first husband*], they didn't like that! PAINED: And it's like one thing after another, always wanting their approval, not getting it, feeling terrible, doing something else—I wouldn't say worse—but right along the line always doing something that made me feel *terrible* about myself later on. [That's what] the outcome was. At the time when I made the decision, I always felt, well, this will either get me out of this at the time or this is the right thing to do, or whatever. HURT: And in the end of almost every decision, I have always felt bad and terrible, that I couldn't make the right decision, and that I just wasn't given the opportunity to make decisions in my life. And I see that now and feel badly about that [*sigh*].

[*Author's note: To save space, I have eliminated two areas of content here. Both, like all of this excerpt, were strongly emotional. In the first, Ann elaborated on the restrictions placed on her independent decision making by her mother. In the second, Ann described how, several years back, due to a brief lapse in her oversight of her child, her father succeeded in performing a sexual act with Ann's young daughter, and Ann, full of fury, described her determination never to leave the two of them alone again. These were all part of a continuous heart-wrenching monologue, without comment from the therapist or Bob. She then went on as follows.*]

DETERMINED: And the children's self-esteem is so important to me, and I praise them and I make them feel good about themselves! EMPHATIC, CONVINCED: Because I don't like myself! No matter what I do [*pausing, thinking*]—being a good mother, having you so proud of me about different things that I do (even though I don't feel they're any big deal), it doesn't make any difference. Somehow, there's never gonna be enough stuff that's gonna make me feel good about me!

This cathartic self-exploration led Ann to the insight that her continual demands on Bob, and her unwillingness to acknowledge his efforts and his love, stemmed from her own extremely poor self-image. She realized that in order to prevent herself from acknowledging her own poor self-image, she kept telling herself that everything would be okay if only Bob would make all of these changes. She indicated that she *needed* to not acknowledge his progress in any significant way, because she needed to feel that he was in continual need of improvement. That way she was able to avoid looking at her own self-contempt. As long as it was *he* who needed improvement, and as long as they were working on *him*, she could go on avoiding facing her own poor self-concept. But she had also recognized later in that same session that she was totally a victim and had no real basis for any self-contempt. As she put it, "I was born into the family that I was born into, and I was essentially doomed because there *was* nothing I could do.... When you were born into that family, that's it!" As a result of the cathartic experience and resulting insights, both her self-concept and the couple's relationship improved dramatically. Her self-confidence, and even the way that she groomed and dressed, improved very quickly and noticeably. And with respect to Bob, she said she was determined to relate to him as a husband, not as a child who needed constantly to be monitored and improved. Ann's use of a projective defense mechanism—it was Bob, not she, who was so unworthy—probably had its beginning very early in the relationship with what I call the Groucho Marx syndrome. Groucho said, "I wouldn't belong to any club that would have me as a member." Ann probably thought early in their marriage, "Bob can't be very worthwhile/lovable if he wants somebody as unworthy/unlovable as me." By virtue of its power to help her forget the second part of that thought, thereby reducing the anxiety with which her self-contempt was associated, the first part of the thought was strongly reinforced and would be called into play whenever the self-contempt threatened to surface.

CONCLUDING COMMENT

This case illustrates two things. The first is that in encouraging Ann to pursue her darkest, most dreaded feelings, the RE therapist pursues emotional truth fearlessly, no matter how dark or negative it may appear. This really is an application in one specific area of the broader (Rogerian) principle that the RE therapist seeks to help clients reveal and face whatever is true for them at the moment, regardless of where that threatens to lead. I think this is not as trivial or as much of a cliché as many readers might think: it is not always easy to resist the temptation to offer reassurance, or to "reframe" the moment's phenomenological truth in the presumed service of promoting "marital adjustment," "problem solving," or "personality development." I believe that in the long run the unfailing pursuit of the deepest levels of emotional truth does not really conflict with promoting better adjustment. But that is not always the way it seems at the moment. So, for a neophyte RE therapist, until it can gain credence based on case experience, this particular aspect of RE practice must derive from faith in this undergirding, this philosophical principle of following truth wherever it threatens to lead.

Second, the case illustrates the way in which the RE theoretical framework integrates aspects of humanistic, psychodynamic, behavioral, and interpersonal principles and practices into a skill-training, multilevel system framework. In the case example, recognition that defense mechanisms probably were at work, and that a cathartic experience possibly would lead to insight, is based on psychodynamic theory. All the empathy and compassion Ann had experienced, especially from her husband, throughout the therapy, freed her enough from fear and imparted her with enough emotional strength to experience catharsis. Of course, the empathy and compassion were there because of humanistic (Rogerian) theory and techniques. The methods used in RE to teach that empathy and compassion derive from social-learning and reinforcement theories. The entire idea of using spouses as psychotherapeutic agents for their own relationship and to promote personality change is rooted in interpersonal theory. The idea that one can change the individual system (Ann) by changing a relationship system (Ann-Bob), derives from family system thinking. And, finally, the idea that one also can change a family system, or as in this case, the Ann-Bob couple system, by changing the intrapsychic component of an individual system (Ann) is best expressed in a multilevel Living System Treatment Framework (Guerney & Ford, 1993).

REFERENCES

Dollard, J., & Miller, N. E. (1950). *Personality and psychotherapy.* New York: McGraw-Hill.

Ford, D. H. (1987). *Humans as self-constructing living systems: A developmental perspective on behavior and personality.* Hillsdale, NJ: Erlbaum.

Fraillon, J. M. G., Guerney, B. G., Jr., Kirschner, D. A., & Kirschner, S. (1990). The adopted sister: Case study and points of contention and convergence. In J. C. Norcross & N. Saltzman (Eds.), *Therapy wars: Contention and convergence in differing clinical approaches* (pp. 218ff). San Francisco: Jossey-Bass.

Guerney, B. G., Jr. (1969). *Psychotherapeutic agents: New roles for nonprofessionals, parents, and teachers.* New York: Holt, Rinehart & Winston.

Guerney, B. G., Jr. (1977). *Relationship enhancement: Skill–training programs for therapy, problem prevention and enrichment.* San Francisco: Jossey-Bass.

Guerney, B. G., Jr. (1982). The delivery of mental health services: Spiritual vs. medical vs. educational models. In T. R. Vallance & R. M. Sabre (Eds.), *Mental health services in transition: A policy sourcebook* (pp. 219–255). New York: Human Sciences Press.

Guerney, B. G., Jr. (1983). Marital and family relationship enhancement therapy. In P. Keller & L. Ritt (Eds.), *Innovations in clinical practice: A source book* (Vol. III, pp. 40–53). Sarasota, FL: Professional Resource Exchange.

Guerney, B. G., Jr. (1989). *Relationship enhancement manual*. State College, PA: IDEALS.

Guerney, B. G., Jr. (1991). *The dozen deadly sins*. Unpublished one-page document.

Guerney, B. G., Jr., & Ford, D. (1993). *Family therapy and a multi-level Living Systems Framework*. Unpublished manuscript.

Guerney, B. G., Jr., Stollak, G., & Guerney, L. F. (1970). A format for a new mode of psychological practice: Or, how to escape a zombie. *Counseling Psychologist, 2*(2), 970–1005.

Snyder, M., & Guerney, B. G., Jr. (in press). Brief marital/family therapy: The relationship enhancement approach. In R. Wells & V. Giannetti (Eds.), *A casebook of brief psychotherapies*. New York: Plenum.

Staats, A. W., & Eifert, G. H. (1990). The paradigmatic behaviorism theory of emotions: Basis for unification. *Clinical Psychology Review, 10*, 539–566.

SECTION C

Systemic Approaches

7

Emotion in the Context of Systemic Marital Therapy

SHARON GLICK MILLER

The popular notion of marital therapy brings to mind images of noisy, arguing couples or those resigned to lives of quiet despair. Indeed, the marital therapist enters an emotional arena. With its absence being indifference, emotion is connection, and the patterns of emotional expression determine the quality of that connection. Yet, while emotion is key in work with couples, so too are other forms of behavior. In fact, emotion overlaps with other realms of functioning: it is the somatic girding of our behavior, it is a source of information, and it is a means of communication.

This chapter will focus on the issue of emotion in marital therapy. Essential aspects of emotion and their implications will be outlined. Some of the affective issues that present in various stages of therapy and their management will then be highlighted and illustrated with a case example.

A SYSTEMIC VIEW OF EMOTION: IMPLICATIONS FOR THERAPY

Talking about emotion as distinct from cognition or behavior poses a dilemma. These traditional categories imply a more rigid division than may have originally been intended (Zerubavel, 1991), in which connections between them and the way in which living systems operate are obscured. Yet, at the same time, such distinctions are essential to making sense of life, and when we view emotion systemically, the complex reciprocal process between the many interdependent variables comes into view. Emotion may be viewed as a system in its own right, incorporating processes ranging from the neurophysiology of emotional arousal to the cultural shaping of emotional experience and expression, existing in a temporal and relational context (Campos, Campos, & Barrett, 1989; Greenberg & Safran, 1987). The individual-in-context is the basic unit for analysis, as emotion is an appraisal of our rela-

151

tionship to the environment (Lazarus, 1991).   Functionally, the following premises are recognized as essential to our understanding of emotion, and each has implications for therapy.

1. *Emotions have a biological basis.* Darwin (1872/1965) first drew attention to the universality of emotions and their role in survival. Extensive cross-cultural research suggests the universality of such emotions as anger, disgust, fear, happiness, sadness, and surprise (Ekman, 1980, 1984). While cultural factors shape our experience and provide different elicitors, display rules, and coping skills, these emotions all present with a distinct pattern of facial, postural, vocal, behavioral, autonomic, and central nervous system responses. The experience of physiological arousal is a necessary condition for the experience of emotion (Berscheid, 1983). Genetics is also a factor underlying individual differences in temperament or emotionality (Buss & Plomin, 1975; Plutchik, 1988).

These physiological underpinnings of emotion must sometimes be addressed by the therapist. For example, to alter a sequence in which an individual reactively lashes out, the therapist may direct attention to somatic feelings of arousal that signal increasing tension: "Can you tell when you are beginning to get upset? What do you feel in your body?" By focusing on the somatic precursors to the usual response, the client is more able to interrupt the sequence and substitute a different action.

Individual differences in temperament also need to be recognized and addressed. In some cases, it is necessary to help individuals become aware of their proneness to a high level of emotionality and identify those conditions that exacerbate it (such as alcohol intake or sleep deprivation). There are other times when an extreme affective response may benefit from pharmacological intervention.

2. *Emotion provides important information about the self in interaction with the environment.* Emotion may be regarded as "a type of information processing" (Greenberg & Safran, 1987, p. 147). This information has a motivational and organizational function. It amplifies goals and energizes behavior (Safran & Greenberg, 1991; Frijda, 1986; Campos & Barrett, 1984). Although our experience would suggest that emotion comes and goes in relation to certain behaviors or events, it is ever present. We are usually most aware of it, however, when a shift occurs, as when movement toward a goal is frustrated or when we have conflicting goals (Efran, Lukens, & Lukens, 1990; Berscheid, 1983).

Given that the emotions provide important information about oneself in relation to a context, the therapist will want to be alert to difficulties individuals may have in attending to their emotions. Wishes or feelings that remain unexpressed cannot be met or addressed. Over time, this may contribute to individual and/or marital unhappiness. The "processing" or "languaging" of emotional experience in the context of marital therapy can lead to new information for both spouses and the emergence of a more adaptive response (Daldrup, Beutler, Greenberg, & Engle, 1988; Efran et al., 1990; Greenberg & Johnson, 1988; Greenberg & Safran, 1987).

The therapist also accesses information from his or her own emotional system and uses it as a guide in therapy. Much of clinical instinct is the use of such information within the context of a conceptional model of therapeutic intervention.

3. *Emotions dispose us to action.* Emotions play a role in motivating and organizing our behavior. Clinicians frequently see emotional response patterns that have developed in one context and, while adaptive in that context, are maladaptive in another. For example, withdrawing in fear at the first sign of upset may have been an adaptive emotional response for a child with an alcoholic parent, but such avoidance will impede conflict resolution in a subsequent marriage. Making this conceptional link for individuals, along with outlining a new behavioral strategy, is often sufficient to elicit change.

4. *Emotion, like all behavior, is communication.* Like any communication, a display of emotion gives both a report and a message about the report, or metacommunication (Watzlawick, Beavin, & Jackson, 1967). The report, conveyed digitally with words, is interpreted in light of the analogic information accompanying it, conveyed through such things as voice tone, gesture, and gaze. Emphasis has been placed on the need for the clinician to clarify ambiguities or discrepancies between the digital and analogic levels of communication. This may be true with emotional messages as well. For example, while the content of the message may be an angry attack, nonverbal cues may indicate hurt. Here the clinician would clarify both messages: I am hurt: hurting me will not be tolerated. Without amplifying the report of hurt and without removing the metacommunicational command, one is confronted with the paradoxical message "I am hurting you to show you that hurtful behavior will not be tolerated" and a partner who is likely to respond with symmetrical conflict-escalating behavior. Expressing the message in a softer way facilitates a more desired response from the partner and allows both to examine the transaction. Sometimes nonverbal cues will indicate that the expression of a feeling has an instrumental or manipulative intent. Here, too, clarification by the therapist may facilitate change.

5. *Emotions have a cultural basis.* We are cultural beings. We live in a world of culturally constituted symbols (words, rituals). To understand our behavior, we need to understand these symbols and the meaning we attach to them. Feelings are aroused from the meaning we attribute to these symbols. Because we are products of different cultural training, especially at the level of the family culture, this meaning and the feelings it arouses may not be shared by our spouse. Clarifying the misunderstandings that arise from the different interpretations given to the same event, as well as introducing new meaning, is an important part of therapy.

The cultural shaping of emotions can supersede biological impulses. Even a strong drive like hunger can be ignored in the face of culture, as when Jews or Moslems fast on designated religious holidays, or when some women severely restrict their food intake to achieve the cultural norm of thinness. Culture also shapes our perceptual abilities. People "develop culture-specific perceptual skills that enable them to detect subtle cues that outsiders are unlikely to notice" (Bock, 1988, p. 9). Experienced clinicians respond to subtle nuances in tone and gestures that may be imperceptible to the student. In a similar fashion, the spouse of an abusive partner may be exquisitely sensitive to signs of potential conflict.

6. *Emotion is a part of an interactive process in human functioning.* Cognitive and behavioral appraisal fuels our experience of emotion. There is concordance between feelings, thoughts, and actions. When people say they think one thing and feel another, they are reporting conflicting desires, one of which they label rational and the other emotional. It seems that when we can provide deductive reasoning, we call it thought, and when we cannot, we call it emotion. Perhaps emotion is best regarded as nonlineal cognition.

The interplay between affect, behavior, cognition, and the relational environment has been addressed in a significant body of work (e.g., Lazarus, 1991; Safran & Greenberg, 1991; Campos, et al., 1989; Greenberg & Johnson, 1988; Bandura, 1986; Lazarus, Coyne, & Folkman, 1982). Different models of marital therapy also reflect this interplay, although more implicitly than explicitly. For example, a cognitive-behavioral approach may clearly address affective issues (e.g., Baucom & Epstein, 1990). The overlap in the techniques used in behavioral marital therapy and insight-oriented marital therapy also speaks to this issue (Jacobson, 1991). Further, behavioral approaches that do not integrate an emotional focus may not be as effective in sustaining improvements in marital satisfaction (Snyder, Wills, & Grady-Fletcher, 1991).

7. *Emotion is a relational process.* Emotions have a regulatory function in relationships (Campos et al., 1989). Emotional display or expression becomes part of a complex feedback process in a social system. A's emotion has an impact on B, whose response has an impact on A. One may delineate a sequence of provocation, response or reaction, and outcome. Marital therapists intervene to alter this sequence.

From this initial review, we see that emotion is a biocultural phenomenon that provides information to the individual-in-context. Some emotional issues that manifest in marital therapy will be reviewed next.

EMOTIONAL ISSUES IN SYSTEMIC MARITAL THERAPY

Many issues in marital therapy may be framed as emotional. Here I chose to discuss some that emerge when there is only marginal commitment to the marriage. Although such cases are common, the process by which one engages and maintains ambivalent couples in therapy is not often discussed. A case example is used to illustrate this process. First, however, the framework that guides this work will be reviewed. It is shaped by the principles of systemic therapy, goals that emerge from a model of marital functioning, and some of the emotional issues that present in the various stages of therapy.

Definition of Systemic Therapy

Systemic therapy applies systems thinking to clinical practice. It is an orientation and not a specific set of techniques. While family therapy was one of the first applications of systems thinking to the clinical domain, other approaches and disciplines have now integrated some of these principles (Ford & Lerner, 1992; Liddle, 1991; Capra, 1982).

Functionally, systemic therapy may be defined as "an approach in which a therapist (or a team of therapists), working with varying combinations and configurations of people, devises and introduces interventions designed to alter the interaction (process, workings) of the interpersonal system and context within which one or more psychiatric/behavioral human problems are embedded, and thereby also alters the functioning of the individuals within that system, with the goal of alleviating or eliminating the problems" (Stanton, 1988, p. 9). Key components in this definition are the active stance of the therapist (who determines with whom to meet and introduces interventions) and the focus on process and interpersonal context. Also implied, and more explicitly addressed elsewhere, is the focus on improving the functioning of both the individuals and the interpersonal system, such as the marriage or family (Gurman, 1988). Systemic therapy necessitates a multidimensional approach (Liddle, Dakof, & Diamond, 1990), in which there is a focus on each individual as a system, the system that is the primary interpersonal context in which the problem is embedded (marital or family), as well as the other related systems (e.g., family of origin, work, therapeutic).

From within a systemic view, the boundary between individual and marital therapy becomes blurred as self and system are seen as coevolved or reciprocally determined. A change in individual functioning changes the context of the marriage and vice versa. Change is therefore targeted at both the self (subsystem) and the marital system.

To talk about targets of change may be a convenient way to code therapist behavior, but it imparts an inaccurate view of intervention. Therapists do not act upon a system. They act as part of a newly formed therapeutic system composed of client(s) and therapist. Some of what they bring to the system may generate change. However, because living systems are self-organizing and self-generative, what impacts a system and what is generated from such impact are not predictable. Although we may act in a way that generates change, we cannot say that the intervention caused the change.

Why then all focus on intervention techniques? Just because we cannot introduce change in a cause-and-effect way does not mean that we should be inert or neutral, even if that were possible. As long as we understand that we "cannot anticipate that everything will work out as expected" (Efran et al., 1990, p. 191), we can continue to strategize. There are enough commonalities in how we function that we may proceed with guidelines.

While a systemic approach tempers some notions we may have about changing others, it expands interventions by recognizing the multiple pathways to change. To have any impact, the therapist must act in a way that is congruent with a particular system at a particular time (de Shazer, 1984; Anderson & Stewart, 1983). This implies a wide repertoire. The pragmatism that has been an essential feature of family systems approaches has resulted in the development of many interventions, as well as the incorporation of interventions from other modalities.

Delineating Therapeutic Goals

The issue for any therapy is what to do, in what order, and by what means. While the determination of what to do is situation specific, certain redundancies help us formulate a model of effective couple interaction and identify therapeutic goals. Core issues present around (1) autonomy, (2) conflict resolution, and (3) intimacy.

Autonomy

From a systemic perspective, autonomy refers to a state of being *within* a relationship. This should not be mistaken for something that exists at the expense of intimacy or connectedness. Autonomy is a relative term, since one cannot be independent of one's environment. The self, while in constant interaction with the environment and defined in relation to that context, has some degree of organization that is autonomous. For example, one can have goals that may be seen as (more) internally defined. While infants and young children are extremely dependent upon external control, this lessens with maturation.

Implied in the notion of autonomy is responsibility (Foerster, 1984). Functionally, it is the willingness and ability to understand one's own contribution to an interactional sequence and to take responsibility for one's feelings and actions. Although transactions are reciprocally determined, the degree to which one simply reacts, as opposed to responding in a more planful way, can vary depending on one's level of autonomy.

Increased autonomy is always a therapeutic goal. It is often one of the first targets for therapeutic change in that a certain degree of autonomy is a prerequisite for work on dyadic issues.

Conflict Resolution

Communicating clearly and directly about issues, as well as being able to resolve conflicts, is key to marital satisfaction. Problems with conflict resolution can reliably distinguish distressed from nondistressed couples (Markman, 1984; Billings, 1979; Gottman, 1979). Although stated in behavioral terms, this has affective implications. To be able to articulate clearly one's feelings implies an ability to access and appraise them. To be able to engage in joint problem solving about emotionally charged issues implies an ability to contain negative affect or express it in a way that does not escalate the conflict. It also implies the ability to be empathic to the feelings of the other. Differences are tolerated without one feeling threatened and/or criticized.

Intimacy

Some understanding of how to achieve and maintain intimacy in a marriage can also be important. Intimacy may be defined as the "inconstant subjective side of relatedness, the sharing of personal feelings, fantasies and affectively meaningful experience ...the multi-faceted, elaborated relatedness for those who have grown beyond the basic stage of attachment and care-giving" (Wynne, 1989, p. 310).

There are several prerequisites for the development of intimacy. Problems with autonomy, communication, and conflict resolution will hinder its development. The secure sense of self that is associated with autonomy facilitates relating to others in an intimate manner. Fears of intrusion or of being "swallowed up" by the personality of the other, as well as anxiety about aloneness, impede the development of intimacy. Similarly, problems with communication or conflict resolution will prevent the increased mutuality that emerges from the exchange of personal feelings and mutually satisfactory joint problem solving. Because autonomy, communication, and conflict resolution are prerequisites to the development of intimacy, marital therapists will usually address problems in these areas first.

There is also a structural or behavioral prerequisite to intimacy in that a couple must spend some time together or the relationship will erode. Many dual-career couples spend their free time as family time, leaving the spouses with little time for each other. Unless the couple is ambivalent about the relationship and would find spending time together stressful, the therapist may address this structural arrangement immediately by suggesting that a couple spend some ritualized time together. This needs to be a time where both can feel relaxed and somewhat protected from the pressure of outside demands. Decreased tension and a feeling of increased closeness can result from this change alone, while therapy then addresses the (other) problems that brought them to therapy.

Structurally, then, the couple must have adequate access to each other. They must be able to share intimate feelings and resolve conflict. Any psychological impediments to intimacy, such as fears of dependency, rejection, or intrusion, must also be addressed.

When we highlight these issues, a static notion of the marital dyad as a system is conveyed inadvertently. Living systems are certainly not static. As such, a couple may be seen as a system (of "selves") evolving through time, and it is helpful to view the presenting problems within a temporal context. One may track the coevolution of the onset of problems and/or the timing of seeking help with other events in the system. This can provide important clues as to what may need to be addressed in therapy. In the case illustrated below, the husband sought therapy after the death of his father. It emerged that his choice of marital partner had been influenced by his father's approval and now he "felt free" to reconsider his marriage.

Temporal issues also affect how a client experiences a situation. Feelings about the past or the future impinge on present behavior. When there is a history of long-term marital unhappiness, it is not uncommon to hear expressed a fear that "working on the relationship" will lead to "being stuck in a bad marriage" with "no energy to try to leave again." This fear of where therapy may lead is an example of when feelings about the future must be addressed in therapy. Fears that therapy might propel one toward divorce or leave one dealing with the loss of the fantasized future relationship with another are additional examples.

In a similar fashion, feelings from the past can influence behavior in the present. There is a strong link between emotions and memory. A "reaction to stimulation may last as little as a fraction of a second, but an emotional response may endure for hours, days, or even longer and thus prolong the stimulation that leads to behavior" (Scott, 1988, p. 25). This potentially adaptive function of memory may become problematic and a focus of therapy.

Not only do we experience process across time, we also experience it across space, in different contexts. Each spouse participates in outside systems (e.g., work, peer group, family of origin) that may influence the marriage. Concerns about the job performance, concentration on career development to the neglect of personal and family well being, a friend's reinforcement of a spouse's negative traits, and turning more to a friend than to one's spouse are all examples of participation in these other systems, which clearly influence the marital dyad.

The marital dyad itself is also influenced by issues in the family. Problems with merging different parenting styles and goals, coping with the inevitable worries and frustrations, or dividing a myriad of tasks to the mutual satisfaction of both partners are potential negative influences. Confronted with such stressors, many couples resort to blaming each other. Feelings of loss or failure in the face of infertility or miscarriage can also precipitate marital distress.

Emotional Issues as They Present in Key Stages of Marital Therapy

There are many emotional issues that are a common feature of therapy. They operate not only between the two partners, but also between the therapist and each member of the marital dyad. Some of these issues will be discussed as they emerge in various stages of therapy: (1) engagement, (2) stabilization, (3) clarification, and (4) resolution. It should be remembered that such a demarcation of stages is an arbitrary punctuation of a flow of experience.

Engagement

The development of a positive working relationship between the therapist and client(s) is seen as essential in all forms of therapy (Bordin, 1976; Marguiles & Havens, 1981; Marzali, Marmar, & Krupnik, 1981; Luborsky, McLellan, Woody, O'Brien, & Auerbach 1985). Any impediments in developing such an alliance should therefore be addressed, as should any "ruptures" that may occur in the ongoing process of the therapy (Safran & Segal, 1990).

Feeling understood is primary for the client to develop a positive working alliance. Merely reflecting what the client has said, or providing words of support, will usually not result in empathy. Rather, it develops when the therapist conveys that he or she understands by, to some degree, feeling what the client is feeling, validating those feelings (while not necessarily the behaviors associated with them), and conveying willingness and sureness in working with them.

The direction provided by the therapist is a key element in the successful formation of a working alliance, perhaps because it contributes to feelings of trust. Providing insufficient structure or direction in the early phase of marital therapy is associated with negative outcome (Gurman & Kniskern, 1978). The direction offered should not only reflect the conceptual map of the therapist for therapy, but also evolve from where the couple is emotionally and what the emotionally salient issues for each member are.

"Joining" is the term coined by Minuchin (1974) and used in the family therapy literature to connote the process of engagement and development of a working alliance. Through the use of the verb form, emphasis is placed on the process and the role of the therapist in it. Underlined is the fact that the therapist must join the family, trying to experience it as an insider. It is only from this "inside" position that change is seen as possible (Minuchin, Rosman, & Baker, 1978). However, while in the same boat as the family, the therapist must also steer the course. Thus, joining is actually a process of joining, disjoining, and rejoining in a differentiated way (Minuchin & Fishman, 1981).

Different issues will present during the engagement phase in couples therapy depending on the nature of the presenting problem (e.g., alcoholism, a recently discovered extramarital affair), the duration of the conflict, and individual coping styles. In general, cases in which commitment to the relationship is weak necessitate a primary emotional focus. Here, individuals have conflicting impulses around staying or leaving the relationship. Such cases make joining somewhat more difficult. There may be a fear that working on the marriage will leave one stuck in a bad marriage, while at the same time there is distress at the thought of divorce. It is rare that both parties will express the same degree of ambivalence about the relationship. Although each may be pessimistic, if one expresses this sentiment, the other will present a more positive stand, as if some systemic equilibrium is at play. Each spouse seems to sense that if he or she echoes the negativity expressed by the other, there will be a certain divorce.

Ambivalence and the emotions underlying it are what is most alive for a couple in this situation. To try to engage them to work on dyadic issues is premature when one or both may be feeling uncertain as to whether that is what they want. Sometimes this lack of commitment to working on the relationship is not articulated explicitly, but will manifest as a lack of progress in the marital therapy until it is addressed by the therapist.

These feelings of ambivalence can be validated and a course of therapy proposed in accordance with them. Validation recognizes that if people have been unhappy for many years, it is understandable that they may be reluctant to commit to more of the same. When there has been little experience of change, there is little faith that anything can change. After these feelings have been validated, a course of therapy is proposed that would be the same whether or not the couple wanted to stay together or to separate. In this way, the ambivalence is sidestepped. The suggested goal of therapy is to sort out the couple's feelings and thoughts and then to articulate them clearly. In the process, some problems may be resolved. After the issues have been clarified, a decision can then be made about continuing to work on the relationship. Most couples experience increased commitment to the marriage. For those who decide to divorce, the process of separating is less vituperative. Perhaps they are aided by an understanding of the issues between them. Perhaps in the process of discussion, there is a shift from breach of contract to a renegotiated one. Knowing that the process may be helpful no matter what the outcome, the therapist can underline that this work should be done whether or not the decision is to stay together or divorce. Because a commitment cannot be made to the marriage, a commitment is made to this work and this process.

Stabilization

One of the therapist's primary tasks is to provide structure and control when needed. This role is usually mentioned when there is risk of potential suicide or violence, but it is also important in less severe and dramatic situations. Therapy must be a safe place emotionally for the articulation of feelings, both within and outside of the office. Mutual recriminations hurled between husband and wife do not facilitate the exploration or resolution of issues. For this reason, teaching and reinforcing conflict-containment skills is often an initial goal in therapy.

When a couple presents with long-standing marital distress, hopeless resignation and distancing may have replaced noisy battles. Stabilization may still be needed, but it usually must address what has been a subtle escalation of interpersonal distance. The partner who has been more overtly distancing is not asked to get closer to the other spouse (which would be too threatening at this point), but is asked to stop distancing. If there is an extramarital relationship, it should be ended, or at least put on hold while the therapy is ongoing. (When there has been an affair, part of stabilization requires individual sessions to help each spouse deal with his or her respective feelings around this.)

Also, as noted above, it is usually one partner who more actively distances while the other assumes the complementary position of wanting the marriage to continue, which may be expressed as "I don't want a divorce, but I don't want things to be the same either." A partner who is guarding against the possibility of divorce may not feel it is safe to raise issues. The therapist should therefore provide reassurances by having the distancing partner commit to the process and put the issue of divorce on hold. The treatment plan, outlined above as part of the engagement process with ambivalent couples, must be rearticulated repeatedly.

The nondistancing spouse may also be reactively angry. Having decided years ago not to act on the fact that many wishes and needs were unmet in the relationship and to somehow make do, he or she may be angry when the other partner now questions the viability of the marriage. Under the anger may be many feelings, such as fear about the future, guilt about not having done more for the other, and doubts about self-worth. Blaming of the other or reactively distancing ("we might as well divorce now") can be interrupted and contained by the therapist. While the intensity of the feeling is validated, the individual is invited to express the "softer" feelings of fear and self-doubt, which alters the dialogue between the couple.

When couples are ambivalent about the relationship and/or on the brink of divorce, it is also helpful to remind them that taking the temperature of the marriage minute to minute is not helpful. What is emphasized instead are key markers of change that will evolve over time. For example, often the first marker of progress is increased autonomy—articulating, exploring, and clarifying issues, and taking responsibility for one's own behavior in the relationship.

The therapist must also be alert to the effect of the partners sharing marital details with others outside of the marriage. Especially when a couple is very distant, one would want to encourage this sharing to be done with each other. Also, other systems that are privy to the couple's intimacies may negatively influence the marital work. For example, in the case below, the husband began to share details with his secretary and entertained fantasies of how easy marriage to her would be compared with his wife. Meanwhile, she shared details with a friend still bitter over her own divorce.

Clarification

Unacknowledged and unarticulated feelings and wishes may underlie much individual and marital distress. Acting or reacting in a way that is protective (e.g., withdrawing) but that does not lead to the desired goal (conflict resolution or intimacy) is a related phenomenon. Therefore, a core component of marital therapy is to help both partners explore these feelings in themselves and their spouse, expressing them in a way that facilitates resolution of conflict and/or promotes intimacy.

There are many ways in which the therapist guides the process to achieve this. Usually, the therapist will begin by framing any reactive transaction that occurs within the session. Such transactions are common in the early phases of therapy, when couples are reactive, have little self-focus, and have little skill in articulating their feelings from an "I" position. For example, when one partner blames the other or rages about some behavior, the therapist shifts the focus to feelings underlying the anger: "Help me understand why that is an issue for you." This intervention contains the implicit assumption that the spouse's behavior may not be problematic for someone else. With help, the feelings and thoughts are clarified and expressed in a nonblaming manner. Raising issues in this way not only facilitates resolution, but also allows individuals to feel empowered by the ability to be less reactive.

Many clients ignore their feelings. Again, questions become interventions as the therapist slows the process down and asks questions that help the individual focus on his or her experience, as for example, "What does that feel like for you?" Nonverbal behavior may also be reflected back, as for example, "You seemed to stiffen when she said that."

In a similar fashion, the therapist targets core beliefs about the relationship, tracking both their origin (e.g., family of origin experience) and their maintenance (dyadic transactions that currently support them). The feelings associated with these beliefs are also addressed. Tapping into this emotional system is usually necessary for change to occur (Safran & Segal, 1990; Greenberg & Johnson, 1988). For example, in the case illustrated below, the husband came to realize that he anticipated his wife's displeasure when he engaged in solo leisure activities and that this came more from his projection than from her behavior. However, change occurred only after he experienced and explored the myriad of emotions he felt when engaging in such activities. Prior to that point, although he was aware of his cognitive distortion and its origin, he commented that there was "a link still missing" for him.

In cases of long-standing marital distress, one often hears a global statement about unhappiness in the marriage rather than specific complaints. Here clients are likely to need the help of the therapist in attending to their affective process to explore the source of their unhappiness. The therapist may use the information provided by his or her own emotions in the session to track the emotional domain for the client. The therapist must empathically understand the experience of the client, who requires the therapist's help in eliciting and articulating feelings.

The exploration of feelings is not limited to an experiential focus within the session. Between-session tasks may be used to amplify the focus on feelings. For example, couples may be given a structured communication task in which designated times are set aside during which the other listens without interruption. Only personal feelings are to be expressed, from an "I" position. Any reference to the behavior of the other must be in terms of how such behavior is an issue for the speaker. This traditional behavioral task used to encourage communication skills also addresses emotional issues. It underlines the need to attend to feelings and to articulate them in a specific way, in a context in which they will be received without challenge. The task helps to maintain a focus on tracking feelings between sessions and can provide useful feedback for the therapist. Difficulty in the performance of such tasks can invite a subsequent exploration of the feelings or thoughts inhibiting the behavior.

Resolution

Change is a focus from the first contact with a client. The therapist listens to how the problem is framed and takes care not to reinforce what may be problem maintaining. A slightly different frame may be introduced to elicit new thoughts and feelings. When the therapist probes how one spouse feels in response to the partner's transaction, a step toward change may be made. Something that may have been previously overlooked is framed as significant. While a more detailed treatment plan evolves over time, the therapist can identify and work toward initial goals derived from knowledge about the common impediments to marital satisfaction noted above. When the therapist encourages changes that allow the couple to work together on identified issues, the way is opened for other changes to occur. Attending to previously unacknowledged feelings and/or behaving in new ways alters one's self-perception and one's perception of the other. Therapy tries to elicit such changes and then builds upon them.

Not all cases will have the emotional realm as a central focus. Dramatic results can occur from minimal behavioral intervention. For example, a physician and his wife reported in the first session that their marriage was "in intensive care with a little chance of making it." They felt distant from each other and reported minimal contact. Their distance seemed to result from a rapidly escalating symmetrical cycle. Preoccupied and worried by problems at work, the husband appeared unavailable to his wife, who felt taken for granted as she was trying to cope with the demands of child care. Hurt and angry, she distanced herself. Perceiving her distance as a lack of support at a time when he most needed it, he sought support from colleagues and appeared even more remote, resulting in further reactive distancing by his wife. Therapy consisted of pointing out this escalating pattern and urging both often to at least "stand still" when they felt like distancing. This brought immediate change. The remaining three sessions were used to help this couple understand conceptually what had taken place and learn alternative strategies in order to prevent its reoccurrence. Although behavior change was the primary focus, feelings were expressed and addressed, facilitating a further closeness between the couple. Which domain of intervention assumes a primary focus will be problem-determined, although therapy will address the multiple realms of functioning (Liddle et al., 1990).

In the case illustrated below, emotions assume a primary focus. Why does one case have a predominantly behavioral tone and another, with the same therapist, have more of an emotional focus? This is an important question for process research. One factor may be that the two couples in question "languaged" their problems very differently. In one, the language was very behavioral; emphasis was on action taken and what should be done. By contrast, the presentation of the other couple was replete with affective statements: being in pain, feeling stuck, feeling depressed. In each case, initial attempts to alter transactions were framed with the given emphasis ("stand still," "focus on feelings"), giving one more of a behavioral focus and the other more of an emotional one. Although, again, multiple realms of functioning were addressed in each case before resolution was achieved.

CASE ILLUSTRATION

Overview

In the following case, emotional issues assume a primary focus. Here, one spouse dismissed much of what he felt. His way of coping with his unhappiness in the marriage was to shut down his feelings and not attend to them. While this was a pattern he learned in his family of origin, his wife's negative reactivity reinforced it. She perceived his expression of negative affect as an existential threat and reacted accordingly. Therapy helped her become more autonomous and less reactive, making the expression of feelings by her husband safer for both. He was helped to elicit and articulate his feelings in this more supportive context. While this generated some warmer feelings between the couple, unresolved conflicts also surfaced and were subsequently resolved in therapy. The case underlines a therapist's need to integrate affective, behavioral and cognitive approaches and reflects the process of tracking and intervening on both the individual and marital levels.

Initial Presentation

Mr. and Mrs. D. had been married for 18 years when they first entered therapy. Both were tearful as they described their present life together. It was painful to be in the marriage; it was painful to think about divorce. Mr. D., a 45-year-old executive, was worried that therapy might result in his "settling" for an unsatisfactory marriage. Mrs. D., a former teacher who was now at home with their two children, was more afraid of the likelihood of divorce.

The couple was unable to resolve conflicts between them. Mrs. D. believed that she could not raise issues directly, and that it was necessary to "work around" her husband. Mr. D. believed that he had capitulated on many issues as his way of resolving conflict.

Tracking their relationship over time, one could see traces of this pattern in their early years together. Many issues between them remained unresolved, and over the years many hurts had accumulated. Children and finances were deterrents to a dissolution, but neither wanted to continue the way they were and both were pessimistic about change.

Engagement and Stabilization

Mr. and Mrs. D. were each in a very different place emotionally. To engage then in therapy, this had to be considered. Mr. D. was less interested in working on the relationship than in addressing his own unhappiness, his uncertainty about wanting to stay in the marriage, and his fear that he would "settle" for an unhappy marriage rather than have the courage to leave. Although Mrs. D. had also been unhappy in the marriage and had contemplated divorce, she responded to her husband's recent talk of ending the marriage and his increased distancing with feelings of anger and panic. She had difficulty focusing on the issues at hand. Following an initial conjoint interview, each was seen separately.

It was suggested to Mr. D. that whatever his eventual decision about the marriage, he needed to be clear about the issues. His current state of dysphoria was connected with his tendency to ignore much of what he was feeling. His global disdain for his marriage was explored with an attempt to extract more specific complaints. The reported irritants were magnified within the session (Why might this be an issue for him? Did he express this to his wife?). The purpose was to underline the depth of his feeling around what he considered trivial events and the fact that his complaints were never even raised with his wife. He agreed with a focus of therapy that would help him take better care of himself in this regard, something that he would need to be able to do in any relationship. He understood that this would be the initial focus of therapy, that any decision to stay or leave the marriage would be put on hold, and that he would make a commitment to stay in the marriage for now to sort out his issues within that relationship.

This plan was also outlined to Mrs. D. With her, it was important to emphasize that therapy was a process over a span of time, with ups and downs, so as to mitigate her assessing and reacting to the status of the marriage minute to minute. She was given more global markers to indicate progress and assured that these would be pointed out by the therapist as they were attained, as would any impediments to the process. Mrs. D. had a more reactive coping style with a low threshold for frustration. She wanted to work on the marriage, but only if assured her husband was doing so. She welcomed help in assuming a more autonomous stand and behaving less reactively ("I know what I feel, but I don't know what to do with it").

The initial phase of therapy, which dealt primarily with issues of engagement and stabilization, involved a combination of individual and conjoint sessions. The conjoint sessions determined targets for individual changes. They also provided some needed help with communication skills and monitored dyadic transactions. The couple was encouraged to share feelings or thoughts that arose from their individual work to mitigate the distance between them:

Mr. D.: I did share some things about me that I worked out since last time...
Mrs.D.: When you shared that with me, it felt good.

This increased closeness worried Mr. D. about "getting stuck" in the marriage. In the next individual session, he reported:

Mr. D.: We talked this morning. There was a softening of feelings for her. But I don't want to compromise myself. I think my relationship with [my wife] can probably improve, but I don't think it can ever improve to the point that I want it. The whole thing is very scary to me. I know it is going to be a compromise if I stay.
Therapist: That is nine steps ahead. We have to work in slow steps. Maybe the relationship will improve enough, maybe not. We have to work so you will be okay either way.

As noted earlier, individuals who are ambivalent about their relationship often need such reassurance and a reminder of the initial contract to focus on behaviors that would be problematic in any relationship and/or to clarify some of their thoughts and feelings.

A Multilevel, Multidimensional Focus

Both the individual and marital levels of intervention were constantly monitored. Although much of the initial work was at the level of the individual, its impact on the couple was anticipated and tracked.

A nodal point for change in the couple's transactions was the husband's lack of articulation of many of his wishes and feelings. Because this couple seemed to work best in a more emotional realm, this was framed affectively as needing to access his feelings. A more behavioral frame could have emphasized the articulation of feelings, and a cognitive one could have focused on the belief that impeded such articulation, namely that in a relationship articulation results in one's hurting the other or being hurt. All realms were eventually addressed in therapy, but overall this case had primarily an emotional focus. Even "behavioral" interventions, such as a focus on communication skills were responded to with an affective focus. For example, when the couple related an altercation early in the therapy, the incident was used within the session both to clarify their feelings and to introduce more effective ways of communicating them. In the process of stating her feelings, Mrs. D. became quiet and, as if lost in thought, began to talk about having similar feelings dealing with her mother.

Mrs. D.: When I think about it, my mother had lots of questions, but when it came down to it, you never got to feelings. I had this thing with her [*relates the incident*].
Mr. D.: Was the way I handled my questions...
Mrs.D.: Yeah, it was like my mother! I realize that I tried not to get into hassles with her [*a pattern replicated with her husband*]. She can't be sup-

portive of me. I can't see sharing with her. She would just be upset and hurt. I never shared feelings with her.

Here, a focus on communication generated some emotional information that was important to the wife.

Similarly, a transaction simply meant to clarify communication was enlightening for Mr. D. His nonverbal reaction to a statement made by his wife suggested that he had misheard it. When asked what he had heard her say, he realized his error. In the next session, he remarked:

MR. D.: That was a breakthrough. That day, when you were very directive, and leaned forward and asked what I heard [my wife] say and I came out and said something different from what she had said, that bugged me because I had interpreted and put a little flag on something that wasn't there. [*He shared the incident with his brother.*] My brother said that my parents were such strong guilt givers that I wouldn't hear what is really being said. Mom would say to us, "You're killing me. You're putting nails in my coffin. Wait till your father comes home." So [my brother and I] learned to lie in our household. When we would fight and if we damaged something we would stop the fight and make up a lie to explain, because it was better to lie than to face "You're going to put nails in my coffin." (*He related several more examples.*)

THERAPIST: So you realize, just to state it in a different way, what?

MR. D.: I realize that some of my reactions are not necessarily based upon my relationship with my wife. It is patterns that I had developed as a child, fear patterns, interaction patterns. I don't know how to phrase it, but I am able to separate it somewhat now.

Clarification of Affective Issues

Emotional issues for both Mr. and Mrs. D. were an important focus of the therapy. For brevity, only the process by which Mr. D. came to explore and clarify some of his feelings will be highlighted here. His internalized style was central to the couple's problems. Helping someone begin to attend to feelings is a gradual and, as illustrated above, unpredictable process. The therapist must make multiple attempts, in multiple ways.

For example, when it was learned that his father had recently died, an attempt was made to elicit Mr. D.'s feelings about this event, as a recent parental death is often related to increased marital distress. Here the first attempt to explore a possible connection yielded a flat response and a dismissal of this issue: "I had gotten close to my father before he'd gotten ill... Once he was so ill, his death was a relief." Yet at a later point in therapy, he would express the pivotal role of his father's death.

To facilitate an increasing focus on feelings, a between-session assignment was given. It was suggested that he read Napier's (1988) *The Fragile Bond*, a text that underlines an experiential focus on feelings within a marital relationship. The reading provoked some memories, which he shared with his wife.

MR. D.: I was a real crier as a kid. I cried very easily. My family and the teachers in school would try to get me to stop by punishing me, which probably leads me to believe that I learned to repress feelings as a result of that. I do remember this one incident...I was 7 years old when I told my mother "I hate you" and I got the cold shoulder for at least 3 or 4 days...I felt real sad and I felt badly that I was getting punished for that. It was another indication that you were supposed to repress your feelings. And I am a real pleaser, which all makes sense.

Over time he remembered his mother's warning that his behavior was "putting nails in her coffin," especially significant in light of the fact that she first developed cancer when he was 8 and that "she was a believer that stress caused cancer." He remembered his father chastizing him for "wanting to play all day" when he did not want to help with the yard work and connected this to his anticipation of his wife's upset ("I approach her with my guns blazing") if he went to play golf or did not want to work in the yard.

Yet, Mr. D. indicated that his awareness only touched the surface:

MR. D.: There is a link that I am missing. I see the connection between "nails in her coffin" and my approach to my wife. I mean it is all there. But I can't put it together.
THERAPIST: When you do something pleasurable, you will feel it kick in. So when you are doing something pleasurable, I would like you to pay close attention to what you feel and what you say to yourself. [*Given the lateness of the hour, this was suggested as a between-session focus. However, it sparked something in Mr. D. and some well-spent minutes were taken*]
MR.D.: You don't know how interesting that is! [*He begins to relate an incident with great feeling.*] I just became aware of it! [*Referring to the experience of it within the session.*] So it is not enough to know I have the feeling, I have to understand it.

For Mr. D., it was necessary to experience the emotion in order to understand it.

Mr. D. was now very much engaged in the therapy. As he learned to process his emotions, he reported feeling better and no longer "in pain." Mr. D. came to work through many of the feelings surrounding his mother's death. He also became aware of how the death of his father symbolized freedom for him. There had been strong paternal pressure about dating someone from the same ethnic background, and his wife symbolized his father's choice. In this way, his father's death sparked his move out of his marriage.

Resolution

As Mr. D. became aware of these feelings, his view of his marriage became less negative.

MR. D.: It wasn't really bad for 18 years. It wasn't as bad as I said. It was just the pain that was so horrible that it seemed like it was all bad. It wasn't 18 years of hell. There were good times. There were bad times, but our bad times were really bad, because of the way we interacted, because of my father's garbage that I carried with me, or my wife's garbage.

The focus then shifted to emphasize taking care of one's feelings in a relationship. Mr. D. had been raised in an authoritarian household where little psychological autonomy was granted. He had no experience of negotiating issues, but rather a sense that "one hurts or is hurt." Initial attempts to deal with this were frustrated by Mr. D.'s anxiety about getting closer to his wife. He repeatedly expressed the worry that if he allowed himself to get closer to his wife, he would end up "settling." He lacked the secure sense of self associated with autonomy that would free him to relate more intimately. The solution he sought was to move to his own apartment for several months. During this time, Mr. and Mrs. D. successfully worked out many old unresolved issues between them, as well as new issues that came up between them. By the end of therapy, Mrs. D. was more autonomous and less reactive. She had fewer problems dealing with her husband directly and had even worked out a more satisfactory relationship with her mother. Mr. D., also more autonomous and no longer emotionally constricted, felt that he was truly choosing to be married to his wife and felt closer to her.

Case Summary

When Mr. and Mrs. D. presented for therapy, their complaints were non-specific. They felt distant from each other and headed toward divorce. The lack of conflict resolution in their relationship was salient. The precise impediments to conflict resolution for this couple determined the initial therapeutic goals. Here, core factors included Mr. D.'s dismissing many of his feelings and his belief that articulating feelings would result in "hurting or being hurt." Also impeding conflict resolution was Mrs. D.'s reactive style, which reinforced her husband's belief that expressing his feelings would hurt her. Intervention therefore needed to target affective, cognitive, and behavioral realms of functioning.

Although individual work was necessary to remove impediments to conflict and intimacy, it was carefully woven in with work at the relationship level. The initial high level of reactivity between the couple did not allow individual work to be done in the presence of the other. However, given the emotional distance between the couple and the vulnerability of the marriage, it was key that the results of work done in individual sessions were shared in subsequent conjoint sessions.

The weaving between the individual and dyadic levels was also instrumental in the engagement process. One cannot engage a system per se, but the individuals that make up a system. In this case, that meant being sensitive to the different concerns each member of the system brought to therapy.

SUMMARY

Emotion provides essential information about the self in interaction with the environment, provided it is accessed and used. Feelings that are not acknowledged cannot be addressed. Previously unacknowledged feelings, once explored, can lead to cognitive, behavioral, and emotional changes.

Because marriage is the primary relationship to which most adults turn to satisfy basic emotional needs, any problem in processing, articulating, or tolerating emotion, will have serious ramifications. Marital therapy that addresses such affective issues will also have to focus on related realms of functioning, such as behavior and cognition, in their relational context. Any of these realms may assume a predominant focus at different points in therapy. A systemic orientation, with its focus on interdependence and complexity, necessitates such a multidimensional approach.

REFERENCES

Anderson, C., & Stewart, S. (1983). *Mastering resistance: A practical guide to family therapy.* New York: Guilford.

Bandura, A. (1986). *Social foundations of thought and action: A social cognitive theory.* Englewood Cliffs, NJ: Prentice-Hall.

Baucom, D., & Epstein, N. (1990). *Cognitive-behavioral marital therapy.* New York: Brunner/Mazel.

Beach, S., Sandeen, E., & O'Leary, K. D. (1990). *Depression in marriage: A model for etiology and treatment.* New York: Guilford.

Berscheid, E. (1983). Emotion in close relationships. In H. Kelley, E. Berscheid, A. Christensen, J. Harvey, T. Huston, G. Levinger, E. McClintock, L. Peplau, & D. Peterson (Eds.), *Close relationships.* New York: Freeman.

Billings, A. (1979). Conflict resolution in distressed and nondistressed married couples. *Journal of Consulting and Clinical Psychology, 47,* 368–376.

Bock, P. K. (1988). *Rethinking psychological anthropology: Continuity and change in the study of human action.* New York: Freeman.

Bordin, E. S. (1976). The generalizability of the psychoanalytic concept of the working alliance. *Psychotherapy: Theory, Research, and Practice, 16,* 252–260.

Bruner, J. (1990). *Acts of meaning.* Cambridge: Harvard University Press.

Buss, A. H., & Plomin, R. (1975). *A temperament theory of personality development.* London: Wiley.

Campos, J., & Barrett, K. (1984). Toward a new understanding of emotions and their development. In C. Izard, J. Kagan, & R. Zajonc (Eds.), *Emotions, cognition, and behavior.* New York: Cambridge University Press.

Campos, J., Campos, R., & Barrett, K. (1989). Emergent themes in the study of emotional development and emotion regulation. *Developmental Psychology, 25,* 394–402.

Capra, F. (1982). *The turning point: Science, society and the rising culture.* New York: Bantam Books.

Daldrup, R. J., Beutler, L. E., Engle, D., & Greenberg, L. (1988). *Focused expressive therapy: Freeing the overcontrolled patient.* New York: Guilford.

Darwin, C. (1965). *The expression of the emotions in man and animals.* London: Murray. (Original work published 1872)

de Shazer, S. (1984). The death of resistance. *Family Process, 23,* 11–17.

Efran, J., Lukens, M. D., & Lukens, R. (1990). *Language, structure, and change: Frameworks of meaning in psychotherapy.* New York: Norton.

Ekman, P. (1980). *Face of man: Universal expression in a New Guinea village.* New York: Garland.

Ekman, P. (1984). Expression and the nature of emotion. In K. Scherer & P. Ekman (Eds.), *Approaches to emotion.* Hillsdale, NJ: Erlbaum.

Foerster, H. von (1984). On constructing a reality. In P. Watzlawick (Ed.), *The invented reality.* New York: Norton.

Ford, D. H., & Lerner, R. M. (1992). *Development systems theory: An integrative approach and the living systems framework.* Newbury Park, CA: Sage.

Frijda, N. (1986). *The emotions.* New York: Cambridge University Press.

Geertz, C. (1973). *The interpretation of cultures.* New York: Basic Books.

Gottman, J. M. (1979). *Marital interaction: Experimental investigations.* New York: Academic.

Greenberg, L., & Johnson, S. (1988). *Emotionally focused therapy for couples.* New York: Guilford.

Greenberg, L., & Safran, J. (1987). *Emotion in psychotherapy: Affect cognition and the process of change.* New York: Guilford.

Gurman, A. (1988). Issues in the specification of family therapy interventions. In L. Wynne (Ed.), *The state of the art in family therapy research: Controversies and recommendations.* New York: Family Process Press.

Gurman, A., & Kniskern, D. (1978). Deterioration in marital and family therapy. *Family Process, 17,* 3–20.

Jacobson, N. (1991). Behavioral versus insight-oriented marital therapy: Labels can be misleading. *Journal of Consulting and Clinical Psychology, 59,* 142–145.

Lazarus, R. (1991). *Emotion and adaptation.* New York: Oxford University Press.

Lazarus, R., Coyne, J., & Folkman, S. (1982). Cognition, emotion and motivation: The doctoring of Humpty-Dumpty. In R. W. J. Neufeld (Ed.), *Psychological stress and psychopathology.* New York: McGraw-Hill.

Liddle, H. (1991). Empirical values and the culture of family therapy. *Journal of Marriage and Family Therapy, 17,* 327–348.

Liddle, H., Dakof, G., & Diamond, G. (1990). Adolescent substance abuse: Multidimensional family therapy in action. In E. Kaufman & P. Kaufman (Eds.), *Family therapy with drug and alcohol abuse.* Boston: Allyn & Bacon.

Luborsky, L., Mclellan, A. T., Woody, G. E., O'Brien, C. P., & Auerbach, A. (1985). Therapist success and its determinants. *Archives of General Psychiatry, 42,* 602–611.

Margulies, A., & Havens, L. (1981). The initial encounter: What to do first? *American Journal of Psychiatry, 138,* 421–428.

Markman, H. J. (1984). The longitudinal study of couples' interactions: Implications for understanding and predicting the development marital distress. In K. Hahlweg & N. S. Jacobson (Eds.), *Marital interaction: Analysis and modification.* New York: Guilford.

Marzali, E. M., Marmar, C., & Krupnik, J. (1981). Therapeutic alliance scales: Development and relationship to psychotherapy outcome. *American Journal of Psychiatry, 138,* 361–364.

Minuchin, S. (1974). *Families and family therapy.* Cambridge: Harvard University Press.

Minuchin, S., & Fishman, H. C. (1981). *Family therapy techniques.* Cambridge: Harvard University Press.

Minuchin, S., Rosman, B. L., & Baker, L. (1978). *Psychosomatic families.* Cambridge: Harvard University Press.

Napier, A. (1988). *The fragile bond.* New York: Harper & Row.

Plutchik, R. (1988). The nature of emotion: Clinical implications. In M. Clynes & J. Panksepp (Eds.), *Emotions and psychopathology.* New York: Plenum.

Safran, J., & Greenberg, L. (1991). *Emotion and the process of therapeutic change.* New York: Guilford.

Safran, J., & Segal, Z. (1990). *Interpersonal process in cognitive therapy.* New York: Basic Books.

Sahlins, M. (1976). *The use and abuse of biology: An anthropological critique of sociobiology.* Ann Arbor: University of Michigan Press.

Scott, J. P. (1988). Genetics, emotions and psychopathology. In M. Clynes & J. Panksepp (Eds.), *Emotions and psychopathology.* New York: Plenum.

Snyder, D. K., Wills, R. M., & Grady-Fletcher, A. (1991). Long-term effectiveness of behavioral versus insight-oriented marital therapy: A 4-year follow-up study. *Journal of Consulting and Clinical Psychology, 59,* 138–141.

Stanton, M. D. (1988). The lobster quadrille: Issues and dilemmas for family therapy research. In L. Wynne (Ed.), *The state of the art in family therapy research: Controversies and recommendations.* New York: Family Process Press.

Watzalwick, P., Beavin, J. H., & Jackson, D. D. (1967). *Pragmatics of human communication.* New York: Norton.

Wynne, L. (1989). *The epigenesis of relational systems: A model for understanding family development.* New York: Family Process Press.

Zerubavel, E. (1991). *The fine line: Making distinctions in everyday life.* New York: Free Press.

8

Emotion and Family Living: The Perspective of Structure Determinism

JAY S. EFRAN and MARC J. BLUMBERG

The subject of emotion deserves to be at or near the top of any list of confusing themes in the mental health field. The topic of emotional experience perplexes mental health professionals almost as thoroughly as it baffles their clients. Moreover, it is a domain in which clients and therapists, both steeped in much the same culture of myths and half truths, regularly reinforce each other's misperceptions.

It is bad enough that therapists give their professional stamp of approval to some of their clients' most misguided beliefs. Worse yet, therapists tend to embellish those beliefs with additional interpretations and suggestions that are also of dubious validity and value. Some clients therefore leave therapy with more excess conceptual baggage than they had when they arrived. Instead of life having become more transparent for them, it has become even more complex and burdensome.

The truth of the matter is that few therapists have received specific training in the realm of the emotions, and most have virtually no understanding of the underlying physiology. Schools of thought that emphasize the *vocabulary* of emotion do not necessarily provide adequate definitions of the terms they use and have not evolved an integrated and workable amalgam of theory and technique. Thus, most therapists remain ill equipped to do much more than reflect and amplify the current, received view of emotional life—the very set of beliefs and assumptions that is already creating so much difficulty. Unfortunately, even therapists who are convinced that they have a good grasp of emotional issues tend to fall back on familiar-sounding but loosely defined notions that are theoretically outmoded and scientifically indefensible.

STRUCTURE DETERMINISM

In this chapter, we will sketch our own point of view about the emotions and present some ideas about working with couples. Our approach draws heavily upon the biological and cybernetic perspective Maturana calls *structure determinism* (Efran & Lukens, 1985; Maturana, 1980; Maturana & Varela, 1987). Structure determinism underscores the centrality of language in determining how human beings interact with one another and create an experience of life for themselves. Words and symbols are viewed as integral to our functioning as social, biological beings. Moreover, from this point of view, language does not simply reflect a preexisting reality—it generates a unique reality that could not have been brought into existence without language. This language-created reality includes those circumstances we label "predicaments," as well as the patterns of interaction we consider to be "solutions." Finally, structure determinism provides new answers to basic questions about our status as "autopoietic" (i.e., self-producing) biological entities. Because structure determinism is an abstract theory that is difficult to tackle head-on, we will try to come at it obliquely by indicating how a structure determinist might overcome some of the conceptual dilemmas that have plagued other theorists and clinicians. We will begin by examining the problems inherent in two opposite perspectives that have dominated thinking in this area—"rational supremacy" and "irrational supremacy."

RATIONAL SUPREMACY

In our culture, people are generally convinced that human beings can and should behave rationally and logically. As Mahoney (1991) reminds us, many people subscribe to the *doctrine of rational supremacy*. It asserts that "reason and rationality can and should control everything 'below' them in the human organism, especially feelings and actions" (p. 446). In this view, emotions are cast in the role of "spoilers"—separate and mischievous processes that periodically sabotage the good works of the intellect. Carl Jung was one of the first to warn of the dangers of this sort of conception. He suggested that Westerners dwell in a skyscraper of the intellect that lacks a proper foundation of feelings and intuitions. Because of its inadequate base, that skyscraper is in perpetual danger of toppling over (Progoff, 1953). Despite Jung's warning, rational supremacists continue to equate cool, deliberate ratiocination with maturity and mental health, and they conceptualize emotional impulses as obstacles to responsible living. Emotions are to be kept strictly under control, or banished to small pockets of life—for example, Mardi Gras or special cathartic rituals—where they can safely be "released" without causing much actual damage. A person who generally "acts on impulse" or does things "for no particular reason" is considered eccentric or pathological.

The rational supremacist model includes the proposition that a person will ordinarily listen to reason, and that, unless something is drastically wrong, he or she can be expected to solve problems by sitting down and figuring them out logically. Based on this model, rational-emotive therapists explicitly use "disputational" methods. The therapist directly contests the client's "irrational" or "maladaptive" assumptions. Many other therapists do the same thing, although not as explicitly. They point out to the client, in a hundred different ways, the advantages of being more *reasonable*. This can be veiled ("That's something you might want to take a look at") or more pointed ("Why don't you just tell your husband that you resent having to care for the children by yourself, even when he is home on the weekend," or "Do you see how your withdrawing causes her to be angrier?").

Ironically, the platitudes many therapists offer their clients may be similar to the ones that those same clients would suggest to their own friends and relatives. That is why it is not unusual to hear a client say, "Gee, that's exactly what I say to other people." Recently, a client chastised one of our student therapists by saying, "Look, don't you think I haven't thought of *that* before?" It is likely that many other clients have had similar thoughts but were either too polite or too intimidated to say so. Although stating the obvious can sometimes be a useful stratagem, it is rarely sufficient. If it were, people would cure themselves by reading fortune cookie homilies. People are not necessarily in difficulty because they are unable to envision a rational course of action. Often they know perfectly well what to do but may still be unable to do it. Consider, for example, how often people stand helplessly by and listen to their mouths utter the very thoughts their brains had just decided it would be sensible to withhold.

Therapists often "language-up" commonsense interventions so that they sound more technical and esoteric. Thus, a client's "just plain stupid" ideas become, in the hands of the cognitive-behavioral therapist, a set of "maladaptive cognitions." A young man's uncle advises him to just face his fear, but the therapist instead prescribes a regimen of "in vivo exposure." The commonsense admonition is to "take things one step at a time," but the professional proposes "graded exposure" or "systematic desensitization." (The film *What About Bob?* with its notion of "baby steps," comically strips these maneuvers of their professional veneer.) These strategies have value, but they are not particularly novel. Methods like *assertiveness training* or rehearsing *positive self-statements* can be made to sound like technical advances, but, in reality, they may just be trivial rephrasings of the advice traditionally offered by Dale Carnegie, Norman Vincent Peale, and Émile Coué.[1] Perhaps this is why columnist George Will chides social science for "doing what it so often does, stumbling upon the obvious with a sense of discovery" (1989, p. A-14).

A coworker might advise an angry colleague to think twice before telling the boss off. The psychoanalyst makes much the same point by interpreting hostility toward an employer as a derivative of prior *authority issues* (Rabkin, 1970). In this context, we are reminded that noted child psychiatrist Robert Coles, near the outset of his career, asked his own analyst whether he should take retaliatory action for an affront he had suffered. He was concerned that he might just be "acting out." With refreshing candor, his analyst replied that he himself had never been clear about where acting out ended and living began.

RATIONALITY AS HANDMAIDEN

To the structure determinist, people are *not* rational creatures, ruled by the intellect. In fact, it can be shown that all of the systems of logic on which people rely—from mathematics to mechanics—are actually based on *arational* starting premises—ordinary human preferences. Explanatory systems are human-made. They do not exist in nature. They are sets of organizational principles invented by people for practical purposes, such as counting or measuring. People have devised different systems that fit different tasks. Binary numbers work well in the realm of computers, but a decimal system is needed for banking. However, as the mathematician Gödel has proven, no system can "get going" without an initial starting point that has been chosen by a human being. That first premise cannot be shown to be ultimately correct (Hofstadter, 1979). One could always have begun elsewhere, perhaps with still better outcomes. From time to time, radically different premises *are* chosen and their implications explored. We mention this to demonstrate that even those human activities that people consider the most "cerebral" originate from a basic aesthetic choice—a human hunch or predilection. In human affairs rationality is never king. It is handmaiden to our preferences. Film director Orson Welles (1915–1985) put it this way: he said that man may be a rational animal, but, then again, he "always loses his temper when called upon to act in accordance with the dictates of reason."

Experienced trial lawyers know that jurors rarely decide cases by a careful and logical review of the evidence. Rather, the jurors get a sense—an intuition—of whether or not the defendant is guilty and then seek facts and evidence that will support or justify the decision toward which they have been leaning. Therefore, successful trial strategies must take into account the likely subjective reactions of the jurors and not just the weight of the objective evidence. Something similar occurs in decisions people make about whom to marry, where to work, when to have children, and where to live. They may feel a little bare unless they bolster their hunches with lists of reasons. However, when the tally from a list of pros and cons does not happen to agree with a person's intuition, it is generally the list that gets revised.

In their daily lives, people hardly operate as if rationality were supreme. They stuff themselves at a restaurant, bemoan having eaten so much, vow never to do it again, and then repeat the entire sequence on the very next outing. Similarly, at the start of each semester, students resolve never to slip back into the old pattern of postponing their assignments. However, as the semester wears on, they again find themselves starting each paper the night before it is due, or waiting until the very last minute to cram for an examination. An individual claims to be seriously pressed for time yet easily rationalizes taking time out to watch a favorite television show, look at a magazine that has just arrived, or sort a pile of papers that has nothing to do with the task at hand. It is amazing how much housework gets done as a project deadline approaches.

People who lose their keys generally look repeatedly in places they have already checked. One of the authors recalls not only having emptied his dresser drawer of all its contents but also running his hand along the edges of the bare wood, as if he expected the keys to somehow pop out of some cleverly designed secret compartment. This hardly seems like rational behavior. The expression "cutting off one's nose to spite one's face" is a cultural acknowledgment of how often our rationality is subservient to other forces. Moreover, learning theory research shows that we rarely act so as to maximize rewards (e.g., Herrnstein, 1990; Rescorla, 1988; Zinbarg, 1990). We are prone to the gambler's fallacy and are notoriously susceptible to being swayed by small, short-term payoffs. There are far more airplane phobics than automobile phobics, although, rationally speaking, it ought to be the other way around. To get people to wear seatbelts to protect themselves, states had to pass statutes with heavy penalties attached. Even today, despite the advertising campaigns and the enactment of laws, there are still individuals who steadfastly refuse to buckle up.

These are ordinary examples. We have avoided discussing areas such as attraction and sexuality, in which changing moods and preferences are the rule rather than the exception. A romantic gesture that seems perfect at one moment seems ridiculously out of character the next. At any stage of life, sudden and intense attractions are difficult to explain logically. They lead to the sort of situation W. C. Fields might have had in mind when he mentioned that "few things in life are more embarrassing than the necessity of having to inform an old friend that you have just got engaged to his fiancée." Then there are those life-dislocating shifts from undying devotion to utter disdain or outright hatred. Recently in the news there was a report of a woman who was being prosecuted for attempting to arrange the assassination of her husband, whom she had come to loathe. What is most surprising in this case is that even as she sat in jail awaiting trial for his attempted murder, the husband claimed to have tender feelings for her and was hoping that somehow or other this "rift" could be mended. His case is extreme, but we have all been known to extend ourselves, over and over again, to people who have shown themselves to be untrustworthy.

The picture that emerges from the brain-research laboratory is even more strikingly discrepant from what rational supremacists would predict. According to Ornstein (1991), "The mind is a squadron of simpletons. It is not unified, it is not rational, it is not well designed" (p. 2). Rationality is a component of the mind, but one that is "used rarely, and in a very limited area" (p. 3). In most situations there simply isn't time for the mind to examine a "truth table" of possibilities in order to arrive at the most sensible choice. *The mind acts first and explains later.* Portions of the mind are given little information about what other "modules" are doing (Gazzaniga, 1985, 1988). In fact, research shows that neurons fire in anticipation of an action, and before we are consciously aware of what we are about to do. Brain activity associated with particular actions occurs before those actions begin and even before we are conscious of the *desire* to act. Furthermore, these are specific patterns of neural activity, not just general "preparatory" rumblings of the system. In other words, although we think our actions are "up to us," we are more like observers who notice aspects of our minds operating "on their own authority" (Ornstein, 1991, p. 147). Although we have been brought up with the belief that we are the authors of our thoughts and sentences, a little introspection reveals that we become privy to the details of what we have to say in the process of speaking. Eavesdrop, for example, on a typical telephone conversation. Each participant is apt to say good-bye several times over. Just as one person is about to hang up, more thoughts emerge that need to be said. It is as if those thoughts control when he or she finally hangs up. Nevertheless, the illusion that we are "in charge" persists. That illusion is a by-product of our ability to use past experience to predict what we are likely to do next. Even so, there are plenty of last-minute surprises.

LANGUAGE AS SOCIAL ACTION

It is also important to recognize that our thoughts and desires do not belong entirely to us as individuals. They reflect the times in which we live, and how we are *structurally coupled* (Maturana, 1988) to others in the language community. Structural coupling points to the fact that entities (living or nonliving) that are in close proximity become more congruent over time. It has often been noted that life in a family gradually accommodates to the needs of a pet dog, while at the same time the dog increasingly takes on the attributes of family members. This is structural coupling in action, and it operates at every level of organization, including the societal. "Everything said is said from a tradition" (Varela, 1979, p. 268). Tradition shapes and gives meaning to each of our responses. Even our private thoughts and self-evaluations reflect the ongoing communal dialogue. Structure determinists do not view words and thoughts as disembodied or individually created abstractions. Instead, they consider language a specialized form of community coordination. Thoughts are part of the social choreography. People could not have the thoughts they do if they were somehow excluded from the "dance" around them. That is why Maturana makes the initially startling proposition that language and all the other so-called higher cortical functions do not take place inside a person's skull—they take place in the space of the community. Of course, in order to participate in the communal dance, one needs to have the proper basic "equipment," including the kind of highly plastic nervous system that human beings possess. However, the dance itself is never contained "in" any of the dancers.

A ramification of this way of thinking is the recognition that people cannot go elsewhere and remain the same. They are not self-contained packages that travel well. An individual who moves to another culture begins to change *into* that culture—new and different thoughts emerge, as do alternative sets of values, beliefs, and habits of living.

In the military, such a transformation begins the moment a recruit steps off the bus. Drill sergeants refer to this as "shock" day, and with good reason. The recruit's head is shaved, he is issued a uniform, and he begins to operate "the army way." Although inductees may react in different ways to this new *structural coupling*, depending on their background and their other relationships, no one remains unaffected.

The notion of the "independent thinker," who does exactly what he or she pleases in all circumstances, is largely a Western cultural invention. In our society, much of what passes for "rugged individualism" is merely subgroup conformity. Consider, for instance, the teenage boy who assumes that deciding to get a "mohawk" haircut demonstrates his independent thinking.

Given the abundance of personal and scientific evidence that contradicts the doctrine of rational supremacy, why does this viewpoint persist? A major factor is that our actions, regardless of how and where they originate, are quickly woven into self-narrative that casts us in the starring role. These stories are told and retold, both to ourselves and to others. They help perpetuate the illusion that our lives are sensible, well planned, and individually controlled. Even obvious lapses of good sense or sudden changes in direction can be quickly smoothed over and incorporated into the ongoing yarn. It is in this storied life (Bruner, 1986, 1990; Howard, 1991; Sarbin, 1986) that we literally and figuratively *make sense*. As Anderson (1990) puts it, "Mind is a tireless and not altogether careful fabricator of stories about everything, infinitely inventive of making up connections between events and creating causes to fit effects" (p. 72). Our tales are engineered to coordinate with those of our neighbors, which gives them an added plausibility. At the same time, our collective social structures ensure that we are all moving along roughly parallel pathways. We tend to support each other's assumptions, generating a consensual cocoon of explanatory fictions. Language bolsters an illusion of self-control and orderliness. At the same time, it equips us with terms like "procrastination" that help to rationalize—*literally, to render rational*—instances when we are obviously not following the announced program.

CELEBRATING IRRATIONALITY

It should be clear that we believe that laypersons and professionals alike have overestimated the role of rationality in everyday life. On the other hand, in some circles, the role of *irrationality* has also been exaggerated. Advocates of what we have chosen to call the *doctrine of irrational supremacy* are properly skeptical about people's ability to intellectually understand and explain themselves. They consider verbal statements potentially superficial and unreliable indicators of a person's status. Instead, they look to "feelings" and "intuitions" to reveal a person's true intentions. They prize expressions that seem to arise from the "gut" as opposed to those originating in the "head." From our point of view, this orientation has a number of severe disadvantages. It perpetuates the awkward practice of conceptually separating the intellect from the emotions, reinforcing a false dichotomy between "inner" and "outer" space (Rabkin, 1970). Furthermore, because of the heavy focus on *internal* dynamics, it distracts attention from potentially determinative features of the social environment.

Proponents of the doctrine of irrational supremacy are frequently wedded to both a *hydraulic model*, which we will discuss shortly, and a *depth metaphor*. The depth metaphor includes the notion that there are various "layers" of personality and feeling. It usually involves a belief in an entitized unconscious, which may be assumed to be a storehouse of repressed wishes and memories as well as a wellspring of primitive drives and impulses. Life's "surface" disruptions are often attributed to an underground warfare of competing mind entities (Rotter, 1954). This complex model of the psychic apparatus is not supported by findings from contemporary neurological research. In Penfield-type experiments, for example, electric probes are used to directly stimulate areas in the brain. Under these conditions, subjects often report vivid and presumably intact memories of childhood scenes. This was originally cited as evidence that portions of the brain did, indeed, serve as storage areas for significant early occurrences. More recently, however, it has been determined that the memories reported with electrical stimulation are not literal recordings of past events. They are influenced by snippets of operating-room chatter and contain images of locations and events that were never actually part of the person's past (Ornstein, 1991).

Emotional Hydraulics

Therapists of humanistic persuasions who are interested in the expression of feelings often advise their clients to "get the feeling out" by pounding a pillow, screaming at an imaginary adversary, attempting to elicit tears, or dredging up and disclosing memories of past traumas. This is thought to free people from social constraints that normally inhibit the expression of "genuine" emotions. More likely, it just trades one set of situational demand characteristics for another. The shift in social rules may be useful for certain purposes, but not because it assures direct access to submerged feelings or repressed material. Nothing does that.

Therapists who favor cathartic methods usually subscribe, sometimes unwittingly, to some version of the archaic but highly popular theory of *emotional hydraulics*. The underlying notion here is that feelings are substances that "build up" in the system and, if not properly released or drained, can cause ulcers and a host of other maladies. This view of emotion gives a therapeutic imprimatur to the cultural wisdom that emotions are stored inside the body and that people need to have emotional "safety valves." This is sometimes called "steam kettle" thinking because it conjures up an image of the body as a kind of container, like a pressure cooker or a boiler. At the same time, it reifies emotions into substances that obey the principles of hydraulics—for example, when emotions are blocked in one direction they presumably push for release in another. This crude theorizing is neither supported by the findings of research programs on cathartic effects (Bohart, 1980; Efran & Spangler, 1979; Nichols & Efran, 1985; Nichols & Zax, 1977; Ryle, 1959) nor consistent with contemporary understandings of human anatomy and physiology. However, steam kettle thinking persists because the metaphor has a rough-and-ready correspondence with everyday experience. In other words, everyone intuitively understands what it is like to be "under pressure," to keep a "tight lid" on anger, to "bottle up" grief, to "vent" outrage, and to feel "drained" after a good cry. People less often recall or think about those instances in which the folk remedies that derive from this sort of metaphor do not work or actually make matters worse. They have a limited understanding of the mechanisms that give the steam kettle model its apparent validity. When the nostrums do not work, no one is quite sure why.

Workers in our field also pay too little attention to the origin and history of many of the practices they espouse. The concept of emotional release, central to steam kettle approaches, can be made to sound modern, but it actually harks back to the ancient practice of using purgatives to rid the system of toxins. It has a family relationship to trephining the skull to release evil spirits and attaching leeches to the body to purify the bloodstream.[2] Draining the emotions to improve mental health is not much more sensible than draining blood to remove infections. Although such methods ought to have been relegated long ago to the archives of medical superstition, an investigator can still walk into almost any community mental health clinic in the country and identify remnants of the purgative approach, sometimes in very direct and obvious form. It is well to keep in mind that we can always make our current practices *sound* reasonable. When bloodletting was popular, physicians would not have had any difficulty producing striking testimonials of its effectiveness. Then, as now, failures and exceptions are easily ignored or rationalized away. In science and medicine there is an unfortunate tendency to poke fun at past practices while smugly assuming that we are now too sophisticated to make similar or parallel mistakes. Steam kettle theorizing, in myriad forms, is still alive and well, and continues to permeate popular and professional thinking about the emotions.

A Cathartic Treatment That Failed

Steam kettle treatments can simply be distracting, delaying the implementation of better approaches, or they can lead therapists to go in entirely the wrong direction. Not long ago we were asked for advice in the case of an adolescent girl who had been treated at a center using "cathartic" methods. The family had become alarmed because with each "regressive" session her behavior seemed to deteriorate still further. The more she was encouraged to express her emotions in the consulting room, the more confused she seemed to be when she emerged. She interacted less and less with peers and ceased doing her schoolwork altogether. She frequently retreated to her room for periods of silence or bouts of histrionics, such as screaming at the top of her lungs, throwing her belongings around the room, and walking around without clothes. When she started making suicidal gestures, her cathartic treatment was abruptly canceled and she was committed to a nearby inpatient adolescent facility.

Apparently, in this case, "getting her feelings out" not only was unproductive but may have inadvertently contributed to her "going off the deep end," as her parents would later describe it. Initially, this young woman's complaints about living were framed in rather ordinary language, but as regressive therapy proceeded, she began to talk in increasingly mysterious and suggestive terms about spirits, auras, and bad karma. (This is ironic, given the close association throughout history between cathartic techniques and religious conceptions of demonic possession.)

According to the diagnostic workups at the inpatient facility, there was no evidence of schizophrenia, and, in our opinion, the young woman was operating with roughly the same emotional equipment the rest of us possess. Considering that she was *not* the sort of person who was reluctant to express herself, it is not clear why anyone thought she needed special training in emotional release.

Reconstructing Childhood Events

Of course, there can always be hidden agendas in families that make communicating about particular topics difficult. However, her cathartic treatments were individual sessions and were not aimed at improving family communication. As is typical in such treatment strategies, there was an emphasis on retrieving repressed memories and "abreacting" associated feelings. During her regressive sessions, it can be inferred that her guttural sounds and oblique, "coded" messages were greeted as evidence that genuine feelings were bubbling up from within and that the residuals of an early trauma were resurfacing. However, as we noted, evidence on brain stimulation, as well as research on implanted memories and the therapy-aided recall of childhood events, makes it clear that not all such presumed revelations can be taken literally. In particular, those elicited in a cathartic context may be partially or wholly manufactured to meet the demand characteristics of the situation. Contrary to what one hears these days in the popular press, childhood recollections are *always* highly susceptible to suggestion and social manipulation (e.g., Loftus, 1980, 1991, 1992; Loftus & Loftus, 1980). In many instances a "remembered event" simply could not have occurred as the person described it because it combines elements from different times and settings into a single image or narrative fragment. For example, a person might report being on the porch of a childhood home when, in fact, that house did not have a porch. The porch image may have been "borrowed" from a relative's house, from a house to which the family later moved, or even from a scene in a motion picture. Such client confabulations can also include bits and pieces of relatives' stories, images from photo albums, reports from television news, fragments of book plots, and therapist-suggested themes and hypotheses. Unfortunately, the accuracy of such recollections does not correlate with either the vividness of the image or his or her faith in its veracity. It is therefore a mistake to think of feelings and stories that emerge in such sessions as being intact retrievals from some sort of internal storehouse of past memories and feelings. Although aspects of events from the past may be incorporated into these recollections, the recollections are contemporary social constructions that are highly responsive to current expectations, including prevailing patterns of belief. Recollections are admixtures of fact and fable. Thus, there is a germ of truth to William Ralph Inge's (1860–1954) wry observation that "events in the past may be roughly divided into those which probably never happened and those which do not matter."

"Loosening" and the Loss of Self

The therapist in the case described above was encouraging the young woman to amplify each feeling or impulse that floated by and was simultaneously deemphasizing the ordinary social connections that sustain living. She was given implicit permission to elaborate internal associations and fantasies—a process Kelly (1955) referred to as "loosening." In effect, this changes the person's relationship to the processes that usually keep him or her sane. Human beings need to be immersed in a stable set of social structures in order to maintain their equilibrium. When such structures dissolve, or are set in opposition to one another (what we will later label "emotional contradiction"), people lose their sense of who they are. In other words, a little loosening can go a long way.

Examples of the effects of loosening can be found in everyday life. Some people find that their vacations are unexpectedly disorienting because they have to suspend their usual routines. Such individuals may experience discomfort while attempting to relax on the beach. They soon get an itch to return to work, to be back in familiar surroundings, or to spend time with their associates, children, and neighbors. They even find themselves missing things they thought they wanted to get away from. As a result, some people actually cut their trips short. As one such individual put it: "I guess I'm just not the vacation type. I don't feel right when I'm not working."

The reader may have experienced a transient "loss of self" when attending a movie alone or when wandering alone in an unfamiliar city or country. Sailors frequently complain about the difficulties of being on liberty in unfamiliar ports. Unless they remain aboard ship or are able to stick together with others who are going ashore, they may be overwhelmed by a sense of anomie that can easily develop into full-blown depression. Although they may have looked forward to shore leave, they now discover in themselves a strong desire to pull up anchor as quickly as possible. Especially for sailors, who are expected to conform to the stereotypical macho role of being footloose and fancy-free adventurers, these insecurities can prove disconcerting and socially awkward. Because the sailors may not be able to share such sentiments with their shipmates, they may believe that everyone else is off having fun, and that they are the only ones beset with disturbing feelings of isolation and alienation.

Emotional Hydraulics vs. Social Structure

These examples illustrate how actions and events that are often construed in internal steam kettle terms might be better understood by focusing on a person's changing role in a social ecology. Matters that at first blush appear to be a function of inner dynamics may actually reflect fluctuations of communal structure. A too exclusive focus on intrapsychic experience by client *or* therapist can prevent either one from understanding the relevant social contingencies. For instance, the adolescent we described above improved greatly during her inpatient stay mainly because of the effectiveness of the institution's inherent structure. The program she was in required that she dress herself each morning and participate in various group meetings and activities. She was expected to make her bed and bus her own food trays. Although she complained at first about the regime, her mood improved and she began to look better, sleep better, and act more like her "old self."

Most important, she found herself forming friendships with people her own age who, having been around the block once or twice themselves, were neither overly shocked by—nor particularly interested in—her talk of auras and incantations. She was able to compare her family experiences with those of others and to recognize that her grievances about her family were not extraordinary. She also met a boy who was attracted to her, and with whom she felt comfortable. Under those felicitous circumstances, prior problems melted away rather quickly. Themes that had seemed immensely significant only a few days before faded into relative unimportance.

Changes in social structure modify who we are. Problems are not fixed entities; they are language formulations that fluctuate depending on who we are with, what we are doing, and how we talk to ourselves. That is why even Freud was of the opinion that if one wanted a person to change rapidly, he or she should be placed in a very different environment, perhaps by being sent on vacation or given large sums of money. He recommended psychoanalysis mainly as an aid to self-examination—not as the most efficient tool for changing behavior (Rieff, 1959).

We have to wean ourselves from the belief that we possess an independent internal world filled with fixed feelings, memories, and meanings, which, if properly tapped, will lead to emotional and mental health. Any exploration of "inner space" is simultaneously a remapping of interpersonal space (Rabkin, 1970). Introspective activities are simultaneously social and "political" repositionings. Even daydreams shift social equations. For instance, a young man's fantasy of being rejected may cause him to hesitate to ask for a date. On the other hand, recalling his winning home run may give him sufficient courage to initiate the phone call. In both cases, something usually considered "internal" has become an essential aspect of how an encounter unfolds. Therefore, to the structure determinist, it is unwise to attempt to decide where an internal image leaves off and an actual encounter begins. Images, dreams, and fantasies are part of social and biological reality.

NATURAL DRIFT

As you can see, the structure determinist celebrates neither rationality nor irrationality. A system operates primarily on the basis of *arationality* and what Maturana calls *natural drift*. He gives the analogy of a boat, without sails or rudder, tossed about by the wind and the waves. Depending on its shape and the path that evolves, it comes to have a particular history. Sooner or later, it will meet up with a "destructive interaction" that causes it to sink or break up sufficiently so that it will no longer be recognizable as a boat. Until then, it participates in a structure-determined voyage. If the boat had mechanisms of self-awareness and could speak, it would surely attempt to explain where it was, where it had been, and where it was going. In other words, it would discover pattern and meaning in the drift, just as we are accustomed to doing. However, despite what the boat might say, an outside observer would still characterize what is happening as a meaningless drift because the boat's location and trajectory, at each moment, would be fixed by the way its shape happens to interact with the prevailing conditions.

We, too, drift through life. As Austrian poet Karl Kraus (1874–1936) once put it, "Life is an effort that deserves a better cause." However, as we have also suggested, we exist in a society that demands that *everything* be given an explanation. This is because we developed language and, along with it, the recursive ability to talk to ourselves *about* ourselves. Therefore, we narratize the *drift* and simultaneously become the audience for our own narrations. This complicates matters because, unlike the simple case of the boat, what we say about ourselves makes a difference—it becomes one more determinant of how the drift evolves. For instance, a wife concludes, perhaps correctly, that her mother-in-law disapproves of how she is parenting her toddler. Therefore, she is edgy and defensive when the mother-in-law is watching. The increased tension adversely affects her ability to respond patiently and flexibly to her child's needs, reconfirming the mother-in-law's worst suspicions. The mother-in-law mentions her concerns to her son, who, in turn, feels obliged to take the matter up with his wife, precipitating a fight between them and reinforcing the wife's feelings of vulnerability to her mother-in-law's negative appraisals. Throughout the sequence, the way the matter is being construed and discussed affects the way the participants interact, and vice versa. Life is still a drift—as it is for the boat—but language adds an extra twist to the equation. Talking about the possibility of a bank failure can precipitate one. Worrying about getting enough sleep can keep one up nights. Declaring one's innocence can create an impression of guilt. Showing jealousy can sow the seeds of infidelity.

Nervous System Closure

When living is conceptualized as a structural drift, certain traditional distinctions lose their significance. For example, it becomes apparent that inner and outer space are not really separable. They are the front and back of the same coin. An organism and its environmental niche mutually specify one another. A modification of one results in the readjustment of the other. In fact, the distinction between what is inside the skin and what is outside, although socially convenient, has little reality for the biological system itself. This is partly because the nervous system is a closed neuronal network that, as we shall see, pays attention only to its own promptings. We like to think we can escape the confines of our nervous system and peer at ourselves from an outside, objective perspective. However, what we take to be an outside view of ourselves is simply more of our own circuitry at work.

Because the nervous system "listens" only to itself, paradoxes arise. For example, after a leg has been amputated, the amputee may still experience it itching and may feel impelled to scratch the invisible limb or to repeatedly check beneath the blanket to verify visually that there is nothing there. In this so-called phantom limb experience, the nervous system continues issuing proprioceptive messages, much as it did before the leg was removed. It is not concerned with logic or changes that may be apparent to an external observer. Eventually the system readjusts because of the changed relations among various nervous system modules. In the meantime, however, the person is forced to cope with contradictory "knowings." As a member in good standing of the language community, he or she knows that the leg has been lost and can never return, yet at the same time "knows" that it is wiggling just beneath the sheets.

Family Complications

The phantom limb experience is a striking example of the imperatives of the nervous system, and the paradoxes created when it causes one aspect of "reality" to conflict with another. The structure determinist recognizes that all of us face such dilemmas every day of our lives because the facets of our various "knowings" are rarely fully coordinated. Family living adds yet another level of complexity because it requires several people to attempt to live together in close proximity and coordinate their various "knowings" into a shared reality. One of the authors used to be driven to distraction by a high-frequency hum produced by a television set. No one else in the family heard it. Only politeness kept them from accusing him of having lost his mind. When the repairman arrived, he verified that there was nothing wrong with the set, but he did explain that certain high-voltage transformers emit air-stream disturbances to which some people are especially sensitive. What was an intolerable noise to one person in the family simply did not exist for the others. They thought he was just imagining things. Obviously, even simple aspects of personal reality cannot necessarily be understood by others. Each person has different "equipment" and operates with a different background of experience.

Couples often have to reconcile very different conceptions of marriage and reality. Even husbands and wives who started out thinking they were in basic agreement about what to expect from marriage and from life may later discover they have been operating from totally different sets of assumptions. As we point out to couples, they come from different "tribes" in which different "stories" have been taken for granted. Moreover, each tribe is now expecting the new couple to abide by *its* tribal rituals. This is why family therapist Carl Whitaker maintains that "marriage is when families exchange hostages" (Gustafson, 1992, p. 75). In the protracted negotiations that often follow, both spouses may have dual allegiances—to their partner and to their family of origin.

Understanding this dynamic, family therapists have emphasized establishing and maintaining clear boundaries—markers that will separate one subgroup from another, thereby helping to minimize psychological (and sometimes physical) bloodshed. Some have cast these issues in terms of a lack of communication skills or emotional sensitivity. We do not see it that way. Family members who have difficulty being civil with one another may, in other settings, demonstrate great tact and skill in dealing with others. Furthermore, they are not necessarily ignorant about the feelings and sentiments of other family members. In fact, they may know each other well—too well, in some respects. They know where to poke and where to prod. They can anticipate the other person's moves, playing an excellent game of conversational "fill in the blanks." In this respect, it would be well to keep in mind the advice Whitaker gives concerning the operation of families and marriages. He asserts that families operate at a primitive level "where social conventions, consistency, and communication are of little need and are often counterproductive" (Gustafson, 1992, p. 165).

The disputes that arise— those that really count—quickly take on a moral tone because each individual wants and expects his or her worldview to be *privileged*. These are not fights about *opinions*—they are confrontations about what should be acknowledged as "real" and correct. Maturana calls what happens in such debates "conversations of accusation, recrimination, and characterization" (Mendez, Coddou, & Maturana, 1988). The struggle over whose story shall prevail can continue beyond the grave and down through many generations. Moreover, such feuds—even in their milder forms—are not usually cleared up by providing training in making "I statements" or instructing people to mirror the position of the other before responding.

BEING RIGHT

In conversations of accusation, recrimination, and characterization, there is invariably the feeling that the other person is being unnecessarily stubborn or is acting out of sheer malice. The conversation becomes *personal*. Once that happens, it can be difficult for either party to reverse engines and be conciliatory. A client reported being unable to find the car his wife parked in a parking lot. Although he knew better, he could not shake the hypothesis that she had "hidden" it in some obscure spot just to annoy him. The more he stalked up and down the aisles, the more furious he became. He finally found the car in a very obvious location—he had gone right past it the first time around. As often happens, the problem was solved but he remained upset—his adrenaline level had not yet returned to baseline levels. He found himself searching his mind for some "good reason" to continue blaming his wife for the incident, although he knew that, in the end, it was going to turn out to be his own fault. People involved in automobile accidents react the same way. Even though they backed up into a parked car, they want to know "who's the jerk that put that damned car there," as if someone else was doing it to them. We want to be right, even if it means making people we like and admire, wrong. This can create instances of "emotional contradiction," a topic to which we will return.

It is remarkable how regularly we opt for trouble. We can know rationally that others are trying to work out a compromise, but even with a settlement in sight, we insist on uttering that one final barb that serves to sabotage everything that has gone before. We raise delicate issues at the worst possible times, when the other person is frazzled, in the midst of other battles, or when expecting dinner guests. We pick away at a partner bit by bit until a full-blown conflagration becomes inevitable. We are rarely willing to leave well enough alone. What we want, more than anything else, is *to be right*. It is said that people will commit suicide in order to have the last word in an argument or to ensure that *their* version of the story is accepted. The fights that destroy relationships are not about material goods, social arrangements, or sex, although any of those "commodities" can become pawns in the struggle. The fights are more basically about issues of entitlement, about who was "right" all along.

Therapists sometimes act as if they thought these wars were over *territory*, when they are actually about *religion*. It is not just that the family room is a mess, that there is a sock missing, or that the person is once again late for dinner. It is not even about whether or not there has been an extramarital affair. It is about the underlying "theology"—for instance, whether it isn't morally repugnant that any one human being could make *such* a mess, be *that* lazy, or be *so* inconsiderate of another's feelings?

These interpersonal collisions are rooted in the belief that there is a discernible objective reality and an ultimate and standard meaning to life. The resulting angst is exacerbated by the assumption that, under ordinary circumstances, an appeal to logic or human decency should suffice—that "instructive interaction" works (Maturana & Varela, 1987). In other words, when you tell people something, they ought to listen and mend their ways. If they do not, there is clearly something wrong with them. They are sick or evil, mad or bad. However, given that the neural system is informationally closed, people *never* listen, except to their own interpretations. Similarities in our structure and background make it *seem* as if we are paying attention—this is consensus and social coordination—but it is only an illusion of direct instructive interaction.

When a mother says, "Someday you'll understand," she is speaking the truth. Such statements are typically uttered in anger or out of frustration and disappointment. However, they embody the wisdom that people comprehend only what they are able to experience themselves. Everything else is just theory and hearsay. Readers, using authors' words, have a running conversation with themselves. That dialogue determines their experience of the material. Similarly, in college, there are as many different "courses" being taught as there are "nervous systems" sitting in the classroom. Each person interacts uniquely with the process. The professor, thinking he or she is transferring intact *information* from one organism to another—the usual telephonic model of communication—is shocked to see what appears on the final examinations. "Did I say that?" "Were we in the same classroom?" To the structure determinist, the answer to both questions is always *no*, even for students who get good grades. Information is never passed directly from one person to another. All education, including the special form we call psychotherapy, is "conversation," not instructive interaction (Goolishian & Anderson, 1987, 1988).

Objective Imperialism

Being told what to experience simply does not work. However, in Western epistemology, we think of our eyes as windows on the world. Moreover, once we have taken a look at what is out there, we feel inclined to share our insights with others—not as opinions, but as facts. In the example we reported earlier, the author didn't simply *believe* the TV set was humming, he *knew* it for a fact. Others in the family were just as positive that it was "all in his head." Gustafson (1986) notes that "we are living near the center of an equivalent to the Roman Empire, where we Instruct the World" (p. 200). Being at the center, we are largely oblivious to the problems this imperialistic epistemology creates, many of which are manifest in our relationships.

Even in areas that we take to be "solid," such as color perception, the objectivist stance is indefensible. The colors we see are nervous system *enactments*, not isomorphic translations of spectral hues (Varela, Thompson, & Rosch, 1991). You can test this for yourself by closing your eyes and pressing lightly on your eyelids. You will be able to generate, without any help from the spectrum, the very colors people ordinarily attribute to the outside world.[3]

ORTHOGONALITY—THE KEY TO THERAPEUTIC CHANGE

Ultimately, experience is neither objective nor subjective. Both of those terms, which are reciprocals of each other, are epistemologically obsolete. The reality of our experience is "participatory" (Varela, 1979). Yalom (1989) makes a similar point: "How disquieting to realize that reality is illusion, at best a democratization of perception based on participant consensus" (p. 172). In working with couples and family members, it is important to give each person an opportunity to experience *that* insight, not as an abstraction, but in personally relevant forms (Mendez, et al., 1988). The therapist is like a "coach" who arranges interaction so that this sort of discovery becomes more probable. The conversation that occurs, if it is to have unique value, must be "orthogonal"—in other words, as we explain below, it must break up the patterning to which the person has become accustomed.

People belong to a variety of interpersonal "clubs," each of which has its own membership requirements and rules of operation. People have already worked out accommodations to existing club affiliations. The current problem is a derivative of the contradictions those multiple couplings create. Moreover, when a structural coupling is solid, little about its nature or the details of the surrounding medium can be noticed—it is taken for granted.

Not long ago, a colleague visited the office of one of the authors. He happened to ask about a painting on the office wall. In turning to see what the visitor was referring to, the author "saw" the painting once again, as if for the first time. It had become psychologically invisible over the years—"part of the furniture." By borrowing the visitor's perspective, the author was able to make the painting focal. A therapist plays a similar role for a client. When the status quo is disturbed, assumptions that had been hidden can be brought back into focus and reevaluated. By borrowing the therapist's "eyes," a client becomes a visitor in his or her own life space.

This process always requires what Maturana (1988) calls *orthogonal inter-action*. Orthogonal interaction involves relating to a person in such a way that he or she must generate a new or infrequently used response. The client's club rules are purposely bypassed by the therapist to generate interaction to which the client's system has not yet accommodated. *Such perturbations force new patterns to emerge.* We recall a client, a veteran of several previous thera-pies, who was ruminating aloud about whether he should propose marriage to his present girlfriend. He added that he knew that since "therapists never give direct advice," he would have to figure this out for himself. The thera-pist said, "Of course, you should propose to her, and this week wouldn't be at all too soon." This led to an abrupt change in the client's usual obsessive pattern, including an exploration of all kinds of assumptions about therapy, risk taking, and certainty in life. Incidentally, the client married the woman within the year, and the couple invited the therapist to the wedding.

The new pattern is not always that dramatic, and it does not inevitably lead to a happy ending. On the other hand, to the extent that therapeutic interaction merely replicates preexisting patterns, nothing happens. Once clients have been changed by having participated in orthogonal interactions, they may return to their other "clubs" and operate differently in them. This often forces far-reaching realignments. For example, as a result of therapy, a mother announces to her spouse and children that she intends to go "off duty" for a certain portion of each evening. This automatically precipitates a vari-ety of role shifts in the immediate family, and perhaps in the extended family as well. The relevant cybernetic principle is that a change in any one compo-nent of a system produces changes in all the others.

SEEING BEYOND THE TRIPARTITE SCHEME

Orthogonal interaction does not need to be categorized as verbal or non-verbal, cognitive or emotional, practical or theoretical. Those opposites meld together in this view because any change in a system constitutes a structural change. There are no separate intellectual, affective, and behavioral changes. Traditional theorists are often blindsided by their allegiance to an old-fashioned functionalism, particularly the tripartite scheme of the ancient Greeks. As Kelly (1969) puts it, the division of human activity into thoughts, feelings, and actions "confuses everything and clarifies nothing" (p. 91). Once clinicians or theorists accept that sort of division, they are locked into a series of largely fruitless debates concerning how these "functions" might interrelate. In other words, once Humpty Dumpty has come apart, how is he to be fit back together? Do thoughts come before feelings, or do feelings precede thoughts? Can one have a feeling without an accompanying cognitive appraisal? If a person behaved differently, would he or she then automatically think different thoughts or experience different feelings? What if a person just *pretended* to think like someone else? Would he or she become like that person? In our view, these are not very useful questions, and they have not yielded particularly satisfying answers. To repeat, they presuppose a separation that is artificial and misleading.

As structure determinists, we argue that it is a mistake to take Humpty Dumpty apart in the first place. Our mechanistic urge to parse entities and impose distinctions on integral systems creates an array of false issues. In social science and medicine, there is always the danger of "vivisecting the nightingale to probe the secret of his note" (Thomas Bailey Aldrich, 1836–1907). Why not approach the system as a unity rather than as a collection of discrete parts and functions? Of course, it is both permissible and necessary to make conceptual distinctions in order to map a terrain, but these cleavages must be acknowledged as human-made and artificial. They should be maintained only as long as they are useful to the task at hand. As Bateson (1979) notes, "The division of the perceived universe into parts and wholes is *convenient* and may be necessary, but no necessity determines how it shall be done [emphasis added]" (p. 42). Good science always involves the freedom to entertain multiple perspectives. However, when shifting the turret of a microscope to a lens of a different power, one must recognize that this provides merely another perspective on the same problem, not the discovery of new and intrinsically separate functions, factors, or mechanisms.

Consider, as an example, a person who wants to study the psychotherapy process. He or she might consider what goes on in therapy either as an integral aspect of the person's life or simply as a separate "perch" from which the person's life can be observed and analyzed. Both perspectives are defensible. In such matters, it is often advisable to be "two-headed"—to try it both ways and see what happens. The therapy process itself can also be dissected into any number of components, such as sessions, treatment phases, interpersonal themes, and so on. Here again, each division is apt to yield fresh perspectives. The investigatory microscope can focus on the role of the identified patient, or the activities of the family as a whole, or the community. With an even wider angle lens, the entire enterprise can be viewed as a philosophical, medical, financial, or political venture. Woody Allen quips that when he was preparing his income tax return, he wasn't sure in what category to list the expense of his psychoanalysis. He first considered listing it as a medical expense. After some consideration, however, he wondered if it would be better to label it entertainment. He finally settled on calling it a religious contribution!

Any of these ways of parsing therapy might yield useful information. However, no set of divisions is mandatory, none is exhaustive, and none is "correct." Similarly, it is legitimate for a clinician or an investigator to track a client's verbal utterances, heart-rate changes, or telephone bill. However, these records in no way reveal the operation of separate cognitive, affective, and behavioral subsystems. They are simply different ways to focus the microscope.

AN ALTERNATE VIEW OF EMOTION

Before we decide to give up the traditional categories of thoughts, emotions, and actions, we need to look at the question of whether such terms have any utility. In some ways it might be better to throw them out and begin with a fresh slate. For the moment, however, we will content ourselves to redefine them. As we have already indicated, "thinking" is a form of social action. Thinking is behaving, even if the person who is doing the thinking is not moving around much. Lying in bed and deciding which of several applicants should be offered a job constitutes vigorous "action," even though the next phase of the plan—making the phone call—has not happened yet. Maturana suggests that language activity, such as thinking and speaking, is for human beings what grooming is for chimps. It shapes and maintains the community structure, establishing who will do what for whom. It is in language—which includes both words and symbols—that we have names and reputations, pose questions, and receive answers. Problems are in language. In other words, a problem is not simply a set of circumstances. It must include a social "discussion" or conversation about those circumstances. As the discussion changes, the problem changes.

Emotions, by contrast, are the shifting bodily configurations that support any and all action states, including activities that are primarily linguistic, and those that some would categorize as "rational" or "cognitive." Bodily predispositions underlie everything we do (Frijda, 1986, 1988). Emotions, in this usage, are not turned on or off, although there are constant readjustments of hormonal levels, body posture, and other parameters (Efran & Fauber, in press). Our lives flow through a succession of emotional states, which, in turn, make different sorts of actions and thoughts more or less likely to occur. Unlike in other conceptions, the emotions are considered to be neither substances that are stored or released, nor a subsystem that is only sometimes occupying center stage. Emotions are not simply signals from a system working behind the scenes or beneath the skin, although we do "feel" differently in different postures and are sensitive to shifts in the calibrations of the body. The flow of emotional postures is a large part of who we are, and enactments cannot move forward unless our bodies cooperate by assuming appropriate configurations. However, in this view of biological organization, there is no danger that the emotions will be ignored, given short shrift, or repressed.

By definition, emotions are expressions. They form the foundation of moment-to-moment operations. Therefore, the idea of an unexpressed or repressed emotion is a contradiction in terms. It is a metaphor left over from steam kettle thinking. What people seem to mean when they talk about unexpressed emotion are circumstances that lead to periods of *emotional contradiction*, to which we will now turn our attention.

LIVING IN EMOTIONAL CONTRADICTION

At times we are caught between two modes of action. We simultaneously want to stay and go, fight and make up. We are torn—literally stretched—between two opposing action tendencies. These are instances of *emotional contradiction*, when the body is being asked to support, in close proximity, several competing orientations. The attempt to serve more than one master is stressful and demanding. However, it should be noted that these are instances of unresolved conflict, not failures of the emotional system. Nevertheless, enactments are apt to be awkward and stilted, like a person with a knee injury attempting to play tennis. The player has chosen to remain on the court but is favoring the injured leg to avoid pain and the possibility of additional damage. Thus, movements that are ordinarily executed automatically and forcefully are restrained or avoided altogether. The person cannot play full out. Similarly, a husband trying to be diplomatic about the quality of his wife's cooking may either be so tactful that the point never gets across or—despite his attempt to be gentle—cause her to end up hurt and insulted.

When circumstances result in emotional contradictions, neither of two alternatives can be fully enacted and neither can be abandoned. People often talk about such dilemmas as if they constituted a fight *between* their head and their heart, or between two conflicting emotions, but these are simply figures of speech. The conflict is between two divergent options, not one part of the system and another. It is more social than organismic (Akillas & Efran, 1989). If a student cannot decide whether to continue to hit the books or to put them aside to join his buddies for a beer, the struggle is only *figuratively* between the superego and the id or the intellect and the animalistic. It is more accurately described as a choice of two paths of action, each of which entails costs and benefits.

These conflicts can be short-lived or long-term. Here is an example of a relatively delimited but painful scenario: Because a man wants to appear flexible and cooperative, he readily agrees to go and see the film his date has picked out. She assumes it is a movie in which he also has some interest. He would rather have gone to see an action adventure, but he did not say so. When the film is over, trouble begins. She loved the film and is eager to compare notes. He wants to avoid revealing his negative reactions and would just as soon move on to another topic of conversation. She notices that he has shut down but is not sure why. They both feel the strain, but neither is willing to take steps to put the hidden agenda squarely on the table. They make some awkward attempts to get the evening back on track, but the rhythm has been lost—and, with it, optimism about future interactions.

Let's examine a more chronic problem. A husband may try to be "modern," but members of his family of origin bristle at the idea that his wife is earning more money than he is. The family did not even like the idea of her working. Behind his wife's back, they criticize him for failing to "wear the pants" in the family. When he tries to defend his wife against their attacks, they laugh about how thoroughly she has him brainwashed. He is continually caught between conflicting sets of values and different "club" operating rules. The coward's way out—moving out of town or avoiding contact—is only a temporary solution. Meanwhile, he experiences daily reminders of these issues. Even the possibility of her receiving a further promotion, ordinarily a happy event in family life, becomes part of a pattern of emotional contradiction.

Actions have consequences, and often the social payoffs and costs are ambiguous, changing, or mutually inhibiting. For example, a wife would like to leave her abusing husband but fears that he will discover her intentions prematurely, putting her at even greater risk of physical harm. She could inform the authorities, but she has no guarantee that they would issue a restraining order or that, if they did, it would protect her from his wrath. Therefore, she continues to live through a severe emotional contradiction, perhaps even forced to pretend that she desires sexual intimacy with this person she is trying to control, outsmart, and keep at a distance. Of course, there are instances that are even more consternating, because some battered wives *do* have strong desires for sexual contact with their abusing husbands. The wife caught in that sort of predicament may silently admonish herself for being weak willed or depraved. She may come to believe she is the "slut" he accuses her of being. Again, these are not problems of the emotions, per se, nor fights between rational and irrational modes of operation. If the subjectively available options were charted—perhaps in a decision matrix—the resulting behaviors might seem perfectly understandable. Therefore, it is almost always a disservice to suggest to clients that they are acting "impulsively" or are unable to express their true selves or emotions. They are unlikely to be able to use such information. Such assessments are made from a perspective outside the system. They do take account of the preferences an individual actually experiences at the time the situation is unfolding. It would be far more useful to provide a therapy forum in which all of clients' preferences—including those they would rather forget—are acknowledged as having been fully legitimate. Preferences are instances of system functioning. They may have unfortunate consequences, but they do not have to be defended.

The Role of Preferences

It was American humorist James Thurber (1894–1961) who said, "All men should strive to learn before they die what they are running from, and to, and why." We think he was talking about the desirability of accepting one's preferences—positive and negative—and finding ways to realize at least some of them. Contrary to clinical folklore (with which many therapists collude), preferences are rarely hidden from us, although we may decide to keep them hidden from others. More often, we dismiss them as being trivial or unimportant. The rationalistic culture in which we live demands that, except at Mardi Gras, people tailor their desires to fit into socially acceptable categories and, whenever possible, be made to sound virtuous and orderly. This is not an evil plot. It is a side effect of our broader desire to live together in socially coordinated patterns. However, whenever a person becomes more concerned with justifying choices than enacting them, he or she takes a step away from self-understanding and satisfaction. The antidote is the courage to acknowledge preferences with a minimum of social defense, and to lie responsibly about most of the rest. This is usually called "being appropriate" and judicious. Maturana puts it more bluntly by pointing out that in any culture thus far invented, people have been forced to save their lives many times over through hypocrisy (Efran & Heffner, 1991)!

Being appropriate works. On the other hand, trying *not* to want what one wants virtually guarantees a condition of emotional contradiction, accompanied by periods of increased stress, inefficient functioning, incompletions, and self-doubts. Attempting to want what someone else expects one to want is another variation on the same theme. Thus, it is very important to distinguish, in one's languaging, between wanting something and *wanting to want* it. One reason "quit smoking" programs have notoriously high dropout and relapse rates is because they often fail to distinguish between those two categories. They indiscriminately lump together people who want to stop and those who simply *wish* they wanted to stop. Most of those who actually want to stop, just do (Schachter, 1982). The others "quit" over and over again.

As we have indicated, our definition of emotion includes support for the quiet moments as well as the dramatic moments. Relaxing requires bodily adjustments just as clearly as does fleeing from an enemy, making love, or playing tennis. The supposition is that particular skeletal and hormonal adjustments facilitate given actions and inhibit others, and that there is a criss-crossed flow between the realm of language and the corresponding adjustments of the "bodyhood" (Maturana, 1988). The postures required for problem solving do not coincide with those needed for falling asleep. In the morning, when the telephone rings and wakes you up, there is at least a short period of emotional contradiction. You may want to get off the phone as quickly as possible so you can return to sleep and finish a pleasant dream. Under these circumstances, your conversation is usually less than scintillating, and you may find yourself entering into agreements you do not really understand and may later forget—anything to get the other person off the phone.

The body apparatus takes time to change from one mode of operation to another. In the meantime, you do the best you can. For instance, you may be geared up for a fight, and then the social circumstances shift rapidly, making it inappropriate to continue along that particular pathway but difficult to know what else to do. One of the authors recalls returning a broken wrist-watch to a jewelry store. Unfortunately, the clerk immediately agreed to repair the watch. There was no room for the argument that the author had already begun on the way to the store (playing both parts himself). The author, unable to shift gears, continued to grumble under his breath about "quality control" and so on, despite the fact that the adversary had long since vanished.

A person returning home after a tough day at work, may be unable to "recalibrate" immediately. However, other family members may have difficulty understanding why the person is not in a better mood. Actually, such moods are not either good or bad, they are simply postures that happen to be appropriate or inappropriate to the task at hand. When you are being attacked, it is useful to defend yourself or to counterattack. However, the attack mode interferes with attempts to be playful or affiliative.

PERPETUATING FAMILY MYTHS

Most of us no longer live within the social structure of a tribe or in the tight-knit community of a small village. At the shopping mall, public school, or business office, people from many backgrounds intermingle, each pursuing a somewhat different agenda. In the tribe, there were only a limited number of ways to be, and there were customs and rites of passage to help people move from one stage of life to another. There was little flexibility, but there was also a minimum of confusion. The postmodern world presents the opposite condition—a vast array of "design-it-yourself" alternatives, but also a lot of personal confusion. In this sense, couples come by their disagreements "honestly" (Shapiro, 1965). Spouses have fundamental disagreements about whether or not to have children, whether or not to move away from relatives, whether or not to support more than one career, and so on. These used to be givens. Again, the conflicts that arise in these domains are not really problems of communication, in the usual sense, nor do they result from a failure of one party or another to adequately process emotional cues. They are more likely the interpersonal fallout of creaky social arrangements, some of which are tied to the fact that we are in a period of rapid social change.

Unfortunately, therapists can make such matters worse when they give in to the temptation to psychologize and pathologize these problems. People are caught in a sociological crossfire, but when they seek treatment, clinicians look for evidence of deficient or broken personal and interpersonal "machinery." Therapists easily spot "dysfunction" and, in the process, promulgate a mythological standard concerning ordinary family ties and emotional closeness. The mythology they endorse creates false hopes and expectations, and causes individuals to continue blaming themselves and their family of origin for failing to have a storybook romance. Ironically, the self-blame that results creates new problems and complicates old ones. As we indicated earlier, how problems are languaged and symbolized can determine, to a considerable degree, the course of events.

Consider, for example, the now prevalent myth of the sensitive male. Although sightings of such creatures are only a little less rare than those of the Loch Ness monster, marriage and family counselors talk as if all normal husbands are expected to share their "inner feelings" with their spouses and to listen attentively, patiently, and sympathetically as the day's happenings are described. It should come as no surprise that the average husband would much prefer to escape to the safety of the television set rather than endure a prolonged exchange about either his wife's emotional state or his own. This may not be a laudable state of affairs, but it is quite ordinary in the culture, hardly a reason to reach for the *Diagnostic and Statistical Manual*. Many families with the same pattern do quite nicely, without anyone feeling a need to seek treatment. Frankly, a husband willing to come in for therapy in the first place is already something of an exceptional specimen, which may be why he is willing to sit and discuss being more emotionally sensitive. Many males, particularly in the lower socioeconomic groups, would be unwilling to have anything to do with such a potentially effete venture. Even in middle-class groups, female clients outnumber males by over 2 to 1 (Sharma, 1986). Mental health workers on the front lines report that they often have to coax a husband to take an interest in family treatment, and if he does show up for a session or two, it may be with considerable reluctance and skepticism. On the ride home, he may have some choice comments to make about the session—and the therapist. In this area, at least, he does not lack emotional expressivity.

What is surprising is that therapists often endorse ideals that they, themselves, have not experienced in their own relationships. Moreover, their friends show many of the same "dysfunctional" patterns they pathologize in clients. For some reason, therapists' common sense often goes out the window when they close the door to the consulting room. Family theorist Salvador Minuchin (1974) puts it this way:

> In spite of sociological and anthropological studies of the family, the myth of placid normality endures…This picture of people living in harmony, coping with social inputs without getting ruffled, and always cooperating with each other, crumbles whenever one looks at any fam-

ily with its ordinary problems. It is therefore alarming that this standard is sometimes maintained unchallenged by therapists, who measure the functioning of client families against the idealized image. (pp. 50–51)

Let's keep in mind that when it comes to being in a family and raising children, most of the world operates on the basis of very different standards and assumptions than we do. At professional conferences, and in sessions, therapists talk as if current child-rearing and marital practices have been established to be biologically and psychologically correct, and as if deviations from these patterns are destined to produce unhappiness and psychopathology. This is a professional myth—widespread, comforting, smug, and wrong. Obviously, we do not recommend a wholesale return to the ways of previous generations, but an occasional look backward in time (or outward toward other cultures) might help us wake up from the slumber of provincial perspectives. Until comparatively recently, for example, excess children used to be routinely given or sold to the church, sent to a workhouse or orphanage, or abandoned altogether. "Parenting consisted largely of attempting to break a child's inherently evil spirit....The idea of loving children upon birth is a relatively recent concept. It is not universal and it is not instinctual" (Spector, 1992, p. A-19).

If we trace the notion of romantic love, particularly as a basis for forming long-term relationships, we would again see that this is a recent, and, in many ways, *peculiar* invention, which has by no means been demonstrated to produce greater fulfillment, more stable or long-lasting relationships, or an overall increase in happiness. In fact, some consider it one of the worst possible bases on which to found a family. French essayist André Maurois is reputed to have said, "We owe to the middle ages the two worst inventions of humanity—romantic love and gunpowder."

A while back, sex manuals added to the burden of guilt people experienced by suggesting that simultaneous orgasm was the sine qua non of sexual adequacy and was necessary to mental health. As a result, partners all over the country blamed themselves and each other for inadequate performance, and they either suffered in silence or sought various forms of therapy and sex counseling. Unrealistic standards concerning high degrees of emotional attunement in marriage can have similar deleterious effects on people's morale. In addition, therapists seem to do little to educate couples about the role and operation of sex in marriage. If anything, they reinforce misconceptions. For example, when therapists hear that sexual desire has diminished over the years of a marriage, they often offer fancy explanations in terms of faulty communication patterns, midlife crises, misplaced projective identifications, repressed memories of childhood sexual abuse, and so on. But it is a well-established pattern in mammals that intensity of interest decreases as novelty wears off and familiarity sets in. It is true of rats, chimps, and other mammals, including human beings (see, for example, Wilson, Kuehn, & Beach,

1963). As we indicated earlier, structural coupling of any sort leads to a decrease in focal attention.

Attraction is usually most intense when there is limited access, such as when there is a chaperone to avoid, a wall to climb, or even a danger or guilt to be overcome. A recent survey by the National Opinion Research Center of the University of Chicago indicates that 9% of married individuals report that they were sexually abstinent during the year preceding the survey, and it is estimated that 10% to 25% of all married couples are celibate at some point during the marriage (Avna & Waltz, 1992). Well-known sex researcher C. A. Tripp (1987) summarizes the issue of diminishing attraction this way:

> The fact that sexual motivations founder or simply prove impossible once a fairly critical distance between partners is violated in either direction turns out to be the key to many a locked-up secret in human relations....Conspicuous by its absence is the love-story dream: the on-going, sexually vivid, delicately intimate monogamous tie. It exists—like mermaids, perpetual motion, and heaven itself—in the human imagination" (pp. 60–61).

Yet couples rarely hear this side of the story from their therapists. Instead, they are left to wonder what is wrong with them as individuals or as a couple. They may be given "sensate focus" exercises to do, but the results will only be temporary. As the novelty of trying something new wears off, the biologically determined trend will continue. Again, in the situation we have described, we are dealing with nature, not psychopathology. People's basic biology was simply not designed with current practices in mind.

LOVE

For Maturana (1985)—love defined as the passion or preference for living in close proximity—is the fundamental emotional stance of human beings. It is the affiliative posture that makes civilization possible, and, in turn, has made possible the development of language and the other higher cortical functions. However, the opposite of love is not hate—it is indifference. Therefore, it is not inconsistent that in our desire to live together, we experience many moments of emotional contradiction. The expression "Can't live with 'em, can't live without 'em" is an acknowledgment of the struggle. Therapy ought not promise that a bit of behavioral contracting, past-history exploration, or experiential focusing will eliminate the roller coaster ride that is a relationship. On the other hand, marriage does not have to be constant "work," as some therapists grimly warn. Marriage is a constantly changing codrift. It is always a matter of "What's next?" If not taken too seriously, or artificially forced to remain in static configurations, it can be a quite rewarding and exciting "venue" within which to experience life.

A CLINICAL VIGNETTE

A book chapter can never be a course in psychotherapy. Moreover, structure determinism is not a theory that urges a particular set of clinical tools and techniques. Structure determinism provides an integrative perspective that makes it easier to think through problem of living and relating. We close with a brief clinical vignette in order to help concretize, in the reader's mind, how we work with couples. It is offered "as is"—without accompanying commentary and interpretation. As with any such segment, many interpretations of what transpired are possible. Some would be incorrect, but none would be complete or final.

One of the authors saw an articulate married couple who complained that their discussions of even routine household tasks quickly deteriorated into bitter conflagrations. The wife complained that her husband was never willing to sit down and discuss "their problems." The husband countered that she was not interested in discussing problems—she was interested in getting her own way. In their fights, a common pattern emerged: the husband felt attacked and withdrew, sometimes by becoming silent, sometimes by leaving. The wife would get more incensed and begin packing his belongings, throwing them around the room, or, on one occasion, out the second-story window.

The husband and wife were seen for a number of joint sessions, but they were also seen individually. When everyone is always in the room together there can be too much bickering, defending, and cross-complaining to generate fresh perspectives. In one of his individual meetings, the husband asked, "What am I supposed to tell her when she criticizes?" The therapist said, "Why tell her anything? Why not invite instead of responding? Take her to dinner and let her make you wrong over soup or salad. Besides, how can you reply if you have no idea what she is asking?" They got into a discussion about people needing to "be right" and the reciprocal need to make someone—anyone—wrong. They also came back to the issue of what, in the husband's view, their marriage was supposed to be about. What purpose was it supposed to serve?

Often, people become so invested in surviving daily struggles that they forget about the bigger picture. As someone once noted, the trouble with life is that it is so continuous. Therefore, it is hard to stop and see how you got to where you are, and even more difficult to contemplate a route to someplace else. Therefore, orthogonal interaction often consists of moving to a higher plane of discourse—peering at the *frame that forms the context for the problem* rather than at the problem itself (Efran & Clarfield, 1993; Efran, Germer, & Lukens, 1986). In this connection we should add that we virtually never ask a person how he or she "feels" about some event. That phrasing seems to rivet the person into the narrowest possible frame of reference—just the reverse of what we want to have happen (Efran, Lukens, & Lukens, 1990). Even asking "What are you thinking?" or "What is your thought in connection with that?" does a better job of producing relevant and evocative material. Ironically, it was reevaluation counselors, who concentrate on "discharge" patterns, who discovered the advantage of avoiding the term "feeling" in such questions (Jackins, 1965).

In discussing "the big picture," the therapist mentioned something about the fact that in this form of therapy we were not all that concerned about day-to-day problems. That statement struck the client as odd, because he was sure the opposite was true—that therapy was supposed to tell you how to manage immediate difficulties. He did not quite understand what the therapist meant, but something about the statement stuck with him after the session.

During the week that followed, the husband was in a different mood than usual.[4] He felt a little looser—not quite so afraid of an imminent attack. He had no better idea of how to proceed, but there seemed to be more "slack" in the system. At a point when his wife mentioned that he had not yet fixed the closet clothes rack, although he had promised to, he did not feel a need to defend himself. In fact, it felt as if she was just saying something that needed to be said, or something she wanted to announce. As he later indicated when thinking back over the incident, it was as if she was talking to someone else in the room or to no one in particular. He did not respond to her comment about the closet, but he did propose they bring in pizza for dinner instead of bothering to prepare something at home. This surprised her, because he rarely made such a suggestion without prompting. She found herself agreeing to the plan. As he was taking her order—finding out if she wanted pepperoni, extra cheese, and so on—he moved closer and gave her an affectionate nudge. It was not a planned attempt to be strategic—it just happened.

It is characteristic of our work that we almost never give clients direct "homework assignments" or suggest that they take particular actions that feel artificial just to produce a given effect. We do not have much faith in the outcomes of those forms of manipulation. On the other hand, out of the "conversation" that occurs in a session, there are frequent surprising twists, in which the grip of a problem seems to loosen or the person rather suddenly comes to see a situation very differently. In this particular case, both people were able to move in directions they neither had predicted nor, several days before, had considered very likely.

SUMMARY

Traditional theories of emotions fall into two broad categories: cathartic approaches that perpetuate the belief that emotions are internally stored substances, and rational supremacist approaches that overemphasize the intellect and the ability of individuals to select motivational or cognitive states. The alternate view presented here proposes that the attempt to parse human functioning into the traditional categories of thoughts, emotions, and actions is inherently flawed and counterproductive to psychological theorizing as well as to clinical practice. The theory of structure determinism, which posits that people are essentially arational beings embarked on a structural *drift*, emphasizes the central role of language in the creation and resolution of problems. From this point of view, the term "emotion" is redefined: it refers to the shifting body "postures" (including skeletal and hormonal adjustments) that support enactments. Even action sequences that are linguistic, involving primarily words and symbols, cannot be initiated or completed without appropriate adjustments of the "bodyhood." Attention is focused on patterns of communal interaction, especially those moments of *emotional contradiction* when individuals are attempting to pursue conflicting preferences and goals. Orthogonal interaction, which renders hidden assumptive structures visible, is offered as the key to therapeutic change in working with couples and families.

ACKNOWLEDGMENTS

The authors wish to thank Elsa R. Efran and Aaron T. Hogue for their assistance in the preparation of this chapter.

REFERENCES

Akillas, E., & Efran, J. S. (1989). Internal conflict, language and metaphor: Implications for psychotherapy. *Journal of Contemporary Psychotherapy, 19*, 149–159.

Anderson, W. T. (1990). *Reality isn't what it used to be*. San Francisco: Harper & Row.

Avna, J., & Waltz, D. (1992). *Celibate wives*. New York: Lowell House.

Bateson, G. (1979). *Mind and nature*. New York: Dutton.

Bohart, A. C. (1980). Toward a cognitive theory of catharsis. *Psychotherapy: Theory, Research, and Practice, 17*, 192–201.

Bruner, J. (1986). *Actual minds, possible worlds*. Cambridge, MA: Harvard University Press.

Bruner, J. (1990). *Acts of meaning*. Cambridge, MA: Harvard University Press.

Efran, J. S., & Clarfield, L. E. (1993). Context: The fulcrum of constructivist psychotherapy. *Journal of Cognitive Psychotherapy: An International Quarterly, 7*, 171–180.

Efran, J. S., & Fauber, R. L. (in press). Radical constructivism: Questions and answers. In R. A. Neimeyer & M. J. Mahoney (Eds.), *Constructivism in psychotherapy*. Washington, DC: American Psychological Association.

Efran, J. S., Germer, C. K., & Lukens, M. D. (1986). Contextualism and psychotherapy. In R. L. Rosnow & M. Georgourdi (Eds.), *Contextualism and understanding in the behavioral sciences: Implications for research and theory* (pp. 169–186). New York: Praeger.

Efran, J. S., & Heffner, K. P. (1991). Change the name and you change the game. *Journal of Strategic and Systemic Therapies, 10*(1), 50–65.

Efran, J. S., & Lukens, M. D. (1985). The world according to Humberto Maturana. *The Family Therapy Networker, 9*(3), 23–25, 27–28, 72–75.

Efran, J. S., Lukens, M. D., & Lukens, R. J. (1990). *Language, structure, and change: Frameworks of meaning in psychotherapy*. New York: Norton.

Efran, J. S., & Spangler, T. (1979). Why grownups cry: A two-factor theory and evidence from "The Miracle Worker." *Motivation and Emotion, 3*, 63–72.

Frijda, N. H. (1986). *The emotions*. New York: Cambridge University Press.

Frijda, N. H. (1988). The laws of emotion. *American Psychologist, 43*, 349–358.

Gazzaniga, M. S. (1985). *The social brain: Discovering the networks of the mind.* New York: Basic Books.

Gazzaniga, M. S. (1988). *Mind matter.* New York: Houghton Mifflin.

Goolishian, H., & Anderson, H. (1987). Language systems and therapy: An evolving idea. *Psychotherapy, 24*(3S), 529–538.

Goolishian, H., & Anderson, H. A. (1988). Human systems as linguistic systems: Preliminary and evolving ideas about the implications for clinical theory. *Family Process, 27,* 371–393.

Gustafson, J. P. (1986). *The complex secret of brief psychotherapy.* New York: Norton.

Gustafson, J. P. (1992). *Self-delight in a harsh world: The main stories of individual, marital, and family psychotherapy.* New York: Norton.

Herrnstein, R. J. (1990). Rational choice theory: Necessary but not sufficient. *American Psychologist, 45,* 356–367.

Hofstadter, D. R. (1979). *Gödel, Escher, Bach: An eternal golden braid.* New York: Basic Books.

Howard, G. S. (1991). Culture tales: A narrative approach to thinking, cross-cultural psychology, and psychotherapy. *American Psychologist, 46,* 187–197.

Jackins, H. (1965). *The human side of human beings.* Seattle: Rational Island Publishers.

Kelly, G. A. (1955). *The psychology of personal constructs* (Vols. 1 & 2). New York: Norton.

Kelly, G. A. (1969). *Clinical psychology and personality: The selected papers of George Kelly* (B. Maher, Ed.). New York: Wiley.

Loftus, E. F. (1980). *Memory: Surprising new insights into how we remember and why we forget.* Reading, MA: Addison-Wesley.

Loftus, E. F. (1991). *Witness for the defense: The accused, the eyewitness, and the expert who puts memory on trial.* New York: St. Martin's.

Loftus, E. F. (1992, August). *The reality of repressed memories.* Frederick Howell Lewis Distinguished Lecture presented at the 100th Annual Convention of the American Psychological Association, Washington, DC.

Loftus, E. F., & Loftus, G. R. (1980). On the permanence of stored information in the human brain. *American Psychologist, 35,* 409–420.

Mahoney, M. J. (1991). *Human change processes: The scientific foundations of psychotherapy.* New York: Basic Books.

Maturana, H. R. (1980). Biology of cognition (1970). In H. R. Maturana & F. J. Varela (Eds.), *Autopoiesis and cognition: The realization of the living.* Boston: Reidel.

Maturana, H. R. (1985). Reflexionen über liebe [Reflections on love]. *Zeitschrift für Systemiche Therapie, 3,* 129–131.

Maturana, H. R. (1988). Reality: The search for objectivity or the quest for a compelling argument. *Irish Journal of Psychology, 9,* 25–82.

Maturana, H. R., & Varela, F. J. (1987). *The tree of knowledge: The biological roots of human understanding.* Boston: Shambhala Publications.

Mendez, C. L., Coddou, F., & Maturana, H. (1988). The bringing forth of pathology. *Irish Journal of Psychology, 9,* 144–172.

Minuchin, S. (1974). *Families and family therapy.* Cambridge, MA: Harvard University Press.

Nichols, M. P., & Efran, J. S. (1985). Catharsis in psychotherapy: A new perspective. *Psychotherapy: Theory, Research, and Practice, 22,* 46–58.

Nichols, M. P., & Zax, M. (1977). *Catharsis in psychotherapy.* New York: Gardner.

Ornstein, R. E. (1991). *The evolution of consciousness: Of Darwin, Freud, and cranial fire: The origins of the way we think.* New York: Prentice Hall.

Progoff, I. (1953). *Jung's psychology and its social meaning.* New York: Grove.

Rabkin, R. (1970). *Inner & outer space: Introduction to a theory of social psychiatry.* New York: Norton.

Rescorla, R. A. (1988). Pavlovian conditioning: It's not what you think it is. *American Psychologist, 43,* 151–160.

Rieff, P. (1959). *Freud: The mind of a moralist.* New York: Viking.

Rotter, J. B. (1954). *Social learning and clinical psychology.* Englewood Cliffs, NJ: Prentice-Hall.

Ryle, G. (1959). Feelings. In W. Elton (Ed.), *Aesthetics and language.* Oxford: Basil Blackwell.

Sarbin, T. R. (Ed.). (1986). *Narrative psychology: The storied nature of human conduct.* New York: Praeger.

Schachter, S. (1982). Recidivism and self-cure of smoking and obesity. *American Psychologist, 37,* 436–444.

Shapiro, D. (1965). *Neurotic styles.* New York: Basic Books.

Sharma, S. L. (1986). *The therapeutic dialogue.* Albuquerque: University of New Mexico Press.

Spector, A. (1992, October 9). The "traditional" family is largely a fictional ideal. *Philadelphia Inquirer*, p. A-19.

Tripp, C. A. (1987). *The homosexual matrix.* New York: McGraw-Hill.

Varela, F. J. (1979). *Principles of biological autonomy.* New York: Elsevier North-Holland.

Varela, F. J. (1989). Reflections on the circulation of concepts between a biology of cognition and systemic family therapy. *Family Process, 28,* 15–24.

Varela, F. J., Thompson, E., & Rosch, E. (1991). *The embodied mind: Cognitive science and human experience.* Cambridge: MIT Press.

Will, G. F. (1989, December 11). Odd, isn't it, that history's most developed society has a deep craving for gore. *Philadelphia Inquirer*, p. A-14.

Wilson, J. R., Kuehn, R. E., & Beach, F. A. (1963). Modification in sexual behavior of male rats produced by changing the stimulus female. *Journal of Comparative and Physiological Psychology, 56,* 636–644.

Yalom, I. D. (1989). *Love's executioner, and other tales of psychotherapy.* New York: Basic Books.

Zinbarg, R. E. (1990). Animal research and behavior therapy: Part I. Behavior therapy is not what you think it is. *Behavior Therapist, 13,* 171–175.

NOTES

1. Coué (1857–1926) is best known for having people repeat to themselves, "Every day in every way I am getting better and better." How is this any different from repeating positive self-statements?

2. Actually, leeches are now making something of a comeback in traditional medicine, but in a different role and context.

3. Color palettes are different in different species. Birds, for example, operate with four chromatic dimensions—one more than we use. Therefore, if birds could speak, there would be no agreement about how many primary colors exist or how they could be named. This isn't simply a difference in precision or an argument over labels. There would be no easy way to map their color scheme onto ours, or vice versa. Moreover—and this is the important point—neither species knows what is really "out there," and each is "correct" within its own frame of reference.

4. Our clients frequently report that they leave a session in a very different state of mind, although they do not always recall exactly what was discussed. Moreover, they find notions derived from the session "drifting to mind" at strange moments or in connection with developing circumstances.

SECTION D

Cognitive and Behaviorally Oriented Approaches

9

Emotion and Behavioral Couple Therapy

KELLY KOERNER and NEIL S. JACOBSON

In the current zeitgeist, it is assumed that behaviorism does not have anything useful to say about emotion. Although clinicians may adopt "behavioral" techniques, they frequently reject the behavioral philosophy from which the techniques were derived, primarily because complex behavior such as emotion seems beyond the scope of behaviorism. However, as we hope to make clear in this chapter, behaviorists *are* interested in the study of emotion. In fact, the role of emotion is one of our prime interests as we study the process of change in couple therapy.

Our goal in this chapter is to describe a behavioral conception of the role of emotion in couple therapy that we have found useful in clinical work. In the process, we hope to disengage the caricature of behaviorism from the behavioral ideas that might enrich the applied study of emotion. Our purpose is to provide an alternative view of emotion that contributes to improved efficacy of couple therapy. Although there is evidence that traditional behavioral couple therapy (TBCT) is helpful for some couples, continued improvements are necessary because about one third of couples continue to report marital problems at the end of therapy (Baucom & Hoffman, 1986), and about 50% report relapse at follow-up. These results are comparable to outcome data available on other approaches (Jacobson & Addis, 1993).

We begin with a brief historical presentation of the ideas guiding TBCT in order to then discuss the limitations of this traditional view with respect to what we see as a more meaningful translation of behavioral principles to clinical work. Then we provide a behavioral perspective on the use of emotion in couple therapy, and describe how this conceptual analysis informs clinical work with couples.

HISTORY

The interventions of traditional behavioral couple therapy were derived from a social exchange model of interaction and distress. From this perspective, the behaviors of individuals in a relationship are interdependent such that processes of influence and control are mutual and reciprocal. The probability of a given interaction pattern, then, is determined primarily by social consequences provided within the relationship through the continual interchange of behaviors that are pleasing and beneficial and those that are displeasing and costly.

Distress, in this model, is assumed to be a function of couples' interaction patterns. Inevitably, couples have wants and needs that conflict. Distress results from couples' aversive and ineffectual response to conflict. When conflicts arise, one or both partners may respond aversively by nagging, complaining, distancing, or becoming violent until the other gives in, creating a coercive cycle that each partner contributes to and maintains. In addition to this coercive cycle, "deficits in problem-solving and behavior change skills, reinforcement erosion, stimulus control deficiencies, skill deficits, exogenous factors which increase the attractiveness of alternatives to the marriage, and discrepant preferences in regard to the degree of intimacy desired" (Jacobson & Margolin, 1979, p. 29) make it difficult for couples to resolve conflicts.

Given this model of distress, the goal in traditional behavioral couple therapy is to teach couples more productive and positive means of effecting desired behavior changes in one another. That is, the couple changes distressing interaction patterns between the partners by learning to reduce punishing behaviors and increase reinforcing behaviors. Change here means accommodating to a partner's requests and compromising or collaborating to solve problems. In TBCT there has been an emphasis on skill training and contingency contracting to help couples learn to change each other and themselves.

In traditional cognitive-behavioral couple therapy, changes in emotion have most often been thought of as the by-products of change techniques directed at the cognitions and overt behaviors that elicit unpleasant emotional responses (Baucom & Epstein, 1990, p. 91). The aim, then, in TBCT is to change some "nonemotional" aspect of the relationship (cognitions and overt behaviors) in order for the clients to feel better about one another. A good example of this sort of intervention is behavior exchange. Because global dissatisfaction with the partner and the relationship may be a function of the naturally occurring decrease in positive effects each member of the couple has on the other, the TBCT therapist gives directives that encourage each partner to identify and change the frequency of behaviors reinforced and punished in the relationship. Similarly, love days (Weiss, Hops, & Patterson, 1973) or caring days (Stuart, 1980) are times during which each spouse does extra things to please the other. The intention in interventions such as these is to change overt behaviors, which are assumed in turn to produce changes in emotional reactions.

Emotional changes have seldom been presented as necessary precursors to changes in other aspects of the relationship in TBCT. Rather, TBCT has used emotional communication training as an adjunct to problem solving rather than as a means to change the partners' emotional experience with each other. Successful problem solving in the traditional format depends on the ability of both partners to express negative feelings directly. The therapist in TBCT might conceptualize a partner's difficulties expressing negative feelings as a skill deficit and teach emotional expressiveness (provide a list of feeling words; teach the client to discriminate between feelings such as disappointment and anger, etc.). Increasing explicit verbal expression of emotions was also alleged to foster a more sensitive response in the partner. A cognitive rationale for such training is that feelings can be used as cues to interrupt problematic attributional patterns, for example, as cues to seek clarification from the partner, rather than to jump to the conclusion that the other's motives are negative.

Thus, TBCT has made limited use of emotion as a precursor to change in other aspects of the relationship. However, efforts to improve the efficacy of TBCT have convinced us that, with many couples, an alternative approach is needed. In order to be helpful, especially with the most difficult cases, the therapist must create the conditions that facilitate emotional acceptance of unchangeable aspects of the relationship. Strategies in TBCT are intended to alter problematic interaction patterns through compromise, collaboration, and problem resolution. However, the traditional approach implies undue optimism about the extent of change that is feasible. Mate selection can be fallible, and couples do have some problems that cannot be easily solved, such as where a two-career couple decides to live when one is offered an out-of-town promotion or whose life-style should be altered more to care for an aging parent. In addition, traditional behavioral couple therapy is often overly optimistic about the degree of compromise and collaboration that a polarized couple can muster early in therapy.

The recognition that couples may have limited potential for change has led to additions to and reworking of TBCT (Christensen & Jacobson, 1991; Christensen, Jacobson, & Babcock, 1993; Jacobson, 1992) called integrative behavioral couples therapy (IBCT). In IBCT, rather than working solely to change problematic behavior, the therapist also helps to change the context that makes that behavior problematic, especially in those areas where the change potential is limited by factors unlikely to be amenable to change. Efforts to develop a more effective treatment have led back to basic behavioral principles and, as a result, to the important role of emotional change in couple therapy. In fact, one major area of expansion in IBCT is that the conditions under which emotional changes occur, and the covariation of emotional changes with other behavioral changes, are explicitly analyzed and incorporated into the therapy. Emotional experience and expression become key targets of intervention.

This emphasis on emotion may seem at odds with common perceptions regarding behaviorism. In developing our conceptualization of emotion in the following section, we will begin by making clear the basic assumptions of behavioral theory that distinguish it from other approaches.

BEHAVIORAL CONCEPTUALIZATION OF EMOTION

As stated above, behaviorists are interested in explaining the same subject matter as are thinkers from other approaches. Adopting a behavioral theory in no way rules out the study of emotion. Contrary to popular misconceptions, as behaviorists we do not consider emotion epiphenomenal; rather, emotions constitute some of the most interesting behavior to study. A behavioral approach to the study of emotion does, however, differ from other approaches in two important ways. First, behaviorists define behavior as anything an organism does, including both public behavior that is observable to others and private behavior that is observable only to the behaving individual. Private behaviors include those that occur within the person's body as well as those occurring when the person is alone. By convention, behaviorists categorize behavior as motor (movements of the skeletal muscles), cognitive-verbal (e.g., thinking; perceiving; attending; imaging; spoken, written, and gestural communication), and physiological (activity of the CNS, glands, and smooth muscles); all of these may be either public or private. The behavioral position we espouse avoids the inherent dualism of reified hypothetical constructs (that is, the differentiation of "mental" phenomena from other organismic responding) by considering all organismic responding to be behavior. We see no a priori reason to assume that the extent of public accessibility to behavior means that the factors influencing private behavior are necessarily different from those influencing public behavior. The extent of public accessibility is related to the methods one adopts to study behavioral phenomena but in no way invalidates the status of behavioral phenomena for scientific study (Moore, 1980).

A second aspect of behaviorism that differentiates it from other approaches is a nearly single-minded emphasis on pragmatic criteria for evaluating explanations. As with other approaches, explanations should allow "prediction and control with adequate scope and precision" (Hayes & Brownstein, 1986, p. 179). However, from a behavioral perspective, the adequacy of an explanation is judged primarily with respect to its ability to generate effective action (influence or control). That is, "A term, concept, or statement of a relation is not true or false simply according to public agreement about the correspondence between it and other events, but according to the impact that the use of the term, concept, or statement has on dealing successfully with the phenomena of interest" (Hayes & Brownstein, 1986, p. 177).

This pragmatic criterion for judging explanations leads to analysis of environmental factors because these are the only variables to which the therapist and researcher have direct access and, therefore, the only variables through which the researcher and therapist can directly effect change. Thus, what is often viewed as rigid or arbitrary insistence on describing environmental causes of behavior is actually requisite for intellectual integrity, when one adopts prediction and control as the goals of one's analysis. Of course, there are times when variables affecting a given phenomenon are beyond control for technical reasons. Nevertheless, behaviorists insist that "an adequate explanation or interpretation be based on events that are of the same kind as those permitting control" (Hayes & Brownstein, 1986 p. 179); in other words, the variables must at least in principle be amenable to control where control is technically possible.

Combining pragmatic criteria to evaluate explanations with the assumption that the same sorts of explanations should be sought for both public and private behavior results in a unique approach to the study of emotion. Behavioral explanations are made in terms of the antecedents and consequences that covary with the experience and the expression of emotion rather than in terms of hypothetical or mediational constructs. Our assumption is that both the experience and expression of emotion are behavior and, thus, are subject to the same influences that govern other behavior. Two types of contingencies influence behavior: phylogenetic and ontogenetic. Phylogenetic influences are those factors that have favored properties and functions of emotional expression and experience that have been adaptive for the species. Such properties and functions are considered to be somewhat "hard wired" in the sense that they are innate, patterned response predispositions. Ontogenetic influences on behavior have to do with the ways that individuals' emotional experience and expression are modified as they adapt to physical and social environments during their life. We will tend to emphasize the factors that influence individual adaptation rather than species adaptation in this discussion, despite the recognition that both are important.

Behaviorists discuss individual adaptation in terms of functional analyses, that is, by describing environmental antecedents and consequences unique to an individual that identify the conditions under which behavioral covariations occur. In this approach, one behavior (overt behavior or emotional response) is not explained by some other behavior (e.g., some cognitive mediator such as an activated schema). Rather, the goal of a functional analysis is to identify aspects of the social (or physical) environment that influence the relationships among cognition, emotion, and overt responding.

We will use the term "emotion" to mean complex covariations of physiological/somatic, cognitive, and overt behavioral responses that occur when an event interrupts an individual's typical chain of behaviors in a particular situation (Kelley et al., 1983). Experimental manipulation of events that lead to emotional arousal has shown that emotional arousal and mood states correlate with changes in diverse factors such as concepts of the self, self-attributions, perceptions of control, learning and performance on various tasks, patterns of self-reward, and delay of gratification (Izard, Kagan, & Zajonc, 1984). Reviews of the research on the relationships between emotional states and various cognitive processes (Bower, 1981; Gilligan & Bower,

1984) also indicate that emotional states are associated with mood congruent bias in memory and can bias interpretation, fantasies, projections, free associations, personal forecasts, and social judgments so that they are congruent with current mood. In other words, there are certain changes in conditions that lead to broad shifts in feelings, thoughts, urges, preferences, and other patterns of responding.

The division of behavior into overt, cognitive, and physiological categories is arbitrary and made for conceptual clarity rather than in response to evidence that these response modes actually function as separate systems. This point is especially relevant given that basic research on emotions demonstrates that cognitive, affective, and motor response systems do not correlate perfectly but rather may overlap yet remain somewhat independent (Derryberry & Rothbart, 1984). It is exactly such discrepant covariations among response systems that make an analysis of the conditions that give rise to behavioral covariation useful. In this view it is the *conditions* under which emotions are felt, expressed, inhibited, dissociated, and so on that are of interest. Said differently, relating one type of behavior (emotion) with another type of behavior (cognition or overt action) is limited unless the conditions that link cognition-emotion-action are specified because the particular combinations are determined by interpersonal context. For example, the thought "This is unfair" in one context may lead to anger, in another to sadness, and in another to a state of calm.

From a behavioral point of view, specifying the interpersonal context and personal history that influence the relationships among different response systems is necessary not only for a more complete understanding of emotion but also because it is at the level of interpersonal context that the therapist has influence. Delineating the antecedents and consequences associated with the variation in links of emotion-cognition-action is important clinically. For example, to work successfully with couples who are violent, it is important to know the conditions under which an argument is likely to escalate into violence. These couples often have heated arguments that do not result in violence, and so the conditions that differentiate violent from nonviolent interactions are important. A husband who is jealous and angry that his wife comes home late from work is likely to remember other times when he felt neglected or mistreated by her, and is likely to be more suspicious of her explanations than he would be when he was not angry. The content of the argument, and the thoughts and feelings of each partner, may be the same in any argument, regardless of whether the argument ends in violence. The covariation of a husband's feeling angry and actually striking his spouse during an argument may be more a function of variables that block disengagement from conflict—for example, arguing in a car. An explanation of the husband's violence only in terms of his concurrent cognition or emotional arousal is incomplete. Instead of positing emotion or cognition as *causes* of observable behavior, we would want to understand how emotional experiences and observable behaviors with which they are associated are a *function* of events in the environment.

Certain changes in conditions, such as loss, seem universally associated with emotion, that is, with broad behavioral reorganization that allows for rapid adaptation to the changed social or physical environment. The pattern of reorganization (and maybe even the particular aspects of situations that are evocative) is probably a function of evolutionary contingencies.

However, unique experiences over the course of one's life modify the pattern of individual emotional experience and expression. For a given individual, certain emotional responses occur only when some events or objects are present and not in the presence of others. The term "stimulus control" is used to describe this differential influence of some events or objects on behavior. A stimulus can be simple (a gentle nod of the head) or complex (a therapist's vivid metaphor that incorporates important aspects of a whole course of therapy). The valence or value of the stimulus is determined by interpersonal context and personal history. A partner's gentle nod of the head may be reassuring and occasion the other's further self-disclosure in one context, whereas in another context it is experienced as a hurtful criticism. Identifying the differential stimulus control of events that precipitate and maintain shifts in emotional experience and expression is helpful.

For example, one partner's interest in the other's work and thoughtful efforts to make the other comfortable at the end of the day may usually enhance intimacy and closeness. That is, the caring, attentive behavior may serve the stimulus function of setting the occasion for self-disclosure as well as that of increasing the probability that approach, interest, and caring are more likely to occur in the future. However, after an argument, all efforts to be attentive, efforts to make the other happy, and so on, may fail to enhance intimacy. In fact, often the same behavior that once drew the partners together now actually drives them apart. Each attempt at asking about work is a reminder of how that partner is avoiding the real issue (e.g., conflict resolution). Small kindnesses that once were viewed as thoughtful demonstrations of love are seen as manipulations and diversions. In other words, under some conditions what was once reinforcing becomes punishing, and a different complicated sequence of interaction becomes more likely. An argument both evokes emotional responding and changes the usual effects or meanings of other events. Such changes in the social environment (1) lead to broad behavioral reorganization that changes the probability of diverse related behaviors (e.g., the partner becomes more likely to do all of the things one does when angry) and (2) lead to broad changes in stimulus control and stimulus functions (e.g., what is reinforcing in the throes of an argument is often different from what reinforces when partners are getting along well).

The point we are making here is that because emotional experience and expression are under stimulus control, the therapist can identify and change aspects of the interpersonal context (i.e., change stimulus control) that influence emotional experience and expression to help couples become genuinely more flexible and intimate with each other. Because the changes in conditions that evoke emotion are also those that result in broad reorganization of behavior that simultaneously alters the meaning or valence (stimulus function) of many aspects of the interpersonal context, interventions that change contingencies regarding emotion are likely to have wide-ranging impact. From a behavioral point of view, understanding the changes in context that lead to the sort of broad reorganization that occurs under emotional arousal is interesting and worthwhile. Rigor in understanding the antecedents and consequences of emotional experience and expression should refine our ability to alter the context such that what was experienced as inducing suffering, alienation, and distance can instead be experienced as painful but not divisive. Because the conditions that evoke emotion naturally lead to reorganization of broad classes of behavior, identifying and more systematically making use of these contingency changes could increase the effectiveness of therapy.

This is the crux of the role of emotion in IBCT, developed by Jacobson and Christensen (Jacobson, 1992; Christensen, Jacobson, & Babcock, in press). We believe that the resolution of numerous couples' problems is better approached by changing the context that makes the behavior problematic than by changing the problematic behavior. The conditions associated with reorganizations of behavior and the changes in stimulus function that accompany emotionality are the conditions that the therapist must access to be effective with these couples. The specific contextual changes we are interested in creating are ones that reorganize behavior to foster a shift to more open, nonblaming, and nondefensive communication about problems, in addition to some accommodation of each partner to the other's specific needs. We would like for couples to experience the partner's behavior in a new way, such that what was offensive or blameworthy is now more understandable and tolerable or even seen as a valuable, though at times unpleasant, difference. Emotional acceptance results when there is a shift in context such that the behavior that was problematic no longer needs to be changed. The idea is to devote effort to identifying and changing the conditions that help create a change in the emotional response of the partner making the complaint about the other's problematic behavior, in addition to, and sometimes instead of, focusing on changing the other's problematic behavior. In IBCT various means are used to alter the stimulus control of the situation so that problems or differences come to be experienced and are responded to more flexibly and openly. A brief example of fostering emotional acceptance is provided here to illustrate a situation in which the IBCT therapist would try to change the stimulus context to foster emotional acceptance instead of changing the differences or problems that may be resistant to change.

A couple come into therapy because they are constantly arguing. The husband, who was originally attracted by his wife's emotional strength and independence, now thinks that she is cold and distant and feels unloved and unsupported. He would like her to do small favors and show little kindnesses such as thinking to pick up his dry cleaning if she is in the area, bringing him coffee, and showing affection in public. He believes that if she really loved him, she would spontaneously do these things. She, on the other hand, thinks he is vaguely demanding and irritatingly indirect. While once he seemed to appreciate her strengths, especially as being different from his mother, she now feels imposed upon, criticized, and unaccepted. To foster emotional acceptance, the IBCT therapist would neither encourage her to change by assigning behavioral exchange exercises nor use cognitive techniques to change the husband's desire to be taken care of sometimes. Rather, the goal would be to change the context so that this difference stops driving them apart. The therapist might help the husband to more actively take care of his own needs for nurturing, thereby making it somewhat less painful when his wife does not. The therapist might label the interaction pattern to highlight each partner's vulnerability so that when the wife feels criticized by the husband for not being more giving, this is a signal for her to commiserate and maybe show caring in other ways that are more comfortable to her. These are just two ways the therapist might try to achieve change in aspects of the situation that help the couple drop the struggle to get the other to change.

Couples inevitably have differences and some problems that will not change as much as they would like over the course of marital therapy. For some couples, the differences themselves are not nearly as problematic as their efforts to resolve the differences. Both partners' well-intentioned efforts to solve the problem often elicit problematic behavior in the other that, in turn, elicits problematic behavior in themselves. For example, one partner may be jealous of the amount of time the other spends with work and friends. In an effort to accommodate a jealous husband, the wife declines an offer to go out with coworkers one night, privately considers how to rearrange work commitments to make time for a weekend away, and then cuts short a phone conversation to greet her husband at the door. The husband, thinking of their recent discussions about jealousy, asks, "Who was that on the phone?" in what he hopes is a neutral tone of voice. Although slightly annoyed that he asked who was on the phone, she tries to avoid upsetting him and answers, "Oh nobody," and changes the topic. The casual "Oh, nobody" actually makes it seem that she does not want to tell him who it was, and when she describes how she turned down an offer to go out with coworkers, he feels jealous and guilty that he is restricting her, and he minimizes the importance of her concession by expressing his doubt that she really wants to be with him anyway: "I know you'd rather be out with your friends—maybe you could still go."

In cases in which requests for change are not granted or are granted in an ambivalent manner, or when the contingencies of a problem are subtle or difficult for either the therapist or client to access, typical TBCT interventions are unlikely to be helpful. The typical problem-solving format is unlikely to help couples negotiate changes such as increasing the amount of trust between them, their interest in sex, or their respect for each other's achievements. As well, negotiated problem solving where both partners give something up usually entails negative reinforcement and punishment, which may be experienced as aversive.

Rather, in these instances, we would like for couples to have a conversation in which they have the experience of commiserating about the problem, understanding how the problem causes both of them pain. The point is to get them to talk about the pain they experience as a consequence of the other person's actions, without blaming the other person for it. Emotional acceptance results when there is a shift in context such that the behavior that was problematic no longer needs to be changed.

Acceptance often connotes resignation. This is not what we mean. The idea is to help the couple become as fully aware of relevant aspects of the problem as possible (e.g., the hurt and disappointment each feels about the other's actions), without deluding themselves that the pain caused by these differences will stop because the other person will change. For example, if the partners have differing strong values about how each should balance commitments to work and family, the idea in IBCT is to help each partner fully understand and acknowledge the other's values. Rather than the only options being for the partners to divest themselves of their own values or blame and criticize the other for the wrong values, the partners respectfully accept each other's opinions and make decisions about remaining together based on their willingness to accept the effects that different values have on their partnership. The idea is to help the couple see each other as clearly as possible, so that decisions to stay together are based not on wishful thinking regarding changes the partner will make but on a clear assessment and acceptance of the limits of change.

We have described somewhat the theoretical background guiding our approach to the use of emotion in IBCT and how this differs from more traditional interventions in TBCT. The next section describes in detail how interventions we label emotional acceptance are used.

EMOTIONAL ACCEPTANCE IN IBCT

Emotional acceptance work is a modification and expansion of what Jacobson and colleagues have described elsewhere as troubleshooting (Jacobson & Holtzworth-Munroe, 1986; Wood & Jacobson, 1985). Couples seeking therapy tend toward rapid, reciprocal, and often explosive escalations of negative affect (e.g., Gottman, 1979; Margolin & Wampold, 1981) that are often unchanged by seemingly successful courses of therapy (Hahlweg, Revenstorf, & Schindler, 1984).

For many years, our attention was focused on clinical strategies that could be used to stop these arguments. We attempted to induce couples to generalize their communication–problem-solving skills to these naturalistic occurrences. Many couples simply failed at this endeavor, despite being excellent communicators and problem solvers in other situations. The next step involved attempts to teach cognitive coping skills that could be employed during the argument to promote deescalation (Epstein, 1982; Schindler & Vollmer, 1984). For example, after learning to recognize the early signs of an angry altercation, spouses might be trained to emit self-statements to calm themselves down and redirect the conversation. Based on our clinical experience, these techniques were usually unsuccessful. Couples had little trouble producing such self-statements outside the emotional context, but it often seemed that when embroiled in the heat of battle, neither was sufficiently willing or able to disengage from the process long enough to engage in coping skills. When asked about their lack of utilization after the fact, at times spouses would say that they forgot about the coping skills, and at other times they remembered but chose not to employ them. It often seemed that other reinforcers prevailed, despite the spouses' ability after the fact to recognize that these quarrels had a destructive impact on the relationship. (Jacobson & Holtzworth-Munroe, 1986, p. 61)

The lack of success at diffusing and interrupting coercive interactions led to the development of troubleshooting to improve the efficacy of therapy. In troubleshooting no explicit effort is made to directly inhibit escalation processes, but rather the goals are to (a) explore thoughts and feelings that occur during the escalation process and (b) examine alternatives that exist in highly charged emotional interactions. In troubleshooting as originally conceived, the first step is to induce the couple to "get into" one of their common and prototypical disputes during the session. This can be done either by having each partner provide an account of a distressing interaction from the week or by using some problem that recurs during the session. Next, the therapist interrupts any escalation that occurs during the interaction by engaging in dialogue with each partner. The therapist attempts to elicit the interaction's meaning by having each partner thoroughly elaborate reactions at the time, especially any unexpressed thoughts and affect. Finally, the therapist and client retrospectively analyze the escalation with the aim of generating alternatives that might improve the course of future arguments. While the steps of troubleshooting have been refined and expanded in emotional acceptance work, the goals of such interventions have undergone significant modification in recent years.

The goal in emotional acceptance is to change the context that makes a given behavior problematic, whereas the goal in troubleshooting has been to change the problematic behavior by identifying alternative behaviors of each partner that could make the interaction go differently in the future. To foster emotional acceptance, the therapist does not modify the existing behavioral capabilities but rather strives to create a context that naturally draws out the existing positive repertoire of each partner. The therapist does this by altering the stimulus control of the situation in such a way that each partner actually comes to experience the other's previously aversive behavior in a different way, which allows for intimacy-enhancing dialogue about problems and differences.

Said differently, the specific context of the problem that must be changed varies from couple to couple. But, in general, changing the context means that the therapist attempts to make changes in the behavior of the spouse who has the complaint so that he or she can give up the struggle to change the other's relatively unchangeable behavior. There are four types of interventions used to promote emotional acceptance in IBCT: empathic joining around the problem, turning the problem into an "it," increasing tolerance of the partner's aversive behavior, and enhancing self-care. The therapist may promote dialogue about the problems and issues that divide the couple in ways that enhance intimacy (emotional acceptance via increased empathy). The therapist may encourage the couple to view problems as a common enemy they share rather than something one *does* to the other (turning the problem into an "it"). The therapist may intervene strategically by prescribing the problem and through this ritualization alter the interaction to counter the attribution of malicious intent and accompanying emotional pain (tolerance building). Or the therapist may help the complaining partner to find alternative ways of getting needs met or may help that partner become clear about his or her bottom line and the ultimate sequence of events that would lead to the dissolution of the relationship (self-care). The idea in all of these interventions is to help the client give up the struggle to change the other partner.

The therapist is guided by two principles in emotional acceptance work. Most people have long histories of approaching, comforting, commiserating with, and working to help relieve the distress of a loved one. At its simplest, emotional acceptance amplifies emotions that are likely to encourage such behavior and that compete or interfere with simultaneous blame, anger, defensiveness, and distancing. That is, the therapist (1) attempts to alter stimulus control just enough to generate competing responses and (2) identifies and makes maximum use of the naturally occurring contingencies in the couple's relationship. Said differently, the therapist blocks the couple's usual responses to the problem in ways that promote alternative behaviors that receive positive reinforcement. The therapist does this in various ways, but always the intent is to generate intimacy and compassion for the partner by drawing attention to and making salient those aspects of the situation that engender compassionate understanding.

Empathic Joining

Empathic joining around the problem, a reworking of troubleshooting from TBCT, has much in common with reframing in emotionally focused couple therapy (EFT) (Greenberg & Johnson, 1988). As in troubleshooting, empathic joining typically involves generating a discussion about the original problematic behavior or, in some cases, asking the couple to fight in the session. The therapist encourages both partners to tell their own version of what happened, reflecting and summarizing so that each feels understood. To gather information about the thematic similarities among the couple's disputes, the therapist asks questions to ascertain what each intended to communicate and what actually was communicated during the fight. For example, the therapist might ask, what was the meaning for one partner when the other said no to lovemaking? How does the partner express interest and what is the meaning of that to the recipient? It may be that one partner's enthusiastic or repetitive expressions of interest in sex mean to the other that nothing but sex matters, that the former offers affection but does not value the latter as a person.

As the therapist develops an idea of the thematic similarities among the couple's conflicts, he or she is active, using various strategies to alter the stimulus control properties involved in the disputes. The therapist encourages both partners to say more about how they felt and to say it in a different way than they did during the fight. The therapist selectively draws out those aspects of the conversation that were not said or that were not really heard by the partner that might lead the partner to better understand or feel closer to the other. If the person cannot say those parts of the conversation that were left out, then the therapist does. Therapist comments amplify and distill the affective part of the communication and separate this from the blame. The therapist may do this with or without explicitly acknowledging that the communication is modified.

Therapist encouragement to express feelings is intended to lead to a "softening" of each partner toward the other. By softening we mean that there is less rigid stimulus control—the person is able to attend to and be affected by many aspects of the situation rather than only those aspects congruent with upset mood. This softening may facilitate both partners' flexibility in solving the problem and may also generalize to interactions outside of therapy. However, in emotional acceptance work, it is more important that the couple have an intimate conversation than that they solve the problem. Also, in IBCT the emphasis of expressing feelings is *inter*personal, that is in the service of generating more compassion in the partner. This is a slightly different emphasis than in EFT, which seems to emphasize *intra*personal discovery of experience more than IBCT.

Another way the therapist alters what the couple attends to is by providing verbal descriptions that are alternatives to critical or blaming client accounts. When the therapist has heard both partners and has a good grasp of the interaction pattern, he or she offers an interpretation of the thematic similarities across arguments, emphasizing the reciprocal nature of the interaction and encouraging the couple to help develop an accurate theme. The best formulations describe how each partner contributes to the pattern and balance the roles that each plays in the interaction. The therapist should clearly demonstrate with examples how each partner is caught in a self-defeating and unavoidable trap, as the behavior leads to the opposite of what is wanted. Each person is trapped in the sense that his or her responses to the partner actually produce more of the behavior that drives the other person away. The therapist uses vivid language and metaphor to convey to the other partner an emotionally compelling account that captures the other's phenomenological experience. The therapist is careful to acknowledge the negative features of the behavior but also points out any positive features that are being ignored, which under other circumstances are, or at other times in the relationship were, valued by the couple. The therapist may do this by highlighting the ways that particular differences are inevitable, understandable, complementary, good, initially what attracted them to each other, and so on.

Throughout the discussions about the theme, the point is to sensitize the couple to the whole, complex interaction sequence by providing a thematic description that unifies seemingly disparate situations. The therapist would like for the distressing interaction to become externalized as an "it," as something separate from both partners about which they can commiserate rather than blame the other.

The therapist, whenever possible, should practice "low-impact" therapy (similar to "minimal-impact" or "no-trace" camping, in which hikers attempt to alter the environment as minimally as possible during their trip). Here the therapist's goal is to encourage the conditions that naturally lead to increased intimacy with as little arbitrarily introduced format and structure as possible. Client compliance that is dependent on therapist instructional control is relatively insensitive to fluctuations in the relationship and therefore may interfere with intimacy.

Another way that the therapist establishes different stimulus control is to block and resist either partner's efforts to generate solutions as premature prior to a full understanding of how both are trapped in a pattern from which they cannot escape. The therapist does not endorse a particular solution but rather persistently points out and refines the pattern until the couple endorses the interpretation that describes their mutual contribution to the interaction, and until the couple can identify it and talk about it with each other.

Turning the Problem into an "It"

A second set of interventions seeks to shift the couple from blaming each other for problems, toward a less emotionally charged experience of problems as something that happens to both of them. The therapist uses various tactics, such as humor and putting the problem in an empty chair, in order to create emotional distance from it, so that the couple works as a team against a common enemy.

To illustrate with a case example, Linda and Carla have been partners for several years. The couple recently moved when Linda was accepted to graduate school in creative writing, and Carla has had a difficult time making friends and finding work (she is a carpenter). Linda comes home one night feeling irritable and somewhat withdrawn as she enters the apartment. Carla has friends over with whom she hopes her partner will interact, and Linda's withdrawal feels like a put-down. Carla withdraws, too, and later, after a heated argument, leaves the apartment.

In the session, the therapist might encourage each partner to express her private reactions during the argument in detail. As the therapist asks each about her perspective of what happened, the partners are initially polarized: Linda accusing Carla of being too sensitive and insecure and making too big a deal out of the whole incident; Carla counterattacking by blaming Linda for making her unhappy with the move and then refusing to spend time with her friends because they are not good enough. The therapist first attempts to get the couple to pay attention to different aspects of the situation by drawing out those aspects of the conversation that went unsaid. It may come out that Linda constantly feels guilty that she has uprooted Carla and made her unhappy, and that when she came home and saw Carla interacting with her new friends, it just reminded her of how much she had forced Carla to give up. As Carla expands on how difficult the move has been and how unwilling Linda has been to do even the smallest things to make the transition easier, the therapist may draw out how worried Carla is that the relationship will fall apart because Linda will want someone who is more of an intellectual.

The therapist has the choice of whether to pursue change-oriented strategies to help the couple reach a compromise agreement about how Linda could find ways to spend more time with Carla. However, given the highly emotional nature and pervasiveness of the closeness versus distance theme, the therapist might prefer to block Carla's efforts in this direction, and instead introduce the idea of acceptance: First, the therapist might validate Carla's concern by talking about her complaint with Linda. Second, the therapist might try to get Carla to consider a less accusing and blaming way of communicating her unhappiness with Linda. Third, the therapist might validate Linda's position and label emotions that tend to draw compassion from others (e.g., "How sad it is that your choosing to pursue this dream of becoming a writer has caused you also to have to bear this cross of making the person who is most important to you unhappy," or "Carla's criticisms of you must feel like a blade penetrating to your soul"). Finally, the therapist might offer advice about how Carla can change her part of the communication. The hope would be that Linda would soften, become less defensive and more willing to listen to Carla's concerns. The therapist offers the idea of acceptance in a way that allows the partners to commiserate about the problem as an "it"—pointing out that this life change would strain any relationship. Rather than getting either partner to do things differently, the therapist suggests that the realization that this is a painful transition for both of them is more important.

One caveat: expressions of vulnerability by one partner do not necessarily lead to shifts in the other partner's behavior, and worse, in some cases may generate responses opposite to the desired move toward compassion. There is no guarantee that attempts to generate compassion or softening will be successful. Under some conditions, the therapist might not want a husband to make himself vulnerable by, for example, expressing tender feelings of how unloved he feels, because he may not trust the wife to respond sensitively (e.g., the wife's response might be to defend her own position, thereby punishing openness and vulnerability). Given certain family backgrounds, a husband's expressing tender feelings may actually evoke a wife's disgust at his weakness. The key is to remember that individual assessment of the conditions associated with approach, intimacy, and compassion are needed.

Increasing Tolerance

Another means the IBCT therapist uses to foster emotional acceptance is to increase tolerance toward the problematic behavior or interaction that causes distress. Increasing tolerance means that when the problematic behavior or interaction occurs, one or both partners experience it as less aversive and become more able to refrain from making things worse by contributing their half of the problematic interaction pattern. Some increase in tolerance naturally happens during conversations that develop the theme of the couple's arguments when the therapist seeks to increase empathic joining. When the therapist points out how differences are inevitable, understandable, and complementary, this makes the actions that cause pain more benign and predictable and, therefore, more tolerable. Tolerance also is increased in conversations developing the theme when the therapist helps the clients externalize the problem as an "it."

The primary ways the therapist increases tolerance and thereby promotes emotional acceptance are through ritualization of the problematic interaction pattern and planning for slipups. To ritualize the problem the therapist may "prescribe the symptom" by asking the clients to fake the problematic behavior (by doing it at a time when the client does not really feel like doing it) for a brief time before telling the partner, "I'm just doing the assignment." For example, the therapist may ask a husband to respond defensively to his wife's request (when he in fact feels like meeting her request) in order to observe more objectively the way that his defensiveness affects her. In addition to increasing his understanding of his wife, the goal of this intervention is to change the meaning of the problematic behavior (husband's defensiveness) for the recipient (the wife), since the recipient can no longer be certain if it is the real thing or just the therapy assignment. In other words, here again the therapist works to change the stimulus context by changing the valence or meaning of the behavior so that it is no longer problematic, even though it may continue to occur.

A second way the IBCT therapist works directly to increase tolerance is to plan for slipups. Slipups are instances of recurrence of the problematic behavior despite each person's best efforts. The therapist consistently communicates the message that despite improvement, there will inevitably come a time when they will fall back into their old habits. The therapist works to develop ways that the couple can cope with the inevitability of slipups without becoming distressed. The therapist's statements that relapse is a normal process of change, and statements that help the couple predict when relapse will occur, change the meaning of slipups so that they are more tolerable.

Increasing Self-Care

Another way that IBCT fosters emotional acceptance is through increased self-care. Here the therapist helps clients clarify needs, wants, and their own best interest within the relationship and helps clients develop resources to satisfy needs and wants independent of the relationship. Within the relationship partners may fail to attend to what is in their own best interest, for example, by consistently putting the other's needs before their own or by placing minimal requests on the partner to avoid conflict. While one partner may be inattentive to his or her individual needs in order to maintain a relationship, frequently such efforts paradoxically create a context that inhibits intimacy. Therefore, in IBCT the therapist encourages both partners to identify and appreciate the importance of their needs within the relationship. Simultaneously, the therapist encourages both partners to take personal responsibility for seeing that their own needs are met, and encourages them to seek resources outside the relationship. Deprivation fuels the intensity of the struggle of one partner to get the other to change. That is, within the context of primary reliance on one's partner for satisfying one's sense of purpose and emotional well-being, a lack of time spent together in meaningful conversation or joint activities is experienced as deprivation of responses one needs from others (reinforcement) and deprivation of one's own opportunities to give to and care for another (response deprivation). In the context of deprivation, even subtle instances of the unavailability of the partner become significant. To increase self-care, then, the therapist may encourage the partners to find alternatives that reduce the stress on the romantic partner. For example, with a couple in which one partner has a drinking problem but is unlikely to get treatment, self-care interventions might include helping the nondrinking partner to seek support groups such as Alanon and discussing the conditions that would lead him or her to leave the relationship.

To summarize, the therapist's main goal in emotional acceptance work is to change the context such that what was problematic comes to be experienced as less distressing and is responded to with more openness and flexibility. The therapist changes stimulus control through (1) empathic joining around the problem (by amplifying affect that encourages contact, providing alternative descriptions and reframing client accounts that are blaming, and by blocking any understandable but problematic "solutions" to differences); (2) turning the problem into an "it" so that the couple gain emotional distance and unite in efforts to cope with a shared burden; (3) increasing tolerance by ritualizing the problematic and planning for inevitable slipups; and (4) increasing self-care. The therapist's primary job in emotional acceptance work is to create different stimulus control. Successful changes from emotional acceptance work depend on the extent to which changes in stimulus control actually foster behavior that is incompatible or competes with problematic behavior.

COMPARING IBCT TO OTHER COUPLE THERAPIES

Labels can be misleading when substantiating differences among various approaches to couple therapy (Jacobson, 1991). Given the shared goal of increasing couples' flexible, intimacy-enhancing patterns of responding, the interventions of various therapies may significantly overlap. Effective couple therapies, regardless of whether they are called emotionally focused (Greenberg & Johnson, 1986, 1988), insight oriented (Wills, 1982), or integrative behavioral, may be more similar than different. Differences may result more from differences in emphasis than in content or practice. A thorough comparison of the differences among these three approaches is beyond the scope of this chapter and would most usefully be based on videotapes of actual work rather than based on written description in articles or manuals. Nonetheless, comments highlighting at least the major similarities and differences are in order.

The intent of IBCT is to be a comprehensive treatment package that integrates behavioral, experiential, and family-of-origin–type interventions in a theoretically consistent fashion. Many of the techniques in emotionally focused therapy (EFT) and insight-oriented marriage therapy (IOMT) are compatible with IBCT. For example, EFT describes two therapeutic tasks: accessing emotional experience underlying the interactional pattern to discover new aspects of the self that are not currently influencing the relationship and using this emotional experience and expression to evoke new responses and change in interactional positions to redefine the relationship. In EFT equal emphasis seems to be placed on the *intra*personal and the *inter*personal effects of emotional experience. In IBCT less emphasis is placed on the intrapersonal effects. The skillful IBCT therapist works as the EFT therapist does to increase the range of experience available to each partner, and to help the couple be open to and influenced by as many relevant aspects of their situation as possible. However, in IBCT increasing the range of emotional experience is primarily in the service of facilitating emotional expression with the other partner in order to generate intimacy.

Similarly, the skillful IBCT therapist works as the IOMT therapist does to engage the couple in discussion of how their interaction patterns relate to lessons learned about intimacy in their families. However, again, the IBCT therapist does this interpretive work more for its interpersonal effects than for its intrapsychic effects, for increasing emotional acceptance of the other rather than for inducing individual personality restructuring. For example, the purpose of discussing how a wife's pattern of conflict avoidance comes from maneuvering around an unpredictably angry and rejecting father is to increase the husband's compassion rather than to foster insight for the wife.

The way that IBCT differs from EFT and IOMT is that it more systematically encompasses the behavior change technology of traditional behavioral marital therapy. At the theoretical level, IBCT seems to differ in the importance it places on environmental determinants of behavior and on emotional acceptance. As discussed earlier, there is a theoretical preference for the description of variables in terms of behavior–social environment contingencies rather than hypothetical constructs such as schema or intrapsychic conflicts. The belief is that by seeking variables in the social environment one is less likely to reify concepts and more likely to identify the variables maintaining problems at the level at which interventions are most usefully targeted. In addition, IBCT seems to differ in the emphasis on or the importance given to emotional acceptance, that is, the focus on helping couples accept what is unchangeable about each other and their relationship so that their differences are less divisive and emotionally painful.

CONCLUSION

Future theoretical and experimental work is needed to identify specific conditions associated with broad changes in stimulus function and behavioral reorganization. Integrative behavioral couples therapy is an attempt to integrate basic behavioral principles with basic research on emotion and apply these to enhance the efficacy of couple therapy.

REFERENCES

Baucom, D. H., & Epstein, N. (1990). *Cognitive-behavioral marital therapy*. New York: Brunner/ Mazel.

Baucom, D. H., & Hoffman, J. A. (1986). The effectiveness of marital therapy: Current status and applications to the clinical setting. In N. S. Jacobson & A. S. Gurman (Eds.), *Clinical handbook of marital therapy* (pp. 597–620). New York: Guilford.

Bower, G. H. (1981). Mood and memory. *American Psychologist, 36*, 129–148.

Christensen, A., & Jacobson, N. S. (1991). *Integrative behavioral couple therapy*. Unpublished treatment manual.

Christensen, A., Jacobson, N. S., & Babcock, J. (1993). *Integrative behavioral couple therapy*. Manuscript submitted for publication.

Christensen, A., Jacobson, N. S., & Babcock, J. (in press). Integrative behavioral couple therapy. In N. S. Jacobson & A. S. Gurman (Eds.), *Clinical handbook of marital therapy* (2nd ed.). New York: Guilford.

Derryberry, D., & Rothbart, M. (1984). Emotion, attention, and temperament. In C. Izard, J. Kagan, & R. Zajonc (Eds.), *Emotions, cognition, and behavior* (pp. 132–166). Cambridge, England: Cambridge University Press.

Epstein, N. (1982). Cognitive therapy with couples. *American Journal of Family Therapy, 10*, 5–16.

Gilligan, S. G., & Bower, G. H. (1984). Cognitive consequences of emotional arousal. In C. E. Izard, J. Kagan, & R. B. Zajonc (Eds.), *Emotion, cognition, and behavior* (pp. 547–588). Cambridge, England: Cambridge University Press.

Gottman, J. M. (1979). *Marital interaction: Experimental investigations*. New York: Academic.

Greenberg, L. S., & Johnson, S. M. (1986). Emotionally focused couples therapy. In N. S. Jacobson & A. S. Gurman (Eds.), *Clinical handbook of marital therapy* (pp. 253–276). New York: Guilford.

Greenberg, L. S., & Johnson, S. M. (1988). *Emotionally focused therapy for couples*. New York: Guilford.

Hahlweg, K., Revenstorf, D., & Schindler, L. (1984). Effects of behavioral marital therapy on couples communication and problem-solving skills. *Journal of Consulting and Clinical Psychology, 52*, 553–566.

Hayes, S. C., & Brownstein, A. J. (1986). Mentalism, behavior-behavior relations, and a behavior-analytic view of the purposes of science. *Behavior Analyst, 9*, 175–190.

Izard, C. E., Kagan, J., & Zajonc, R. B. (1984). *Emotion, cognition, and behavior.* Cambridge, England: Cambridge University Press.

Jacobson, N. S. (1991). Behavioral versus insight-oriented marital therapy: Labels can be misleading. *Journal of Consulting and Clinical Psychology, 59*, 142–145.

Jacobson, N. S. (1992). Behavioral couple therapy: A new beginning. *Behavior Therapy, 23*, 493–506.

Jacobson, N. S., & Addis, M. E. (1993). Research on couples and couple therapy: What do we know? Where are we going? *Journal of Consulting and Clinical Psychology, 61*, 85–93.

Jacobson, N. S., & Holtzworth-Munroe, A. (1986). Marital therapy: A social learning-cognitive perspective. In N. S. Jacobson & A. S. Gurman (Eds.), *Clinical handbook of marital therapy* (pp. 29–70). New York: Guilford.

Jacobson, N. S., & Margolin, G. (1979). *Marital therapy: Strategies based on social-learning and behavior exchange principles.* New York: Brunner/Mazel.

Kelley, H. H., Berscheid, E., Christensen, A., Harvey, J. H., Huston, T. L., Levinger, G., McClintock, E., Peplau, L. A., & Peterson, D. R. (1983). *Close relationships.* New York: Freeman.

Margolin, G., & Wampold, B. E. (1981). Sequential analysis of conflict and accord in distressed and non-distressed marital partners. *Journal of Consulting and Clinical Psychology, 49*, 554–567.

Michael, J. (1982). Distinguishing between discriminative and motivational functions of stimulus. *Journal of the Experimental Analysis of Behavior, 37*, 149–155.

Moore, J. (1980). On behaviorism and private events. *Psychological Record, 30*, 459–475.

Schindler, L., & Vollmer, M. (1984). Cognitive perspectives in behavioral marital therapy: Some proposals for bridging theory, research and practice. In K. Halweg & N. S. Jacobson (Eds.), *Marital interaction: Analysis and modification* (pp. 309–324). New York: Guilford.

Stuart, R. B. (1980). *Helping couples change: A social learning approach to marital therapy.* New York: Guilford.

Weiss, R. L., Hops, H., & Patterson, G. R. (1973). A framework for conceptualizing marital conflict, a technology for altering it, some data for evaluating it. In L. A. Hamerlynck, L. C. Handy, & E. J. Mash (Eds.), *Behavior change: Methodology, concepts and practice* (pp. 309–342). Champaign, IL: Research Press.

Wile, D. B. (1981). *Couples therapy: A nontraditional approach.* New York: Wiley.

Wills, R. E. (1982). *Insight-oriented marital therapy.* Unpublished therapy manual. Lafayette Clinic, Detroit.

Wood, L. F., & Jacobson, N. S. (1985). Marital distress. In D. H. Barlow (Ed.), *Clinical handbook of psychological disorders.* New York: Guilford.

10

Toward an Integrated Model of Negative Affectivity in Marriage

STEVEN R. H. BEACH and FRANK D. FINCHAM

A review of the literature on emotion and its potential for illuminating marital dynamics by Bradbury and Fincham in 1987 highlighted the relative paucity of empirical work on emotion and marriage at the time. Since then, considerable progress has been made in clarifying the various functions of emotion, and data on individual differences in emotional experience have grown exponentially. The present chapter draws upon these recent developments and offers a framework for understanding the development of marital discord that might serve as a springboard for further empirical research on emotion and marriage. Using the recently proposed "marital discord model of depression" (Beach, Sandeen, & O'Leary, 1990) as a point of departure, we illustrate the potential power of the framework by showing how it can increase understanding of the development of depression among spouses in maritally discordant dyads. Our central thesis is that research on individual differences in affective experience or affective styles may help us better predict not only which couples are at greatest risk of developing marital discord but also which member of the discordant dyad is at greatest risk for developing a depressive disorder.

The chapter is divided into five sections. Following this introduction, we review briefly the structure, stability, and function of affect. The third section presents a framework that emerges from our review and describes a topology that is useful for understanding marital interaction and the development of marital discord. In the fourth section, we illustrate how our framework contributes to understanding the development of depression. The chapter concludes by summarizing the major features of the analysis offered.

STRUCTURE, STABILITY, AND FUNCTION OF AFFECT

The review offered in this section is not intended to be exhaustive. Rather, it provides the basis for our subsequent discussion of the way affective style may influence marital interaction and the course of marital satisfaction over time. It also lays the groundwork for predictions of individual differences in affective response to marital discord.

Structure of Affect

A model that has achieved considerable prominence in the past decade organizes emotions in terms of orthogonal positive and negative dimensions (Watson & Tellegen, 1985). According to this view, the basic two-dimensional affective space can be represented as a circumplex model, with the various terms descriptive of affective experience being arranged around the perimeter of the circumplex (see Figure 10-1). The high end of the positive affective dimension is defined by affects such as active, elated, enthusiastic, while the high end of the negative affective dimension is defined by affects such as distressed, fearful, hostile. Conversely, the low end of the positive affective dimension is defined by affects such as irritable, sluggish, and drowsy; the low end of the negative affective dimension is defined by affects such as calm and relaxed. Thus, high negative affect and high positive affect are not polar opposites, but rather orthogonal dimensions (Watson & Clark, 1984). Importantly, it appears that the "fundamental emotions" proposed by Izard (1972, 1977) can be organized by the two higher order factors described as positive and negative affect. Likewise, alternative constructions of affective experience that posit a pleasant-unpleasant dimension and an engagement-disengagement dimension (Russell, 1978, 1980, 1983) appear to be only an alternative rotation of the circumplex, rather than a fundamentally divergent characterization of human affect (Watson & Tellegen, 1985). The literatures spawned by the work of Watson and Tellegen, Izard, and Russell therefore provide complementary views of the basic structure of emotion rather than fundamentally divergent descriptions.

The two-dimensional structure of affective space appears to be maintained across studies of observed facial and vocal expressions (Green & Cliff, 1975), analysis of affect terms (Russell, 1983), and reports of affective experience (Watson & Tellegen, 1985). In addition, the structure remains unchanged when affective experience of the moment, the recent past, or a longer time frame is described (Watson, 1988). It is preserved across analyses of pure emotion terms, emotion-related physical sensations, and emotion-related cognition (Mayer, Salovey, Gomberg-Kaufman, & Blainey, 1991), and is found in self-reports of emotion languages other than English (Watson, Clark, & Tellegen, 1984).

It appears, then, that discussions of affect in marriage, whether the domain is expressed emotion or self-report of experienced emotion, should be guided by the strong likelihood that affective experience in marriage is char-

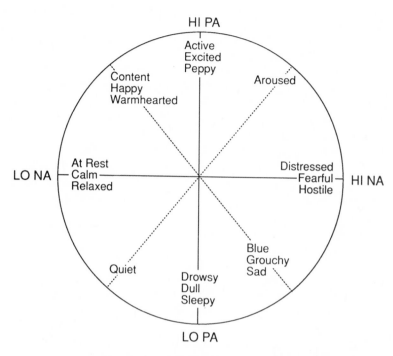

Figure 10-1. A two-factor affective circumplex (PA = positive affect; NA = negative affect). From "Toward the Structure of Affect" by D. Watson and A. Tellegen, *Psychological Bulletin*, 98, 219-235. Copyright 1985 by the American Psychological Association. Adapted by permission.

acterized by two primary dimensions. Decisions as to whether to use a pleasant-unpleasant dimension along with an arousal dimension or dimensions of positive and negative affect should be guided by their utility in a given context. In either case, however, it may be more informative for researchers to ask persons to express their feelings about their partner along two primary dimensions rather than assessing a unidimensional satisfaction or adjustment dimension. By doing so, researchers may move closer to capturing clinically important differences between couples and provide an empirically sound way of classifying discordant couples. Because of its heuristic value across a wide range of potential applications, we adopt Watson and Tellegen's (1985) model, where positive affect and negative affect define separate dimensions of affective experience.

Stability of Affect

Marital discord and depression represent affective states that are negatively valenced. One might conclude that they are related simply on the basis of response style. However, this view cannot easily explain the increasing correlation between level of marital satisfaction and depression over the first few years of marriage (e.g., Beach & O'Leary, 1991; Schaefer & Burnett, 1987). How is it, then, that negative affect in marriage comes to be increasingly intertwined with depression over time?[1]

Of particular relevance for answering this question is the considerable stability of positive and negative affect over time (Schuerger, Zarrella, & Hotz, 1989). The traitlike nature of affective experience has been captured by the terms "negative affectivity (NA)" and "positive affectivity (PA)." Indeed, average stability coefficients for report of affective state over different time periods (ranging from less than 1 year to over 20 years) were found to be .64 for NA and .72 for PA (Schuerger et al., 1989). Further, the constellation of traits correlated with each measure suggests that they have considerable overlap with earlier personality conceptions such as Eysenck's (1967) dimensions of extraversion (PA) and neuroticism (NA). Persons high in NA are therefore prone to experience anxiety and tension, but also anger, feelings of rejection, and sadness. In addition, they may be more reactive to stimuli that induce negative affect (Larsen & Ketelaar, 1991) and are likely to be self-critical and introspective and to dwell on their own mistakes. Conversely, persons high in PA are prone to experience well-being, but also social dominance, energy, and adventurousness (Clark & Watson, 1991) and may be more responsive to stimuli that induce positive affect (Larsen & Ketelaar, 1991). Elevated PA is also related to interest in social interaction, sex, and achievement.

Given the apparent relevance of greater anger and feelings of rejection (NA), or greater interest in social interaction and sex (PA), for marital interaction, it seems reasonable to posit a relation between the dimensions of NA or PA, on the one hand, and feelings toward the partner or marital behavior, on the other (for further discussion, see Bradbury & Fincham, 1989). Supporting this speculation, Kelly and Conley (1987) in a 45-year longitudinal study of 278 marriages found that neuroticism (or alternatively NA) was related longitudinally to poor marital adjustment. Similar findings have been obtained over a 12-month period (e.g., Bradbury, Leddick, & Fincham, 1989). However, as O'Leary and Smith (1991) point out, the mechanisms involved are not well understood and require theoretical and empirical attention. Similarly, Markman, Duncan, Storaasli, and Howes (1987) note that psychopathology of husbands appears more consequential overall for the longitudinal prediction of marital satisfaction, but that level of depressive symptomatology (High NA, Low PA) premaritally in either husbands or wives is the single best "individual pathology" predictor of lower marital satisfaction longitudinally. We believe the literature on positive and negative affectivity provides a theoretical context that can support theory and research linking individual affective/personality style with the development of marital discord. As we will argue below, a theoretical framework derived from the literature on positive and negative affectivity may also help further explicate specific vulnerability to the depressogenic properties of marital discord.

Function of Affect in Marriage

The significance of emotion for behavior and cognition has been highlighted by a number of authors (e.g., Livesey, 1986), and the conception of negative and positive affectivity as stable traits underscores the potential importance of this relationship. Given recent advances in our understanding of the intra- and interpersonal functions of affective displays and emotional experience, a stable affective component to personal functioning would be expected to pull many cognitive and behavioral elements of personal functioning in its wake. Indeed, the once popular idea that emotion was epiphenomenal to the more substantive concerns of cognition and behavior, or an inconvenient by-product of cognition and behavior, has been laid to rest on several fronts. At least four major roles have been proposed and documented for emotion.

First, emotions can prompt attention, influence cognitive capacity, and recruit cognitive material that is most relevant to the situation (Bower, 1981, 1991; Clark, Milberg, & Ross, 1983; Forgas, Bower, & Moylan, 1990; Mandler, 1984; Pietromonaco & Rook, 1987). These processes can profoundly affect social judgments. Of particular relevance for marital discord and the emergence of depression in the context of marital discord is the likelihood that High NA may facilitate recall of affectively congruent material and so intensify negative reactions in conflict situations. Conversely, High PA may facilitate recall of previous positive couple interactions and so facilitate positive reactions to the spouse, greater couple cohesion, and greater ease of exiting from coercive exchanges. For example, it seems likely that High NA spouses, being more negatively engaged and aroused in conflictual situations than Low NA spouses, may be more prone to recall previous anger- (or anxiety-) provoking situations, and to do so more rapidly and with less effort (cf. Blaney, 1986). Likewise, it seems plausible that High NA spouses will find their attention more readily drawn to small negative behaviors or mannerisms than will Low NA partners, further fueling their negative reactions. High NA spouses may be particularly likely to recall and react to partner behavior that is nonsupportive or critical of them, further fueling their negative affective response to conflictual marital interactions.

In addition, and perhaps of more consequence, High NA individuals may be more likely than Low NA individuals to provide negatively valenced responsibility attributions for negative partner behavior (i.e., infer negative intent, harmful motivation, and blame), a hypothesis that has gained some preliminary empirical support (Bradbury, Fincham, & Scott, 1989). Indeed, High NA individuals are characterized as often feeling unjustly treated and criticized. Because spouses' attributions for marital difficulty correlate with negative marital behavior (Bradbury & Fincham, 1992; Fincham & Bradbury, 1988a, 1992), are strongly related to marital satisfaction (Fincham, Beach, & Nelson, 1987), and can influence negatively their subsequent marital behavior (Fincham & Bradbury, 1988b), the facilitation of this cognitive material in High NA individuals could strongly influence the course of marital satisfaction. To the extent that a particular affective style facilitates the recall of material that stimulates more intense negative affect or potentiates less functional ways of evaluating the partner's behavior, it may come to be associated with discord over time. Consistent with this viewpoint, Smith (1992) has presented preliminary data indicating that negative affectivity in husbands correlates with the occurrence of the demand/withdraw pattern in couples.

Second, emotions or changes in emotions may cause the behavior of the actor and thereby play a role in signaling a need for increasing or decreasing the probability of a behavior or class of behaviors in the future (Carver & Scheier, 1990; Klinger, 1975; Clore & Parrott, 1991; Wood, Saltzberg, & Goldsamt, 1990). Of particular interest for the marital discord–depression relationship is the possibility that persons with High NA and Low PA (i.e., high levels of depressive symptomatology but not necessarily diagnosable depression) are disposed to experience more intense negative reactions to conflictual interactions with a partner, but not to experience as much positive reaction to subsequent nonconflictual interaction. Thus, persons with this affective style would be at greater risk for experiencing spousal contact as severely punishing and only weakly rewarding. Under these circumstances, avoiding or withdrawing from conflict and not initiating subsequent attempts at positive interaction with the spouse would be functional in terms of reducing discomfort in the short term. Indeed, following an argument this could place High NA, Low PA individuals at risk to avoid interactions, or adopt interactional styles that involve muted expression and minimal exchange.

Recent findings that husbands or couples displaying elevated levels of withdrawal during conflict situations experience deteriorating marital satisfaction (e.g. Gottman & Krokoff, 1989; Smith, Vivian, & O'Leary, 1990) highlight the potential importance of the withdrawal pattern. In fact, Markman and colleagues' (1987) finding that level of depressive symptomatology predicts lower levels of marital satisfaction longitudinally may reflect the operation of precisely these processes. Again, to the extent that an individual's affective style produces emotional responses that reinforce the use of maladaptive interaction patterns such as withdrawal, or fail to reinforce adaptive interaction patterns such as facilitative problem solving, the affective style that occasions those responses may come to be associated with marital discord over time.

The remaining two roles proposed for emotion concern interpersonal rather than intrapersonal processes. Specifically, emotional displays may prompt or inhibit the action of others, as when crying by a baby prompts parental caretaking (Biglan, Hops, & Sherman, 1988; Coyne, 1976; Darwin, 1872/1972; Nelson & Beach, 1990). Similarly, emotional displays may bring about the behavior of others and thereby play a role in increasing or decreasing the probability of partner behavior in the future (Patterson, 1982; Weary & Williams, 1990; Tetlock & Manstead, 1985).

In the current context, one salient example of the direct role of emotion in interpersonal processes would be the use of angry, aggressive behavior to coerce spousal compliance. When the spouse complies, the aggressive behavior is terminated, negatively reinforcing the spouse for compliance. The high exchange rate of negative behavior that can result from this type of co-ercive process is the signature of dysfunctional relationships (Weiss & Heyman, 1990). Presumably, this pattern would be most likely to character-ize couples in which there are two High NA individuals, both of whom would be prone to respond in kind to negative partner behavior.

A second type of behavior germane to interpersonal processes is the dis-play of depressive behavior. Biglan, Lewin, and Hops (1990) note that de-pressive behavior can serve as a means of controlling aggressive behavior in the family, and may well be maintained through mutually reinforcing coercive processes. For example, depressive behavior has been shown to suppress negative/aggressive spousal behavior in the context of problem-solving discussions (Biglan et al., 1985; Nelson & Beach, 1990), and complain-ing can delay or suppress the occurrence of a family member's aversive behavior in naturalistic settings (Hops et al., 1987). Schmaling and Jacobson (1990) failed to replicate the suppression effect in their investigation of mari-tal interaction. However, they did find a distinctly different pattern of re-sponse to depressive than to aggressive behavior, again suggesting that the two types of behavior are functionally distinct and should be analyzed sepa-rately. Indeed, given the Low PA component of depressive behavior, it is likely to be inherently more submissive and less threatening to a partner than an-gry/confrontational behavior. It is also likely to be less suited to facilitating resolution of the problems confronting the couple. Again, to the extent that the use of depressive behavior is associated with short-term influence over the partner, but longer-term deterioration in marital satisfaction, the affec-tive styles that support its use will come to be associated with marital dis-cord over time. It is predicted that High NA, Low PA individuals will be most likely to engage in depressive behavior when confronted with potential disagreements with their partner, and more likely to do so than persons with other affective styles. Indeed, this may be one mechanism by which they are ultimately placed at higher risk for affective disorder.

As we discuss further the emotional displays, interaction patterns, and cognitive processes hypothesized to characterize various affective styles, it will become clear that each of the four roles of emotion discussed assumes importance in the context of marriage. In addition, each can be seen as part of the interacting system that produces discord and depression and causes marital satisfaction and depressive symptomatology to become more highly related over the course of the marriage (Beach & O'Leary, 1991).

Summary and Caveats

Current conceptions of emotion provide for two higher-order dimensions of emotional experience, with changes on either dimension potentially serv-ing any of four different functions in the relationship. Although this may seem like a rather simple model, it should be noted that even in its simplest form there is no presumption that the same facets of the "three systems" of emotion (verbal report or subjective experience, facial or other behavioral display, and physiological response; Hugdahl, 1981) will necessarily correlate highly with each other or function equivalently for intrapersonal and interpersonal effects. Indeed, it should be noted that the three systems of emotion are often only modestly correlated (Craske & Craig, 1984). This may be important for certain individuals. For example, persons with compulsive personality traits may report high positive affect and low negative affect, while an observer would rate their behavior as reflecting low positive affect and high negative affect. Likewise, one could imagine a dependent individual who might report experiencing considerable negative affect, but display copious "forced" positive affect during interactions with others. Thus, it is possible that in important special cases an individual's affective style may differ depending on whether it is assessed via self-report or observation. In some cases self-report may be more valid, while in others careful observation may yield a more accurate assessment of affective style. In keeping with work on affectivity to date, our predictions assume valid self-report of emotional experience.

An additional complication arises from the fact that even when the experience and overt display of an affect are congruent, it could have a functional effect in one domain while having an undesirable effect in another, or a functional effect vis-à-vis marital functioning but a dysfunctional effect vis-à-vis mood. For example, high negative, low positive affect occurring during a marital interaction might signal a need to change the relationship in some way (a functional effect), but facilitate behaviors that reduce the probability of effectively changing the relationship (e.g., dysfunctional withdrawal), leading to a decline in marital satisfaction over the longer term. Thus, the impact of affective style on marital interaction may be complex. Further, while emotional experience is apparently organized by two underlying factors, it should be noted that specific affects situated in the same dimensional space can be discriminated from each other (Clark & Watson, 1991). Indeed, it is most reasonable to assume that differentiation among specific emotions with a High NA component is particularly likely among intimates. For example, anger may be discriminated from anxiety and may show somewhat different interpersonal and intrapersonal effects, despite being located at the same approximate location on the affective circumplex.

Finally, three factors may be needed to describe affective style adequately, with constraint (or withdrawal) being the third independent factor (cf. Clark & Watson, 1991; Smith, Vivian, & O'Leary, 1990). Most major systems of personality have required a third factor to account for important aspects of human functioning (e.g., Eysenck, 1967; Millon, 1981). The third factor of constraint (Tellegen, 1985), if included along with positive and negative affectivity, would comprise a dimension ranging from the tendency to respond with caution and timidity on the one hand to recklessness and boldness on the other. Thus, when the third factor is included, High PA does not necessarily imply boldness and Low PA does not necessarily imply meekness. If this should ultimately be shown to be a better way of conceptualizing affect in marriage, the outline that follows of the effects of affective style on marital interaction, the development of marital discord, and the emergence of depression will be slightly oversimplified. Conversely, the two-factor model is better supported by the current data, is less subject to current debate as to its basic characteristics, and contributes to clarity of presentation. Accordingly, we offer predictions on the basis of this model, recognizing that it may be necessary to reconceptualize these predictions in terms of a three-factor model in the future.

As we hope is now clear, the current model of affect and emotion as it relates to interaction is simple only in its outline. Although providing a simple framework for organizing information and offering clear predictions regarding individual interpersonal behavior, it nonetheless suggests a multiplicity of pathways from affective states to effects on marital interaction, marital satisfaction, and vulnerability to depression. In addition, while suggesting broad effects of underlying dimensions of affectivity on cognition, and one's own and partner behavior, it allows for the possibility that additional variance may be accounted for by finer discriminations between specific negative affects or by examining additional specific personality traits within affective styles.

TOWARD AN INTEGRATED MODEL OF NEGATIVE AFFECTIVITY IN MARRIAGE

Basic Topology

It is possible from current descriptions to construct a topology, representing the four quadrants of Watson and Tellegen's (1985) circumplex, that describes the basic affective styles (see Table 10-1). The topology is offered for illustrative purposes only, and no implication is intended that positive and negative affectivity are bimodally distributed. Indeed, for most applications it will be more appropriate to retain the dimensional structure of NA and PA. For current purposes, we focus on four points of the circumplex. Thus, it is possible to be High NA but either High or Low PA. Likewise, an individual who is Low NA may be either High or Low PA. Depression is characterized by low levels of positive affect in conjunction with high levels of negative affect. Accordingly, it is persons in the High NA, Low PA cell who would be expected to be at greatest risk for dysphoria and depression.

High NA individuals are expected to notice more negative aspects of their relationships and to react to these negative areas with more intense negative affect. To the extent that more intense negative reactions are correlated with report of greater impact of negative partner behavior, Markman's (1981) longitudinal results suggest risk of further decline in marital satisfaction from premarital levels. These more intense negative affective reactions to the partner may or may not also dispose High NA individuals to engage in various types of negative behavior that are problematic in the long run (cf. Smith et

Table 10-1. *Interactional Style for Each of Four "Affective Types"*

High PA, Low NA	High PA, High NA	Low PA, High NA	Low PA, Low NA
1. Approach oriented	1. Approach oriented	1. Conflict avoiding	1. Conflict avoiding
2. Calm	2. Hostile	2. Grouchy	2. Passive
3. Dominant	3. Dominant	3. Easily alienated	3. Non-responsive
4. Easily satisfied	4. Angry	4. Prone to feel mistreated	
	5. Reactive		
	6. Hard to please		

al., 1991), but High NA is likely to be associated with behaviors that are strong cross-sectional correlates of lower marital satisfaction. Accordingly, the cognitive and behavioral effects of High NA seem to pull in the direction of less marital satisfaction both initially and over the longer term.

Conversely, High PA would be expected to produce greater positive affect in response to partner positive behavior and work against behavioral disengagement, while Low PA should be associated with the tendency to withdraw, or avoid others in a conflictual situation. Thus, according to Smith and colleagues (1990), the longitudinal impact of Low PA (as defined by Watson & Tellegen, 1985) should be in the direction of lower marital satisfaction. In addition, other cognitive and behavioral effects of High PA should pull in the direction of more positive behavior of the sort related cross-sectionally to greater marital satisfaction.

However, the style one would expect to be characteristic of persons falling into each of the quadrants of the circumplex (see Table 10-1) is less clear from the basic literature. It seems reasonable, however, to suppose that High PA, High NA individuals are less affectively stable and more prone to see themselves as being mistreated than their High PA, Low NA counterparts. Likewise, while being more wary of others, they should share with their High PA, Low NA counterparts the general disposition to be dominant. High PA, Low NA individuals would presumably be likely to remain calm and unconcerned in the context of interpersonal conflict, and recover rapidly from any angry exchanges. Although such individuals might be characterized as "easy going," they would also be expected to be self-assured and prone to take charge. Again, one would expect reactive affect in response to the partner, but little chronic hostility or anxiety. Low PA, High NA individuals would be expected to be prone to withdraw from negative interactions. While submissive, they would also be expected to be prone to feel resentful and mistreated. Finally, Low NA, Low PA individuals would neither be expected to express marital dissatisfaction, nor be particularly exuberant about their marital relationship. They would presumably be relatively affectively stable, but with little social motivation or drive for dominance or achievement. However, the lack of emotional responsiveness could create obstacles for the development of intimacy and negatively affect the other partner's perception of caring and involvement, particularly if the other partner was High NA, and so disposed to read ambiguous feedback as negative. Accordingly, in some marital contexts this Low NA, Low PA style might prove problematic, while in others it might be associated with relatively stable positive affect.

. To date there is no literature on how individuals of one affective style interact with those having another style. Accordingly, we now consider "couple affective styles" and their implications. On the basis of what is already known about the individual characteristics and tendencies of persons with different affective styles, predictions are derived about marital interaction and the development of marital discord.

Couple Styles

It is possible for a person in any of the four "affective style" cells to be married to someone else in any of the four cells, resulting in 10 unique combinations or "couple affective styles." For example, it is theoretically possible for a High NA, Low PA individual to marry someone who is not similar on either affective dimension, similar on one dimension only, or similar on both dimensions. While the bulk of the available evidence suggests that assortative mating for similar personality style is the norm, persons with dissimilar personalities may be overly represented among the maritally discordant (O'Leary & Smith, 1991). Accordingly, we examine below predicted interactional patterns for both matched and mismatched partners and their role in the development of marital discord. Again, it should be noted that the 10 "types" are discussed for illustrative purposes only. In fact, the underlying dimensions are most accurately thought of as continuously distributed.

Development of Marital Discord

Before outlining our analysis, it is important to provide an overview of what is currently known about marital interaction and the development of marital discord. This digression has two important advantages. First, it provides a context that will allow the contribution of the proposed framework to be better understood. Second, it shows that current findings can easily be accommodated in our analysis.

Marital Behavior and the Development of Marital Discord

Until recently it was widely accepted that negative marital behavior (e.g., angry interchanges during marital interaction) is related to greater discord for couples, while positive behavior (e.g., emotional acceptance and positive listener behaviors) is related to greater marital satisfaction (e.g., Billings, 1979; Gottman, 1979; Margolin & Wampold, 1981; Revenstorf, Hahlweg, Schindler, & Vogel, 1984). Given the robust cross-sectional effects reported over two decades of research, this seemed the safest of conjectures (cf. Weiss & Heyman, 1990). However, this conjecture has recently been the subject of considerable controversy as a result of a series of longitudinal studies that suggest that concurrent correlates of marital discord fail to predict subsequent change in marital satisfaction. That is, positive behavior may not lead to greater marital satisfaction, and negative behavior may not result in the deterioration of marital satisfaction. This controversy is directly germane to the task of predicting the likely effects of affective style. Accordingly, we review briefly the main longitudinal results and their possible implications.

An early hint that longitudinal results might not parallel cross-sectional findings was offered by Markman (1981, 1984). In a 5-year follow-up of couples who had been assessed premaritally, he found that the perceived negativity of impact of partner behavior was a significant predictor of subsequent decline in marital satisfaction but did not correlate with concurrent marital satisfaction. Several subsequent longitudinal studies also found different patterns for concurrent and longitudinal predictors of marital satisfaction. Filsinger and Thoma (1988) found that several negative behaviors (interruptions by either spouse) predicted dyadic adjustment 5 years later despite being uncorrelated with adjustment cross-sectionally. Bradbury (1991) found that observed sadness during an interaction predicted satisfaction 24 months later. Levenson and Gottman (1983) found that an index of husbands' arousal predicted change in marital satisfaction despite showing little relationship to satisfaction cross-sectionally. Smith and colleagues (1990) reported that a measure of "disengagement" (being quiet, sluggish, silent) during problem-solving interaction was unrelated to current marital satisfaction but predicted negative change in marital satisfaction. Finally, Gottman and Krokoff (1989) found that a number of negative behaviors (e.g., anger) were correlated with lower marital satisfaction cross-sectionally but *greater* marital satisfaction longitudinally (for a review of longitudinal findings, see Bradbury & Karney, 1993).

Obviously, there is a paradox in the longitudinal work on marital interaction. If some "negative" behaviors predict better relationship functioning longitudinally, this should cause us to rethink our interpretations of what is good and bad for couples. However, these findings need to be interpreted cautiously (Smith et al., 1991). In addition to statistical issues beyond the scope of our current review, Smith and colleagues (1991) note that longitudinal work has typically predicted relatively small amounts of change in marital satisfaction. The bigger story in all these data sets has been the stability of marital satisfaction over time. For example, Gottman and Krokoff (1989) report that the stability of husbands' marital satisfaction was .96 over the 3 years of the study. Thus, even if one were to accept the finding that some negative behaviors predict (slight) positive change in marital satisfaction, it is far from clear that this would compensate for the robustly lower marital satisfaction shown by some individuals initially. As Smith and colleagues (1991) note, it is in the first 18 months of marriage that substantial change in marital satisfaction is likely to be found. Accordingly, it may be most prudent for the time being to be guided primarily by the results of longitudinal studies that assess couples premaritally. These studies find that some negative behaviors may be more important than others in predicting subsequent decline, but typically find some relationship between various negative behaviors at premarital assessment and dissatisfaction later in marriage. Thus, while the longitudinal effects are not entirely clear-cut, it is probably premature to assert that negatively valenced behaviors result in high marital satisfaction.[2]

The available longitudinal evidence suggests that negative behavior is associated with poorer concurrent marital satisfaction. In the absence of outside intervention, this level of discord is likely to be chronic once it has been established, with the couples most dissatisfied early in marriage being the ones who are particularly likely to be most dissatisfied later. A strong case can be made that an affective style high in negative affectivity may put some couples at risk for negative behavior and also put them at risk to respond with more distress as their relationship becomes discordant. In this view, the relationship of negative marital behaviors and negative marital cognition to marital discord is not an artifact of the relationship between affective style and each of the other marital variables; yet their relationship is not inconsequential either. Rather, affective style is expected to be related to each of these facets of marital functioning, but over time each of the facets of marital functioning is expected to exert influence on the others, bringing them into greater correspondence. If so, better understanding of the processes involved could advance our understanding of the etiology of marital discord.

The Interpersonal Circumplex

A number of hints about the typical interpersonal behavior of persons with varying affective styles are available in the literature on positive and negative affectivity and have been alluded to earlier. However, it may be possible to generate additional hypotheses about the likely interactions of couples with various affective styles by attending as well to the literature on the interpersonal circumplex (e.g. Kiesler, 1991; Leary, 1957; Strong et al., 1988; Wiggins, 1982). Specifically, it has been noted that interpersonal styles and affective styles have the same basic structure, and it appears possible to plot both sets of terms within the same semantic space (Kiesler, 1991). If so, it seems probable that the dimension in interpersonal circumplex models related to interpersonal control (dominance-submission) could be superimposed on the dimension of positive affectivity in affective circumplex models. Supporting this possibility, Clark and Watson (1991) have noted that positive affectivity is strongly associated with social dominance. Likewise, it seems probable that the dimension in interpersonal circumplex models related to affiliation (friendliness-hostility) could be superimposed on the dimension of negative affectivity in affective circumplex models (or perhaps rotated slightly). In this case, support for the conjecture can be derived directly from defining descriptors of high negative affectivity that include "hostile" (Watson & Tellegen, 1985). Although the extent to which affective and interpersonal circumplex models can be integrated remains to be demonstrated empirically, the correspondence is sufficiently striking to warrant further attention. In addition, it allows for a rich pool of potential hypotheses about the interpersonal behavior of couples with various affective styles. It should be noted, however, that the dimensions of the interpersonal circumplex may represent a somewhat different rotation of the factor structure, and so the characteristics associated most strongly with the primary dimensions of the interpersonal circumplex may be moderate to weak correlates of positive and negative affectivity.

The use of the interpersonal circumplex (Strong et al., 1988) to supplement predictions about the likely interactional styles of persons with different affective styles provides the following suggestions. Persons in the High PA, Low NA quadrant would be expected to be sociable, outgoing, and helpful. In its more extreme forms, this style is likely to be associated with intrusive, patronizing, and overprotective behavior. In contrast, persons in the High PA, High NA quadrant would be expected to be dominating, competitive, condescending, and critical. In its more extreme forms, this style might be characterized as detached, abusive, sarcastic, and arrogant. Persons in the Low PA, Low NA quadrant might be characterized as trusting, content, gentle, and agreeable, and in more extreme forms persons displaying this style might be described as gullible, clinging, and passive. Finally, persons in the Low PA, High NA quadrant would be expected to be timid, self-doubting, and distrustful, or in more extreme forms suspicious, brooding, self-derogating, and helpless. In sum, the suggestions derived from the interpersonal circumplex about the likely interpersonal styles of persons with various affective styles seem quite consistent with information available in the empirical literature relating interpersonal behavior to affective style. Accordingly, in our discussion of couple styles we use both the affectivity and interpersonal literatures to inform our predictions.

Using Affective Styles to Predict Couple Styles

In this section, we consider the couple interactional style and its implications for marital discord and depression that emerge when a High NA, Low PA spouse is married to each of the four possible types of partners (High NA, High PA; High NA, Low PA; Low NA, Low PA; Low NA, High PA). This focus on the High NA, Low PA spouse reflects both our interest in persons at risk for depression and evidence in the longitudinal literature on newlyweds that High NA, Low PA behaviors may predict decline in marital satisfaction (e.g., Negativity of impact, NA, Markman, 1981; Negative reciprocity, NA, Filsinger & Thoma, 1988; quiet, sluggish behavior, Low PA, Smith et al., 1990; Depression premaritally, High NA-Low PA, Markman et al., 1988).

High NA, Low PA/High NA, High PA. For the High NA, Low PA spouse with a High NA, High PA partner, one would predict avoidance of potentially conflictual interactions by the High NA, Low PA partner. However, the High

NA, High PA partner should be disposed to approach conflict and pursue potential areas of disagreement. This could be dealt with early in the relationship by the High NA, Low PA partner expressing uncertainty and acquiescing in areas of disagreement. Premaritally, this type of couple might appear relatively happy, albeit not quite as happy as the average couple about to marry. However, since the High NA, Low PA partner should be prone to resentment and hurt, resentful reactions to spouse behavior would be expected to increase over time. As the pattern of avoidance and suppressed conflict became more established, the High NA, Low PA partner increasingly would be at risk for feeling unjustly treated and victimized. This could, in turn, prompt attributional activity leading to negative responsibility attributions for marital events, and overgeneralizations about the source of partner behavior. Accordingly, despite apparently positive marital adjustment early in the relationship, the High NA, Low PA partner could find himself or herself becoming increasingly emotionally reactive, experiencing a variety of intense negative affective states including anger, tension, dissatisfaction, and guilt as the relationship continued. Thus, the High NA, Low PA partner would be expected to experience rapid decline in marital satisfaction early in the marriage. Eventually, this would manifest in sullen, complaining, or even overtly angry behavior.

The High NA, High PA partner, when faced with stressful marital interactions, would also be predicted to be quite reactive. Angry outbursts and feelings of being mistreated would be predicted for the High PA, High NA partner as well. However, here the dominant reaction would be punishing, critical, and disdainful. While the angry feelings of the High NA, High PA partner would be expected to dissipate if submissive behavior was initiated, and the High NA, Low PA spouse would be predicted to provide this type of behavior, he or she would be predicted to become increasingly maritally dissatisfied and continue to withdraw, tending to perpetuate the High NA, High PA partner's dissatisfaction as well. The resulting stalemate and chronic marital dissatisfaction would be expected to further constrict the limited positive affect experienced by the High NA, Low PA partner. Conversely, the High NA, High PA partner could easily be at risk of pursuing alternative sources of positive stimulation, whether this was simply more time away from home or involvement in extramarital relationships. In either case, the High NA, High PA partner would be expected to report substantial erosion of satisfaction at some lag following the dissatisfaction of the High NA, Low PA partner. If the stresses within the relationship continued to increase and the level of positive, supportive interaction continued to decrease, this could precipitate a sharp increase in NA for the High NA, Low PA partner. The increase in level of negative affect combined with the decrease in positive affect is likely to set the stage for the onset of a diagnosable depressive disorder.

High NA, Low PA/High NA, Low PA. Also of interest is the High NA, Low PA dyad. Because both partners possess the same basic affective style, one would expect a general agreement (spoken or unspoken) to avoid discussion of potentially conflictual material. Perceived similarity in style should allow for empathy and perceived support. However, since neither partner is likely to push the other to engage in pleasant activities together, or initiate self-disclosure and greater intimacy, the relationship might be expected to be somewhat emotionally flat and unfulfilling. However, the couple might experience few real symptoms of either marital discord or depression unless external events created problems requiring joint solutions. In the face of external stressors, or an emergent disagreement that could not be avoided, the couple would be expected to have difficulty mobilizing effective coping or joint problem solving. Reactive negative exchanges in the context of attempts at problem solving could lead to feelings of resentment and marital dissatisfaction. In turn, the breakdown in marital satisfaction and increase in aversive interactions could lead to increased depressive symptomatology for one or both of the spouses. However, it is likely that if the couple were to present for therapy they would report high levels of caring for each other, and blame their problems as much on their own faults as on the partner. Accordingly, this type of couple might be expected to present with a less bitter or intense type of marital discord.

High NA, Low PA/Low NA, Low PA. Couples with a High NA, Low PA spouse and a Low NA, Low PA partner would be expected to show a similarly negative course over time to that described above, with the exceptions that (a) only the High NA, Low PA spouse would be predicted to become depressed, (b) the Low NA, Low PA spouse would not be expected to express very much marital dissatisfaction, and (c) as a result of the lack of shared reactions to events, the level of perceived intimacy in the relationship would be expected to be slightly lower. Again, both members of the dyad would be expected to avoid conflict, leading to an emotionally flat couple with neither partner being likely to take the initiative with regard to joint positive activities. However, the Low NA, Low PA spouse would be expected to defer on issues of importance to the High NA, Low PA partner, decreasing the likelihood of recurrent, intense negative interactions. The Low NA partner is likely to have little inherent basis for empathy with the High NA partner's affective reactions. This would be expected to make the High NA, Low PA partner feel even more isolated and decrease the probability of perceived understanding and support.

The relationship dynamic described above might induce sufficient discomfort in the High NA, Low PA spouse to prompt whining/demands for attention or evidence of concern on the part of the Low NA, Low PA partner. Acquiescence to these demands would probably be accompanied by some discomfort and self-protective withdrawal on the part of the Low NA, Low PA spouse. Presumably, an intractable vicious cycle could be established under these circumstances of the sort described by Coyne (1976). That is, the depression-prone partner (High NA, Low PA) might seek assurance from the other partner, who provides it verbally but shows various nonverbal indications of withdrawal. The nonverbal indications of rejection or withdrawal then prompt further depressive behavior and whining/demands for reassurance or attention. Accordingly, a couple with one High NA, Low PA partner and one Low NA, Low PA partner might present for marital therapy with the depressed partner complaining about the other partner's emotional inadequacy and lack of love, while the nondepressed partner maintains that there is little problematic about the relationship other than the depressed partner's incessant and unreasonable demands for attention.

High NA, Low PA/Low NA, High PA. Couples with a High NA, Low PA spouse and a Low NA, High PA partner might be expected to fair the best, relative to the couple types considered so far. The nonhostile, reassuring style of the Low NA, High PA spouse would be expected to counteract the tendency of the High NA, Low PA spouse to withdraw from conflict. In addition, the relatively self-doubting, modest style of the High NA, Low PA spouse would be expected to facilitate the acceptance of positive couple activities initiated by the High PA partner, thereby tending to counteract some of the lack of positive experience that would otherwise be the case. The High NA, Low PA spouse might well feel taken care of by the take-charge style of the partner, while the Low NA, High PA spouse would potentially feel nurturant, potent, and satisfied with being important and having complete say in couple decision making. In the presence of external stress, the Low NA, High PA spouse would be expected to take charge with the passive acquiescence of the High NA, Low PA spouse. Thus, this type of couple potentially could weather even periods of depression in the High NA, Low PA spouse without experiencing serious marital discord.

Presumably, however, marital discord could develop if the Low NA, High PA partner's behavior began to appear irresponsible and undependable. If the High NA, Low PA partner were to conclude that the other could not be counted on, and was domineering without providing safety and caring, this could prompt upset, anxiety, and anger, along with a rapid decrease in marital satisfaction. Conversely, marital discord could be initiated if the Low NA, High PA spouse became bored or frustrated with the High NA, Low PA partner and began to engage in outside activities that promised more excitement and stimulation, leading to declines in marital satisfaction for both spouses. In either case, once present, marital discord would result in the perception of lost support and an increase in depressive symptomatology in the High NA, Low PA spouse.

Development of Discord in Other Couple Types

Three additional couple types are discussed to illustrate those in which both members of the dyad have the High NA, High PA affective style, those in which both members of the dyad have the Low NA, Low PA affective style, and those in which one spouse is High NA, High PA while the other is Low NA, Low PA. These couples are of interest because they highlight potential alternative pathways from affective style to marital dissatisfaction, and help identify subtypes of couples who may present with particularly chaotic marital interactions, particularly stable and lifeless marital interaction patterns, or dramatic demand/withdrawal patterns. In addition, from the standpoint of accounting for the development of depression in the context of marital discord, these couple types are examples of cases in which greater amounts of negative marital interaction and lack of marital support would be required before any excess of diagnosable depression would be predicted to result. Accordingly, like the three couple types involving the Low NA, High PA partner, these couple types lead one to hypothesize cases in which "negative" marital interaction may not lead to depression and so highlight the possibility that affective style might moderate the effect of marital discord on depression (Beach et al., 1990). For couples sharing the High NA, High PA style, increased marital discord might lead to exit from the relationship rather than depression. For couples sharing the Low NA, Low PA style, depression might fail to feed back into marital discord; and for couples with a High NA, High PA partner and a Low NA, Low PA partner, marital discord might be reported by one spouse with the other reporting little marital upset. Depression, if it occurred in the Low PA, Low NA partner, would be likely to be transient in nature, whereas if it occurred in the High NA, High PA partner it would be strongly tinged with anger and resentment. A more likely scenario, however, would be an attempt by the Low NA, Low PA partner to placate the High NA, High PA spouse. We discuss each of these partial exceptions to the original marital discord model below.

Both Spouses High NA, High PA. Spouses sharing the High NA, High PA affective style would be expected to be energetic, assertive, or aggressive, and oriented toward being dominant in interpersonal interactions. However, they also might be expected to display more anger, hostility, and criticism in the context of conflict. Accordingly, this type of couple is likely to have periods of relative marital happiness interspersed with intense conflict. Of all the couple types, these couples are hypothesized to have the most variable level of marital satisfaction over time. Once a conflict developed, both spouses would rapidly escalate the conflict, become belligerent and punishing, and display considerable negative affect. As a result, their reported marital satisfaction would plummet. Although the high level of negative affect reciprocity would be expected to generate heated discussions about conflict areas, if resolved it would result in strong bursts of positive affect (cf. Berscheid, 1983). Accordingly, either conflicts would be thoroughly aired, leaving the couple feeling extremely good, or else the couple would be at high risk to terminate the relationship during one of their periods of intense conflict. Over time, this pattern might not produce an excess of maritally dissatisfied spouses. Rather, it might be associated with a bimodal distribution of divorce-prone couples who eventually split up, on the one hand, and couples who report relatively high levels of marital satisfaction most of the time, on the other. Couples of this sort would not be expected to produce depressed spouses as frequently as couples involving High NA, Low PA partners.

Both Spouses Low NA, Low PA. At the other end of the spectrum are couples in which both partners share the Low NA, Low PA affective style. These couples are expected to show little desire for stimulation or dominance. Neither partner would be expected to initiate activities, leading the couple to do little together, living essentially parallel lives, and expecting little else. Their marital satisfaction would most likely be stable and in the low satisfied range. Few conflicts would be expected, and if some conflict were experienced, it would be dealt with by emotional withdrawal. Although some dysphoria might be reported, members of such couples would not be at particularly high risk for depression unless severe stress external to the relationship were to occur. Even if one partner were to become depressed, the other would not be expected to report much marital dissatisfaction. Such couples would seem unlikely to present for therapy unless some external stressor presented a threat to the integrity of the relationship. If such a couple were to present for therapy, it is likely that marital work would focus on mobilizing marital support for coping with the external stressor, and perhaps increasing positive marital interactions. These couples are interesting from the perspective of the marital discord model of depression since they represent cases in which low levels of marital support could co-occur with marital satisfaction and no increased risk of depression.

High NA, High PA/ Low NA, Low PA. Couples in which one spouse is High NA, High PA while the other is Low NA, Low PA would be predicted to show a particularly dysfunctional interaction pattern. Early in the relationship, it would be expected that the High NA, High PA partner would be dominant in many decisions. Since the Low NA, Low PA partner would be expected to acquiesce, this arrangement might result in little difficulty for the couple over the short run. However, the high levels of critical, punishing behavior by the High NA, High PA partner could begin to pull the other partner in the direction of High NA over time. Eventually, the Low NA, Low PA partner could begin to display depressive behavior, particularly self-derogating, helpless behavior. This would lead the High NA, High PA spouse to view the other partner as weak and unworthy. Since there would be rough comparability in each spouse's view of the situation, both might be likely to see the problem as residing primarily within the Low PA, Low NA spouse, and neither might report particularly strong marital dissatisfaction. From the standpoint of the marital discord model, this type of couple is interesting because it highlights a case where spousal criticism might influence the development of depression in the absence of clear, overt marital discord.

The three remaining couple types are not considered further because they are expected to be underrepresented among couples having a depressed partner. These couple types all include a Low NA, High PA partner. In each case the Low NA, High PA partner is expected to serve as a brake on rapid escalation of conflict and contribute to relatively rapid recovery of positive feelings in the aftermath of conflict. Thus, couples with a Low NA, High PA partner along with either another Low NA, High PA partner, or a Low NA,

Low PA partner, or a High NA, High PA partner are all expected to maintain their level of marital satisfaction fairly well, with the person higher in NA expressing somewhat more dissatisfaction with the relationship. In addition, it is possible that problems in the relationship could arise secondary to the Low NA, High PA partner's desire for social stimulation. In particular, the High PA, Low NA partner might become bored with the relationship. If the Low NA, High PA partner engages in affairs or spends time elsewhere to gratify social needs, this could precipitate marital problems and marital instability. However, even if marital problems develop, Low NA, High PA partners are not expected to be especially vulnerable to prolonged depressive symptomatology.

Boundary Conditions and Caveats

The Role of Cognition. As stated earlier, the affective styles that spouses bring to their marital relationships do not account entirely for the development of dysfunctional patterns of interaction or for the development of depression. To understand more fully the exacerbation of marital discord once a negative pattern has been established, one must consider key cognitive processes and the way in which affect recruits and maintains congruent cognition. Consideration of these key cognitive processes should help account for some of the variability in level of marital satisfaction that is present within each couple type. Again, however, persons with certain affective styles are likely to show characteristic ways of thinking about conflict, and these cognitive styles will further reinforce the impact of affective styles on the development and maintenance of marital discord and of depression. In particular, High PA should be related to confidence and dominance in interactions. In combination with High NA, this would seem to put the individual at risk for attributing more blame to the partner than to the self. Thus, the High NA, High PA partner should be most prone to make negative attributions of responsibility for partner behavior. However, there is likely to be variability in responsibility attributions among all affective styles. Accordingly, a couple's initial tendency toward marital discord could be markedly exacerbated or dampened depending on the attributional style of each member of the dyad.

Early on in a relationship, partners may begin to form stable attributions regarding the conflict in their relationship. For couples in which there is considerable conflict, such as High NA, High PA couples, the understanding each spouse has of the conflict may profoundly influence its course over time. In particular, we propose that attribution of blame becomes increasingly important. Partners may become so focused on blaming their spouse and exacting retribution for perceived wrongdoing that the potential for constructive problem engagement becomes almost nonexistent. Indeed, once discordant, couples are quite willing to attribute blame to each other (e.g., Fincham, Beach, & Baucom, 1987; for a review, see Bradbury & Fincham, 1990) and do so with a high level of certainty (Noller & Venardos, 1986). For spouses who make more negative responsibility attributions, the couple's propensities for negative interactions will be intensified. On the other hand, dysfunctional patterns of interaction will not increase over time when spouses make more benign attributions of responsibility for their conflict behavior.

Dynamic System. While there is considerable stability in the affective system both in the short term and over the long run, it is nonetheless clearly a dynamic system capable of both rapid and gradual change over time. In particular, levels of negative affect are capable of sudden sharp spikes in intensity when individuals are followed over time (Zevon & Tellegen, 1982). Indeed, it seems likely that much of what happens in successful marital therapy is designed to help spouses experiencing elevated NA return to their more usual level of negative affect over the course of therapy. Obviously, this dynamic quality complicates the analysis of the effect of NA and PA on marital interaction over time. To the extent that some individuals show great lability in their affective systems, this may render their "average" level of NA or PA relatively meaningless. It may be the variance in level of NA over time that proves more consequential for such persons.

It should also be clear that even persons who are not especially labile may experience constellations of circumstances that are capable of producing shifts in their mood and in turn influencing both their cognition and behavior. Thus, a person who is known to be typically Low NA could experience a series of stressors that would gradually shift him or her in the direction of higher levels of negative affect. As this occurred, it might be expected that the behavior patterns typically associated with High NA would become more dominant. Accordingly, relatively Low NA individuals could nonetheless come to experience high negative affect and display the behaviors associated with High NA. It follows from this consideration that there is a probabilistic relation between couple affective style and dyadic interaction and that changes in external circumstances might be anticipated to exert substantial influence on the couple's interaction.

Implications for Intervention. We have used the positive and negative affect dimensions to generate couple types and have predicted different marital trajectories for each type. Importantly, we have not argued simply that High NA will be associated with more complaints about the partner and less reported marital satisfaction. Rather, we have argued that substantive processes beyond self-report response bias link affective style with the development of discord. Accordingly, we predict that some couple types will show more change in marital satisfaction after marriage than others.

It is not surprising, however, that the dimensions of NA and PA translate into interactional terms since NA and PA do not simply represent an affective thermostat, but a stable constellation of interpersonal style variables, cognitive variables, and affective variables that serve to maintain each other. If true, early intervention aimed at the most malleable aspect of these styles could potentially change the implications of the affective style for later marital satisfaction. In particular, interventions that interrupt the dysfunctional withdrawal tendencies of some couples and the negative attributional styles of others may go far toward disrupting the negative trajectory of some couples at risk for marital discord and/or depression.

It follows from our characterization of the High NA, Low PA group that preventive marital intervention for this group is particularly important. This group seems likely to benefit from interventions that facilitate their ability to engage their partners constructively in conflict situations, enhance the probability that they have their needs met, and increase couples' ability to engage in positive shared activities. It seems likely that such interventions would go far in reversing any discord-inducing properties of their "affective style." Indeed, one might hypothesize that successful change in interactional style might work to change the dysfunctional "affective style" itself over time. Accordingly, programs for the prevention of marital discord such as PREP (Markman, Floyd, Stanley; & Storaasli, 1988) could be very effective at alleviating the worst effects of affective style on vulnerability for both marital discord and depression, particularly if they were tailored specifically to the problematic areas most characteristic of these couples. Alternatively, to the extent that there is an affective thermostat of some sort, it is possible that this type of intervention would last only for a short time before its impact was attenuated. The question of premarital prevention of depressogenic processes in marriage is a tantalizing area for future inquiry.

Notwithstanding its limitations, the framework we offer has broad applicability to a number of marriage-related phenomena. In the next section, we illustrate one such application by examining depression that develops in the context of marital discord.

APPLICATION: UNDERSTANDING THE DEVELOPMENT OF DEPRESSION

The marital discord model of depression (Beach et al., 1990) was predicated on the observation that there is a robust relationship between marital discord and depression. Indeed, about 50% of depressed persons are maritally discordant, and about 50% of the maritally discordant are depressed. Why do only 50% of discordant couples meet criteria for depression? The marital discord model, however, does not discuss in detail the role of individual diatheses for depression. That is, it does not provide a detailed account of who will be most vulnerable to the depressogenic effects of marital discord. The current formulation suggests that an important reason for the strong covariation of marital discord and depression is that persons who are high in negative affectivity and low in positive affectivity are more prone to develop and complain of marital discord than are many others. In addition, these individuals may also be more prone to develop depressive symptoms. Further, persons high in negative affectivity and low in positive affectivity are likely to be more stress reactive (cf. Beach & O'Leary, 1991). Thus, in the context of the marital discord that results, in part, from their own behavior, these individuals are likely to have large spikes in their level of negative affectivity and may show decreases in their level of positive affectivity. This spike in negative affectivity probably marks the beginning of the episode of depression in many cases.

In the current model, marital discord emerges as part of a larger process leading to depression. The more complete process is depicted in Figure 10-2. It can be seen that the marital discord model (Beach, et al., 1990) is incorporated into this model. In addition, this model is responsive to Coyne and Downey's (1991) admonition to consider the possibility that only some persons are vulnerable to depression. The model begins with the affective "type" of the couple and indicates that this is related to the emergence of discord in the relationship. In addition, it is predicted that different types of couples will be most likely to engage in low levels of the supportive behaviors (High PA), which tend to mitigate depression, and high levels of the stressful (High NA) marital behaviors, which tend to contribute to depressive symptomatology. Further, it is predicted that individuals' affective style will influence their risk for depression both directly and indirectly. Thus, affective style enters the model in three places: as it contributes to the development of discord initially, as it directly predisposes to the development of depression, and as it contributes indirectly by increasing reactivity to stressful marital interactions. It is also hypothesized that factors outside the marital relationship can influence the development of depression.

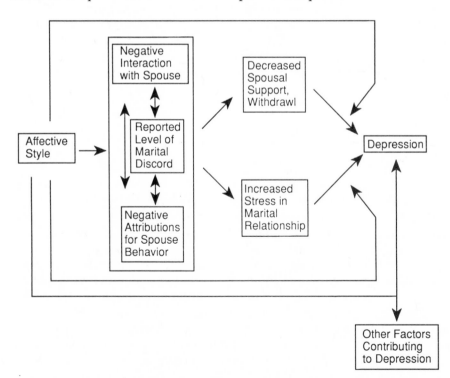

Figure 10-2. Negative affectivity in marital discord and depression.

The current integrated model has several advantages over the original marital discord model of depression. From the standpoint of research and prevention, its greatest advantage is its suggestion that the robust association between marital discord and depression will be greater for some classes of individuals than for others. That is, affective style will moderate the relationship between marital discord and depression. Further, it suggests that couple types that are at risk for both marital discord and depression may be identified, and that they can be identified before these negative outcomes occur. Accordingly, to the extent that modification is possible in the problematic constellation of affect, cognition, and behavior that predisposes them to difficulty, it should be possible to reduce their risk.

From the standpoint of understanding the marital context of depression, the current elaborated model also identifies couples who may be at risk for severe marital discord but relatively impervious to depression. These couples would contribute unexplained error variance in attempts to test the original marital discord model, but within the framework of affective styles, this type of couple may be better accounted for.

Accordingly, the amount of variance in depressive symptomatology accounted for longitudinally should increase using the current model, and the implications for preventive intervention are clearer. Indeed, using affective styles as a component of models accounting for marital behavior and cognition, or the development and deterioration of relationships over time, seems likely to provide richer descriptions of couple processes, greater predictability of marital discord, and new implications for prevention and therapeutic intervention. The intersection of affective styles and couple processes represents both an exciting and unexplored domain for future investigation and an area that promises large returns on current theoretical and empirical investment.

CONCLUSION

This chapter began by outlining the structure and function of affect and reviewed recent research that showed affective dispositions are stable and consequential. When the construct of affective styles is applied to marriage, there appear to be far-reaching consequences for our understanding of marital dynamics and the development of marital discord. The implications for marital interaction are underscored by the overlap between circumplex models of affect and circumplex models of interpersonal behavior. We elaborated the couple dynamics that might be expected when individuals with particular affective styles marry and form characteristic affective/interpersonal environments. Although the model outlined is meant to have general applicability, its relevance for understanding the development of depression in the context of marriage is particularly salient. Indeed, it provides a series of guidelines for predicting which couples and spouses within couples are at highest risk for experiencing marital discord and/or depression. Implications for prevention were also outlined.

The current analysis represents a step toward the goal of a more complete, integrated model of negative affectivity in marriage. Realization of this goal requires greater cognizance of the basic empirical literature on emotion, which will, in turn, influence the conceptualization and measurement of marital discord and the understanding of its origins. These changes necessarily bring with them advances in the way we conceptualize remediation and prevention of marital discord. At a minimum, it focuses attention on increasing positive affect in marriage as a goal distinct from decreasing negative affect. In addition, it facilitates greater sensitivity to the varying needs of couples composed of different types of individuals. Perhaps the framework provided by an integrated model of negative affectivity in marriage could provide the context required for a more empirically grounded, flexible approach to marital intervention. Accordingly, the value of continuing openness on the part of marital theorists and therapists to the basic literature on affect seems clear.

ACKNOWLEDGMENTS

The authors thank Thomas N. Bradbury for his helpful comments on an earlier draft of this chapter. Preparation of the chapter was supported, in part, by NIMH grant MH41487-05 awarded to Abraham Tesser and Steven Beach, and by NIMH grant MH44078, a grant from the Harry Frank Guggenheim Foundation, and a Faculty Scholar Award from the W. T. Grant Foundation awarded to the second author.

NOTES

1. Throughout, we focus on the explication of substantive, potentially causal, pathways from affective style to marital discord to depression, and spend little time explicating the obvious shared variance in marital discord and depression attributable to response style (e.g., complaint vs. defensive response styles).
2. Should future work find that some types of angry displays (or other "negative behaviors") are functional in some newlywed couples, it seems likely from the perspective of affective styles that this will be true only for displays of angry behavior that occur in the context of relationships that are positive in tone overall (a situation that may well pertain for many couples premaritally), or in which only brief angry displays are necessary to accomplish their purpose. This viewpoint is consistent with Smith and associates' (1990) finding that the interaction between negative affect and positive affect predicts subsequent marital satisfaction. Angry behavior could nonetheless be dysfunctional in the context of high levels of chronic, reciprocated angry exchanges or low levels of positive affect.

   In this view, it is the failure of negative affect regulation that is problematic for relationships rather than the display of negative affect per se. Specifically, if affective reactions convey information to partners in early stages of relationship development or at transition points in relationships and are functional for this reason, when they become repetitive and highly frequent, they will become uninformative and so dysfunctional. Thus, to the extent that negative affective displays are functional longitudinally, we predict that this circumstance most likely holds true only for the limited circumstance described above.

REFERENCES

Beach, S. R. H., & O'Leary, K. D. (1993). Marital discord and dysphoria: For whom does the marital relationship predict depressive symptomatology? *Journal of Social and Personal Relationships, 10,* 405–420.

Beach, S. R. H., Sandeen, E. E., & O'Leary, K. D. (1990). *Depression in marriage.* New York: Guilford.

Berscheid, E. (1983). Emotion. In H. H. Kelley, E. Berscheid, A. Christensen, J. Harvey, T. L. Huston, G. Levinger, E. McClintock, A. Peplau, & D. R. Peterson (Eds.), *Close relationships.* New York: Freeman.

Biglan, A., Hops, H., & Sherman, L. (1988). Coercive family processes and maternal depression. In R. D. V. Peters & R. J. McMahon (Eds.), *Social learning and systems approaches to marriage and the family* (pp. 72–103). New York: Brunner/Mazel.

Biglan, A., Hops, H., Sherman, L., Friedman, L. S., Arthur, J., & Osteen, V. (1985). Problem-solving interactions of depressed women and their husbands. *Behavior Therapy, 16,* 431–451.

Biglan, A., Lewin, L., & Hops, H. (1990). A contextual approach to the problem of aversive practices in families. In G. R. Patterson (Ed.), *Depression and aggression in family interaction* (pp. 103–129). Hillsdale, NJ: Erlbaum.

Billings, A. (1979). Conflict resolution in distressed and nondistressed married couples. *Journal of Consulting and Clinical Psychology, 47,* 368–376.

Blaney, P. H. (1986). Affect and memory: A review. *Psychological Bulletin, 99,* 229–246.

Bower, G. H. (1981). Mood and memory. *American Psychologist, 36,* 129–148.

Bower, G. H. (1991). Mood congruity of social judgements. In J. P. Forgas (Ed.), *Affect emotion and social judgements* (pp. 31–54). Oxford, England: Pergamon.

Bradbury, T. N. (1991). Marital interaction and marital satisfaction: Longitudinal findings. Paper presented at the Annual Meeting of the Western Psychological Association, San Francisco.

Bradbury, T. N., & Fincham, F. D. (1987). Assessment of affect in marriage. In K. D. O'Leary (Ed.), *Assessment of marital discord* (pp. 59–108). Hillsdale, NJ: Erlbaum.

Bradbury, T. N., & Fincham, F. D. (1989). Behavior and satisfaction in marriage: Prospective mediating processes. *Review of Personality and Social Psychology, 10,* 119–143.

Bradbury, T. N. & Fincham, F. D. (1990). Attributions in marriage: Review and critique. *Psychological Bulletin, 107,* 3–33.

Bradbury, T. N., & Fincham, F. D. (1992). Attributions and behavior in marital interaction. *Journal of Personality and Social Psychology, 63,* 613–628.

Bradbury, T. N., Fincham, F. D., & Scott, C. (1989). Attributions and marital satisfaction: The role of depression and negative affectivity. Paper presented at the 61st Annual Meeting of the Midwestern Psychological Association, May, Chicago.

Bradbury, T. N., & Karney, B. R. (1993). Longitudinal study of marital interaction and dysfunction: Review and analysis. *Clinical Psychology Review, 13,* 15–28.

Bradbury, T. N., Leddick, K., & Fincham, F. D. (1989). Depression and negative affectivity in marriage. Paper presented at the 61st Annual Meeting of the Midwestern Psychological Association, May, Chicago.

Carver, C. S., & Scheier, M. F. (1990). Origins and functions of positive and negative affect: A control-processing view. *Psychological Review, 97,* 19–35.

Clark, M. S., Milberg, S., & Ross, J. (1983). Arousal cues arousal-related material in memory: Implications for understanding effects of mood on memory. *Journal of Verbal Learning and Verbal Behavior, 22,* 633–649.

Clark, L. A., & Watson, D. (1988). Mood and the mundane: Relations between daily life events and self-reported mood. *Journal of Personality and Social Psychology, 54,* 296–308.

Clark, L. A., & Watson, D. (1991). General affective dispositions in physical and psychological health. In C. R. Snyder & D. R. Forsyth (Eds.), *Handbook of social and clinical psychology* (pp. 221–245). Tarrytown, NY: Pergamon.

Clore, G. L., & Parrott, G. (1991). Moods and their vicissitudes: Thoughts and feelings as information. In J. P. Forgas (Ed.), *Emotion and social judgements* (pp. 107–124). Oxford, England: Pergamon.

Coyne, J. C. (1976). Toward an interactional description of depression. *Psychiatry, 39,* 28–40.

Coyne, J. C., & Downey, G. (1991). Social factors and psychopathology: Stress, social support, and coping processes. *Annual Review of Psychology, 42,* 401–426.

Craske, M. G., & Craig, K. D. (1984). Musical performance anxiety: The three-systems model and self-efficacy theory. *Behavior Research and Therapy, 22,* 267–280.

Darwin, C. (1972). *The expression of emotions in man and animals.* London: Murray. (Original work published in 1872)

Eysenck, H. J. (1967). *The biological basis of personality.* Springfield, IL: Charles C. Thomas.

Filsinger, E. E., & Thoma, S. J. (1988). Behavioral antecedents of relationship stability and adjustment: A five-year longitudinal study. *Journal of Marriage and the Family, 50,* 785–795.

Fincham, F. D., Beach, S. R. H., & Baucom, D. H. (1987). Attribution processes in distressed and nondistressed couples: 4. Self-partner attribution differences. *Journal of Personality and Social Psychology, 52,* 739–748.

Fincham, F. D., Beach, S. R. H., & Nelson, G. M. (1987). Attribution processes in distressed and nondistressed couples: 3. Causal and responsibility attributions for spouse behavior. *Cognitive Therapy and Research, 11,* 71–86.

Fincham, F. D., & Bradbury, T. N. (1988a). The impact of attributions in marriage: Empirical and conceptual foundations. *British Journal of Clinical Psychology, 27,* 77–90.

Fincham, F. D., & Bradbury, T. N. (1988b). The impact of attributions in marriage: An experimental analysis. *Journal of Social and Clinical Psychology, 7,* 147–162.

Fincham, F. D., & Bradbury, T. N. (1992). Assessing attributions in marriage: The Relationship Attribution Measure. *Journal of Personality and Social Psychology, 62,* 457–468.

Forgas, J., Bower, G., & Moylan, S. (1990). Praise or blame? Affective influences on attributions for achievement. *Journal of Personality and Social Psychology, 59,* 809–819.

Gottman, J. M. (1979). *Marital interaction: Experimental investigations.* New York: Academic.

Gottman, J. M., & Krokoff, L. J. (1989). Marital interaction and satisfaction: A longitudinal view. *Journal of Consulting and Clinical Psychology, 57,* 47–52.

Green, R. S., & Cliff, N. (1975). Multidimensional comparisons of structures of vocally and facially expressed emotions. *Perception and Psychophysics, 17,* 429–438.

Hops, H., Biglan, A., Sherman, L., Arthur, J., Friedman, L., Osteen, V. (1987). Home observation of family interactions of depressed women. *Journal of Consulting and Clinical Psychology, 55,* 341–346.

Hugdahl, K. (1981). The three-systems model of fear and emotion: A critical examination. *Behavior Research and Therapy, 16,* 315–321.

Izard, C. E. (1972). *Patterns of emotions: A new analysis of anxiety and depression.* New York: Academic.

Izard, C. E. (1977). *Human emotions.* New York: Plenum.

Kelly, L. E., & Conley, J. J. (1987). Personality and compatibility: A prospective analysis of marital stability and marital satisfaction. *Journal of Personality and Social Psychology, 52,* 27–40.

Kiesler, D. J. (1991). Interpersonal methods of assessment and diagnosis. In C. R. Snyder & D. R. Forsyth (Eds.), *Handbook of social and clinical psychology* (pp. 438–468). Tarrytown, NY: Pergamon.

Klinger, E. (1975). Consequences of commitment to and disengagement from incentives. *Psychological Review, 82,* 1–25.

Larsen, R. J., & Ketelaar, T. (1991). Personality and susceptibility to positive and negative emotional states. *Journal of Personality and Social Psychology, 61,* 132–140.

Leary, T. (1957). *Interpersonal diagnosis of personality.* New York: Ronald.

Levenson, R. W., & Gottman, J. M. (1983). Marital interaction: Physiological linkage and affective exchange. *Journal of Personality and Social Psychology, 45,* 587–597.

Livesey, P. J. (1986). *Learning and emotion: A biological synthesis.* Hillsdale, NJ: Erlbaum.

Mandler, G. (1984). *Mind and body: Psychology of emotion and stress.* New York: Norton.

Markman, H. J. (1981). Prediction of marital distress: A 5-year follow-up. *Journal of Consulting and Clinical Psychology, 4,* 743–749.

Markman, H. J. (1984). The longitudinal study of couples' interactions: Implications for understanding and predicting the development of marital distress. In K. Hahlweg & N. S. Jacobson (Eds.), *Marital interaction: Analysis and modification* (pp. 253–281). New York: Guilford.

Markman, H. J., Duncan, S. W., Storaasli, R. D., & Howes, P. W. (1987). The prediction of marital distress: A longitudinal investigation. In K. Hahlweg & M. Goldstein (Eds.), *Understanding major mental disorder: The contribution of family interaction research* (pp. 266–289). New York: Family Process.

Markman, H. J., Floyd, F. J., Stanley, S. M., & Storaasli, R. D. (1988). Prevention of marital distress: A longitudinal investigation. *Journal of Consulting and Clinical Psychology, 56,* 210–217.

Margolin, G., & Wampold, B. E. (1981). Sequential analysis of conflict and accord in distressed and nondistressed marital partners. *Journal of Consulting and Clinical Psychology, 49,* 554–567.

Mayer, J. D., Salovey, P., Gomberg-Kaufman, S., & Blainey, K. (1991). A broader conception of the mood experience. *Journal of Personality and Social Psychology, 60,* 100–111.

Millon, T. (1981). *Disorders of personality.* New York: Wiley.

Nelson, G. M., & Beach, S. R. H. (1990). Sequential interaction in depression: Effects of depressive behavior on spousal aggression. *Behavior Therapy, 21,* 167–182.

Noller, P., & Venardos, C. (1986). Communication awareness in married couples. *Journal of Social and Personal Relationships, 3,* 31–42.

O'Leary, K. D., & Smith, D. A. (1991). Marital interactions. *Annual Review of Psychology, 42,* 191–212.

Patterson, G. R. (1982). *Coercive family processes.* Eugene, OR: Castilia.

Pietromonaco, P. R., & Rook, K. S. (1987). Decision style in depression: The contribution of perceived risks and benefits. *Journal of Personality and Social Psychology, 52,* 399–408.

Revenstorf, D., Hahlweg, K., Schindler, L., & Vogel, B. (1984). Interaction analysis of marital conflict. In K. Hahlweg & N. S. Jacobson (Eds.), *Marital interaction: Analysis and modification* (pp. 159–181). New York: Guilford.

Russell, J. A. (1978). Evidence of convergent validity on the dimensions of affect. *Journal of Personality and Social Psychology, 36,* 1152–1168.

Russell, J. A. (1980). A circumplex model of affect. *Journal of Personality and Social Psychology, 39,* 1161–1178.

Russell, J. A. (1983). Pancultural aspects of the human conceptual structure of emotions. *Journal of Personality and Social Psychology, 45,* 1161–1178.

Schaefer, E. S., & Burnett, C. K. (1987). Stability and predictability of quality of women's marital relationships and demoralization. *Journal of Personality and Social Psychology, 53,* 1129–1136.

Schmaling, K. B., & Jacobson, N. S. (1990). Marital interaction and depression. *Journal of Abnormal Psychology, 99,* 229–236.

Schuerger, J. M., Zarrella, K. L., & Hotz, A. S. (1989). Factors that influence the temporal stability of personality by questionnaire. *Journal of Personality and Social Psychology, 56,* 777–783.

Smith, D. A. (1992). An individual differences approach to marital interactions. Paper presented at the 64th Annual Meeting of the Midwestern Psychological Association, May, Chicago.

Smith, D., Vivian, D., & O'Leary, K. D. (1990). Longitudinal prediction of marital discord from premarital expressions of affect. *Journal of Consulting and Clinical Psychology, 58,* 790–798.

Smith, D. A., Vivian, D., & O'Leary, K. D. (1991). The misnomer proposition: A critical reappraisal of the longitudinal status of "Negativity" in marital communication. *Behavioral Assessment, 13,* 1–17.

Strong, S. R., Hills, H. I., Kilmartin, C. T., De Vries, H., Lanier, K., Nelson, B. N., Strickland, D., & Meyer, C. W. III (1988). The dynamic relations among interpersonal behaviors: A test of complementarity and anticomplementarity. *Journal of Personality and Social Psychology, 54,* 789–810.

Tellegen, A. (1985). Structures of mood and personality and their relevance to assessing anxiety, with an emphasis on self-report. In A. H. Tuma & J. D. Maser (Eds.), *Anxiety and the anxiety disorders* (pp. 681–706). Hillsdale, NJ: Erlbaum.

Tetlock, P. E., & Manstead, A. S. R. (1985). Impression management versus intrapsychic explanations in social psychology: A useful dichotomy? *Psychological Review, 92,* 59–77.

Watson, D. (1988). The vicissitudes of mood measurement: Effects of varying descriptors, time frames, and response formats on measures of positive and negative affect. *Journal of Personality and Social Psychology, 55,* 128–141.

Watson, D., & Clark, L. A. (1984). Negative affectivity: The disposition to experience aversive emotional states. *Psychological Bulletin, 96,* 465–490.

Watson, D., Clark, L. A., & Tellegen, A. (1984). Cross-cultural convergence in the structure of mood: A Japanese replication and a comparison with U.S. findings. *Journal of Personality and Social Psychology, 47,* 127–144.

Watson, D., & Tellegen, A. (1985). Toward the structure of affect. *Psychological Bulletin, 98,* 219–235.

Weary, G., & Williams, J. P. (1990). Depressive self-presentation: Beyond self-handicapping. *Journal of Personality and Social Psychology, 58,* 892–898.

Weiss, R. L. & Heyman, R. E. (1990). Observation of marital interaction. In F. D. Fincham and T. N. Bradbury (Eds.), *The psychology of marriage* (pp. 87–117). New York: Guilford.

Wiggins, J. S. (1982). Circumplex models of interpersonal behavior in clinical psychology. In P. C. Kendall & J. N. Butcher (Eds.), *Handbook of research methods in clinical psychology* (pp. 183–221). New York: Wiley.

Wood, J. V., Saltzberg, J. A., & Goldsamt, L. A. (1990). Does affect induce self-focused attention? *Journal of Personality and Social Psychology, 58,* 899–908.

Zevon, M. A., & Tellegen, A. (1982). The structure of mood change: An idiographic nomothetic analysis. *Journal of Personality and Social Psychology, 43,* 111–122.

11

An Agenda for Marital Therapy

JOHN M. GOTTMAN

A great deal of clinically oriented research on marriage has been based on the dream that the correlates of marital dissatisfaction would suggest which processes should be changed by therapists. Thus, the dream was that the correlates of marital dissatisfaction would be a source of therapeutic goals. The extent to which this idea has actually been put into practice is another question, one that need not concern us here. I will call these empirically derived therapeutic goals the "agenda" for marital therapy. It is not necessarily the job of such research to address the issue of how to best create the suggested change.

In this chapter, I will continue this dream, with one modification. For the past 10 years, the general question that has motivated much of my work is a longitudinal one: How do marriages change over time? Gottman and Krokoff (1989) reported that correlates of concurrent marital satisfaction and change in marital satisfaction may be different. Indeed, it seemed to be the case that while some behaviors predicted both concurrent unhappiness and deterioration in marital satisfaction, others predicted concurrent unhappiness but *improvement* in marital satisfaction. If this finding holds up upon replication, it throws into question the empirical strategy of considering the correlates of marital dissatisfaction as the only source of a possible agenda for marital therapy.

In the past several years, my laboratory has broadened its interest from change in marital satisfaction to marital stability or instability. In this chapter I ask the question, What would marital therapy look like if its goals came only from variables that predict marital stability or dissolution? I will begin with some recent unpublished results from my research about what predicts marital stability versus marital dissolution. I believe that these results can be used in the spirit of suggesting one possible research agenda for marital therapy. Not surprisingly, this agenda will have a lot to do with emotion.

Marital therapists certainly do not claim that their goal is to keep their clients' marriages intact. Yet, despite the fact that marital stability is only one of many goals one might select, it might be an interesting exercise to consider what might be recommended with marital stability as the goal. Marital stability is certainly not an unreasonable goal. Consider the facts. There are currently over one million divorces a year in the United States alone. Current estimates are that the divorce rate is close to 50% (Cherlin, 1981). Furthermore, marital dissolution is well documented as a clinical issue of serious consequences in terms of the mental and physical health of spouses (Levinger & Moles, 1979) and their children (Emery, 1988). Given these considerations, marital stability may not be a bad place to start. I leave it to others to select another goal, and to play a similar empirical game. We will also see that empirical evidence exists to support the notion that there is a cascade of events that involve marital instability, and so stability will turn out to be rather a broad goal.

OVERVIEW ON METHODS

The approach R. Levenson and I have taken to the study of emotion in marriage and families may be called a *social psychophysiological* approach (see Kaplan, Burch, & Bloom, 1964; Cacioppo & Petty, 1983). This approach has guided the design of our laboratories. In our various laboratories, we obtain synchronized physiological, self-report, and behavioral data from interacting families. Some, but not all, of these behavioral data are concerned with emotion. The primary goal of our current research is to test a model of specific marital processes that predict marital dissolution.

Subjects

We began in 1980 with a cohort of 30 couples from Bloomington, Indiana, who varied widely in marital satisfaction. We followed this in 1983 with a cohort of 79 couples, also from Bloomington, who also varied widely in marital satisfaction and in years married (we call this the 1983 cohort, based on when we started the data collection). Most of the results in this chapter will be based on this 1983 cohort. Since then, we have begun studying couples at specific stages in the family life cycle. Currently, we are collecting data from six additional cohorts of married couples. One of the cohorts are newlyweds, of 120 couples in our laboratory in Seattle. Two of the other cohorts are from Illinois and from Seattle; they are families that have a preschool child (we call these the 1986 and 1989 cohorts) and have been married approximately 8 years. Two additional cohorts are being collected in collaboration with R. Levenson and L. Carstenson, and involve approximately 80 couples in their forties and approximately 80 couples in their sixties. In each sample, we will have obtained synchronized video and physiological data from both spouses during conflict resolution at Time-1, and the same observational coding of the Time-1 interaction. The physiological data vary from study to study. For the most part, we have collected peripheral autonomic data such as heart rate and skin conductance. However, in one collaboration we are also collecting immunological and endocrinological data.

OVERVIEW ON EMOTION

An Agnostic Approach

I must admit that my "approach" to emotion was initially quite dustbowl empirical, or what might be called "agnostic." That is, I did not know which theoretical approach was the right one, assuming a "right one" exists at all. The only caveat was that I wanted to study emotion during actual, reasonably naturalistic marital interaction, and not employ some laboratory simulation unless it was addressed to a specific theoretical issue (which I assumed would arise later in our research program).

Thus, R. Levenson and I attempted to collect a data base on emotion during marital interaction that would make it possible to tap all the domains of emotion that researchers had studied: physiological, self-report, and behavioral. We developed and validated (Gottman & Levenson, 1985) a video recall method for self-report data that synchronized these data to the physiological and behavioral record. We used or developed observational systems that varied from quite microanalytic (Ekman and Friesen's Facial Action Coding System [FACS] to macroanalytic (the author's Specific Affect Coding System [SPAFF]), as well as coding systems that were less specifically designed to study emotion, but more focused on communicative skill or problem-solving ability (coding visual gaze direction, the Marital Interaction Coding System [MICS], the Couples Interaction Scoring System [CISS], the Rapid Couples Interaction Scoring System [RCISS]).

Our particular view of the literature on emotion theory was that, unfortunately, more theory than data had been generated, and more heat than light was the result. Thus we reasoned that while it might be useful to employ (for example) a neo-Darwinian orientation to emotion in terms of facial expression from a *measurement* standpoint, this orientation to emotion did not have to be taken as religious dogma. The proof of the pudding is in the eating, and so we thought that the usefulness of a particular theoretical orientation would ultimately lie in how good were the numbers that it generated for us.

Let me give you an example to clarify this point. The example is about the definition of "emotion." A Darwinian perspective, exemplified by Ekman and Friesen and Izard, would admit a potential candidate (for example, pride or worry) as an emotion only if it satisfied criteria of cross-cultural universality in recognition and production. Ekman and Friesen have other criteria with respect to timing and behavioral flexibility (vs. stereotypy) that led them to suggest that the startle is a reflex rather than an emotion, and that depression is a mood state, not an emotion.

Hence, the investigator needs to consider what to code as an emotion. Are pride and worry emotions? If not, ought they to be ignored? One could argue that it does not make sense to ignore some action as emotional just because it is not cross-culturally universal. One could argue that one ought not to care if it is a universal action. The argument is simply that an action ought to be taken as emotional if in this culture, at this time, cultural informants can reliably tell us that this action means, say, sadness. Feld (1987) studied the Kaluli culture in New Guinea and noted that they employ vestiges of the musical sounds of tropical birds that surround them to denote their own feelings. Hence, a Kaluli who said, "My mother-in-law is coming for a visit" and felt sad about it would say the sentence with one set of musical notes and intonation, while if the feeling were excitement, would employ another set of notes. Only a competent Kaluli could decode these feelings. Our approach to these and other issues in emotion theory is agnostic. We have employed two observational coding systems, one based on a cultural informants approach (called SPAFF), and one based on cross-culturally universal actions (Ekman and Friesen's EMFACS). If there is a horserace, the test between the two is empirical: Which gives us the best information in terms of some criterion we are concerned about?

This highlights my particular bias. For the most part, I am not interested in emotion. I am interested in marriage. If emotion can tell me something about marriage, then I am interested in emotion. If not, then I am not interested in emotion. As you will see, it turns out that emotion can tell us a great deal about marriage. Over time it has also become clear to me that a general positive/negative emotion categorization, although important, is probably not going to be adequate for describing what goes wrong in an ailing marriage. We are probably going to have to get more specific.

OVERVIEW ON MARITAL DISSOLUTION

Research has been quite unsuccessful at predicting in which marriages the couple will separate or divorce. Research has also not specified which marital interaction processes are antecedents of the dissolution of marital relationships (for a review, see Newcomb & Bentler, 1981); hence, we currently have little understanding of what patterns of marital interaction lead to marital dissolution.

The lack of predictive knowledge stems, in part, from the fact that researchers have primarily been concerned with the effects of marital dissolution. Only a handful of studies have been prospective longitudinal studies that have attempted to predict separation and divorce (Block, Block, & Morrison, 1981; Constantine & Bahr, 1980; Bentler & Newcomb, 1978; Kelly & Conley,

1987). These studies have found either no results, or weak results, and the pattern of results has not suggested a clear theoretical picture of the dissolving marital relationship.

Furthermore, to date, neither observational methods nor physiological variables, which may provide some descriptive and theoretical clarity, have been applied in a prospective longitudinal design. Therefore, there is currently a lack of research that describes those marital interaction processes that are predictive of marital dissolution.

THE CONCEPT OF OUTCOME AND PROCESS CASCADES

In a great deal of the short-term longitudinal high-risk research, one is confronted with the problem that the criterion of greatest interest occurs relatively rarely. This is true, for example, in research on heart attacks. To deal with this problem, very expensive large-scale collaborative studies have been funded that recruit a very large sample. A less expensive alternative exists if there is some orderly progression toward the criterion of interest, and if the precursors are less rare than the criterion of interest. For example, in the case of heart attacks, silent ischemia, angina pain, or other variables may be precursors. If this is so, then, at the end of a short-term longitudinal study, one could say that a particular subject, while not a heartattack victim, did show evidence of some progression toward cardiovascular disease. This would increase the power of the design, and require a much smaller sample.

Low Base Rate Problem

In a similar way, a major problem in predicting separation and divorce is that base rates tend to be low in short-term longitudinal research. Kelly and Conley (1987) studied 278 couples who were married in 1935 for 35 years. Of the 278 couples, 50 divorced in the 35 years, or 0.5% per year. There are well-known cohort effects in this literature, so that divorce is clearly more likely among contemporary cohorts. Unfortunately, few estimates of longitudinal divorce rates are currently available for contemporary samples. Most divorce statistics are only an estimate of the true longitudinal divorce rate. Nonetheless, current estimates are that nearly 50% of all couples who marry will eventually divorce across the entire life of the marriage (Cherlin, 1981), although these estimates have yet to be definitively tested. However, there is some evidence that these high estimates are valid. In the Constantine and Bahr study, the rate was 2.5% per year. The couples had married in the 1960s. This rate is considerably higher than the 0.5% per year reported in the Kelly and Conley study. Our results suggest that current estimates are considerably higher, at 3% to 4% per year.

MARITAL OUTCOME CASCADE

Hence, R. Levenson and I suggest that one solution to the low base rate problem is the Outcome Cascade Model of marital dissolution. While separation and divorce are relatively low base rate events, this structural model of marital dissolution provides a Guttman-like scale of events (Guttman, 1950) that lead up to separation and divorce. The model suggests that there is a cascade phenomenon that most couples undergo in marital dissolution, and provides added power in shifting the prediction to the precursors of dissolution, as well as to the prediction of separation and divorce.

At first glance, this hypothesized cascade toward marital dissolution may not seem conceptually very profound. It may seem obvious that couples who divorce are likely to have previously separated, and before that to have considered dissolution, and before that to have been unhappily married. However, this seemingly obvious fact has yet to be empirically demonstrated. Additional reflection should reveal that other progressions are possible. For example, it is currently unknown (and the source of some controversy) whether the dissolution of marriages is part of the same process as marital dissatisfaction (as was suggested by Lewis & Spanier, 1982) or whether these are independent processes. An independence between marital dissolution and deterioration of marital satisfaction would be consistent with a phenomenon noted by others (e.g., Lederer & Jackson, 1968) that many quite unhappily married couples continue to stay together for a variety of reasons (e.g., religiosity; see Bugaighis, Schumm, Jurich, & Bollman, 1985).

A MARITAL PROCESS CASCADE MAY BE RELATED TO THE OUTCOME CASCADE

The model to be tested in our laboratory is that couples at Time-1 vary in terms of their location on a set of marital processes, and that these processes may predict the probability that couples will move toward dissolution. There is no need for these processes to form a cascade, but it would be elegant if this were the case. Indeed, it seems plausible that there is a cascade of process variables that are related to the outcome cascade.

In this chapter, I will report the results of our preliminary analyses of the prediction of marital dissolution. Three points will be made:

1. Marital outcomes do indeed form a cascade. Hence, we can describe a couple as on a cascade toward marital dissolution, or not. Furthermore, we claim to be able to predict precursor variables more easily than the rarer variables of separation and divorce.
2. In what might be called "expensive prediction," we will report that there are a set of marital interaction processes and physiologi-

cal variables that are strongly related to this cascade toward marital dissolution.

3.   In what might be called "inexpensive prediction," using six variables from an interview with the couple about the history of their marriage and five self-report questionnaires, we can identify measures that are related to both behavior and the cascade toward marital dissolution; we will show that these measures taken from the interview and from the questionnaires have validity in predicting the cascade toward marital dissolution over time.

Related to point No. 3, I hope that this inexpensive form of measurement will prove useful to clinicians and to clinical researchers.

EVIDENCE FOR AN OUTCOME CASCADE MODEL OF MARITAL DISSOLUTION

I will report a new analysis based on our 1983–1987 study with 79 couples that resulted in a cascade model. Before the structural equations modeling is introduced, some simple statistical tests will suggest that we are on the right track. Our data were consistent with a Guttman-like scale (Guttman, 1950) notion. Note that, conceptually, couples who divorce could be independent of couples who separate; that is, some couples who divorce also separate, but others do not; similarly, some couples who separate do not divorce. Nonetheless, the data show a great deal of dependence. In our data, couples who had divorced were more likely to have separated than those who had not, $\chi^2 (1) = 22.80$, $p < .001$. In addition, couples who had separated were more likely to have considered dissolution than those who had not, $\chi^2(1) = 15.59$, $p < .001$. Finally, couples who had considered dissolution were more likely to be lower in marital quality in 1987, $t(55) = 7.27$, $p < .001$, and in 1983, $t(62) = 5.84$, $p < .001$, than those who had not.

Structural Model

To explain the statistics of structural modeling, if the model fits the data, the chi-square must be *nonsignificant*. In Figure 11-1, path coefficients are displayed, with their z-scores in parentheses. A z-score of 1.96 or greater is considered significant at $p < 0.05$. The Bentler computer program EQS was used for these analyses; the program does not assume that the data are normally distributed. This is necessary for the separation and divorce variables, which are likely to be binary or Poisson distributed. The model in Figure 11-1 fits these data well, with a nonsignificant $\chi^2(4) = 7.09$, $p = .13$. We do not assume that the structural model represents a causal path, but simply a Guttman-like ordering of variables consistent with the observed covariance matrix. An alternative model was tested in which there is actually no cascade; that is, that

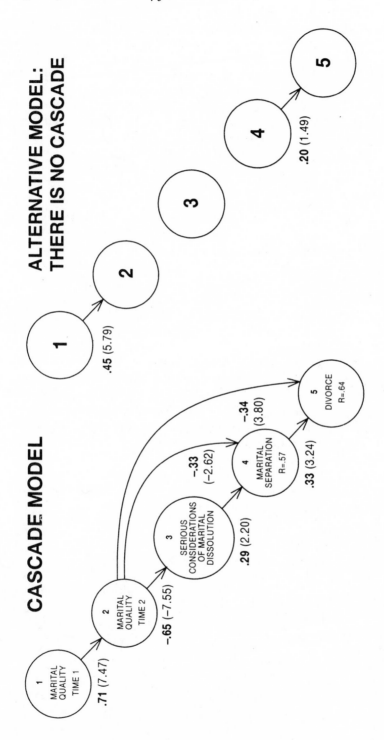

Figure 11-1. With precursor variables, an "outcome cascade" defines a trajectory toward divorce.

we cannot predict the separation and divorce variables from the supposed precursor variables. In this alternative model, only common method variance is represented. This alternative model did not fit the data well, with $\chi^2(4) = 22.59$, $p < 0.001$. With use of generalized least squares (GLS) with Bentler's EQS program, as can be seen from the model in Figure 11-1, the data are well represented by a model that parallels the conceptual model. The model suggests that low marital quality at both time points is related to the couples' serious considerations of dissolution, which is, in turn, related to separation and divorce.

Summary

Preliminary results suggest that there is a Guttman-like scaling of outcome variables, or an outcome cascade related to marital dissolution. Thus, we can expect to be able to predict precursors of final marital dissolution best.

EVIDENCE FOR A MARITAL PROCESS CASCADE THAT COVARIES WITH THE OUTCOME CASCADE TOWARD MARITAL DISSOLUTION

In this section I will focus on our process variables that come from observational and physiological data. Recent evidence available from our laboratory now makes it possible to propose a model of marital processes that covary with the cascade toward marital dissolution. These processes are (1) the Primacy of Negativity, Physiological Linkage, and Physiological Arousal and (2) what I call the "Four Horsemen of the Apocalypse": Complain/Criticize, Contempt, Defensiveness, and Stonewalling.

Primacy of Negativity and a Rough Typology of Couples in Terms of Risk, Using Only One Process Variable

High- and Low-Risk Couples

We will start by defining two groups of couples, high- and low-risk couples, using only one process variable, the Primacy of Negativity (over Positivity). The Primacy of Negativity can be defined as negativity predominating over positivity. This will be assessed with one variable using our Rapid Couples Interaction Scoring System (RCISS). We operationalize this construct using point graphs that cumulate, for each turn at speech, the difference between the number of positive and negative items checked by the observer using the RCISS codes. For example, if the husband got five positive items checked on a turn and seven negative items, his score for that turn would be $5 - 7 = -2$. This score would then cumulate over turns. Figure 11-2 shows a point graph

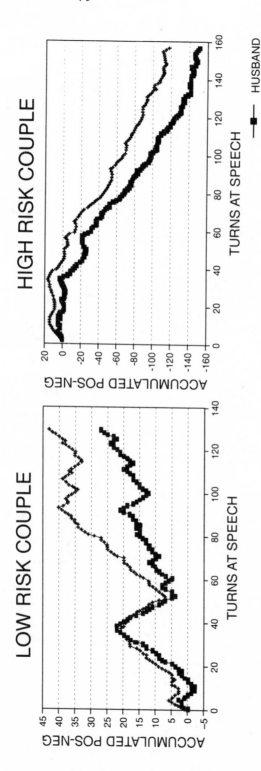

Figure 11-2. The RCISS defines one variable used to predict, from the marital interaction, which couples will be at risk. The low-risk couple has significantly positive husband and wife slopes; all other couples are high risk.

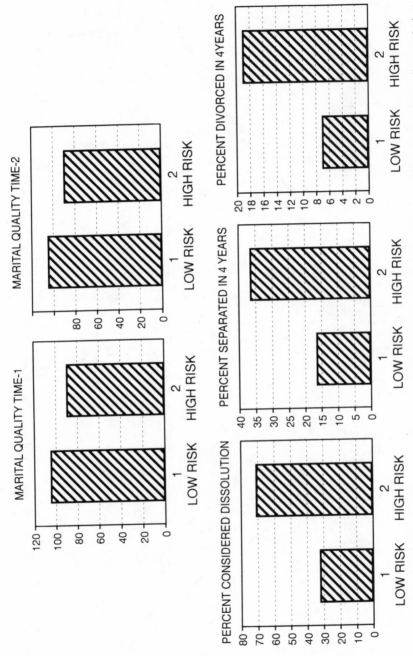

Figure 11-3. Couples at risk (based on their interaction) were significantly more likely to be unhappily married at Time-1 and Time-2, to have seriously considered separaion or divorce, to actually separate, and (marginally) to divorce.

for two different couples, one that can be considered "low risk" (both husband and wife slopes significantly positive) and one that could be called "high risk" (one or both slopes not significantly positive).

If we divide the 73 couples (from the 1983 cohort) into low- and high-risk groups, using only this one process variable, we find the relationship with the variables of the cascade model depicted in Figure 11-3. As can be seen, this relationship suggests that, as expected from the Guttman-like scaling, we can predict the precursors of separation and divorce better than we can predict divorce itself.

Statistical Test of the Primacy of Negativity Component

The multivariate effects in Figure 11-3 are significant. There was a significant multivariate group effect (low/high risk) for the variables of the Cascade Model, $F(5,66) = 2.80, p < .05$. If the variables of the Cascade Model form a Guttman-like scale, we would expect that our typology would do better at discriminating variables lower on the hierarchy. Precursor variables should be easier to predict than the more rarely occurring criterion events. That was indeed the case. The univariate F-ratios (and z-scores for dichotomous variables) showed the expected pattern of decreasing differentiation as lower base rate events were approached on the scale, consistent with the idea that the variables of the Cascade Model form a Guttman-like scale. Table 11-1 shows that high-risk couples were at greater risk for the cascade toward marital dissolution than were low-risk couples on most measured variables. Table 11-1 also portrays the means for 1983 and 1987 marital satisfaction. Compared to low-risk couples, high-risk couples had lower levels of marital satisfaction at both times of measurement.

In summary, we can identify low- and high-risk groups from only one variable taken from the RCISS Time-1 interaction variables. The high- and low-risk groups differ from one another on the outcome variables of the Cascade Model. We now go on to discuss how to sharpen the prediction of risk, and to discuss how to understand the prediction of risk.

Table 11-1. *ANOVA with Variables of the Cascade Model, Based on the RCISS (Rapid Couples Interaction Scoring System) Point Graphs*

Variable	Group F-Ratio	Means Low Risk	High Risk
	Univariate[a]		
Marital Quality			
Time-1	11.03***	104.07	89.65
Time-2	12.50***	103.96	88.87
Considered dissolution.[b]	$z = 3.18$*	33.0%	71.0%
Separation	$z = 1.84$*	16.7%	36.8%
Divorce	$z = 1.57$	7.1%	19.0%

$p < .10.$ * $p < .05.$ ** $p < .01.$ *** $p < .001.$
[a] $df = (1,71)$; degrees of freedom and F-ratios were adjusted to reflect missing data that were estimated.
[b] z-scores for dichotomous data.

Physiological Linkage

Physiological linkage is assessed by performing bivariate time-series analyses using a computer program written by Williams and Gottman (1981). In this analysis, for example, one attempts to use the heart rate of the wife to account for variance in the heart rate of the husband, over and above what can be accounted for by the husband's past. This is called accounting for cross-correlation after controlling for autocorrelation. A summed score of predictability in each direction (husband to wife and wife to husband) is obtained across all physiological channels. We now have sufficient evidence that these processes covary with Time-1 marital satisfaction (Levenson & Gottman, 1983). Levenson and Gottman (1983) found that linkage accounted for over 60% of the variance in concurrent marital satisfaction. In previous research, high negative affect behavioral predictability characterized dissatisfied marriages. This negative linkage is also seen in its physiological counterpart, physiological linkage, which we have found to be associated with negative affect and with cycles of negative affect escalation and deescalation (Levenson & Gottman, 1985). In a recent analysis of the 1986 cohort, L. Bush in our laboratory found that *heart rate physiological linkage* in the first 5 minutes of the interaction significantly predicted divorce and marital stability (point biserial correlation = 0.35, p < .01). Hence, we now have evidence that physiological linkage will correlate with the variables of the outcome cascade.

Physiological Arousal

Wives in high-risk couples had faster heart rates (i.e., shorter cardiac interbeat intervals) and greater peripheral vasoconstriction (i.e., smaller finger-pulse amplitudes) during the problem area interaction than did wives in low-risk couples (see Table 11-2). Husbands in the two types of marriages did not differ physiologically.

Table 11-2. *Comparison of Low-Risk and High-Risk Couples on Dissolution, Other Questionnaire, Physiological, and Affect Rating Dial Variables*

Variable	Low Risk	High Risk	t
Husband			
Cardiac interbeat interval	800.07	811.45	−.43
Activity	.98	.97	.37
Skin conductance	12.34	11.15	.73
Pulse transmission time	243.26	244.03	−.16
Pulse amplitude	7.74	7.87	−.16
Wife			
Cardiac interbeat interval	789.48	731.10	2.08*
Activity	1.78	1.78	−.17
Skin conductance	11.39	8.97	1.50
Pulse transmission time	239.07	233.13	1.41
Pulse amplitude	9.38	6.58	2.11*

More Precision about High-Risk Marital Behavior: The Four Horsemen of the Apocalypse

The use of the one RCISS process variable to predict may be parsimonious, and of some interest, but it is intellectually unsatisfying as a description of the ailing marriage. The process cascade I wish to propose that predicts marital dissolution is the following, which I call the "Four Horsemen of the Apocalypse." This cascade is that *Complaining and Criticizing* lead to *Contempt*, which leads to *Defensiveness*, which leads to *Listener Withdrawal from Interaction* (*"Stonewalling"*). Gottman and Krokoff (1989) found that defensiveness and stonewalling predicted deterioration in marital satisfaction in a 3-year longitudinal study. Contempt, defensiveness, and stonewalling can be assessed with the RCISS. Each scale, which consists of several behaviors, has high Cronbach alpha, and has been validated using as criteria marital satisfaction, other observational coding systems, and conflict interaction at home (Krokoff, Gottman, & Hass, 1989). To check the validity of the RCISS, data were also coded (for the 1983 cohort) by Dr. Robert Weiss at the University of Oregon with the Marital Interaction Coding System (MICS). The MICS summary codes validated by Gottman and Krokoff were employed. In each system, it was possible to define four parallel codes: (1) *Complain/Criticize*; (2) *Defensive*; (3) *Contemptuous*; and (4) *Stonewalling*. For the sake of simplicity, for these analyses, data were summed over husband and wife. Figures 11-4 and 11-5 show that these four variables for both the RCISS and the MICS form a Guttman-like scale. For the RCISS, only the saturated model fit [χ^2 (2) = 0.00, p = 1.00], while for the MICS, something very close to the saturated model fit [$\chi^2(2)$ = 0.82, p = 0.66]. These figures show that there is considerable consistency in this Guttman-like scaling of processes. These analyses show that such a Guttman-like scaling model is consistent with these data.

Table 11-3. *Correlation of the Four Process Variables with the Cascade Model Variables*

	Marital Quality Time 1	Time 2	Considered Dissolution	Separation	Divorce
MICS					
Complain/Criticize	−.34**	−.32**	.23*	.18	.28**
Defensive	−.26*	−.18	.13	.13	.05
Contemptuous	−.27**	−.19	.11	−.01	.01
Stonewalling	−.37***	−.31**	.23*	.06	.09
RCISS					
Complain/Criticize	−.24*	−.09	.11	.18	.16
Defensive	−.31**	−.39***	.25*	.14	.40***
Contemptuous	−.31**	−.35**	.14	.14	.26*
Stonewalling	−.34**	−.43***	.24*	.12	.19

Abbreviations: MICS = Marital Interaction Coding System; RCISS = Rapid Couples Interaction Scoring System.

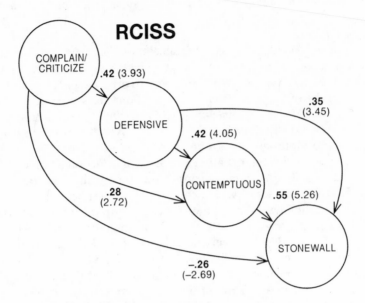

Figure11-4. The RCISS shows that there is a "process cascade" composed of criticism, defensiveness, contempt, and stonewalling.

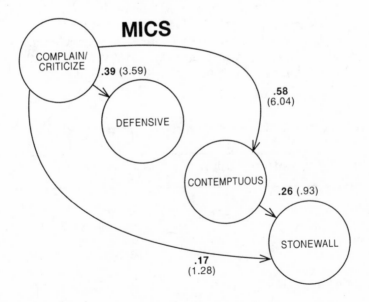

Figure 11-5. The MICS shows that there is a "process cascade" composed of criticism, defensiveness, contempt, and stonewalling.

Correlations with Cascade Model

Table 11-3 summarizes the correlations of these four process variables with the variables of the Cascade Model. For both the RCISS and the MICS, these four processes are able to predict the variables of the Cascade Model. Furthermore, as expected, they do better for the precursors of divorce and separation. In summary, using the four observational variables, we can identify a process cascade:

Complain/Criticize→Contempt→Defensiveness→Stonewalling

that adds to our ability to describe couples at high or low risk for the outcome cascade.

GENDER DIFFERENCES: WOMEN COMPLAIN/CRITICIZE AND MEN STONEWALL

At the ends of the latter process cascade (see Figures 11-4 and 11-5), we see the Complain/Criticize and the Stonewall codes. In this section, we explore gender differences we have obtained for these two codes. In a recent paper (Gottman & Levenson, 1988), we reviewed evidence for a consistent sex difference in the nature of marital complaints. In one of the earliest studies on marriage, for example, Terman, Buttenweiser, Ferguson, Johnson, and Wilson (1938) reported that husbands' marital grievances were most likely to involve their wives' complaining, criticizing, and escalating emotion, whereas wives' grievances were most likely to involve their husband's emotional withdrawal. Similarly, Locke (1951) found that divorced men complained of constant bickering more than did divorced women, and suggested that in unhappy marriages it is the men and not the women who evince withdrawal in terms of reduced demonstration of affection. Komarovsky (1962) noted that unhappily married men conceal their feelings. She noted "a striking tendency on the husbands' part to 'clam up' in the face of conflict" (p. 143) and to withdraw by such means as walking out of the house or silence.

These anecdotal observations raise the question of whether males withdraw more than females during marital conflict. They also raise the question of whether the correlates of male withdrawal involve more negative marital interaction. Anecdotal data support the idea that male withdrawal is related to the intensity of marital conflict. For example, while Komarovsky's data about the history of the marriages are retrospective accounts, many of the quotes from her couples suggest that the husbands were not *always* withdrawn in their marriages. The same anecdotal pattern of husbands' withdrawal in the face of intense negative affect was described by Rubin (1976). To summarize, there is consistent qualitative evidence that, despite marked societal changes in sex roles across the period spanned by these studies, men are perceived by their wives as emotionally withdrawn in unhappy marriages, whereas women are perceived by their husbands as complaining and conflict engaging; also, it appears that male withdrawal may be related to the intensity of the negativity of the marital conflict.

These studies have limited their methods to anecdotal qualitative accounts of these gender differences. When we examined our data quantitatively (using the RCISS), we found that there were indeed significant gender differences for the stonewalling scale, $t(72) = 4.78, p < .001$, with husbands stonewalling significantly more than wives (husbands = 1.09, wives = 0.86). Also, there were differences in the complain-criticize scale, $t(72) = -3.51, p < .001$, with wives complaining more than husbands (husbands = .20, wives = .31). Hence, there is evidence that anecdotally observed gender differences in marital complaints were paralleled by observations of marital interaction in the present study; husbands stonewalled more than wives, while wives complained and criticized more than husbands.

We next assessed whether there were physiological differences associated with the husband's stonewalling and the wife's complaining and criticizing. We found that during marital conflict, for the husband, his gross motor movement was negatively related to his stonewalling ($-0.26, p < .05$), and his skin conductance was positively related to his stonewalling ($0.31, p < .01$); the wife's, cardiac interbeat interval was negatively related to her husband's stonewalling ($-0.34, p < .01$), and her skin conductance was positively related to his stonewalling ($0.30, p < .05$). We also found that although no husband physiological variables were associated with the wife's complaining and criticizing, the wife's cardiac interbeat interval was negatively related to her complaining and criticizing ($-0.26, p < .05$) as was the amplitude of blood in her finger ($-0.31, p < .01$) (Table 11-2). The withdrawal of blood from the periphery (reduced finger-pulse amplitude) is consistent with the general alarm response (probably indicative of greater alpha sympathetic activation).

We next addressed the question of whether male withdrawal was related to the intensity of negative marital interaction. We found that the husband's stonewalling was indeed significantly related to his defensiveness ($0.55, p < .001$), and to his expressions of contempt ($0.57, p < .001$). The husband's stonewalling was also significantly related to his wife's complaining and criticizing ($0.24, p < .05$), his wife's defensiveness ($0.50, p < .001$), his wife's contempt ($0.51, p < .001$), and his wife's stonewalling ($0.78, p < .001$). Thus, it appears to be the case that the husband's stonewalling is related to the intensity of negative codes, and to the listener withdrawal of the wife.

Thus, our results supported the anecdotal reports of gender difference between husbands and wives that have appeared in the marital literature over the past 50 years. We found evidence that during conflictual marital interaction wives complained and criticized more than husbands and husbands stonewalled more than wives.

The Husband's Stonewalling

The relationships we found between the husband's withdrawal from interaction and increases in the wife's heart rate and skin conductance are consistent with the notion that the husband's withdrawal is stressful (i.e., physiologically arousing) for her. This result fits with reports in the literature regarding wives' complaints that they find husbands' withdrawal highly aversive.

The husband's stonewalling was related to the intensity of all the wife's negative codes and his own defensiveness and contempt, as well as his wife's stonewalling. This suggests that stonewalling occurs within a negative interactive context in which both partners are simultaneously withdrawn listeners and complaining, criticizing, contemptuous, and defensive speakers. This interaction can be described as a "hot-withdrawn" or "hostile-detached" pattern.

It is probable that the greater likelihood of male stonewalling is independent of whether the conflictual issue was raised by the husband or by the wife. Recent work by Christensen and Heavey (1990) examined observers' ratings of withdrawal when a child-rearing issue under discussion was raised by the husband or by the wife. In both instances, husbands were significantly more likely to be rated as withdrawing from the interaction than wives.

Physiological Arousal

There was evidence in our data that the husband's withdrawal from hot marital interaction was also associated with his physiological arousal (increases in skin conductance). Since one physiological channel, and not two, is correlated with stonewalling for the male, we may describe male stonewalling as not quite as diffusely physiologically arousing for the male as it is for the female. Stonewalling might represent a "shutting down" by a listener in an attempt to control physiological arousal. However, there is some evidence to suggest that this attempt may be ineffective. For example, subjects who do not facially express emotion during stressful situations have been found to have greater physiological responses than those who do express emotion (e.g., Notarius & Levenson, 1979). In addition, there is evidence that a coping style of repression and denial is associated with heightened physiological responses to stress (e.g., Weinberger, Schwartz, & Davidson, 1979).

Wives, the Somatic Victims of an Ailing Marriage?

Physiological arousal is not just a male phenomenon. In fact, in general, our data support the notion that women, who take responsibility for improving an ailing marriage and who do not withdraw, are more likely to be chronically physiologically aroused than men, who are more likely to withdraw. It is quite likely that what we observe in the laboratory as stonewalling is probably actual avoidance by the male. Our data suggest that, upon 4-year follow-up of the 1983 cohort, it is the wives in high-risk marriages whose health is compromised, not the husbands. These health results could be related to the Time-1 gender effects in physiological arousal during marital interaction.

A QUESTIONNAIRE PACKAGE THAT COVARIES WITH BEHAVIOR AND PREDICTS THE OUTCOME CASCADE

Distance and Isolation

At Time-1 we collected a set of five questionnaires from subjects. These questionnaires were designed in our laboratory to describe a process of increasing distance and isolation. The idea was that the underlying variable driving this increased distance and isolation was a concept called "flooding." The five questionnaires are (1) *Loneliness* (sample item: "Sometimes I feel so lonely it hurts"), internal consistency alphas = .79 and .82, for husband and wife, respectively (abbreviation: LONELY); (2) *Parallel Lives* (sample item: "My partner and I live pretty separate lives"), internal consistency alphas = .95 and .95, for husband and wife, respectively; this scale assesses the extent to which husband and wife have arranged their lives so that they do not interact very much and do not do things together (abbreviation: PARALLEL); (3) *Severity of Problems*, computed from the Couple's Problem Inventory (Gottman, Markman, & Notarius, 1977), based on a subjective estimate of the severity of a set of issues in the marriage, internal consistency alphas = .79 and .75, for the husband and wife, respectively (abbreviation: PROB); (4) *Flooded by Partner's Negative Affect*, a scale that assesses the extent to which spouse A feels that spouse B's negative emotions arise unexpectedly, and are overwhelming and disorganizing to spouse A, internal consistency alphas = .82 and .73, for the husband and wife, respectively (abbreviation: ESCAL); (5) *Works Problems Out Alone, Not with Spouse*, a scale that assesses the extent to which a person thinks that it is better to avoid problems or work them out alone, rather than with the spouse, internal consistency alphas = .88 and .76, for the husband and wife, respectively (abbreviation: PHIL). To review, the theoretical idea behind the design of these measures was that they would tap the increasing distance and isolation that might accompany marital dissolution, and that being flooded by one's partner's negative affect would drive this increased distance and isolation.

We thought that self-report data might add additional conceptual clarity to the constructs we have been developing. Self-report measures also have the advantage of being inexpensive for clinicians or clinical researchers. However, it is important to validate that these measures correlate with both behavior and marital outcome.

Factor Structure

I performed a principal components analysis on the questionnaire data. The following two components were obtained:

Variable	Component 1	Component 2
Husband PHIL	.59	.01
Wife PHIL	.49	.28
H ESCAL	.78	−.11
W ESCAL	.79	−.19
H PROB	.88	−.06
W PROB	.75	−.17
H LONELY	.89	.00
W LONELY	.26	.86
H PARALLEL	.59	−.19
W PARALLEL	.19	.83
Variance	44.00%	16.30%

This analysis suggests that the five questionnaires are primarily one dimension, except for wife Loneliness and wife Parallel Lives, which load on an orthogonal component. It should be noted that the Parallel Lives scale correlates with each person's own Loneliness; for wives the correlation is $0.61, p < .001$, and for husbands, the correlation is $0.59, p < .001$. What this implies is that our couples do not tend to view this state of parallel lives as a desirable state.

Correlation with Behavior

Table 11-4 summarizes the correlations of the questionnaires with behavior. This table shows that the questionnaires correlate quite well with the behavioral measures.

Correlations of Questionnaires with Variables of the Cascade Model

Table 11-5 summarizes the correlations of the questionnaire variables with the variables of the Cascade Model. These data show that the questionnaires correlate with the variables of the Cascade Model in a manner that is consistent with expectations that these variables form a Guttman-like scale in which precursor variables are easier to predict than rarely occurring criterion variables.

Table 11-4. *Correlations of Questionnaires with Behavior*

Variable	Complain/Criticize	Defensive	Contemptuous	Stonewalling
With MICS				
H PHIL	.19	.05	−.05	.19
W PHIL	.22	.11	.11	.17
H ESCAL	.35**	.26*	.43***	.32**
W ESCAL	.38***	.34**	.42***	.40***
H PROB	.26*	.14	.29**	.20
W PROB	.45***	.24*	.49***	.24*
H LONELY	.20	.17	.28*	.18
H PARALLEL	.24*	−.05	.11	.14
With RCISS				
H PHIL	.13	.09	−.03	.10
W PHIL	.22	.15	.19	.04
H ESCAL	.29**	.21	.38***	.35**
W ESCAL	.23*	.39***	.37***	.50***
H PROB	.04	.00	.12	.04
W PROB	.31**	.35**	.39***	.35**
H LONELY	.21	.11	.15	.21
H PARALLEL	.23*	.15	.22	.20

With Point Graph Variables	Husband Positive Minus Negative	Wife Positive Minus Negative
H PHIL	−.15	−.07
W PHIL	−.20	−.25*
H ESCAL	−.39***	−.39***
W ESCAL	−.40***	−.42***
H PROB	−.14	−.12
W PROB	−.36**	−.47***
H LONELY	−.29**	−.27*
H PARALLEL	−.31**	−.14

Abbreviations: PHIL = works problems out alone, not with spouse; ESCAL = flooded by partner's negative affect; PROB = severity of problems; LONELY = loneliness; PARALLEL = parallel lives.

Table 11-5. *Correlations of the Questionnaire Variables with the Cascade Model Variables*

	Marital Quality		Considered	Separation	Divorce
	Time 1	Time 2	Dissolution		
H PHIL	−.45***	−.33**	.17	.12	.15
W PHIL	−.39***	−.30**	.12	.13	.28*
H ESCAL	−.68***	−.46***	.39***	.10	.09
W ESCAL	−.72***	−.59***	.53***	.14	.21
H PROB	−.68***	−.40***	.33**	.05	.17
W PROB	−.62***	−.49***	.48***	.31**	.26*
H LONELY	−.78***	−.43***	.43***	.16	.16
H PARALLEL	−.16	−.24*	.07	.16	.31**

Abbreviations: PHIL = works problems out alone, not with spouse; ESCAL = flooded by partner's negative affect; PROB = severity of problems; LONELY = loneliness; PARALLEL = parallel lives.

The Questionnaires Also Form a Process Cascade

The theoretical idea that motivated the design of these questionnaires was that the perception of one's partner's emotions as overwhelming and unpredictable would be likely to drive the decay of the relationship and lead to avoidance. Using structural equations modeling, there is a model that is consistent with this theory that the experience of being "flooded" by one's partner's negative emotions may lead to withdrawal, the perceptions that the marital problems are severe, and loneliness in the marriage. To simplify the analysis, the ESCAL, PHIL, and PROB variables were added for husband and wife, and the PARALLEL scale was dropped from the analysis. The model in Figure 11-6 fit the data, with $\chi^2(1) = 1.69$, $p = .19$, Bentler-Bonnett Normed index = .998.

In summary, it is possible to identify a set of processes that index Distance and Isolation with five questionnaires assessing: *Loneliness, Parallel Lives, Severity of Problems, Flooded by Partner's Negative Affect*, and *Works Problems Out Alone, Not with Spouse*. These questionnaires form a process cascade, and covary with both behavior and the outcome cascade.

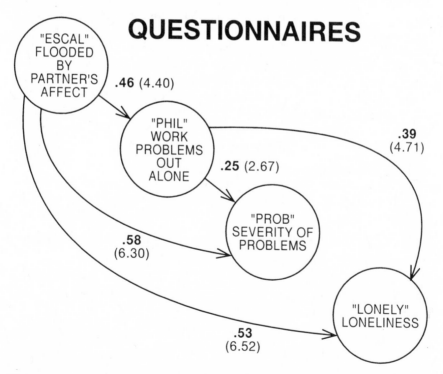

Figure 11-6. There is a "process cascade" composed of flooding, deciding it is best to work out problems alone, viewing one's marital problems as severe, and loneliness.

ORAL HISTORY INTERVIEW

This interview is based on the work of Studs Terkl. Terkl was interested in creating radio programs, so he invented an interviewing style that is very different from a clinical interview. He avoided the usual vocal backchannels ("um hmm," etc.) that clinical interviewers and therapists employ, because these are annoying on a radio show. At the end of the subjects' responses Terkl would gesture and respond with great energy and emotion, and then ask another question and be quiet. He could then splice himself out of the tapes and have a long segment of just the subject talking.

This is a semistructured interview, which means that you will memorize the questions. However, the subjects may answer Question 10 as they are answering Question 2, and that is okay in a semistructured interview. The important thing is to get answers to all the questions, but the order is not important. You will go with the natural course of conversation, and try to get the subjects to be as expansive and involved as possible.

A bad interviewer merely gets answers to the questions, but a good interviewer makes sure to get into the subjective world of the people being interviewed. For example, suppose that a couple describe a period in their relationship when he went to college but she stayed in high school one more year to finish. She says that she visited him a few times during this year. A good interviewer wonders about the inner experience of this period. Was the situation one in which he was embarrassed by her visits, viewing her as a kid or a yokel, and did she feel the rejection? If so, how did they cope with these feelings? Or, was this a situation in which he felt great showing her the world of college and she was proud and excited? We want to know about these inner experiences.

We-ness. You will find some couples who emphasize we-ness in these interviews, while some couples do not. Sometimes one person will be talking about the "we" while the other is emphasizing separateness and difference.

Glorifying the struggle. Some couples will express the philosophy that marriage is hard, that it is a struggle, but that it is worth it.

Gender differences. See if you can identify differences between spouses that relate to gender differences in emotional expression, responsiveness, and role.

Conflict-avoiding vs. conflict-engaging couples. Some couples minimize the emotional side of their marital interaction, either positive or negative af-

(Continued)

fect. They tend to avoid disagreements. They tend to speak about the events of the day in terms of errands rather than feelings. Self-disclosure is minimized. Their roles tend to be fairly stereotyped and prescribed by cultural norms.

PART I: HISTORY OF THE RELATIONSHIP (ABOUT 45 MINUTES)

Question 1. Why don't we start from the very beginning. Tell me how the two of you met and got together.

Do you remember the first time you met? Tell me about it.

Was there anything about (spouse's name) that made him/her stand out?

What were your first impressions of each other?

Question 2. When you think back to the time you were dating, before you got married, what do you remember? What stands out?

How long did you know each other before you got married? What do you remember of this period? What were some of the highlights? Some of the tensions? What types of things did you do together?

Question 3. Tell me about how you decided to get married. Of all the people in the world, what led you to decide that this was the person you wanted to marry? Was it an easy decision? Was it a difficult decision? (Were they ever in love?)

Question 4. Do you remember your wedding? Tell me about your wedding. Did you have a honeymoon? What do you remember about it?

Question 5. When you think back to the first year you were married, what do you remember? Were there any adjustments to being married?

What about the transition to being parents? Tell me about this period of you marriage. What was it like for the two of you?

Question 6. Looking back over the years, what moments stand out as the really good times in your marriage? What were the really happy times? (What is a good time like for this couple?)

Question 7. Many of the couples we've talked to say that their relationships go through periods of ups and downs. Would you say that this is true of your marriage?

Question 8. Looking back over the years, what moments stand out as the really hard times in your marriage? Why do you think you stayed together? How did you get through these difficult times?

Question 9. How would you say your marriage is different from when you first got married?

PART II. THE PHILOSOPHY OF MARRIAGE

Question 10. We're interested in your ideas about what makes a marriage work. Why do you think some marriages work while others don't? Think of a couple you know that has a particularly good marriage and one that you know that has a particularly bad marriage. (Let them decide together which two couples these are). What is different about these two marriages? How would you compare your own marriage to each of these couples?

Question 11. Tell me about you parents' marriages. (Ask of each spouse:) What was (is) their marriage like? Would you say it's very similar or different from your own marriage?

Figure 11-7.

Oral History Interview

Since we thought it would be useful for clinical work to have an interview that could tap processes that were themselves predictive of marital dissolution and make these processes readily observable to the clinician, we developed such an interview. In the 1986 study, we used an interview developed in our laboratory with L. Krokoff, called the "Oral History Interview." The Oral History Interview (see Figure 11-7) is modeled after the interview methods of sociologist/reporter Studs Terkel. It is a semistructured interview in which the interviewer asks a set of open-ended questions. The interviewer asks about the history of the couple's relationship: how they met, how they courted and married, what the bad times were, how they got over these bad times, what the good times were (and what they are today). The interviewer also asks about the couple's "philosophy" of marriage: the couple is asked to select a good and a bad marriage they know of and to talk about the differences. They also describe their parents' marriage and how it compares to their own. We have used the interview as the first thing couples do in our projects, as a way to build rapport with them. Most couples love doing the oral history interview. We have also used it as the last thing couples do in our project, as a way of couples' leaving our laboratory in a good mood.

Recently, K. Buehlman in our laboratory developed a behavioral coding system based on couples' responses in this interview. Her coding system assessed several dimensions of marriage. In particular, she recently selected six variables that she thought would be interesting theoretically and predictive of marital dissolution. She noticed that husbands' behavior during this interview showed a striking degree of variation across couples. Hence, she decided that the husbands' data would provide the best predictors of the longitudinal fate of the marriage. She coded three positive variables: (1) *Husband We-ness*, the amount of "we-ness" expressed by the husband in the recollections and philosophies; part of this construct is the use of "We sentences" rather than "I sentences," so this construct taps how unified the husband feels with his wife; (2) *Husband Expansiveness*, how "expansive" the husband was during the interview, as opposed to constricted; an expansive husband elaborated with detailed recollections and philosophy about the marriage; (3) *Husband Fondness for His Wife*, a simple affective dimension of the degree of affection and pride the husband expressed toward his wife (an opposite example is the husband who cannot think of anything that first attracted him to his wife). She also coded three negative variables: (4) *Chaos*, a rating given to the couple about the extent to which they seem to feel out of control of their lives, buffeted by events outside their control (for example, they got married suddenly because she was pregnant, and this kind of thing seems to characterize their lives); (5 & 6) *Husband and Wife Disappointment in Their Marriage*, which was judged as their having expectations of their marriage that are not met. The overall agreement across coders on these dimensions was quite high, about 80%.

Buehlman found that her coding of the Time-1 Oral History Interview correlated significantly with behavioral coding of the marital interaction, as assessed by both SPAFF and RCISS. Hence, she found independent validation of the codes of the Oral History Interview. She also computed a discriminant function analysis to predict divorce upon the 2-year follow-up of this cohort. The results are summarized in Table 11-6. This strong prediction of divorce (about 94% accuracy) was quite astounding to us. Clearly, it will have to be replicated, and we are in the process of doing so with our other cohorts, who also have participated in an Oral History Interview.

SUMMARY

All the analyses presented in this chapter have shown that preliminary evidence exists for the following facts:

1. The marital outcomes form a cascade. Hence, we can describe a couple as on a cascade toward marital dissolution, or not. We expect to be able to predict precursor variables more easily than the rarer variables of separation and divorce.

2. There are a set of marital interaction processes and physiological variables that are strongly related to this cascade toward marital dissolution. These processes are (1) the Primacy of Negativity, Physiological Linkage, and Physiological Arousal; and (2) the Four Horsemen of the Apocalypse: Complain/Criticize, Contempt, Defensiveness, and Stonewalling.

3. We can identify a set of self-report questionnaire measures that are related to both behavior and the cascade toward marital dissolution. These variables are: (a) *Loneliness* (LONELY); (b) *Parallel Lives* (PARALLEL); (c) *Severity of Problems* (PROB); (d) *Flooded by Partner's Negative Affect* (ESCAL); and (e) *Works Problems Out Alone, Not with Spouse* (PHIL). These questionnaires have thus received some validation for yearly use in following these processes in all couples and predicting the cascade toward marital dissolution over time.

4. From the Oral History Interview, we can see potentially powerful precursors of marital dissolution in such simple affective variables as the amount of disappointment both spouses feel about their marriage.

IMPLICATIONS FOR MARITAL THERAPY

In this section, I will review each of the processes and suggest potential implications of the results for an agenda for marital therapy.

The Primacy of Negativity: A Balance Theory of Marriage

The one variable that was employed to create the low- and high-risk groups was a variable that presumably tapped the balance between negative and positive codes of the RCISS. It is unclear from this analysis which variable is doing the work of discrimination. It could be negativity, it could be positivity, or it could be some balance between the two. It turns out that if one performs discriminant function analyses on the two groups based on the RCISS point graph slopes, the variable that does the best job of discrimination is a balance between positive and negative codes.

In fact, the best discrimination is obtained by a ratio of positive to negative codes. The ratio is about 5.0 for stable marriages, and it is less than one for unstable marriages. One interesting result is that if one uses the specific affect codes (SPAFF), the same ratios hold, and they hold independent of the conversation (whether the couple is discussing a conflict issue, discussing events of the day, or having a positive conversation). The remarkable fact appears that there is a constant of positivity to negativity in both affect and problem-solving codes that needs to hold or be exceeded if a marriage is to be stable.

Steps Toward an Ecology of Behavior

Hence, this suggests that a balance theory between positive and negative may be one thing that contributes to marital stability. I would like to suggest one way to understand this relationship. In population ecology, the survival of various species is modeled by three possible equations: (1) predator-prey; (2) competition for similar food sources; and (3) symbiosis. In the predator-prey equation, predator and prey need to strike a balance or various instabilities will result. For example, if the predator population grows too much, the prey population diminishes until predators start to die as a result of lack of food. In the competition-for-similar-food equation, again there are only certain accommodations that produce stability. The same is true for symbiosis. The two species that are symbiotic also need to be regulated in any given ecology for them ultimately to survive.

Table 11-6. *Predictions of Divorce from Six Oral History Variables*

		Predicted	
		Stable	Divorced
Actual	Stable	37 (92.5%)	3 (7.5%)
	Divorced	0 (0.0%)	7 (100.0%)
	Overall Accuracy:		93.62%

The balance theory of marriage suggests that behavior in a marriage may be viewed as an ecology, with each kind of behavior as a species. Any pair of behaviors may have predator-prey, competitive, or symbiotic relationships. In our initial attempts at applying a balance theory, the "predator" is negativity, and the "prey" is positivity. Relationships that are themselves unstable have a balance that favors the predator of negativity. Relationships that are stable have a balance that hugely favors the "prey" of positive affect.

How far this analogy goes is anyone's guess at this point. For example, one may ask, Is negativity necessary? Surprisingly, the Gottman and Krokoff (1989) results suggest that it may very well be necessary. Much more needs to be learned about conflict engagement and the functions it serves, for example, in the maintenance of intimacy.

The Four Horsemen of the Apocalypse: Complain/Criticize, Contempt, Defensiveness, Withdrawal

We now know that not all negativity is equivalent. Some negative acts are far more corrosive than others. This is true, in particular, for the four that I have called the Four Horsemen. We cannot yet say whether these four variables act together in some kind of sequence. However, the evidence of the Guttman-like scaling of these variables for both the MICS and the RCISS suggests that there may be some kind of chain. In fact, in one analysis to predict divorce, I compared three structural equation models. In one model, defensiveness and contempt acted independently. In another model, defensiveness worked indirectly through contempt to predict divorce. In another model, contempt acted indirectly through defensiveness to predict divorce. Only the latter model fit. So it appears logical and consistent with the data that there is a chain effect of some sort, such as Complain/Criticize→Contempt→Defensiveness→Stonewalling. The Four Horsemen probably are related to physiological arousal, which has implications for the quality of the marital interaction possible. The way this probably works is that diffuse physiological arousal (see Gottman, 1990) negatively affects a person's ability to process information, it leads to reliance on overlearned cognitions and behaviors (particularly hostility and defensiveness), and it makes it harder to access recent learning.

For an analysis of some of this pattern, let us discuss the last horseman, stonewalling. We know quite a lot about stonewalling. First, we know that it is peculiarly a male thing to do. In our 1983 sample, 85% of our stonewallers were male. Second, we know that it is associated with high levels of negativity in the interaction. Third, we know that it is related to physiological arousal of both husbands and wives. How does this work sequentially? We do not know at this point, but we know enough to speculate.

It is likely that the stonewalling we see in our laboratories translates at home to actual avoidance of interaction by the male. This is likely to be related to the couple's inability to regulate physiological arousal in a discussion of problems. Hence, it is reasonable to expect that, in an ailing marriage, the male's inability to soothe himself, and the inability of the couple to soothe one another, are important components of this pattern. A discussion of soothing brings us toward the physiological aspects of the research. This suggests that marital therapy cannot be symmetric with respect to gender!

Physiological Linkage and Physiological Arousal

Let us take a little time to review some physiology. The reason I think this is important is that I will recommend as a new marital therapy agenda some kind of *couples' biofeedback*. What exactly do I mean when I am talking about physiological linkage and physiological arousal? Physiological linkage simply means that person A's physiological responses are predictable from person B's and that the prediction is even better than would be obtained by prediction from person A's past physiology. In other words, there is probably a causal effect of person B's physiology on person A. How is this possible? Well, it is clearly mediated by behavior. Physiological linkage is the physiological counterpart of cycles of negativity in behavior, or what has been called "negative affect reciprocity" (Gottman, 1979).

Behavioral Aspects of Negative Affect Reciprocity

Negative affect reciprocity is very important because negativity becomes what has been technically named an "absorbing state." An absorbing state is one that is difficult to exit once it is entered. The existence of an absorbing state of negativity can have profound implications. The reason is that what an absorbing state implies is that the usual social processes that are present during conflict, some of which elaborate the conflict and repair the interaction (such as metacommunication), do not work in ailing marriages. These processes include feeling probes that explore feelings, information exchange, social comparison, humor, distraction, gossip, finding areas of common ground, and appeals to basic philosophy and expectations in the marriage. Instead, what predominates in dissatisfied couples' use of these social processes is the negative affect. What goes hand in glove is a constriction of social processes and the greater reciprocity of negative affect in dissatisfied couples than in satisfied couples. This means that sequential analyses of the stream of behavior reveal that if one spouse expresses negative affect, the other spouse is more likely to respond with negative affect in a dissatisfied marriage than in a satisfied one. However, the constriction of available social processes is the fascinating structural dynamic that leads to the absorbing state. What happens if a message has two parts, one positive and one negative? For example, the message "Stop interrupting me!" is an attempt to repair the interaction, but it may have been said with some irritation. In a happy marriage, there is a greater probability that the listener will focus on the repair component of the message and respond by saying, "Sorry, what were you saying?" On the other hand, in an unhappy marriage, there is a greater probability that the listener will respond to the irritation in the message and say something like, "I wouldn't have to interrupt if I could get a word in edgewise." In this case, the attempted repair mechanism doesn't work. Negativity being an absorbing state means that all these social processes have less of a chance of working because what people attend to and respond to is the negativity.

What about physiological arousal? Let me take you on a brief tour of necessary physiology to understand one concept, which I call "diffuse physiological arousal," or DPA. The tour begins with a discussion of the autonomic nervous system, particularly with its anatomy. The autonomic nervous system is responsible for the innervation of the internal organs, or viscera, of the body, the supposedly involuntary smooth muscles and involuntary striated muscles such as the heart (for an introduction, see Hassett, 1978).

Anatomy

Our peripheral physiological measures were selected to provide various information about the autonomic nervous system (ANS), which has two anatomically and functionally distinct subsystems, the parasympathetic branch (PNS) and the sympathetic branch (SNS). Both subsystems are characterized by a two-neuron linkage from the brain or spinal cord. The first preganglionic neuron is joined to a second neuron that innervates the target organ. In the SNS, the neural fibers leave the spinal cord from the chest and saddle regions (thoracocolumbar), and in the PNS, the fibers leave the spinal cord from the brain stem and tail regions (craniosacral). In the SNS, the two-neuron chain is short preganglionic and long postganglionic, whereas in the PNS, the anatomy is reversed, long fibers from the spinal cord to the vicinity of the target organ, and then short fibers into the target organ. In the SNS, the short preganglionic fibers go from the spinal cord to a chain (called the sympathetic ganglia) that runs alongside the spinal cord. One implication of these different anatomical features is that there is lots of potential for the mixing of sympathetic ganglia and possibly more "cross talk," which implies that the SNS is capable of diffuse action. For the PNS, on the other hand, the anatomy appears to be designed for little mixing and thus fairly specific action.

Although there are no main SNS nerves because of the amount of SNS mixing, there are two main nerves of the PNS and the organs it serves. The first is the vagus nerve (Xth cranial nerve), which serves the heart, bronchioles of the lung, stomach, small intestine, liver, pancreas, and large intestine. The second is the pelvic (sacral nerves 2, 3, and 4), which serves the colon, kidney, bladder, sex organs, and exterior genitalia. Fibers of the PNS are also found in the following cranial nerves: oculomotor (III), facial (VII), and glossopharyngea (IX).

Chemistry

The two branches of the ANS also differ in stimulation chemistry. Preganglionic fibers in both systems stimulate postganglionic targets using acetylcholine (ACh) released at the synapse. However, in the SNS the primary neurotransmitter from postganglioic fibers to target organs is norepinephrine (NE), whereas in the PNS it is acetylcholine. Two exceptions are (1) the SNS innervation of the adrenal medulla, which is stimulated by SNS preganglionic fibers and hence ACh, and (2) the sweat glands, which are stimulated by SNS postganglionic fibers, but the neurotransmitter is ACh. Hence, sweat gland activity, which in the emotionally responsive eccrine glands is still SNS innervated, has a different stimulation chemistry than, for example, SNS innervation of the heart.

Function

The two branches of the ANS usually act in reciprocal and contrasting fashion throughout the body. However, there are a few well-established gross functional differences that can be described, albeit with some qualifications:

1.   The SNS is a fight or flight system and acts in an energy-expending, or *catabolic*, fashion, while the PNS acts in an energy-conserving, or *anabolic*, fashion. For example, while the SNS is responsible for converting the carbohydrate glycogen stored in the liver to glucose for energy, the PNS is responsible for the conversion of glucose to glycogen.
2.   The SNS can act *diffusely* as well as specifically, while the action of the PNS is usually *specific*.
3.   The SNS has a slow onset, on the order of 2 seconds, while the PNS has a more rapid onset, on the order on 0.5 seconds.
4.   The action of the SNS is longer lasting than the action of the PNS because NE is not degraded as readily by body tissue as ACh is. The time for recovery of some effects of the SNS (for example, on left ventrical contractility, see Berne & Levy, 1981) can be long, for example, on the order of 2 to 3 minutes.
5.   In the cardiovascular system, the main effect of the PNS is on heart rate, while the main effect of the SNS is on myocardial contractility (roughly, how hard the heart contracts; actually both branches affect both aspects of cardiac function).

These general contrasts have to be qualified in some major ways. First, the effects of the two branches of the ANS are usually reciprocal, so that, for example, it is tricky to tell whether a heart rate increase resulted from less PNS activity or more SNS activity. This problem holds throughout. Second, the SNS is quite capable of *specific* functioning. For example, in the human sexual response there is a temporal orchestration of PNS and SNS responding. The excitement phases that regulate the engorgement and lubrication of sexual tissue are usually controlled by the PNS; SNS activation during these phases of the sexual response will result in sexual dysfunction. However, orgasm and ejaculation are regulated by the SNS. It is as if the SNS were the cymbalist who came in at the conductor's signal only at the crescendo and in very specific fashion. Another example concerns the functioning of the PNS and SNS during pure emotions (Ekman, Levenson, & Friesen, 1983). Nonetheless, these general and gross contrasts are useful.

More about Diffuse Physiological Arousal

For purposes such as marital therapy, it is important to have a viewpoint about the nervous system, and I want to propose one organizing variable called diffuse physiological arousal. To understand this variable, consider an ordinal pattern of ANS activation, arranged from high to low:

1. *Emotion-specific Patterning.* I have already noted that both branches of the ANS are potentially able to function with great specificity. The form of action most important to building a theory of marriage is the specificity that results from specific patterns of emotional responding of the kind described by Ekman and colleagues (1983).
2. *Multiple Negative Emotions in Close Temporal Sequence, Constrained Emotions, Negative Emotion Blends.* Here activation in terms of physiology is likely to be more diffuse, so that the specific profiles Ekman and colleagues found are likely to produce a more general elevation of autonomic activity.
3. *SNS Global Discharge.* This kind of general activation of the SNS is the kind that Cannon (1927) described as part of the fight or flight syndrome.
4. *SNS and PNS Discharge.* There is some evidence that the PNS is activated as a negative feedback mechanism to regulate SNS effects of discharge; for example, vagal action can reduce SNS effects on myocardial contractility.
5. *Stress-Related Hormones and Adrenal Involvement.* When the adrenal medulla is activated by the SNS, there is a general increase of systemic levels of stress-related hormones, epinephrine, and NE. There is also evidence that the pituitary-adrenocortical axis is important as a second axis in relation to the body's response to stress (Selye, 1975).

It is reasonable to suggest that DPA is a highly unpleasant and aversive subjective bodily state. The evidence for this contention is weak, but some support comes from the work of Pennebaker (1982) on the psychology of physical symptoms.

There is some evidence beyond our own results to suggest that the DPA construct is useful. For example, Henry and Stephens (1977) suggested that the two adrenal endocrine processes associated with stress are connected to specific emotional states. They reviewed a great deal of human and animal research that supported the notion that the sympathetic-adrenomedullary system (which results in the increased secretion of the catecholamines) is related to anger, hostility, and active coping, whereas the pituitary-adrenocortical system (which results in the increased secretion of cortisol) is related to sadness, depression, and helplessness. Taggart and Carruthers (1971) found that plaque formation in arteries was predicted by both catecholamine secretion (which increases the amount of free fatty acids in the blood) and cortisol secretion. Thus, we may have a fairly interesting emotion-based theory of myocardial infarction due to atherosclerosis, namely, that it is related to chronic life situations that generate blends or temporal sequences of both states (anger, hostility, active coping *and* sadness, depression, helplessness). Unfortunately, as we will see, distressed marriages provide a rich resource for this kind of configuration.

Implication of DPA for Social Interaction

The following hypotheses show why a biologically based theory of marital functioning contributes knowledge that cannot be obtained from a study of social behavior alone. I would like to suggest that the state of DPA has powerful implications for cognitive and social behavior. These implications follow:

1. *DPA reduces the ability to process information.* This distinction is one that is akin to the Lacey (see Coles, Jennings, & Stern, 1984) and Sokolov (1963) stimulus intake/rejection hypothesis in psychophysiology. This hypothesis in psychophysiology has linked the intake of stimuli to cardiac deceleration and the rejection of stimuli to cardiac acceleration (see also Obrist, 1981).
2. *DPA makes overlearned behaviors and cognitions more likely than newly acquired behaviors and cognitions.* If this hypothesis were true, it would explain why it was difficult for marital therapy clients to have access to new learnings during times of heated controversy that resulted in DPA.
3. *DPA increases the likelihood of the same behaviors that are engaged during fight or flight, that is, withdrawal and aggression.* This would make sense as having been the result of past emotional conditioning; it states that, in effect, emotions that result in DPA become linked to the primitive fight or flight diffuse SNS response.
4. *Sex differences exist in recovery time from DPA: Males take longer than females.* There are clear cut implications of this hypothesis, which are spelled out in Gottman and Levenson (1990). These are that

males will be more likely than females to manage the level of negative affect in marital interaction and to take steps to keep it from escalating. In particular, males are more likely than females to inhibit the expression of emotion, to appeal to rationality and compromise (see Raush, Barry, Hertel, & Swain, 1974).

Distance and Isolation

Consider now the questionnaire measures: *Loneliness; Parallel Lives; Severity of Problems; Flooded by Partner's Negative Affect; and Works Problems Out Alone, Not with Spouse.* The theoretical idea behind the design of these measures was that they would tap the increasing distance and isolation that might accompany marital dissolution. The "flooding" concept was believed to be central and causal in increasing this distance and isolation.

Oral History Interview

At one point as a therapist, I began soliciting referrals of marriages that were fairly "loveless" or "dead." A number of couples in marital therapy cases I then saw came to the point of wanting to consider whether or not to stay together. They asked how to go about this decision, and I suggested that they discuss what they once loved about one another and the marriage. Surprisingly, all of these couples had never been "in love," had never gone through a passionate physical attraction, and did not really know how they made the decision to marry. The Oral History Interview was related to this experience.

THERAPY AGENDA

In this section, I will pull together the discussion on the various factors that predict the cascade toward marital dissolution, and summarize these results as recommendations for a marital therapy agenda.

Therapy Agenda with Respect to Our Knowledge about Marital Interaction

Based on our data, the ground rules of marital interaction ought to be the following: (1) Negativity needs to be balanced with positivity by a factor of at least 5 to 1. How this is done ought to depend on the couple's unique idea of what is positive. The therapist can use the Oral History Interview to help the couple achieve this balance. (2) Alternatives need to be found to the Four Horsemen: complaining/criticizing, contempt, defensiveness, and stonewalling; these actions are so corrosive to marriage that they ought to be eliminated from the repertoire (or counterbalanced with an enormous amount of positivity); perhaps the motto can be "Disagreement and anger are okay, but the Four Horsemen are not okay." How is this to be accomplished? For many couples (but not all), I think that basic to these corrosive negative behaviors will be a sense of threat; they will be responding to a sense that this marriage is not a safe place emotionally. Physiological linkage and arousal may be basic to this notion, and I will now discuss this construct.

Therapy Agenda with Respect to Physiological Linkage and Arousal

What are the implications of our discussion of physiology for marital therapy? There are two implications. First, marital therapy sessions ought to reproduce, under more controlled circumstances, the kind of arguments that couples actually have at home that are likely to produce DPA. Too often the marital therapist may jump into a discussion just as it is escalating and teach some communicative skill (such as nondefensive listening). Couples may not have access to this communicative skill when they are at home in a heated state that involves DPA. Second, a goal of therapy ought to be that it is not the therapist who calms the couple down. They have to learn how to do it, and to apply it during moments of DPA.

What is involved in reducing DPA? I can suggest several things. First, the therapist can help the couple identify those issues and ways of acting that serve as DPA "on" buttons. They can try to change their behavior once they have these insights so as to avoid DPA and the Four Horsemen. Greenberg and Johnson's (1988) book has some excellent suggestions for interventions similar to this notion. Second, once DPA is an existent fact, taking a break from the discussion, being apart for a while, with a scheduled reunion, is a good idea. In a research project with N. Jacobson on domestic violence, we have noticed that many physically abusive couples do not seem to have an acceptable way of taking some time apart when the interaction becomes dangerously heated. All this implies that each person needs to have an individual method for self-soothing. The therapist may have to have individual sessions with clients to help teach this skill, or refer individuals for relaxation training.

We have evidence that neutral or positive interaction does reduce the level of the stress-related hormones. This may seem obvious, but in fact the mainstream view on physiology and emotion (based on subjects' urinary responses when viewing films) is that both positive and negative affect will increase stress-related hormones (Levi, 1975). Our data taken directly from marital interaction show that this view is false.

Gender Asymmetric Marital Therapy

Levenson and I have proposed the hypothesis that males differ from females in their greater response to and slower recovery from strong negative affect. There seems to be a fair amount of evidence to support this hypothesis. We have no idea if this difference is the immutable result of biological differences, the result of the differential socialization of the sexes, or a combination of the two. However, it appears to be so widespread that one can suggest to therapists that they discuss these gender differences, and the differential roles the husband and wife play in bringing up issues in the marriage and maintaining a sense of intimacy. Couples may benefit from a discussion of these gender roles. With the video recall procedure, I am currently interviewing male and female newlywed stonewallers to collect information about their thoughts during the stonewalling. My hypothesis is that females will be far more likely to have thoughts of self-soothing and empathy than males, and that males will be more likely than females to rehearse cognitions of righteous indignation and innocent victimhood (mental whining), and to be making plans to both flee and retaliate. If these hypotheses turn out to be valid, the exploration, understanding, and restructuring of these male cognitions should be a goal of marital therapy.

Therapy Agenda Connected with the Questionnaire Data

I suggest that direct discussions of the issues connected with flooding by the partner's negative affect need to be part of processing marital disputes that take place in the therapist's office. How far the couple has progressed in this chain of distance and isolation may determine the entry point into these issues. If the couple has progressed a great deal, the therapist may wish to ask about parallel lives and loneliness in the marriage. My guess is that any entry point will lead back to the key variable of flooding.

Therapy Agenda Connected with the Oral History Interview

The Oral History Interview is the way into several dimensions of a couple's affect about their marriage and philosophy about their marriage. It is a way into their ideas about romance, their pride in and fondness for one another (or its absence), their expectations about the marriage (and their possible disappointments), the nature and role of conflict, their ideas about we-ness versus autonomy, whether they think that chaos rules their lives, whether they "glorify the struggle," cross-generational issues, and even what a good time is for them, and so on. It is a way into the non-conflict-resolving parts of the marriage. We know the least about positive affect in marriage. The idea here is to sensitize the therapist to K. Buehlman's coding manual. Perhaps the Oral History Interview, used as a therapeutic technique, will help open up these dimensions of marriage to therapy.

REFERENCES

Bakeman, R., & Gottman, J. (1986). *Observing interaction: An introduction to sequential analysis.* New York: Cambridge University Press.

Bennett, N. G., Blanc, A. K., & Bloom, D. E. (1988). Commitment and the modern union: Assessing the link between premarital cohabitation and subsequent marital stability. *American Sociological Review, 53*, 127–138.

Bentler, P. M., & Newcomb, M. D. (1978). Longitudinal study of marital success and failure. *Journal of Consulting and Clinical Psychology, 46*, 1053–1070.

Berne, R. M., & Levy, M. N. (1981). *Cardiovascular physiology*. St. Louis: C.V. Mosby.

Block, J. H., Block, J., & Morrison, A. (1981). Parental agreement-disagreement on child-rearing and gender-related personality correlates in children. *Child Development, 52*, 965–974.

Bugaighis, M. A., Schumm, W. R., Jurich, A. P., & Bollman, S. R. (1985). Factors associated with thoughts of marital separation. *Journal of Divorce, 9*, 49–59.

Cacioppo, J. T., & Petty, R. E. (1983). *Social psychophysiology: A sourcebook*. New York: Guilford.

Cannon, W. B. (1927). The James-Lange theory of emotion: A critical examination and an alternative theory. *American Journal of Psychology, 39*, 106–124.

Cherlin, A. J. (1981). *Marriage, divorce, remarriage*. Cambridge, MA: Harvard University Press.

Christensen, A., & Heavey, C. L. (1990). Situation versus personality in marital conflict. *Journal of Personality and Social Psychology, 59*, 73–81.

Coles, M. G. H., Jennings, J. R., & Stern, J. A. (Eds.). (1984). *Psychophysiological perspectives: Festschrift for Beatrice and John Lacey*. New York: Van Nostrand Reinhold.

Constantine, J. A., & Bahr, S. J. (1980). Locus of control and marital stability: A longitudinal study. *Journal of Divorce, 4*, 11–22.

Ekman, P., & Friesen, W. V. (1978). *Facial action coding system*. Palo Alto, CA: Consulting Psychologists Press.

Ekman, P., & Friesen, W. V. (1987). *EMFACS7: Emotional coding of facial action*. Unpublished manual, University of California, San Francisco, Human Interaction Laboratory.

Ekman, P., Levenson, R. W., & Friesen, W. V. (1983). Autonomic nervous system activity distinguishes among emotions. *Science, 221*, 1208–1210.

Emery, R. E. (1988). *Marriage, divorce, and children's adjustment*. Newbury Park, CA: Sage Publications.

Feld, S. (1987). *Sound and sentiment*. New York: Cambridge University Press.

Gottman, J. M. (1979). *Marital interaction: Experimental investigations*. New York: Academic.

Gottman, J. M. (1981). *Time-series analysis: A comprehensive introduction for social scientists*. New York: Cambridge University Press.

Gottman, J. M. (1990). How marriages change. In G. R. Patterson (Ed.), *New directions in family research: Depression and aggression*. Hillsdale, NJ: Erlbaum.

Gottman, J. M., & Krokoff, L. J. (1989). The relationship between marital interaction and marital satisfaction: A longitudinal view. *Journal of Consulting and Clinical Psychology, 57*, 47–52.

Gottman, J. M., & Levenson, R. W. (1985). A valid procedure for obtaining self-report of affect in marital interaction. *Journal of Consulting and Clinical Psychology, 53*, 151–160.

Gottman, J. M., & Levenson, R. W. (1988). The social psychophysiology of marriage. In P. Noller & M. A. Fitzpatrick (Eds.), *Perspectives on marital interaction*. Clevedon, England: Multilingual Matters.

Gottman, J., Markman, H. J., & Notarius, C. (1977). The topography of marital conflict: A sequential analysis of verbal and nonverbal behavior. *Journal of Marriage and the Family, 39*, 461–477.

Greenberg, L. S., & Johnson, S. M. (1988). *Emotionally focused therapy for couples*. New York: Guilford.

Guttman, L. L. (1950). The basis for scalogram analysis. In S. A. Stouffer, L. L. Guttman, E. A. Suchman, P. F. Lazarsfeld, S.A. Starr, & J.A. Clausen (Eds.), *Measurement and prediction: Studies in social psychology in World War II* (Vol. 4). Princeton, NJ: Princeton University Press.

Hassett, J. (1978). *A primer of psychophysiology*. San Francisco: Freeman.

Henry, J. P., & Stephens, P. M. (1977). *Stress, health, and the social environment*. New York: Springer-Verlag.

Kaplan, H. B., Burch, N.R., & Bloom, S.W. (1964). Physiological covariation in small peer groups. In P.H. Liederman & D. Shapiro (Eds.), *Psychological approaches to social behavior*. Stanford, CA: Stanford University Press.

Kelly, L. E., & Conley, J. J. (1987). Personality and compatibility: A prospective analysis of marital stability and marital satisfaction. *Journal of Personality and Social Psychology, 52*, 27–40.

Komarovsky, M. (1962). *Blue-collar marriage*. New York: Random House.

Krokoff, L. J., Gottman, J. M., & Hass, S. D. (1989). Validation of a global Rapid Couples Interaction Scoring System. *Behavioral Assessment, 11*, 65–79.

Lederer, W. J., & Jackson, D. D. (1968). *The mirages of marriage*. New York: Norton.

Levenson, R. W., & Gottman, J. M. (1983). Marital interaction: Physiological linkage and affective exchange. *Journal of Personality and Social Psychology, 45*, 587–597.

Levenson, R. W., & Gottman, J. M. (1985). Physiological and affective predictors of change in relationship satisfaction. *Journal of Personality of Social Psychology, 49*, 85–94.

Levi, L. (Ed.). (1975). *Emotions–their parameters and measurement*. New York: Raven.

Levinger, G., & Moles, O. C. (Eds.). (1979). *Divorce and separation: Context, causes, and consequences*. New York: Basic Books.

Lewis, R. A., & Spanier, G. B. (1982). Marital quality, marital stability, and social exchange. In F. I. Nye (Ed.), *Family relationships, rewards and costs*. Beverly Hills, CA: Sage Publications.

Locke, H. J. (1951). *Predicting adjustments in marriage: A comparison of a divorced and a happily married group*. New York: Henry Holt.

Newcomb, M.D., & Bentler, P.M. (1981). Marital breakdown. In S. Duck & R. Gilmour (Eds.), *Personal relationships* (Vol. 3; pp. 57–94). New York: Academic .

Notarius, C. I., & Levenson, R. W. (1979). Expressive tendencies and physiological responses to stress. *Journal of Personality and Social Psychology, 37*, 1204–1210.

Obrist, P. A. (1981). *Cardiovascular psychophysiology*. New York: Plenum.

Pennebaker, J. W. (1982). *The psychology of physical symptoms*. New York: Springer-Verlag.

Raush, H. L., Barry, W. A., Hertel, R. K., & Swain, M. A. (1974). *Communication, conflict, and marriage*. San Francisco: Jossey-Bass.

Rubin, L. B. (1976). *Worlds of pain*. New York: Basic Books.

Selye, H. (1975). *The stress of life*. New York: McGraw-Hill.

Sokolov, E. N. (1963). *Perception and the conditioned reflex*. Oxford: Pergamon.

Taggart, P., & Carruthers, M. (1971). Endogenous hyperlipidaemia induced by emotional stress of racing driving. *Lancet, 1*, 363–366.

Terman, L. M., Buttenweiser, P., Ferguson. L. W., Johnson, W. B., & Wilson, D. P. (1938). *Psychological factors in marital happiness*. New York: McGraw-Hill.

Weinberger, D. A., Schwartz, G. E., & Davidson, R. J. (1979). Low-anxious, high-anxious, and repressive coping styles: Psychometric patterns and behavioral and physiological responses to stress. *Journal of Abnormal Psychology, 88*, 369–380.

Williams, E., & Gottman, J. (1981). *Users' guide to the Gottman-Williams time-series analysis programs for social scientists*. New York: Cambridge University Press.

PART III

CONCLUSION

12

Emotion in Intimate Interactions: A Synthesis

SUSAN M. JOHNSON and LESLIE S. GREENBERG

Each of the contributors to this volume has presented a perspective on emotion in intimate relationships, as well as a view of how emotion is linked to the development of marital distress, to positive adjustment, and to change processes in marital therapy. In this chapter, we will summarize and synthesize the major themes that have emerged in the previous chapters. We review them in reverse order: behavioral approaches, followed by the systemic, then the more humanistic experiential approaches, and finally the more dynamic perspectives. Two broad questions serve to organize this review: (1) What is the most useful way to conceptualize affect in intimate relationships, and what is the role of affect in the generation of problematic interactions in these relationships? and (2) How can affective experience and expression be modified in therapy, and how can affect then be used to facilitate positive change in distressed relationships?

After summarizing the major themes emerging from previous chapters, we integrate these perspectives with the original principles of Emotionally Focused Therapy (EFT; Greenberg & Johnson, 1988; Johnson & Greenberg, 1994) to develop a more comprehensive perspective on intervening in the emotional system in couples therapy.

COGNITIVE-BEHAVIORAL PERSPECTIVES

From the more behavioral perspective (Koerner & Jacobson, this volume), emotion tends to be viewed as inner behavior, as an activity that is governed by the same factors that influence other kinds of more public behaviors or responses. Since emotion in this view is a physiological, cognitive, and behavioral response to the environment, often occurring when an event interrupts an expected or typical chain of behavior, the therapist focuses upon antecedents to the experience and expression of emotion, or the consequences of the experience and expression. Taking a more cognitive perspective, Beach and Fincham speak of emotional style, a habitual response to others, which can be an antecedent to other behaviors, prompting attention and priming cognition, or a consequent of cognition and behaviors, which can amplify the negative aspects of a partner's behavior. Gottman, adopting an empirical approach to emotion, focuses on motor responses such as facial expression and on physiological arousal and the regulation of this arousal, which impact information-processing, learning, and behavioral responses. The prediction of marital dissolution from such variables is a powerful argument for the primacy of emotion in intimate relationships.

Koerner and Jacobson suggest that by viewing emotion as a behavior they avoid mind/body dualities and debates over mediating variables. The focus then tends to be upon triggers, or stimulus control, and on the results of habitual ways of experiencing or expressing affect. Emotion, rather than being viewed as epiphenomenal or a by-product of cognition, is seen as an important part of the responses that partners have to each other, responses that form the building blocks of interactional patterns.

Emotional responses are seen as potentially problematic and contributing to marital distress by biasing interpretation and meaning creation, influencing, for example, the attribution patterns cueing such behavioral responses as avoidance and aggression, and evoking negative responses from others. As a result, negative emotion may become an absorbing state; negative reciprocity becomes the norm and there is a "constriction of social processes" (Gottman). As Koerner and Jacobson point out, in traditional behavioral approaches, emotional communication was shaped as an adjunct to teaching problem solving. It was not addressed as a key area of change in and of itself or used to change other aspects of the relationship. This is now beginning to change.

How do these contributors view changing emotional experience and expression and using emotion to create change in other aspects of the relationship? One theme involves changing the stimulus control in the relationship. Triggers of specific negative affects are identified and modified so that the "broad behavioral organization" (Koerner & Jacobson) primed by the negative affect does not occur. Gottman suggests that addressing such triggers will help couples manage conflict better in their relationship and avoid being overwhelmed by negative affect.

A second theme is to give partners ways of regulating their affect differently. Gottman suggests partners learn to sooth themselves and manage affect, so it becomes less overwhelming, and less likely to lead to emotional disengagement and processes such as stonewalling, which are a key part of marital dissolution. In addition, it may be necessary to be aware of gender-specific differences in regulating affect, such as the aversiveness of spouse withdrawal for most female partners and the fact that men seem to have greater difficulty recovering from diffuse emotional arousal than do women. Gottman suggests that it is important therefore to allow couples to fight in therapy sessions so that the male partners can learn to deal more adequately with this arousal.

A third theme, and a traditional one in this orientation, is to change affect by changing cognition and/or behavior, which are viewed as the more malleable aspects (Beach & Fincham) of functioning. Thus, changing a partner's negative attributions may help an individual to modify his or her emotional responses to the spouse, or the therapist may structure behaviors in one partner that are designed to create positive affect in the other partner.

A fourth theme is changing the environment, the context of problems, in order to change emotional responses. This may involve identifying not only specific triggers (referred to above) but the antecedents to changes in interaction. Key contextual changes, such as a change in the emotional response of the spouse to the other's problematic behaviors, are encouraged. As a result, the disruptive consequences of problematic behavior may be ameliorated. Modifying such antecedents and/or consequences of behavior is a *traditional* behavioral strategy, and the response of the spouse is perhaps the most powerful contextual variable here. Koerner and Jacobson also, however, incorporate experiential elements into their behavioral approach, focusing on the difficulty of changing behavior when contingencies are subtle and inaccessible. They include strategies that encourage partners to talk about and listen to each other's pain rather than trying to get the other to change. They view this in terms of generating competing responses to problematic behaviors; by evoking emotions such as compassion, for example, they prevent blaming. They also speak of blocking some negative responses and amplifying emotions that encourage contact. These interventions appear quite similar to those in EFT (Greenberg & Johnson, 1988).

This orientation, except when it is integrated with elements from other approaches, represents an essentially outside-in approach to change, whether the emotion is the target or agent of change. However, the line between inner and outer is more permeable, in that emotional responses, particularly of the spouse, are viewed as creating context, and context then creates cues that prompt inner responses. Beach and Fincham speak of affective style helping to create dysfunctional interactions, which then may lead to depression in one of the spouses. They discuss how cognitive processes can prime affect, and affect in turn can recruit and maintain cognition, so that each element mutually influences and determines the other. This moves away from the linear model of causality to one of feedback and self-reflexive mutually influencing variables; that is, it leads us to systems theory.

SYSTEMIC PERSPECTIVES

The systemic tradition, which is, as Miller states, a perspective rather than a specific set of techniques, incorporates many different orientations and in many ways is close to the cognitive-behavioral tradition in that it tends to focus on cognitive worldview, context, and a generally outside-in route to change. In general, systems theorists, especially the strategic interactional therapists, have essentially viewed emotion as disruptive, and as needing to be bypassed or reframed (placed in a different context) in order to change interactions (Fisch, Weakland, & Segal, 1982). Miller, like the previous contributors, sees emotion as another form of behavior—more specifically, behavior that communicates to others. However, she reaches beyond the traditional systems viewpoint and includes the elements of arousal, information processing, and motivation, or a disposition to act, in her view of emotion. Her multidimensional approach, where all elements, feelings, beliefs, and behavior coevolve and reciprocally influence each other, so that self and system reflect each other, stresses emotion as the *connection* between elements. Such a perspective lends itself to seeing and using "multiple pathways to change," of which emotion is but one. She stresses that emotions may need to be contained, reframed, and clarified, as well as incorporated into tasks that are structured to change the way partners interact. Her perspective reflects the concern with relationships between elements in human functioning, the ongoing process of organization of those elements, and the active intervention of the therapist who can enter at many levels to reorganize self or system. The systems view of problems as arising from the inability to reorganize, and to adapt flexibly to a new context, is clearly represented here.

In general, systems theorists tend to view affect as a product of negative interactional cycles, or as a communicative behavior. They tend to focus on what we have termed "instrumental affects" and often attempt to dampen affect by reframing interactions or viewing emotions in terms of their interactive effects. Thus, "feeling" sad or angry would be viewed as "showing" sadness or anger and explored in terms of its communicative significance and effect on the other.

Efran and Blumberg also present a systemic perspective, albeit a very different one, specifically, a structural determinist perspective. They, like Miller, emphasize that cognition, emotion, and behavior are all inseparable elements of one system, and while distinctions may be useful, they are all simply "different ways to focus the microscope," leading to multiple perspectives and realities. These authors frame emotion as a body configuration and predisposition, as an expression, and as a set of preferences implicit in all actions. Love then is a preference for living in close proximity. Central to this viewpoint is the concept that language generates reality, which reflects the ongoing cultural conversation present in one's context; inner life, including emotions, is embedded in context. The line between self and system, "internal image," and "actual encounter" is lost. Emotions in general are seen in a constructivist framework as being more cultural interventions than biological givens. Language is seen as an important constitutive element for emotion, as are cultural rules.

In general, problems then are language formulations, and language reflects context, so couples come from different tribes with different stories that give meaning to events. They therefore fight about what is real and who is right. Therapy is a conversation that enables partners to "see" and experience how they create their realities and that many other realities are possible. There is no mandatory exhaustive or correct viewpoint. More specifically, problems arise from emotional contradictions or competing body orientations, where neither orientation or preference can then be fully enacted. These orientations also take time to change from one mode to another and so may not fit the requirements of context at any one time.

How then is affect modified and used in therapy? In Efran and Blumberg's approach, the therapist helps partners see the "frame that forms the context for the problem" and thus move beyond such contradictions or conflicting preferences. Such emotional contradictions then provide the focus of therapy, but they are not discharged, or contained or changed by reason, but are placed in a new context, a new language, which creates a new reality. These authors take the position that specific interventions cannot be formulated outside of the context of a particular case, and that many interventions can be used depending on the goals specified in that context. The kinds of interventions Miller suggests are more inclusive and similar to more experiential types of intervention, such as helping partners articulate emotional responses and validating them so that "softer" feelings can come to the fore, or setting tasks to evoke or clarify feelings. In general, systems theories do not focus on intervening at the affective level. The authors in this volume have proposed their own unique integration of emotion into a systemic perspective. The general approach usually involves reframing problems and restructuring interactions in order to change communication patterns. Emotional expression is used if and when it helps to restructure interactions or to articulate and consolidate a reframe. Often emotion is viewed as disruptive and as part of the problem that must be recontextualized and reframed. Thus, blaming and jealousy, for example, are worked with as experiences to be changed by means of modifying the interactions and behaviors that support and maintain these dysfunctional states. The focus is predominately on how to change dysfunctional emotional states in which partners are caught. This approach (apart from specific authors such as Miller) appears to advocate that the therapist help the partners cultivate a certain distance from emotion, to see it in a new light, and in this is a dramatic contrast to the experiential/humanistic approaches that follow. It shares with these approaches, however, a nonpathologizing, nonjudgmental approach (preferences are not wrong, sick, or bad) to relationship problems.

EXPERIENTIALLY ORIENTED APPROACHES

The more humanistically and experientially oriented contributors are Pierce, Guerney, and Cusinato and L'Abate. Both Pierce and Guerney emphasize the motivational, action tendency aspect of emotion, and both see emotion as a major lever for change in intimate relationships. There is much in common between these contributors' methods of working with emotion and interventions in our own emotionally focused approach to couples therapy. Most similar is the emphasis on partners *accepting their emotions* and making emotional *contact with the partner* in the session in order to create intimacy (Greenberg & Johnson, 1986a; Dandeneau & Johnson, 1994). Cusinato and L'Abate focus specifically on the role of emotion in the creation of intimacy. Emotions tend to be viewed positively by these contributors, specifically, as adaptive and relationship enhancing. Guerney suggests that emotions protect our psychosocial welfare just as pain protects our physical welfare; that is, they provide vital information, and more specifically, they provide warnings about the significance of environmental cues. Cusinato and L'Abate suggest that problems arise because of how emotions are expressed, while both Guerney and Pierce emphasize the role that avoidance of or defense against the experience of emotion plays in creating relationship problems. Guerney particularly views frustration, arising as a result of unmet needs, as the "archenemy" of marriage.

These authors all view the attempts to control or avoid emotion as creating relationship distress. Pierce states that it is blocked and transformed or distorted emotions that cause problems, for example, a "root" fear response that is transformed into anger, which is then directed at the spouse. He focuses upon the corrosive nature of shame and fear in relationships, and how they result in behaviors that "hide and divide." He also postulates that emotions become distorted because of past negative affect that is restimulated in the present. The fear of experiencing certain emotions—that is, the unacceptable nature of certain emotions to the self, and the fear of showing them to others—results in a *constriction* of experience and of interactive behaviors. Guerney further makes the point that if emotional experiences are defended against successfully, to the point where the person remains unaware of them, they are not then able to be influenced by current experience and circumstances, and they rather tend to color and distort such experience. If intimate relationships are the arena where such distortions are most likely to take place, they are also, Guerney suggests, the place where, because of the powerful emotions created by the partner, they can also be most powerfully and easily corrected. Close relationships then can heal and be a major catalyst for individual growth.

What then are the ways these authors suggest intervening with emotions as targets and agents of change? Since experiential approaches have concentrated on emotion, these authors have the most to suggest in this area.

1. If defense against or avoidance of emotional experience and expression is seen as a major part of the problem, then it follows that acceptance of and involvement in emotional experience is part of the solution. Intense engagement in previously disallowed emotional experience allows the individual to touch "deep" (Guerney) or "root" (Pierce) emotional experiences and express, for example, fear instead of anger and jealousy. The distortion produced by defensive processing is corrected, and past emotions restimulated

by present pain become clarified. Engagement in emotional experience allows an emotion to be processed more fully, to be expanded rather than constricted, with new elements included, thereby allowing emotion to be reorganized and so transformed (Greenberg & Safran, 1987; Johnson & Greenberg, 1994). Guerney stresses, in addition, that in marital therapy, full open and intense emotional expression of previously unexpressed feeling is necessary for change and leads naturally beyond aggression to innate longings for closeness and affection (we would say to basic attachment concerns), or to an acknowledgment of the lack of such desire and a choice to separate.

2. Acceptance and validation in the therapy session provide an antidote to defensiveness, and facilitate the experience and expression of emotion. These authors see the safety created by the therapist as an active ingredient in therapy, not a backdrop to therapeutic interventions. Both Pierce and Guerney refer to the power of empathy and acceptance to facilitate further experiencing in their clients. In fact, it is the deemed unacceptability of, and threat associated with, emotions that necessitate each individual's defensive maneuvers to interrupt and diffuse them. Acceptance between partners is also one of the goals of therapy; Cusinato and L'Abate see the explicit acceptance of vulnerability, fallibility, and neediness as the basis of intimacy.

3. Once emotion is expressed rather than defended against, it is then shared with the partner. The therapist blocks reactivity and facilitates listening in the other. This sharing then creates a new kind of interaction. The therapist directs the dialogue to heighten the expression of previously unexpressed emotions and the process of interaction, sometimes suggesting more heightened and poignant encapsulations of each partner's position. The therapist also blocks the couple's attempt to contain emotion and avoid emotional engagement. Cusinato and L'Abate talk of sharing hurts in particular as the bottom line of love and intimacy.

4. These therapists generally attend to, focus on, listen to, and empathize with partners' emotions, using how rather than why questions, and focusing on body cues as entries into each partner's emotional life. They attempt to keep partners focused on their emotional responses to each other, rather than allowing explanations, stories, and justifications to take time in the session. Empathic responses by the therapist are used to clarify and heighten the emotions of the partners. Empathy is not just identifying with the partner's feelings and ascribing words to the experience. It is the sensitive facilitation of the exploration of meaning by attending to and listening to the other and imagining what it is like to be him or her.

5. Prescribing exercises in the session that change behaviors that function to contain emotions, or asking partners to experiment with new behaviors to elicit emotions that are usually avoided, is also part of this orientation. The therapist then creates experience-inducing situations, as, for example, when a therapist asks a wife to reach out and touch her husband's face to access feelings of tenderness or to explore the anxiety associated with contact.

6. Facilitating positive emotions is also part of this approach, particularly evoking love and caring and emotional engagement (see the case example in the Pierce chapter). This may be achieved by addressing negative emotional responses that seem to block any positive experience and by the direct facilitation of the expression of positive emotions. Also Guerney suggests that inducing positive feelings about the process of therapy, especially hope and confidence, is crucial and arises in part from the nonjudgmental empathy of the therapist, who recognizes and empathizes with each partner's pain.

7. In this perspective, powerful out-of-awareness emotions from the past (which may be framed as unconscious or as unacknowledged) often color or even distort present experience, so that new and different experiences cannot be seen as such. For example, when rage from the past adds to a partner's sense of injury or distrust and blocks any positive acknowledgment of the spouse's attempts to make restitution for hurts inflicted (Guerney's example), these therapists might help a partner to reexperience the pertinent unacknowledged emotion, in order to create "catharsis" in the sense of an emotional restructuring and reorganization of experience. Accessing intense affect allows the emotion to be dealt with in the present, with the partner's or the therapist's help. Spouses then become therapeutic agents for each other and promote adjustment and "personality change."

8. Is there a place in this orientation for the containment of emotions? Guerney explicitly states that in the session there is no need for this; however, in his approach the therapist trains the couple in restraint skills to use at home, to limit negative interactions. Guerney also teaches expressive skills to help people manage and deal with their negative emotions, integrating social learning elements into his therapy. In general, the humanistic/experiential therapist tends not to use skill-building techniques to contain negative emotion or to change interaction, but rather attempts to access more primary emotional responses to replace secondary disruptive defensive emotions.

DYNAMIC APPROACHES

Object relational approaches to couples therapy traditionally work with emotion as an aspect of projection into the spouse (Charney, 1992) arising from developmental deficit or character flaws in the observing partner. In general, emotions are understood in terms of their unconscious origins and motivations.

Wile's ego-analytic approach, however, somewhat more like the approaches of the experiential authors above (particularly Pierce), views problems as occurring when the "pure" emotion evoked by a situation cannot be experienced and expressed, that is, when people cannot "inhabit" their emotions. The experience is then inhibited, and the emotion transformed into other reactions or emotions that people feel less threatened by or more entitled to. The problem is not the emotional responses per se, but the reaction to such feelings. Wile, rather than using mechanisms such as repression, suggests that threatening emotions are often never formulated or constructed in aware-ness. In the case of jealousy, for example, what might be experienced rather than the original jealous anguish is the consequence of the threat, the shame about being afraid/jealous, which then progresses into a sense of righteous rage and motivates an attack on the offending spouse. In this approach, there are no different layers of feeling (here this author is different from Pierce); it is simply that when we cannot inhabit an emotion, it is organized as, or as Wile says "turns into," another emotion, one we feel less uncomfortable with. This is similar to our ideas of primary and secondary emotions, in which primary fear that is not acknowledged is then transformed into sec-ondary anger. Wile stresses that emotions are an opportunity to connect with ourselves and with others, or a route to further alienation. In an ideal rela-tionship, partners can use one another to deal with the "leading-edge" feel-ings that make them uncomfortable. They are able to use each other to deal with and process such feelings and thus generate intimacy and a sense of connection.

How does this dynamic therapist modify and use emotion to help couples change their relationship? He focuses upon formulating and tracking the lead-ing-edge experience of each partner in the here and now of the session or as remembered from the past, and helping the partners communicate these feel-ings to each other. He also demonstrates the conversation they might have had if they had stayed in contact with and formulated these feelings, rather than transforming them into defense and accusation. Emotions are then used as an opportunity to connect with the self and the other. In the transcript, the way the therapist helps the partner formulate emotions is by empathic re-flection, and also by suggesting a range of emotional responses that the part-ner might have felt at a particular moment. The focus appears to be not so much on engagement in emotional experience, as in the more humanistic/experiential therapies, as on gaining a different perspective on that experi-ence. Wile's concern with entitlement also seems to reflect the previous con-tributors' concern with acceptance of one's own and the other's responses, which then helps to render them legitimate and inhabitable.

Kobak, Ruckdeschel, and Hazan present an attachment view of emotion in marital relationships. They, like Wile, focus on the role of defensive distor-tion, in this case on the distortion of normal attachment emotions and the part this plays in the evolution of marital distress. The symptoms of marital distress are here viewed as distorted attachment signals, which tend to cre-ate negative interaction cycles, rather than the desired accessibility and re-sponsiveness naturally elicited by clear emotional signals in attachment relationships. Fear, for example, which normally elicits support in an attach-ment context, is transformed into demands and aggression, which tend to elicit distance. If attachment emotions can be openly acknowledged and sig-nals clarified in therapy, these emotions can then be used to organize appro-priate attachment responses that facilitate contact rather than alienation and aggression. This is a model where attachment fears are seen as constricting information processing. Conversely, attachment security, that is, confidence in the accessibility and responsiveness of the spouse, is viewed as promoting flexible, coherent, and integrated information processing. This then generates clear, open communication between spouses, which fosters intimacy and effective problem solving. In distressed relationships, these authors point out, direct expression of attachment emotions is avoided, and they are then transformed, minimized, exaggerated, or disconnected from attachment concerns, in an attempt to stabilize the relationship and protect the self at the same time.

The interventions specified here, which modify the emotions experienced and expressed and thus reorganize attachment behaviors, are very similar to those used in EFT (Greenberg & Johnson, 1988; Johnson & Greenberg, 1994), which is also based on an attachment model of adult intimacy.

Kobak, Ruckdeschel, and Hazan suggest the following interventions:

1. The therapist focuses on primary attachment feelings (primary as defined by Greenberg & Safran, 1987), for example, fear and sadness arising from the perception that the spouse is unavailable and unresponsive, and uses motor cues to decode attachment emotions implicit in negative interactions.

2. The therapist actively creates safety and validates the emotional responses of partners to reduce the need for self-protection in the session and encourages openness to new information.

3. The therapist explores emotional experience, particularly fear, and accesses core cognitions and insecure attachment models that are linked to such experience. As a result, the role of emotions such as fear, and associated models of self and other in maintaining dysfunctional interactions, becomes clear.

4. Critical affective moments are identified where core assumptions, or working models, are operating and influencing perception, so that these working models can be updated and revised in a way that reflects the present context.

5. Attachment fears can be amplified through evocative responding (as in EFT) until a "processing change" occurs, allowing for greater openness and an open sharing of fears about the other's accessibility and responsiveness.

6. This new information is then integrated into the partners' understanding of the relationship, so that old symptomatic behaviors take on new meaning and do not evoke previous negative emotional responses.

7. Emotional signals, now clarified, can be used to elicit care-giving responses that assuage fears and restore confidence in the partner's availability and responsiveness. Emotions now motivate new behaviors toward the spouse.

INTEGRATION: PRINCIPLES FOR WORKING WITH EMOTION IN COUPLES THERAPY

When these perspectives on how to intervene in the emotional life of couples are integrated with the intervention strategies outlined in EFT (Greenberg & Johnson, 1988; Johnson & Greenberg, 1994), the following set of principles for working with emotion in couples emerges:

1. *Validation and empathic attunement.* Validation and empathic attunement provide a safe environment in which both partners' experience is accepted as legitimate and understandable. Validation affirms people and lets them know that they have been heard. This is particularly important for couples in conflict where both partners tend to discount the other's experience. The therapist attempts to enter the internal frame of reference of both partners to grasp and connect with the personal experience underlying and organizing their responses and interactional position. The therapist remains empathically attuned to each partner's emerging emotional experience in the moment, being especially attentive to nonverbal indicators of shifts in emotional state. This is not simply setting up rapport or providing words so that people can articulate their experience. Rather, it is a process of imaginatively entering the inner world of the other, affectively resonating with it, and then exploring the emerging edges of that experience.

2. *Identification of negative interactional cycles.* The therapist identifies negative interactional cycles related to attachment and control issues, particularly to cycles of critical anger and contempt expressed by one spouse, followed by fearful avoidance and withdrawal by the other. These cycles can be viewed as both the antecedents and the consequences of absorbing states of negative affect, which constrict internal information processing and interpersonal interactions.

3. *Accessing of primary emotions.* It is necessary to access the primary attachment-related emotions that organize the negative interactional cycle. In general, these consist of feelings of fear, sadness, and anger, and the associated desires to be cared for, to be appropriately close, and to have some sense of control over one's own security. Fear and shame are particularly powerful since they evoke disengagement from the partner. Emotions are best accessed by attending to internal experience, body sensations, physiological arousal, and nonverbal expressive signals. Imagery is also useful in evoking emotional experiences.

4. *Acceptance, experiencing, and communication of one's own emotion.* The therapist encourages partners to take a self-focus, accepting and experiencing fully their own primary emotions. The therapist increases the partners ability to inhabit and regulate their affective states by reducing the threat and sense of unentitlement connected to these states and reprocessing them in the safety of the session, as well as by helping partners to express their emotions to each other in a nonblaming manner, which evokes support and acceptance.

5. *Acceptance of the other's emotions and the attachment needs implicit in these emotions.* In the new context provided by partners' affective self-disclosures (the partners' perceived emotional state is the strongest context variable), the therapist promotes the acceptance of each partner's newly expressed emotions and needs, which then modifies how each perceives the other in the relationship. This process also involves the structuring of emotional contact and prototypical bonding events. For example, one partner might express fear and the need for reassurance, which evokes compassion in the other partner, who then responds to the other's needs. This experience of being accepted and understood by one's partner helps to build a secure base where each partner's sense of self can be positively articulated.

6. *Promotion of intrapsychic restructuring when necessary.* The therapist must deal with partners' blocks to the acceptance of their own or the other partner's feelings. It is necessary to address any inability to recognize, accept, and validate their own or their partner's primary attachment-related emotions, and to find ways to soothe and comfort themselves and their partner. Such blocks often occur when past traumatic attachment events are restimulated by present interactions. In the context of present interactions, the therapist helps the partner access the core beliefs or models of self and other implicit in emotional responses, and structures interactions that allow the marital relationship to become a healing arena where one partner can help the other grieve, express fear, experiment with trust, and reprocess rage. The understanding of links between present responses to one's partner and past responses to primary care givers and other intimates is promoted.

7. *Enhancement of intimacy.* The therapist discovers and creates opportunities for emotional contact and promotes attachment-related behaviors that increase the responsiveness of partners to each other's needs for adult interdependence, intimacy, and autonomy. The therapist uses new emotional experience to change interactional positions so that secure bonding can occur.

ISSUES AND QUESTIONS

A number of central issues concerning working with emotion have been raised in the previous chapters and merit further discussion. These are coping with emotion and accepting one's own emotions, acceptance of each partner and that partner's emotional experience by the other, amplification and containment, specific key emotions, positive affect, and combined self and system change.

Coping with Emotion

One prominent theme concerns partners' manner of coping with emotion. How emotions are dealt with or responded to internally creates many of the difficulties in marriage. Often it is the response to, or the defense against, primary attachment-related emotional experience and its expression that fosters the development of problematic interactions. In troubled relationships, both partners' focus is on protecting themselves against their own painful emotions, or the emotions that are expected to arise as a result of the anticipated response of their spouse to their own expressions of feelings and needs. Emotions that are threatening are then transformed, distorted, avoided, minimized or constricted, on both experiential and expressive levels. Responses to the spouse become organized around negative reactive emotions and cycles of behavior that are viewed as providing protection for the self, rather than being organized around engaging the other and meeting attachment needs. In this context, crucial emotional issues remain unresolved, and corrode the relationship, because they are never made explicit but remain buried and hidden.

From an attachment perspective, models of self and other, which in healthy, secure relationships are flexible and "working," that is, open to being revised by new information, now become static, since the preoccupation with self-protection, and coping with the anxiety generated in interactions, limits information processing. There is empirical evidence for the destructiveness of defensiveness in intimate relations (Gottman, 1991, and this volume) and its deleterious effects on the couple's ability to emotionally engage each other. Such engagement has been linked to long-term marital satisfaction (Gottman & Krokoff, 1989; Gottman, this volume). In a positive, secure relationship where emotions can be freely experienced and expressed, the relationship itself and the partner's responses become a source of affect regulation (Tronick, 1989).

From this perspective, it is not emotion per se, even negative unresolved emotion (Gottman & Krokoff, 1989), that is the main villain in the marital story, as some have suggested; rather, it is a certain way of processing emotional experience and constricting emotional expression that fosters negative interactional cycles and hinders the growth of trust and intimacy. The implication is that in marital therapy, primary attachment-related emotion should be accessed, accepted, experienced, and expressed rather than avoided or curtailed.

Coping mechanisms can be viewed in traditional analytic terms as defenses (Guerney), in experiential terms as nonattending, or in information-processing/constructivist terms, as not being synthesized. Authors differ in their view of how this occurs, but all agree that if the experience of an emotion is threatening to us, we tend to interrupt it. This may occur by means of repression, nonattending, avoiding, or reorganizing the experience in a less threatening form, so that the initial response is scarcely formulated and not articulated. The conceptualization of mechanisms may differ, but all contributors seem generally to agree that in intimate relationships such emotion is best accepted and expressed. Direct, open, full emotional experiencing and expression can be referred to as "primary," "true," or "pure" (perhaps untampered with), while defensive emotional responses can be thought of as secondary, incomplete, false, or distorted. In our own work, we prefer what seems to be the least theoretically laden categorisation of emotional responses into primary, or initial, responses; secondary responses, which are reactive or defensive; and instrumental responses.

Emotional experience is presented by many authors as occurring in layers, as in references to deeper root or underlying feelings, and is also seen as varying in the level of awareness accompanying the emotion. Other authors argue against the "depth metaphor" (Efran), and suggest that such distinctions are unnecessary. Wile suggests that there are "leading-edge" feelings, initial emotional responses, which, if they are threatening, are often not formulated in the moment, making mechanisms like repression (where emotion is experienced, stored, and then cut off) unnecessary. This concept of emotional responses being constructed in the present is compatible with a cognitive information-processing view of emotion, which considers any emotional experience as a synthesis of elements. Leventhal (1984), for example, sees emotion as a synthesis of arousal, motor responses, schematic processing, and conceptual processing, which are then organized into a formulated emotion. The concept of leading-edge responses is somewhat similar to the idea of the most alive primary emotions, which are the organism's initial automatic response to the evoking situation (Greenberg & Safran, 1987; Greenberg & Johnson, 1988).

Efran in this volume suggests that emotions are not stored or released but are expressions that are either enacted and completed or inhibited and distorted (expression is part of the organization of experience, not a product). He also surmises that distortion may arise from the occurrence of contradictory emotions, rather than from defense mechanisms. Three mechanisms of "distortion" have then been articulated in this volume: defensive processing, restimulations of past affect that color present experience, and the occurrence of contradictory emotions that then evoke contradictory action tendencies. These are not presented as necessarily mutually exclusive or as sufficient to cause marital distress.

The power of the other's response is also a critical element here. It is not just intrapsychic mechanisms that are involved in the evolution of constricted emotional experience and expression in marriage. The pull of the other's responses must also play a major role here. It is not just if my affect threatens me that I will find it difficult to organize and accept that affect and become defensive in my marriage. This also occurs when my affective response threatens the other, who then responds negatively, creating anxiety in me and a relationship rule or pattern of nonexpression. The power of real interactions, not only anticipated ones, to regulate emotional experiences and expression is often underemphasized. Perhaps this is because psychology started as a discipline that focused upon understanding the individual, rather than on the individual in the context of interpersonal transactions.

One of the main contrasts found in the chapters in this volume is the issue of how fully people should embrace, or own, emotion and how fully the partners should engage in emotional experience in therapy. In general, Guerney advocates immersion in intense emotion, experienced in the moment; Wile appears to work toward creating a metaperspective on emotion, advocating a little more distance from emotional experience; and Efran appears to advocate more distance still. This may of course depend on the personality of the therapist and the type of interventions that fit a particular therapist's style. Perhaps there are times in therapy when each of these styles is appropriate; the question is then, when might each style be particularly useful? One possible answer is that extremely reactive, attack/attack couples, who cannot contain repetitive secondary emotion, may benefit from a more distant approach, in which interactions are reframed or emotions dampened.

Acceptance

A second important theme that emerges is the role of acceptance as a contextual variable, in the form of each partner's acceptance of the other, rather than as an intrapsychic variable, acceptance of one's own inner experience. Defense, as discussed in the section above, essentially involves a lack of acceptance and open processing of one's own inner experience, particularly powerful emotional responses. While only some contributors focus on acceptance by the therapist and acceptance of inner experience by the self, nearly all contributors refer to acceptance between partners in one way or another. Miller speaks of arousing softer feelings and so changing the nature of the dialogue between partners, and Beach and Fincham speak of the positive effects of support and reassurance in countering the negative interpersonal style of one partner. Acceptance can be considered then in terms of how it influences both the construction of each partner's inner emotional experience and the structure of interactions between partners. Blame and criticism, two of the main demons in marital therapy, essentially involve a lack of acceptance of the partner.

Let us first consider acceptance as it refers to *the therapist's acceptance* of each partner and how this operates as a therapeutic agent. The therapist's acceptance of the individual in therapy as he or she is, without judgment or pathologizing, is a cornerstone of humanistic and experiential therapies (Rogers, 1951), where it is seen as an active ingredient in facilitating connection with, and engagement in, intrapsychic experience in therapy. This concept has also been introduced into the behavioral tradition by Linehan (1993). She proposes that rather than attempting to modify a person's behavior, it is important to first validate the person's experience that preceded the behavior. Continuing this development, Koerner and Jacobson refer in this volume to empathic joining by the therapist, as a means of helping the observing partner to feel responses such as compassion.

Guerney, especially, focuses upon the power of the therapist's empathic responding to access the individual's "deepest unstated feeling." He stresses that this empathy is not paraphrasing or labeling of feeling, but an identification with the individual, so that the therapist can "speak for" the other in a way that captures this person's reality more clearly and more profoundly than he or she can verbally formulate it at that particular time. He suggests that compassion and acceptance are necessary for this identification, rather than a diagnostic and analytic stance. The implication is that the therapist has to connect personally with both partners and their experience to help both process their emotional experience further. Emotions openly and fully expressed in a context of safety and acceptance then change. In information-processing terms, this might be described as new elements being accessed and integrated into experience, so that the experienced emotion is reorganized and experienced differently. Anger therefore may expand into rage, which may expand into sorrow, which shifts into longing, which then accesses a sense of connection with the spouse. The essence of Guerney's description of this process, it seems to us, is that the therapist's acceptance of, and engagement in, each partner's experience allows the individual to continue to process the emotion and accept his or her own inner experience. This does not involve just technique but the person of the therapist and the therapist's emotional response to the individual reality of each partner. Therapist acceptance of the partner's emotional reality then provides a context that assuages the need for defensiveness and pulls for an intense involvement in emotional experience. The therapist's empathic response can also counter certain negative responses. Hostility, for example, can be mollified if responded to empathically. More than this, the therapist's empathic connection to each individual's experience evokes the person's further involvement in that experience, which then shifts, expands, and changes.

In addition to empathy, the explicit validation of emotional responses—that is, the acknowledgment of the legitimacy, inherent wisdom, and inevitability of the partner's emotional responses—is a powerful therapeutic tool. Validation goes beyond empathy in explicitly understanding and supporting the individual's meaning system. Attempts by others to change an individual are generally experienced as controlling and are resisted, particularly if the focus of change is behavior that the individual experiences as compelling and out of his or her control. However, validation of the internal experience that leads to particular behaviors without any demand for change tends to empower people. They feel understood and supported, often for the first time. In addition, validation by the therapist facilitates the person's own acceptance of the experience evoking his or her behavior, and once accepted, it is then easier to begin to cope with the experience in adaptive ways. Third, such validation by the therapist establishes a powerful collaborative alliance with each partner. This kind of trust allows the therapist to connect with and intervene with each partner in the most potent way possible.

The second part of this acceptance theme is the power of *acceptance by the spouse*. Guerney makes the point that in an "emotional rebirth," which is a new sense of connection with the self and emotional experience, the best "midwife" is the spouse, and in this process perceptions of self and other are changed. In his approach, Guerney teaches the partners to respond empathically to their spouse, thus facilitating the open processing of emotion and creating a bonding effect as a result of the intimate sharing involved. Cusinato and L'Abate also focus upon this process and see it as the basis for intimacy. The essence of such intimacy is perhaps that one partner allows the other to participate in the processing and construction of his or her emotional experience; intimacy then is not only the sharing of already formulated experience, the product of processing, but the inclusion of the partner in the process of experiencing. Engagement in, or connection with, one's own affective experience and connection with the other then become two sides of the same coin. The articulation and acceptance of self and acceptance by the other influence and reflect each other. The definition of intimacy as the process of trusting self-disclosure followed by empathic responsiveness (Wynne & Wynne, 1986), perhaps the best definition afforded by the literature at present (Dandeneau & Johnson, 1994), fits with this conceptualization.

Koerner and Jacobson present acceptance by the spouse as a crucial change in context in marital therapy that has the power to make differences between spouses and problematic behaviors a source of engagement and intimacy rather than conflict and alienation. If partners can reveal their pain without blaming the other, this may elicit compassion and understanding, rather than anger and coercive attempts to change the other's behavior. As presented in this volume, the behavioral approach of Koerner and Jacobson incorporates an experiential component, for the purpose of amplifying affect that encourages contact. Partners are then able, they suggest, to accept problematic behaviors because they are experienced differently. They make the point that although this kind of intervention is incorporated from experiential approaches such as EFT, there is less fostering of intrapsychic discovery than in EFT. Emotional expression is used specifically to generate new responses, such as compassion, in the other partner. The focus is on communicative effect rather than intrapsychic exploration.

One question that arises here is, what are the necessary steps in the process of evoking this kind of acceptance? This kind of process, where one of the partners expresses pain and thus evokes caring and contact from the spouse, has begun to be addressed in process research into change events in successful marital therapy (Johnson & Greenberg, 1988; Greenberg, Ford, Alden, & Johnson, 1993). This research suggests that the therapist has to help arouse and clarify emotional experiencing, fostering a softening in the blaming stance (Johnson & Greenberg, 1988), and facilitate an explicitly affiliative response from the other spouse to create this new kind of emotional engagement.

Other questions arise as to what it is that should be accepted, and when it is difficult to achieve this kind of acceptance in therapy. Is it the partner's behavior that should be accepted (as suggested by Koerner & Jacobson), or is it the associated attachment-related, primary feelings and/or needs? Accepting differences seems desirable, but can one spouse, for example, compassionately accept behavior from the other, such as continued affairs, even if the first understands that this behavior reflects his or her partner's deep insecurity in attachment relationships? Can a partner accept the other partner's lack of expressiveness, which the latter cannot bring himself or herself to modify, and if so when is this possible and desirable and when is it too difficult and even undesirable? In attachment-oriented therapies where insecurity is seen as the issue, the process of therapy consists of one spouse's emotionally accepting the other's internal experience, and this enhances bonding with the other. This process, when successful, then results in a change in the other partner's experienced insecurity and in associated problematic behaviors. If such change does not seem possible, how much one partner may be able to accept the status quo, which is the implication of the behavioral use of the term "acceptance" in this context, may depend on how threatening the other partner's problematic behavior is to his or her sense of secure attachment.

Amplification and Containment

A third theme that is implicit in the previous chapters is the issue of the containment versus the amplification of emotion, and what ends each might serve. In general, containment is addressed somewhat less than amplification, perhaps because contributors to this book were selected for their interest in the use of emotion in marital therapy. Most authors mention the containment of emotion somewhere; even Guerney, who generally advocates intense expression, mentions that he teaches restraint techniques to curtail the bitter anger some couples express at home. Miller suggests that the structure of the session should be used to contain the couple's emotions. For example, the therapist may interrupt blaming while still validating angry feelings (validation in itself tends to diffuse anger), and then encourage partners to express "softer" emotions. Pierce refers to redirecting negative feelings, specifically, shifting angry blaming statements to ownership-of-feeling statements. Koerner and Jacobson suggest that the therapist block the usual negative responses partners express. Certain techniques also have the potential of usefully distancing couples somewhat from negative emotion, for example, the writing exercises of L'Abate, or taking a break from the discussion, as suggested by Gottman. Gottman specifically speaks of teaching partners to regulate emotion, or self-soothe, by interventions such as relaxation training, to prevent couples from becoming overwhelmed by negative affect. If emotions are differentiated into types, such as primary and secondary, the decision to amplify or contain may depend on the type of emotion occurring in the session. Logically, it is secondary emotions, such as anger that is a reaction to hurt, that need to be contained, and primary responses that may be usefully amplified.

The structure of the session is perhaps the most general device for containing emotion. Several authors refer to the structured ways in which emotion is accessed but then channeled by tasks (Miller) and exercises (Pierce). Pierce also sees the structure of the session as helping partners tolerate the threatening emotions that they have previously avoided by constricting their interactions with their spouse.

Most of the authors here speak of focusing on and heightening emotion generally in terms of creating a reorganization of that emotion. However, there are also some references to traditional concepts of discharge such as catharsis (for example, Guerney), but in this volume even this term has connotations of accessing and expressing in order to reorganize, rather than simply being associated with release. In general, the discussion in this volume appears to move beyond the discharge or control/transcend dichotomy into a more differentiated view of emotional processing. In addition, the authors here focus both on changing emotion itself and on using emotion to change responses to, and presentation of self with, intimate partners.

Key Emotions in Marital Therapy

Emotional theorists refer to six to 10 basic emotions (Izard, 1979; Plutchik & Kellerman, 1980; Ekman & Friesen, 1975). Are some more crucial to the process of change in marital therapy or in the evolution of intimate relationships than others? All authors in the preceding chapters are clear that anger between spouses can be problematic; however, the emotion that stands out as critically important in interaction is *fear*, particularly in the chapters of Gottman, Pierce, Wile, and Kobak and colleagues. This echoes our own view in EFT in which primary vulnerability is seen as central to marital difficulties. A perception of danger and the experience of fear are a necessary ingredient in the evolution of defensive processing of experience and defensive expressive behaviors with the partner, and we have already discussed the powerful effects of defensiveness on marital relationships and its centrality in generating negative interactional cycles. Pierce delineates four fears: the fear of being left, abandoned; the fear of shame, or being found to be bad or incompetent; the fear of being controlled; and the fear of being criticized and attacked. Feldman (1979) also delineates four fears in intimate relationships: fear of being attacked, fear of abandonment, fear of engulfment, and fear of one's own impulses. Fear tends to narrow how information and emotional realities are processed, and how partners perceive and interact with each other. In simple terms, a recognition of threat tends to elicit a fight or flight response, either of which negatively impacts the spouse and often evokes from that spouse the very behaviors that are fearfully anticipated. In EFT it is significant that one of the most powerful events in therapy occurs when, with the help of the therapist, one spouse can look at another and assert, "I am afraid of you when you get angry."

Wile comments that emotions themselves are often threatening or deemed unacceptable to the self or the other, and when this occurs, what is experienced is the sense of threat, rather than the original or simple emotion. Such processes inhibit and transform feelings in destructive ways and ensure that the original leading-edge feeling never gets dealt with in the relationship.

This focus on fear is congruent with research findings that suggest that fear interferes with deriving meaning from verbal cues (Kahneman, 1973), general information-processing skills, communication and problem-solving skills, and people's ability to recognize and learn from new experience (Gurman & Knudson, 1978). In circumstances of fear, it seems logical that emotional schemata (Safran & Greenberg, 1991) are not fluid or flexible and are not elaborated by new experience, but become rigid and automatic, as do the action tendencies implicit in the emotion. This then can be surmised to play a large part in the evolution of the self-reinforcing negative interaction patterns found in distressed couples (Gottman, 1991). On a simplistic level, fear inhibits contact and engagement between people and therefore precludes the development of trust and intimacy.

In attachment terms, fear renders working models static and inflexible, maintaining insecure attachment styles and defining intimate connectedness as dangerous. From an attachment perspective, in a distressed relationship the attachment figure, who should be a natural source of comfort and security and an aid in regulating fear and anxiety, becomes instead a source of anxiety. This results in ambivalent and even bizarre responses to this figure, as the need for contact is distorted by the need to mitigate the anticipated negative consequences of that contact. This perspective echoes the work of Main and Hesse (1990), who suggest that in infants the concurrent activation of both fear and the attachment system produces strong conflict behavior that results in highly ambivalent (approach/avoid) attachment behaviors. Kobak and colleagues focus on how attachment-related fears distort attachment signals to adult partners and help to create marital distress. Fear, which when expressed directly tends to elicit support from the attachment figure, becomes transformed then into coercive demands or avoidance and distance, which further corrode the marital relationship and make accessibility and responsiveness problematic. Kobak and colleagues view attachment fears as interfering with the coordination of levels of information processing involved in emotion and therefore with the appropriate organization of attachment signals and behaviors. Anxiety and the inhibition of emotional signals then result in responses that characterize avoidant and anxious attachment styles, that is, a deactivated attachment system where the spouse is avoided and attachment emotions are minimized, or a hyperactive attachment system where hypervigilance and exaggerated attachment signals are the norm. Partners' emotions also become disconnected from the attachment fears eliciting them (I am angry at your spending habits, not your inaccessibility to me), and permeate more and more areas of interaction, interfering with problem solving and emotional closeness, and leading to rigid interaction patterns such as pursue/withdraw.

Bowlby (1988) suggests that dependency is part of being human and attachment needs and fears are innate and universal. If this is true, such fears would inevitably arise even in relationships where partners have secure attachment styles, that is, basically positive expectations and a high level of confidence in the responsiveness of others. How these fears are handled would then have a great impact on how a relationship evolves.

In terms of interventions, this implies that fear in particular should be focused upon, accessed, and reprocessed in marital therapy. Kobak and his colleagues state that attachment fears must be explicated and linked to the associated working models of self and other. Partners can then openly acknowledge their fears, and this renders symptomatic expressions of such fears unnecessary, and pulls for responsiveness from the partner.

In EFT, attachment fears—fears of loss, rejection, and abandonment; that is, the perceived loss of the accessibility and responsiveness of the spouse—often become the focus of therapy since, in our experience, these are the most powerful emotions underlying the rigid negative positions couples take with each other in distressed relationships. In a "softening," a key change event in EFT, a previously hostile/demanding spouse asks for a response from the partner from a position of vulnerability. This position almost always involves the experiencing of attachment fears and longings, and the direct expression of the need for contact, comfort, and acceptance. The clear expression of such emotions to a responsive partner naturally leads to emotional engagement and a positive bonding event.

Anger is also an important emotion in marital therapy. Often it is a secondary response to the anxiety and distress that result from separation experiences. It is also expressed, along with contempt, as part of the reactive escalating cycle in order to impact the partner and create contact. In addition, as part of blaming, it can be an instrumental expression used to intimidate the other and dominate or control.

However, anger is also a primary response to violation or intrusion and primes the setting of necessary boundaries and assertive behavior. It is often most helpful to help the partner who has withdrawn in the relationship access and express anger at being intruded upon or controlled. This expression is usually tolerated quite well by the more pursuing or critical spouse, who experiences it as emotional contact. Once withdrawn spouses can assert themselves and take some control in the relationship, they tend to feel more secure and become more accessible and responsive to their partner. The therapist has to differentiate between destructive reactive anger, which he or she will often block, reprocess, or reframe, and anger that is an adaptive response to protect the self and assert wants and needs, and can be used as an alternative to withdrawal. As with all interventions, this is a question of process diagnosis (Greenberg & Johnson, 1986), and the therapist has to make a clinical judgment as to how a particular emotional experience and its expression might change interactions and reorganize the emotional bond at a particular time in therapy.

Positive Affect

A fifth theme concerns the role of positive feelings. Gottman suggests that we in fact know very little about positive feelings in intimate relationships; nevertheless he considers a ratio of five to one, of positive to negative feelings, necessary for a marriage to be stable, and many authors speak of arousing softer feelings to replace negative ones. Pierce suggests that the therapist deliberately enhance positive affect by "reromanticizing" relationships, perhaps by talking about previous times when the relationship was going well. He also points out that in general therapists tend to try to modify negative affect and leave the positive to emerge on its own. Kobak and colleagues, using an attachment focus, explicate how emotions activate the attachment system and, if experienced and expressed clearly, facilitate accessibility and responsiveness between spouses. Clear signals such as expressions of vulnerability, if seen and trusted, elicit responsiveness and contact from the spouse. Positive affect in this approach is a natural consequence of intimate contact, comfort, and secure bonding. These authors echo our own change strategies (Greenberg & Johnson, 1988; Johnson & Greenberg, 1994), viewing the most powerful way of eliciting positive feelings to be the accessing of emotions that in an attachment context naturally elicit contact and caring, such as hurt, fear, or sadness. The therapist then can help the other spouse see and respond to these emotions in a caring manner, rather than structuring interactions such as caring days (Stuart, 1980). When this occurs, the responses of the other spouse then help the partner regulate his or her painful affect, and the presence and caring of the other, which constitutes a renewal of the bond, generate security and joy. The responsiveness and accessibility of the partner, while giving the other a sense of felt security in the world, are also a source of fulfillment and happiness in and of themselves; in this sense perhaps attachment theory has more to say about the generation of positive affect than any other theory of intimate relationships. Attachment behaviors—holding, smiling, and general emotional engagement—are innate and powerful elicitors of positive affect.

As Koerner and Jacobson point out, no particular emotion is positive or negative in a relationship; instead, it depends on the context and the meaning given to events, so the other part of creating positive affect is to focus on how events are processed intrapsychically and what attributions are made.

Guerney gives an example of a man listing all the positive feelings and behaviors he had completed to appease his offended wife, which could have been a source of comfort and positive affect for her. She, however, could not respond to them (the tendency of distressed partners to discount the caring behaviors of their partner is phenomenal) because such a response was incompatible with her unspoken, inhibited rage at his betrayal. In this example, her negative emotional response had to be accessed and dealt with before the husband had any chance of eliciting a positive response from her.

Combined Self and System Change

Another theme that permeates the previous chapters is the theme that intrapsychic change occurs in tandem with interactional shifts in marital therapy. As we suggested in the first chapter, intrapsychic and relationship change are usefully viewed as two sides of the same coin. Guerney points out that it is only when therapists can facilitate a change in the "nature of interpersonal interactions with significant others that they produce real and enduring changes in personality," and that the most powerful stimulus for personal growth is the relationship with the intimate partner. From a systemic viewpoint, the boundary between self and system becomes blurred, since both are seen as coevolved and reciprocally determined (Miller). Efran suggests that changes in inner space include a remapping of interpersonal space, and that the line between internal image and actual encounter is hard to find. Wile also makes the point that emotions connect one to the self and to the other, or alienate one from the self and the other. From a more general perspective, people deal with dangerous emotions by constricting their experience and by constricting their interpersonal behaviors, for example, avoiding threatening closeness by withdrawing. Conversely, marital therapy tends to bring more aspects of self into the relationship, and thus expands patterns of interaction. Emotion can be viewed as occurring at the interface between self and system, between inner and outer, simultaneously being an experience and a communication, organizing the self and the other's responses to the self.

In general, the authors included in this volume subscribe to a reciprocally determining, coevolving view of inner and outer, self and attachment context. The self is constantly being defined in relationship to significant others, and the responses of significant others influence how the self is experienced and expressed. A secure positive intimate relationship facilitates the growth and integration of self, not just in childhood but throughout life. Bowlby (1969, 1988) referred to the reciprocal links between working models of self and other. For example, in an anxious, insecure attachment style, the self is seen as unworthy of care and inept at eliciting responsiveness in others. The other, who tends to be seen more positively than the self (Bartholomew & Horowitz, 1991), cannot then be trusted to care for the subject, whose anxious vigilance and insecurity will, in all probability, elicit distancing or rejecting behaviors from the partner, which then confirm the model of self as unworthy.

Given the above, the use of marital therapy to address individual symptomatology, such as depression, makes ultimate sense, but also implies that effective marital therapy has to encompass intrapsychic and interpersonal foci.

SUMMARY: WORKING WITH EMOTIONS

All contributors suggest that couples therapy should produce either a change in the context that elicits negative emotions or a change in how these emotions are processed/experienced. It is almost impossible in couples therapy not to use both, especially since changing context here usually means changing the expressive behaviors of the partner, a basic strategy in marital therapy. There are differences between authors as to how they conceptualize emotion, work with emotion, and use emotion to change relationships. Some authors advocate more engagement by partners in their own emotion than do others. The contributors who place the least emphasis on such engagement would seem to be Efran and Blumberg, who suggest that a new and larger perspective shifts emotion. Contributors such as Pierce, Guerney, and Kobak and colleagues advocate an intense immersion in affective experience to enable the further processing of the emotion so that it becomes fluid and can be reorganized into other responses.

Perhaps the most exciting aspect of marital therapy is that there are many ways in, and many routes to change. To begin to specify the most powerful techniques for changing emotion, it is necessary to take a particular conceptual stance concerning the role of emotion in distressed relationships, and identify different kinds of emotional response that may require differential intervention. If the defended/fully processed dichotomy is used, it may be useful to differentiate different levels of emotional processing here. These might range from dissociated/disowned to incoherently formulated; to formulated but inhibited and unexpressed; to expressed indirectly and not enacted; to openly expressed, completely processed, and inhabited, and integrated into self and system.

If dissociated affect, the most inaccessible level, is considered, some clinicians may focus on cognition and behavior instead, rather than attempt to access these emotions, depending on how crucial they consider the affective dimension to be. Others may attempt to connect the individual with his or her affective experience by techniques such as prescribing exercises that evoke affect (Pierce), or empathetically responding to the deepest unstated feeling the therapist senses in the client and presenting and heightening this feeling (Guerney). In our own approach, we would access emotions by evocatively responding, focusing on (a) the elements of experience unattended to, such as bodily cues like facial expression and tone of voice; (b) recreating and heightening the evoking incident (for example, repeating the spouse's words and reflecting the person's nonverbal responses); or (c) inquiring about the person's sense of his or her response (What happens to you when...). We also direct attention to specific interactional events that seem to have emotional impact, often using images and metaphors to crystallize partners' experience and (somewhat like Pierce in this volume) set up experiments and enactments to heighten emotion. The therapist in EFT also suggests articulations of the partners' experience and elaborates on that experience (Greenberg & Johnson, 1988; Johnson & Greenberg, 1994). The more dissociated and distant individuals are from their affect, the more the therapist will need to intervene as an active partner in helping them to connect with and process that affect.

In terms of using emotional experience and expression to change relationships, therapists in this volume have suggested a variety of ways. Several authors suggest (a) facilitating the communication of previously unexpressed or distorted affect to clarify it and examining the impact of such emotional experience and its expression on the evolution of interactional cycles; (b) facilitating the expression of newly synthesized emotion to evoke new responses in the spouse and shift perceptions of the other; (c) generating competing "soft" emotions that encourage contact rather than disengagement; (d) using emotional experience and expression to access and revise the core models of other, and self in relation to other, that guide perceptions and expectations and organize anticipatory responses; (e) using emotional experience to reorganize the position of each partner in relation to the spouse, considering both control and affiliation dimensions. The reorganization should be in the direction of contact, accessibility, and responsiveness.

Implicit in all the presentations in this volume are positions concerning what is possible in intimate relationships, and the goals the therapist should pursue in marital therapy. From an empirical point of view, a worthy goal is to prevent the Four Horsemen of the Apocalypse (critical complaining, and contempt, followed by distancing and stonewalling defensiveness in the other partner), from taking over the couple's relationship. Interventions need to focus on helping couples deal with the absorbing states of negative affect involved in this pattern. From a theoretical point of view, a general goal might be to short-circuit such negative cycles by helping individuals become more connected to themselves and their emotional responses, and more connected to and engaged with their partners. From an attachment point of view, the therapist should help partners deal with their attachment needs and emotions and express them in such a way as to facilitate a bonding response from their partner.

Efran suggests that therapists may be promoting impossible standards of self-disclosure and sensitive responding, which can create problems rather than resolve them. Taking a concept from Stern (1985), one might ask, is emotional attunement, a truly sensitive emotional responding, necessary, desirable, or even attainable for most married couples? It may be necessary to trim our theoretical and personal perspectives to the objectives and desires of the couple we are treating, and their approach to emotion. The answer to this question may also depend on the person of the therapist. Therapists who are not themselves comfortable with emotions may find it too difficult to connect people with their emotions, or to use emotions therapeutically.

The enormous task of understanding the role of emotion in intimate relationships, and the many ways to therapeutically modify emotional experience and expression, as well as how to enroll emotional processes in the creation of change in intimate relationships, has only just begun. Theorists, researchers, and clinicians are only beginning to grapple with that most fundamental dimension of intimate relationships, emotion. They will continue to do so because, as Mace (1987) states, the hope for the future lies not in an endless stream of technological developments but in the struggle to understand and improve the fundamental quality of human relationships.

REFERENCES

Bartholomew, K., & Horowitz, L. M. (1991). Attachment styles among young adults: A test of a few category model. *Journal of Personality and Social Psychology, 60,* 226–244.

Bowlby, J. (1969). *Attachment and loss: Vol. I. Attachment.* New York: Basic Books.

Bowlby, J. (1988). *A secure base.* New York: Basic Books.

Charney, I. W. (1992). *Existential/dialectical marital therapy.* New York: Brunner/Mazel.

Dandeneau, M. L., & Johnson, S. M. (1994). Facilitating intimacy: Interventions and effects. *Journal of Marital and Family Therapy, 20,* 17–33.

Ekman, P., & Friesen, W. V. (1975). *Unmasking the face.* Englewood Cliffs, NJ: Prentice-Hall.

Feldman, L. B. (1979). Marital conflict and marital intimacy: An integrative psychodynamic, behavioral and systemic model. *Family Process, 18,* 69–78.

Fisch, R., Weakland, J., & Segal, L., (1982). *The tactics of change.* San Francisco: Jossey-Bass.

Gottman, J. M. (1991). Predicting the longitudinal course of marriages. *Journal of Marital and Family Therapy, 17,* 3–7.

Gottman, J. M., & Krokoff, L. J. (1989). Marital interaction and satisfaction: A longitudinal view. *Journal of Consulting and Clinical Psychology, 57,* 47–52.

Greenberg, L., Ford, C., Alden, L., & Johnson, S. M. (1993). In-session change in EFT. *Journal of Consulting and Clinical Psychology, 61,* 78–84.

Greenberg, L. S., & Johnson, S. M. (1986a). Affect in marital therapy. *Journal of Marital and Family Therapy, 12,* 1–10.

Greenberg, L. S., & Johnson, S. M. (1986b). When to evoke emotion and why: Process diagnosis in couples therapy. *Journal of Marital and Family Therapy, 12,* 19–23.

Greenberg, L. S., & Johnson, S. M. (1988). *Emotionally focused therapy for couples.* New York: Guilford.

Greenberg, L., & Safran, J. D. (1987). *Emotion in psychotherapy.* New York: Guilford.

Gurman, A. S., & Knudson, R. M. (1978). Behavioral marriage therapy: A psychodynamic systems analysis and critique. *Family Process, 17,* 121–38.

Izard, C. E. (1979). *Emotion in personality and psychotherapy.* New York: Plenum.

Johnson, S. M., & Greenberg, L. S. (1988). Relating process to process to outcome in martial therapy. *Journal of Marital and Family Therapy, 14,* 175–183.

Johnson, S. M., & Greenberg, L. S. (1994). The emotionally focused approach to problems in adult attachment. In N. S. Jacobson & A. S. Gurman (Eds.), *Clinical handbook of marital therapy* (2nd ed.). New York: Guilford.

Kahneman, D. (1973). *Attention and effort*. Englewood, Cliffs, NJ: Prentice-Hall.

Leventhal, H. (1984). A perceptual motor theory of emotion. In L. Berkowitz (Ed.), *Advances in experimental social psychology*. New York: Academic.

Linehan, M. (1993). *Cognitive-behavioral treatment of borderline personality disorders*. New York: Guilford.

Mace, D. (1987). Three ways of helping married couples. *Journal of Marital and Family Therapy, 13*, 179–185.

Main, M., & Hesse, E. (1990). Parents' unresolved traumatic experiences are related to infant disorganized attachment states: Is frightened and/or frightening parental behavior the linking mechanism? In M. Greenberg, D. Crochetti, & E. Cummings (Eds.), *Attachment during preschool years: Theory, research and intervention* (pp. 161–182). Chicago: University of Chicago Press.

Plutchik, R., & Kellerman, H. (Eds.). (1980). *Emotion: Theory, research and experience: Vol I. Theories of emotion*. New York: Academic.

Rogers, C. (1951). *Client-centered therapy*. Boston: Houghton Mifflin.

Safran, J. D., & Greenberg, L. S. (1991). *Emotion, psychotherapy and change*. New York: Guilford.

Stern, D.N. (1985). *The interpersonal world of the infant*. New York: Basic Books.

Stuart, R. B. (1980). *Helping couples change: A social learning approach to marital therapy*. New York: Aronson.

Tronick, E. Z. (1989). Emotions and emotional communication in infants. *American Psychologist, 44*, 112–119.

Wynne, L. C., & Wynne, A. R. (1986). The quest for intimacy. *Journal of Marital and Family Therapy, 12*, 383–394.

Name Index

Subject Index

Abandonment, 88; fear of, 80

Acceptance: emotional, 216–223, 302, 307, 308, 311–314; of limitations, 117–118

Acceptance-affection-love, 127

Accusatory thinking, 58–59

Action, 11–12, 153; social, language as, 177–178

Action tendencies, 7

Adaptation, 10–11; marital therapy and, 14–15

Adherence, to positives, 112

Adrenal involvement, 287

Affect. *See also* Emotion; Feelings; function of, in marriage, 231–233; negative. *See* Negative affect *entries;* positive, 318–319; stability of, 229–230; structure of, 228–229

Affective styles, and couple styles, 240–246

Affectivity, negative, in marriage, 227–251

Affirmation, of potentialities, 118

Agenda, for marital therapy, 256–291

Aggression, DPA and, 288

Agnostic approach, 258–259

Ambivalence, 159–160

Amplification, 314–315

Anabolic action, 286

Anatomy, of arousal, 285

Anger, 27, 36, 51–52, 53, 54–55, 58, 59, 62, 63, 64, 66, 88, 100–101, 103, 139, 163, 165, 212, 317–318. *See also* Rage; into fear, 77–78; jealous, 32, 33, 34, 37, 38; shame into, 78–79, 84–86

Anxiety, 139. *See also* Fear

Arationality, 184

Arational starting premises, 175

Assertiveness training, 174

Associative processes, 125

Attachment, 46–69, 308; in parent-child relationships, 47–50

Authentic emotional contact, 75–106

Authority issues, 175

Automatic appraisals, 7

Autonomic nervous system (ANS), 285–287

Autonomy, 84, 86, 156, 164–169; loss of, 80

Balance theory of marriage, 282–283

Base rate, low, problem of, 260

Basic concerns, 7

Basic feeling, 77, 85–86

Behavior: cause of, 232; DPA and, 288; ecology of, 282–283; marital, and discord, 237–239; questionnaire package covarying with, 274–277, 281, 291; suggested, 94–96

Behavioral aspects of negative affect reciprocity, 284–285

Behavioral coding system, 280–281

Behavioral conceptualization of emotion, 210–216

Behavioral couple therapy, 207–225

Behaviorally oriented approaches, 205–293

Behavioral theory, 125

Being, versus doing or having, 118

Being right, 187–189

Biological basis, of emotions, 152

Biology, sociology and, 19

Black box, 125